Jens Röhrkasten, Jürgen Sarnowsky (Eds./Hg.)

Monastic Finance

Klösterliche Finanzverwaltung

Vita regularis

Ordnungen und Deutungen
religiosen Lebens im Mittelalter

herausgegeben von

Mirko Breitenstein und Gert Melville

in Verbindung mit:

Giancarlo Andenna (Milano), Rainer Berndt SJ (Frankfurt a.M.),
Michael Cusato OFM (St. Bonaventure, NY),
Nicolangelo D'Acunto (Brescia), Jacques Dalarun (Paris),
Marek Derwich (Wrocław), Albrecht Diem (Syracuse, NY),
Brian Golding (Southampton), Annette Kehnel (Mannheim),
Brian Patrick McGuire (Roskilde), Anne Müller (Eichstätt),
Jens Röhrkasten (Birmingham), Roberto Rusconi (Roma),
Carlos Ruta (Buenos Aires), Hans-Joachim Schmidt (Fribourg),
Steven Vanderputten (Gent), André Vauchez (Paris),
Rudolf Weigand (Eichstätt)

Abhandlungen

Band 81

LIT

Monastic Finance

Studies on the Economy of
Benedictines, Military Orders,
and Mendicants

Klösterliche Finanzverwaltung

Studien zur Wirtschaftsführung der
Benediktiner, Ritterorden und Bettelorden

edited by
herausgegeben von

Jens Röhrkasten
Jürgen Sarnowsky

LIT

Forschungsstelle für Vergleichende Ordensgeschichte (FOVOG)
Research Centre for Comparative History of Religious Orders

Gedruckt mit freundlicher Unterstützung der Fritz Thyssen Stiftung für Wissenschaftsförderung

Gedruckt auf alterungsbeständigem Werkdruckpapier entsprechend
ANSI Z3948   DIN ISO 9706

Bibliografische Information der Deutschen Nationalbibliothek
Die Deutsche Nationalbibliothek verzeichnet diese Publikation in der Deutschen Nationalbibliografie; detaillierte bibliografische Daten sind im Internet über http://dnb.dnb.de abrufbar.

ISBN 978-3-643-15149-0 (br.)
ISBN 978-3-643-35149-4 (PDF)

© LIT VERLAG Dr. W. Hopf Berlin 2022
Verlagskontakt:
Fresnostr. 2   D-48159 Münster
Tel. +49 (0) 2 51-62 03 20
E-Mail: lit@lit-verlag.de   https://www.lit-verlag.de

Auslieferung:
Deutschland: LIT Verlag, Fresnostr. 2, D-48159 Münster
Tel. +49 (0) 2 51-620 32 22, E-Mail: vertrieb@lit-verlag.de

Table of Contents

Monastic Finance – Basic Parameters ... 1

CARLOS MANUEL REGLERO DE LA FUENTE
The Abbey of Sahagún:
Reform, Finances and Society (1000–1230) ... 15

JENS RÖHRKASTEN
English Benedictine Finance and the Crown
Between the Norman Conquest and the Hundred Years War ... 37

CARLOS MANUEL REGLERO DE LA FUENTE
The Administration of the Castilian Benedictine
Monasteries in the First Half of the Fourteenth Century ... 101

JÜRGEN SARNOWSKY
Zur Finanzpolitik geistlicher Ritterorden im Mittelalter ... 123

JÜRGEN SARNOWSKY
Die Finanzen des Deutschen Ordens im 15. Jahrhundert ... 151

PETR HLAVÁČEK
The Bohemian Franciscan Observants in Their
Peculiar 'Economic' Context ... 167

BEATRIX F. ROMHÁNYI
Alms, Preaching, Production and Property:
Mendicant and Pauline Economy in Late Medieval Hungary ... 181

MARIE-MADELEINE DE CEVINS
Les mécanismes de contrôle économique à l'œuvre
dans la province franciscaine observante de Hongrie
à la fin du Moyen Âge (v. 1450–v. 1530) ... 223

INDEX ... 245

Acknowledgements

The articles published in this volume are based on the authors' contributions to two colloquia on 'Monastic Finance' held at the Forschungsstelle für vergleichende Ordensgeschichte at the TU Dresden. The editors should like to thank the Fritz-Thyssen-Stiftung which generously funded the meetings and also enabled us to meet the costs of publication. Our gratitude is also due to the director of the FOVOG at the time, Prof. Dr. Gert Melville, and his staff for hosting these meetings and to Dr. Mirko Breitenstein, his successor, for accepting the volume into the series Vita regularis. Thanks are also due to the FOVOG's student assistant Nathalie Schmidt for her careful work on the text.

Jens Röhrkasten   Jürgen Sarnowsky

Monastic Finance – Basic Parameters

The rejection of the world in favour of a life devoted to God, consisting of contemplation, regular worship and self-denial, was associated with a state of complete personal poverty. More than that, poverty as an element of asceticism was a precondition for a truly religious life – a complete focus on God was only possible if all cares of the world had been left behind. According to Athanasius, already Antonius, farmer of Fayum in Egypt and father of the monks, had been moved to choose the *Vita apostolica* when he heard the words of Matthew 19.21: *Si vis perfectus esse, vade, vende, quae habes, et da pauperibus, et habebis thesaurum in caelo, et veni, sequere me*. A thousand years later, the same words moved Francesco Bernardone of Assisi to make the same decision. His followers, a group of lay people and religious, whose characteristic feature was the renunciation of all possessions – 'pecunia et denarii' – regarded the world as their monastery and yet they abandoned all contact with economic networks and disregarded social conventions related to trade and banking, activities in which the urban merchant class of the Italian towns excelled.[1] The Franciscan 'Regula bullata' of 1223 also contains the more conventional requirement of the novice to abandon all worldly possessions upon entry into the community, however, it went significantly beyond earlier norms by the introduction of collective poverty. This required an economy in a new legal framework. On the other hand, the old principle of individual poverty was a core element of monasticism, being part of the traditional vows expected of a novice. It can be found in the Rule of St. Benedict and the promise of individual poverty remained one of the characteristics of the *Vita religiosa*.[2] Under these conditions it seems only logical that the history of finance or the history of the economy cannot be an issue related to, let alone central to, the study of medieval monasticism and of the history of religious orders.[3]

The poverty practised by the medieval religious was voluntary poverty. The renunciation of all wealth at the time of entry into the religious community was

---

[1] Regula bullata c. 4, St. Francis, Regula bullata, in: Fontes Franciscani, eds. E. MENESTÒ / S. BRUFANI, Assisi 1995, pp. 169–181, at p. 174.

[2] Benedicti Regvla, ed. R. HANSLIK (Corpus Scriptorum Ecclesiasticorum Latinorum 75), Vienna 1960, pp. 90–91.

[3] M. VON DMITREWSKI, Die christliche freiwillige Armut vom Ursprung bis zum 12. Jahrhundert, Berlin 1913; G. SEVERINO, Appunti su povertà e ricchezza nella spiritualità dei secoli XI–XII, in: Bullettino dell'Istituto Storico Italiano per il Medio Evo e Archivio Muratoriano 79 (1968), pp. 149–165; R. MANSELLI, Evangelismo e povertà, in: Povertà e ricchezza nella spiritualità dei secoli IX e XII (Convegni del Centro di Studi sulla Spiritualità Medievale 8), Todi 1969, pp. 9–41; A. VAUCHEZ, La pauvreté volontaire au Moyen Âge, in: Annales ESC 25 (1970), pp. 1566–1573; M. MOLLAT, Études sur l'histoire de la pauvreté (Moyen Age–XVIe siècle), 2 vols., Paris 1974; D. FLOOD (ed.), Poverty in the Middle Ages (Franziskanische Forschungen 27), Werl 1975.

a deliberate act to underline a life-long commitment, devoted to a distinct purpose – *propositum* – the service of God. The Rule of the Order of Grandmont wanted to encourage those who doubted and hesitated with the argument that poverty would leave the individual safely in God's love: *nulla res enim tantopere securum reddit hominem in amore diuino quemadmodum paupertas*.[4] Poverty, however, was not as straightforward a concept as it might seem at first sight. There were different interpretations and definitions which went beyond the mere distinction between total poverty for the individual – which coincided with property held collectively by the community – and a combination of individual and collective poverty, as postulated by St. Francis and his followers. The poverty of traditional medieval monasticism was a poverty of the individual. Collective property was permitted. Many of the older houses had considerable economic assets and their wealth was an attraction to raiders like the Vikings who came to Lindisfarne in 793 or their successors who ransomed the monastery of St. Denis in 858, allegedly spoiling it of 685 pounds of gold and of 3250 pounds of silver.[5]

Part of the definition of poverty were distinctionse made e.g. about the nature of the property held by a religious community. Restrictions were introduced by the Cistercians in their 1134 statutes which contained a list of revenues and forms of wealth which were to be avoided. Everything necessary to sustain life was to be provided by the monks' manual labour. Prohibited was the ownership of parish churches, of tithes, of unfree labourers, of rents and of income from furnaces and mills. Liturgical vestments were to be plain and no vessels needed for the liturgy were to be adorned with gold or precious stones.[6] As Gert MELVILLE has shown, the Rule of the Order of Grandmont expresses similar notions in its clause *De terris non habendis*, where the option of communal property – outside the convent areas – is severely restricted, culminating in the famous clause *unicuique homini, cum mortuus est, tantum terrae sufficit ubi sepeliatur*.[7] The more radical challenge to collective property expressed especially by the Franciscans, led to new definitions of poverty. With the help of legal constructs which made a distinction between ownership and use of an item and which allowed the use of certain

---

[4] Scriptores Ordinis Grandimontensis, ed. J. BEQUET (Corpus Christianorum CC 8), Turnhout 1968, p. 70.

[5] Annales Bertiniani, ed. G. Waitz (MGH Scriptores in usum scholarum 5), Hannover 1883, p. 49.

[6] Statuta Capitulorum Generalium Ordinis Cisterciensis, ed. J.–M. Canivez, 8 vols., Louvain 1933–1941, vol. 1, pp. 14–15.

[7] Scriptores, ed. J. Bequet (note 4 above), p. 72. G. MELVILLE, In solitudine ac paupertate. Stephans von Muret Evangelium vor Franz von Assisi, in: IDEM/A. KEHNEL (eds.), In proposito paupertatis. Studien zum Armutsverständnis bei den mittelalterlichen Bettelorden (Vita regularis. Abhandlungen 13), Münster/Hamburg/London 2001, pp. 7–30; IDEM, What role did charity play in Francis of Assisi's attitude towards the poor? In: IDEM (ed.), Aspects of Charity. Concern for one's neighbour in medieval vita religiosa (Vita regularis. Abhandlungen 45), Berlin 2011, pp. 99–122.

things, the friars were enabled to participate in commercial exchange and a distinctive mendicant economy emerged. Mendicant poverty did not mean that the new orders had no economic structures, it simply meant that the new orders of the thirteenth century had different foundations and that they operated in a manner different from the older orders.

The image of the religious who practised voluntary poverty in complete isolation from the secular world represents an ideal rather than reality for several reasons. Firstly, already the earliest known monasteries in Egypt had held property and had developed their own economy. The minimum requirement for a community of religious was to acquire economic self-sufficiency because only this could provide true independence. But the incomes of monks and nuns could fluctuate due to factors outside their control. Furthermore, encroachments of the external world occurred already at an early stage in the history of a religious community, often in the actual foundation process or when the economic base of a recently founded religious house was enhanced. The creation of a monastic economy required negotiations and possibly the intervention of political authorities or a recourse to law and mediation. Secondly, charity had been seen as a responsibility of many religious already in the fourth and fifth centuries. The rule of St. Benedict defines among the monks' good works *Pauperes recreare, nudum uestire, infirmum uisitare* as well as *in tribulatione subuenire* and *caritatem non derelinquere*.[8] Charity could only be provided if sufficient wealth was available and this required an income beyond the mere needs of the religious community itself. Thirdly, the monastic economy depended on external events, general economic cycles as well as crises phenomena, be they natural disasters or manmade interference. The nature of monastic revenue – which was at its core often agricultural – could lead to cash flow problems and consequently the involvement in financial markets. The possession of estates required constant interaction with the world outside. The imposition of lordship, the enforcement of claims and the control of tenants at different levels required the religious to establish management systems which had an economic as well as a legal and sometimes even a political character. Finance, as part of the wider monastic economy, required the maintenance of intensive and continuous links with the outside world, not least because the element of time is a factor in many financial arrangements. If it is accepted that religious life always emerges out of a wider social context and that it is always tied to external economic conditions, tensions between the religious ideal and the reality of monastic life become apparent. This disparity between ideal and reality was a characteristic feature of the *Vita religiosa*. The need to monitor economic concerns even though this detracted from the *propositum* was not the only structural incongruity in medieval monasticism. The tension between the shared acts of piety as a communal effort to achieve salvation and the actual salvation which

---

[8] Benedicti Regvla, ed. R. HANSLIK (note 2 above), p. 30.

can only be achieved by the individual, is another example of an inherent tension in regular religious life.

Tensions between ideal and reality have already been the starting points for other studies on medieval monasticism and the dichotomy of poverty and monastic finance will be the underlying theme for this volume. Its main purpose is to provide specimens of research into the subject of 'monastic finance' and to assess the approaches of religious communities following different rules and being situated in different part of Europe, i.e. being subject to different economic conditions and political structures. It is important to go beyond the economic structures of one religious order or of monastic institutions in one region, an approach heralded by Kaspar ELM in 1992.[9] This introduces a number of variables which add considerably to the complexity of the subject. Firstly, there is the diversity among the monasteries and the religious orders. The differences between them emerge already in their norms and they go beyond their outward appearance in their habits, their liturgy or the preferred architectural forms of their churches and convent buildings. Secondly attention needs to be paid to the geographical location. The underlying geographical conditions and the location of a convent were as important as the settlement topography which constituted the environment of the religious community. What kind of agriculture was possible? How easy was access to the markets? Was the community isolated or did it enjoy good communications and conditions of transport? Was the religious house located in a town, in a highly urbanised area or in a mostly rural district? These were important underlying factors for the diversity of economic structures in different regions and they determined modes of agricultural production, proximity to markets, and sources of credit. The third variable are the dynamics over time. Chronologically the diversification of the religious movements, the creation of rightly layered monastic landscapes, coincided with the phase of economic expansion in the high Middle Ages. This economic evolution was related to changes in agricultural management and it brought developments in business practices. Apart from the variations in economic conditions and practices, political changes and cultural factors also need to be taken into consideration because they had an impact on attitudes to education, tradition and innovation.

Within this framework of variables, a number of central questions emerge. Even though it will not be possible to address all of them in this volume, a brief survey may provide direction for future research. Monastic finance could operate at different levels. The subject includes accounting procedures within the monastery where responsibilities for certain types of income could be given to obedientiaries. Many different models were developed – in what ways did they differ? How did they evolve? Which control mechanisms were developed? Was their

---

[9] K. ELM (ed.), Erwerbspolitik und Wirtschaftsweise mittelalterlicher Orden und Klöster (Berliner Historische Studien 17; Ordensforschungen VII), Berlin 1992.

creation modelled on other examples or did they represent innovations? How did monasteries interact with the external economy? In what ways, if any, did religious houses participate in the financial markets? How did monasteries or religious orders exist economically between the emerging secular authorities and the different levels of ecclesiastical authority?

Apart from questions relating to the creation of internal structures and the maintenance of external relations there were more general issues. Did monasteries and religious orders pursue economic policies at all? How did monasteries as places of contemplation and seclusion respond to changes in their environment? How did they modify economic structures based on an old-style agrarian economy? Did the diversity between monasteries and religious orders, their different spiritual priorities, have an impact on their economic policies? To what extent did regional diversity create a diversity between monasteries? These questions relate to a number of underlying themes. One of them is the impact of an emerging monetary economy and of new financial processes on medieval monasticism. A related theme is the development of financial strategies of monasteries and religious orders in different European regions in a period characterised by the introduction of modern banking practices. Attention needs to be paid to the improvement of monastic revenues by increasing the efficiency of estate management, by investing into the amelioration of landed estates, by developing industries and by the production of products and commodities for which there was a demand on the market. This volume will provide an insight into monastic financial management in different areas of Europe in different periods of the Middle Ages and it will also allow a comparison of the relative regional importance of monasticism in different European economic and political entities.

The different forms of the *Vita religiosa*, ranging from groups of itinerant preachers to strictly enclosed individuals, from hermits to groups of women or men organising their common life around daily acts of worship, were strongly influenced by their local and regional settings from the very beginning of monasticism. In the Roman Empire the different regions were tied together politically and economically in the decades which saw the genesis and rapid rise of monasticism but this cohesion did not endure. It disappeared at the time when early, eastern, monasticism had spread to the West. The end of the Roman Empire in the West was accompanied by the fragmentation of an integrated economic system linking the Mediterranean with North-Western Europe. This fragmentation included the gradual disappearance of long-distance trade in favour of local and regional networks of exchange and the discontinuation of a centrally controlled coinage. Although the use of coins was gradually resumed on a regional basis in the early Middle Ages, it appears that a barter economy was prevalent in many areas, especially north of the Alps, where rents were mostly paid in kind. This was a subsistence economy based on local or regional exchange of consumables and commodities. It was subject to significant changes from the eleventh century onwards, when economic expansion and the creation new trade networks led to an increasing number and importance of urban settlements and the emergence of new methods of finance which accompanied the reappearance of a monetary economy in most areas of Europe. These changes affected the governments of the nascent European states as well as most sections of society, including the nobility and the regular religious in the monasteries.

From the late eighth century onwards this system suffered temporary disruptions caused by civil wars and invasions affecting localities as well as whole regions. In consequence monasticism disappeared altogether in some areas. However, monasteries survived in other regions and reform initiatives in the tenth century in Burgundy, Lorraine, Flanders and England led to a revival. Demographic expansion, the intensification of economic exchange and the foundation of new towns and markets had a profound effect on religious communities. Monasticism played a prominent role in the process of economic expansion which coincided with the revival of the tenth century and which continued into the second half of the thirteenth century. Part of the attempts to achieve a renewal in this long period were changes in the attitude towards work. Physical labour by the religious gained a new significance, primarily as a part of the religious life, not necessarily as an element of the monastic economy. However, economic concerns were included in reform efforts. Different reform initiatives and visitations usually included the monitoring of the monastic economy. Reform was not restricted to the spiritual sphere, the core of religious life, but extended to other aspects of the monastery, including the economic foundations of the *Vita religiosa*.[10] Steady economic growth and the tremendous expansion of monasticism from the eleventh to the fourteenth century went hand in hand. Monasteries and the first religious orders were not merely beneficiaries of a general trend, the example of the Cistercians shows that they were engines of economic growth. Systematic cultivation of hitherto unused land including assarting and the draining of marshes, numerous foundations of towns, markets and other economic ventures in many parts of Europe were initiated by religious institutions which acted centres of

---

[10] This is not often reflected in the literature on the subject. K. SCHREINER, 'Brot der Mühsal'. Körperliche Arbeit im Mönchtum des hohen und späten Mittelalters. Theologisch motivierte Einstellungen, regelgebundene Normen, geschichtliche Praxis, in: K. SCHREINER (ed.), Gemeinsam leben. Spiritualität, Lebens– und Verfassungsformen klösterlicher Gemeinschaften in Kirche und Gesellschaft des Mittelalters (Vita regularis. Abhandlungen 53), Berlin 2013, pp. 243–290; J. BÖLLING, Reform vor der Reformation. Augustiner–Chorherrenstiftsgründungen an Marienwallfahrtsorten durch die Windesheimer Kongregation (Vita regularis. Abhandlungen 61), Münster 2014, p. 91; S. VANDERPUTTEN, How Reform Began. 'Traditional' Leadership and the Inception of Monastic Reform in Late Eleventh–Century Flanders, in: IDEM (ed.), Reform, Conflict, and the Shaping of Corporate Identities. Collected Studies on Benedictine Monasticism, 1050–1150 (Vita regularis. Abhandlungen 54) Zurich/Berlin 2013, pp. 31–50. The basic introduction into the subject is: K. ELM (ed.), Reformbemühungen und Observanzbestrebungen im spätmittelalterlichen Ordenswesen (Berliner historische Studien 14, Ordensstudien 6), Berlin 1989.

planning and investment. New economic ventures were designed to increase the investors' revenues, however, the economic practices developed in the urban economy and in long-distance trade resulted in more than just an intensification of the traditional exchange of goods. The transition from barter trade to a monetary economy led to new commercial practices in which financial transactions began to play an increasing role. Religious houses – they had traditionally also served as depositaries – could and did join in financial transactions by acting as creditors. Their activities came at a time which saw the genesis of the roots of a modern banking system. By the middle of the twelfth century sophisticated financial transactions were taking place in Genoa, by 1200 some Italian merchants were practically acting as bankers, setting up accounts for customers and providing facilities for credit and investment.[11] International money transfers could be effected cash free and a credit system was in place. Many religious houses made use of these facilities, trying to benefit from the opportunities, sometimes without being aware of the inherent dangers in the system. Not only could uncontrolled debt be a danger but there was also the question of how the involvement in this modern economy affected religious life.

Monastic finance is part of the wider subject of the monastic economy, an area which has been given attention by economic historians as well as by those whose work focuses on the history of monasteries and of religious orders. One of the pioneers of the study of monastic financial and economic policies rather than the more general monastic economy were the French legal historian Robert GÉNÉSTAL whose thesis as a pupil of Charles ESMEIN on the role of the Norman monasteries as institutions providing credit was published in 1901, and Leopold DELISLE, who was one of the editors of the cartulary of St. Victor of Marseille.[12] GÉNÉSTAL, who demanded that the purchase of land and income by monasteries deserved to be studied systematically, focused on the 'mort gage' as an institution of credit. This common method of using land as surety for a loan existed in two forms: 'mort gage' in which the creditor also controlled the income from the land until the debit had been repaid and in this form received an interest, and 'vif gage', the form in which the revenue from the land was used towards the repayment of the loan. GÉNÉSTAL could show that the 'mort gage' was the preferred

---

[11] R. S. LOPEZ, The Commercial Revolution of the Middle Ages, Cambridge 1971; J. A. VAN HOUTTE, Europäische Wirtschaft und Gesellschaft von der großen Wanderung bis zum Schwarzen Tod, in: H. KELLENBENZ (ed.), Handbuch der europäischen Wirtschafts– und Sozialgeschichte Band 2, Stuttgart 1980, pp. 1–149, at pp. 83–95; R. DE ROOVER, Money, Banking, and Credit in Medieval Bruges, Cambridge/MA 1948; P. SPUFFORD, Coinage and Currency, in: M. M. POSTAN / E. MILLER (eds.), The Cambridge Economic History. Volume 2, Trade and Industry in the Middle Ages, Cambridge ²1987, pp. 788–873, at pp. 788–831; R. W. KAEUPER, Bankers to the Crown. The Riccardi of Lucca and Edward I, Princeton 1973.

[12] R. GÉNÉSTAL, Rôle des monastères comme établissements de crédit étudié en Normandie du XIe à la fin du XIIIe siècle, Paris 1901 (also: Caen 1911); Cartulaire de l'Abbaye de S. Victor de Marseille, 3 vols., eds. L. DELISLE / J. MARION / B. GUÉRARD, Paris 1857.

credit arrangement in Normandy, permitting monastic creditors to receive interest on capital they had lent. He was also able to trace the responses to papal prohibitions of contracts involving the payment of interest in the twelfth and thirteenth centuries which eventually led to the development of new economic strategies which were based on the purchase of rent incomes. However, at the centre of GÉNÉSTAL's attention was the legal background of credit arrangements rather than monastic finance as a central element in the economic structure of religious institutions.

A slightly different approach was taken by Robert Hugh SNAPE, fellow of Emmanuel College, Cambridge, and a protegé of the staunchly protestant medievalist George Gordon COULTON, who produced his own study of the monastic economy and of monastic finance.[13] In 1912 SNAPE submitted a study of 'English Monastic Finance in the Later Middle Ages' which appeared as a book in 1926. His study includes chapters on monastic revenues and expenditure, debt and general economic organisation. The intention was to analyse the daily routines of the religious communities, to identify the logistical basis which enabled them to function and to establish how assets were organised and controlled, questions of great relevance still today. SNAPE approached them on the basis of very limited printed sources available at the time. Despite his awareness of the differences between religious orders there was a reluctance to relate variations of economic practice to the specific spiritual orientation of a religious house or of a religious order.

A number of studies on the financial affairs of individual houses conducted by historians in different countries followed. They were based on archival studies as well as on an increasing number of editions of monastic source material from about the middle of the nineteenth century onwards. In France Edgard ALLIX and Robert GÉNÉSTAL published an article on the Benedictine abbey of St. Martin of Troarn in 1904, other examples are Joseph GENNEVOISE's study on the Premonstratensian abbey of Vicogne printed in 1929 or the doctoral thesis by Henri PLATELLE on the temporalities of the abbey of St. Amand.[14] These and later studies could draw on the publication of monastic economic sources from France and Belgium.[15] In England historians began to make use of the numerous

---

[13] G. G. COULTON, Five Centuries of Religion, 4 vols., Cambridge 1923–1950, vol. 3, pp. 149–214, 232–335, 468–506.

[14] E. ALLIX / R. GÉNÉSTAL, Les opérations financières de l'abbaye de Troarn du XIe au XIVe siècle, in: Vierteljahresschrift für Sozial– und Wirtschaftsgeschichte 2 (1904), pp. 616–640; J. GENNEVOISE, L'abbaye de Vicogne, de l'ordre des Prémontré, 2 vols. (Mémoires de la Société d'études de la province de Cambrai 28, 29), Lille/Cambrai 1929; H. PLATELLE, Le temporel de l'abbaye de Saint–Amand des origines à 1340, Paris 1962.

[15] Some early examples are: Cartulaire de l'abbaye de la Sainte–Trinité–du–Mont de Rouen, ed. A. DEVILLE (Collection des documents inédits sur l'histoire de France, Cartulaires 3), Paris 1841; Cartulaire de l'abbaye de Saint–Victor de Marseille, ed. B. GUERARD, Paris 1857; Cartulaire de l'abbaye royale de Notre–Dame–de–Bon–Port de l'ordre de Cîteaux, au diocèse

editions of sources which had become available in some quantity since the middle of the nineteenth century. This material could be divided into two categories. Firstly economic sources from monasteries which had survived the Dissolution of the monasteries in England and Wales. They were often published in county record societies or in the collection informally known as the 'Rolls Series'.[16] Secondly records of the royal Exchequer and of other government institutions. This allowed David KNOWLES to produce his magisterial works on the religious houses and orders in medieval England.[17] Studies of the economy developed by individual houses were already under way while KNOWLES was preparing his books, among them Reginald SMITH's work on Canterbury Cathedral Priory.[18] In the second half of the twentieth century the number of publications on the economy of English monasteries proliferated. Among them were important publications, like KING on Peterborough and HARVEY on Westminster Abbey.[19] However, not all historians searching records of monastic archives were interested in the history of medieval monasticism. Social historians used monastic records to gain an insight into more general economic processes.[20]

---

d'Evreux, ed. J. ANDRIEUX, Evreux 1862; Cartulaire de l'abbaye de Redon, ed. A. DE COURSON, Paris 1863; Cartulaire de l'abbaye Notre–Dame de Léoncel, diocèse de Die, ordre de Cîteaux, ed. U. CHEVALIER, Montélimar 1869; Cartulaires inédits de la Saintonge, ed. T. GRASILIER, 2 vols. (Cartulaires inédits de la Saintonge 1, 2), Niort 1871; Cartulaire de l'abbaye de Malonne, ed. V. BARBIER, in: Analectes pour servir à l'histoire ecclésiastique de la Belgique 20 (1886), pp. 5–48, 129–192.

[16] Registrum Wiltunense, ed. R. C. HOARE, London 1827; Register and Chronicle of Aberconway, ed. H. ELLIS, in: Camden Miscellany i (Camden Society 39), London 1847, pp. 1–23; Historia et Cartularium Monasterii Sancti Petri Gloucestriae, ed. W. H. HART, 3 vols. (Rerum Britannicarum medii aevi scriptores 33), London 1863–1867; Feodarium prioratus Dunelmensis: A Survey of the Estates of the Prior and Convent of Durham Compiled in the Fifteenth Century, ed. W. GREENWELL (Surtees Society 58), Durham 1872; Cartularium Monasterii de Rameseia, eds. W. H. HART / P. A. LYONS, 3 vols. (Rerum Britannicarum medii aevi scriptores 79), London 1884–1893; Cartularium Abbathiae de Rievalle ordinis Cisterciensis, ed. J. C. ATKINSON (Surtees Society 83), Durham 1889; Two Cartularies of the Benedictine Abbeys Muchelney and Athelney in the County of Somerset, ed. E. H. BATES (Somerset Record Society 14), Taunton 1899, pp. 1–112; 113–201; Accounts of the Obedientars of Abingdon Abbey, ed. R. KIRK (Camden Society, new series 52), London 1894.

[17] D. KNOWLES, The Monastic Order in England, Cambridge 1940; IDEM, The Religious Orders in England, 3 vols., Cambridge 1948–1959.

[18] R. A. L. SMITH, Canterbury Cathedral Priory: A Study in Monastic Administration, Cambridge 1943.

[19] E. KING, Peterborough Abbey, 1086–1310: A Study in the Land Market, Cambridge 1973; B. HARVEY, Westminster Abbey and its Estates in the Middle Ages, Oxford 1977.

[20] F. M. PAGE, The Estates of Crowland Abbey: A Study in Manorial Organisation, Cambridge 1934; R. HILTON, Winchcombe Abbey and the Manor of Sherborne, in: University of Birmingham Historical Journal 2 (1949/50), pp. 31–52; IDEM, A Rare Evesham Abbey Estate Document, in: Vale of Evesham Research Papers 2 (1969), pp. 5–10; J. A. RAFTIS, The Estates of Ramsay Abbey: A Study in Economic Growth and Organization, Toronto 1957; C. DYER, Lords and Peasants in a Changing Society. The Estates of the Bishopric of Worcester, 680–1540, Cambridge 1980.

Insights into the evolution of the monastic economy in a wider context were presented in an important article by Cinzio VIOLANTE in 1980.[21] VIOLANTE highlighted the connection between monastic reform and economic reorganisation, focusing on the role of religious houses in the creation of a money economy. He identified a number of factors which had an impact on this process, among them the use of treasures held by monasteries for different purposes. Monastic treasures could be collected as inactive assets or they could be invested in the purchase of land but they were also coveted as taxes or loans by secular leaders or ecclesiastical authorities in times of crisis. However, even if such transactions occurred on a large scale, they did not necessarily have wider economic influences because treasure more or less forcibly extracted from a monastery or invested for construction work or the purchase of land would eventually be replaced because of the circulation of species in the market. Even though the transactions were often disguised in order to conform with canon law, VIOLANTE also found that monasteries were involved in credit deals which involved the payment of interest. He also noted a phase – apparently related to their involvement in the financial markets – during which they went into debt, the old established Benedictine houses earlier than the Cistercians. The analysis of causes brought a number of important insights. Monastic indebtedness was not merely a consequence of increased expenditure on consumption. There were inflationary tendencies which devalued traditional incomes and attempts were made to increase the income by purchasing rents. Another change affecting assets was caused by a gradual transformation of the social groups which traditionally had provided economic assets to monasteries. The rate of donations to monasteries began to slow down from the middle of the twelfth century onwards and the motives and intentions of potential donors and patrons were different from those of earlier generations. Fewer grants were made while the institutions had to adapt to changing economic realities.

The order most closely associated with its economic activity were the Cistercians, who were the ideal objects of historical research because of the survival of relevant sources, because of their economic success and the structured economic policies of their monasteries. There was the notion, or rather myth, of the existence of a specific Cistercian economy. The Cistercians as a religious order with recognisable economic structures may have enjoyed economic success for longer than many traditional Benedictine houses, but "their economic structures were diverse".[22] It is true that many Cistercian communities made better use of available technologies than older monasteries, that they sought a full integration into

---

[21] C. VIOLANTE, Monasteri e canoniche nello sviluppo dell'economia monetaria (secoli XI–XIII), in: Istituzioni monastiche e istituzioni canonicali in occidente (1123–1215) (Pubblicazioni dell'Università cattolica del sacro cuore. Miscellanea del Centro di Studi Medioevali 9), Milan 1980, pp. 369–416.

[22] E. JAMROZIAK, The Cistercian Order in Medieval Europe 1090–1500, London 2013, p. 183.

the urban economy but even though the Cistercians did have their own approach to the economy, they shared the local and regional factors which formed the preconditions for all economic activity with other regular religious institutions: the local geology and landscape, the availability or lack of a transport infrastructure, the variations in the legal, political and social contexts, the dependence on a wider regional economy. Thanks to the work of Robert DONKIN, Adrian BELL, Chris BROOKS, Janet BURTON, Paul DRYBURGH, and others for England and Wales, Constance BOUCHARD for Burgundy, Werner RÖSENER and Winfried SCHICH for the German lands, to name but a few, the regional variations have been identified to reveal rich and diversified economic systems within one religious order.[23] The medieval Cistercians continue to attract attention from historians who publish local studies and source editions as well as analyses with a wider range.[24]

Regional studies with a focus on a particular religious order, are only able to provide limited information and insights into monasticism as a European phenomenom. A comprehensive approach, taking into account different regions and comparing the policies of different religious communities, has the potential to offer results on a Europe-wide scale. The alternative to local and regional studies is a large-scale assessment and analysis of monastic finance in different European regions, primarily the Mediterranean, Central and Western Europe. These areas had important political and economic links with each other while retaining their own distinctive structure. An attempt to achieve coverage of Europe as a whole

---

[23] R. A. DONKIN, Localisation, situation économique et rôle parlementaire des abbés cisterciens anglais, in: Revue d'histoire ecclésiastique 52 (1957), pp. 832–841; IDEM, The Urban Property of the Cistercians in Mediaeval England, in: Analecta Sacri Ordinis Cisterciensis 15 (1959), pp. 104–131; A. BELL / C. BROOKS / P. DRYBURGH, Modern Finance in the Middle Ages? Advance Contracts with Cistercian Abbeys for the Supply of Wool c. 1270–1330: a Summary of Findings, in: Cîteaux 55 (2004), pp. 339–343; A. BELL, 'Leger est aprendre mes fort est arendre': Wool, Debt, and the Dispersal of Pipewell Abbey (1280–1330), in: Journal of Medieval History 32 (2006), pp. 187–211; C. BOUCHARD, Holy Entrepreneurs. Cistercians, Knights and Economic Activity in Twelfth–Century Burgundy, Ithaca/NY 1991; J. BURTON, The Estates and Economy of Rievaulx Abbey in Yorkshire, in: Cîteaux 49 (1998), pp. 29–94; W. RÖSENER, Reichsabtei Salem, Verfassungs– und Wirtschaftsgeschichte des Zisterzienserklosters von der Gründung bis zur Mitte des 14. Jahrhunderts, Sigmaringen 1974; W. SCHICH, Die Stadthöfe der fränkischen Zisterzienserklöster in Würzburg – von den Anfängen bis zum 14. Jahrhundert, in: W. RIBBE (ed.), Zisterzienser Studien 3 (Studien zur europäischen Geschichte 13), Berlin 1976, pp. 45–94; W. SCHICH, Zur Rolle des Handels in der Wirtschaft der Zisterzienserklöster im nordöstlichen Mitteleuropa während der zweiten Hälfte des 12. und der ersten Hälfte des 13. Jahrhunderts, in: Zisterzienser Studien 4 (Studien zur europäischen Geschichte 14), Berlin 1979, pp. 133–168.

[24] J. BRUCH, Die Zisterze Kaisheim und ihre Tochterklöster: Studien zur Organisation und zum Wirtschaften spätmittelalterlicher Frauenklöster mit einer Edition des 'Kaisheimer Rechnungsbuches' (Vita regularis. Editionen 5), Berlin 2013; K. ELM /P. JOERIßEN /H. J. ROTH (eds.), Die Zisterzienser. Ordensleben zwischen Ideal und Wirklichkeit, 2 vols. (Schriften des Rheinischen Museumsamtes 10, 12), Bonn 1980–1982; P. KING, The Finances of the Cistercian Order in the Fourteenth Century (Cistercian Study Series 85), Kalamazoo 1985.

and to include all religious orders was made in a series of conferences organised by Kaspar ELM in the 1980s which resulted in a collection of articles almost amounting to a handbook on the subject.[25] The volume included articles on the Premonstratensians, Cistercians, the Hospitallers, Templars and Teutonic Knights, Hospitals (including the hospital order of St. Anthony) and Secular Colleges as well as the Franciscans. In addition the order of St. Bridget of Sweden and the Sisters of the Common Life were covered. However, with two exceptions all articles focused on the economy of individual convents or – in the case of the Hospitallers – regions. The exceptions were the two contributions on the late-medieval Franciscans and on the Sisters of the Common Life which – instead of case studies – offered more general information on economic trends and policies pursued by the respective religious communities. Geographically the volume covered southern Germany and the Rhineland, northern France and parts of Aragon. The volume was influential. The monastic economy has become a standard topic for modern historians working on the general as well as the regional history of religious orders.[26] These are excellent conditions for a closer analysis of the more specialised field of monastic finance.

This volume can only be a starting point although an attempt is made to achieve a wider geographical and chronological coverage and to present observations over longer periods of time. It begins with a case study of the abbey of Sahagún by Carlos REGLERO DE LA FUENTE who is able to demonstrate the impact of reform on a monastic economy which time and again was affected by periodical political turmoil. Despite these disturbances the abbey lived through and participated in a phase of monetarisation and, like GÉNÉSTAL's Norman monasteries, provided credit facilities already in the eleventh century. Financial relations between the English monarchs and the larger Benedictine houses in the period between the Norman Conquest of England and the beginning of the Hundred Years War are at the centre of the second article. The period saw the emergence of a centralised state with an effective fiscal and judicial administration, institutions which had a profound impact on the monastic economy in this region. Structural parallels to the situation of the Benedictines in England can be found in Castile in the early fourteenth century, as will be shown in the third article. However, the absence of strong interference by a centrally organised administration resulted in important differences, especially a greater autonomy in economic planning. This will be followed by two articles on the military orders.

---

[25] K. ELM (ed.), Erwerbspolitik und Wirtschaftsweise (note 9 above), with contributions by G. MARCHAL, K. WOLLENBERG, J. A. MOL, W. RÖDEL, J. KRIESER, B. JÄHNIG, A. MISCHLEWSKI, U. LINDGREN, B. NEIDIGER, T. NYBERG and G. REHM.

[26] J. BURTON, Monastic and Religious Orders in Britain: 1000–1300, Cambridge 2000; M. HEALE, Monasticism in Late Medieval England, c. 1300–1535, Manchester 2009; G. MELVILLE, Die Welt der mittelalterlichen Klöster. Geschichte und Lebensformen, Munich 2012; C. M. REGLERO DE LA FUENTE, Monasterios y monacato en la España medieval (Estudios/Medieval), Madrid 2021.

The first will deal with the financial structures developed by the three large military orders, the Templars, the Hospitallers and the Teutonic Knights. The second article presents a case study of the Teutonic Knights in the fifteenth century, whose economic administration was first challenged after the battle of Tannenberg in 1410 and then broke down during the Thirteen-Year War (1454–1466). Three studies on the mendicants – among them a contribution including the Hermits of St. Paul – in central and east-central Europe in the later Middle Ages form the final section of the volume. Petr HLAVÁČEK begins with the difficulties faced by the Franciscan Observants during the Hussite Wars and then turns to the problems they faced in individual location and the way in which they managed to finance and organise their provincial chapters. Beatrix ROMHÁNYI provides a survey of the different mendicant orders in Hungary and their economic structures while the legislation and its enforcement are central aspects in the article by Marie-Madeleine DE CEVINS on the Franciscan Observants in Hungary at a time when the kingdom is becoming a borderland to the Muslim world.

The Abbey of Sahagún:
Reform, Finances and Society (1000–1230)

Carlos Manuel Reglero de la Fuente[1]

The Abbey of Sahagún was one of the most important in the kingdoms of León and Castile between the ninth and nineteenth centuries. Situated on the Camino de Santiago, the pilgrims' route to Santiago, a day's horseride from León (65 km),[2] which was the royal residence until the middle of the 12th century. Its name is derived from its original dedication to the martyrs Facundus and Primitivus (Sant Facundo, Sant Fagunt, Sahagún), although, in the second half of the fifteenth century, it came to be known as 'San Benito de Sahagún'. The numerous donations received from kings and nobles over the first few centuries of the abbey's existence formed the base of an extensive manor.[3]

The abbey's chroniclers say that it was founded in the third century, following the martyrdom of its patrons. However, the first reliable reference to it comes in the *Crónica Albeldense*, which narrates its destruction in an Al-Andalus attack in the year 883.[4] It was soon rebuilt, as in the year 904 the abbey received a letter from King Alfonso III, the first in a long list of royal privileges and donations from both lay and ecclesiastical people.[5] Its prosperity was temporarily interrupted by another destruction in the year 986 or 988, during an attack of Almanzor.[6]

---

[1] Universidad de Valladolid. https://orcid.org/0000–0002–3361–1815. This paper forms part of the research project "El ejercicio del poder: espacios, agentes y escrituras (siglos XI–XV)" (HAR2017–84718–P), funded by the MICINN, AEI, UE–FEDER.

[2] Liber Sancti Iacobi: Guía del peregrino medieval (Codex Calixtinus), ed. M. BRAVO LOZANO, Sahagún 1989, p. 21.

[3] J. M. MÍNGUEZ FERNÁNDEZ, El dominio del Monasterio de Sahagún en el siglo X: paisajes agrarios, producción y expansión económica, Salamanca 1980; E. MARTÍNEZ LIÉBANA, El dominio señorial del monasterio de San Benito de Sahagun en la baja edad media (siglos XIII–XV), Madrid 1990; P. GARCÍA MARTÍN, El monasterio de San Benito el Real de Sahagún en la época moderna. Contribución al estudio de la economía rural doméstica en el valle del Duero, Salamanca 1985.

[4] Crónicas asturianas: Crónica de Alfonso III (Rotense y 'A Sebastián'), Crónica Albeldense (y 'Profética'), ed. J. GIL FERNÁNDEZ / J. L. MORALEJO / J. I. RUIZ DE LA PEÑA (eds.), Oviedo 1985, p. 180.

[5] Colección diplomática del Monasterio de Sahagun (Siglos IX–X), ed. J. M. MÍNGUEZ FERNÁNDEZ, León 1976, doc. 6.

[6] M. CARRIEDO TEJEDO, Las campañas de Almanzor contra la ciudad de León (su conquista definitiva en 994 según las fuentes musulmanas y cristianas), in: Estudios Humanísticos. Geografía, Historia, Arte 8 (1986), pp. 165–179, at p. 169. A document from 988 states: *Et dum*

After the year 956, there are several indications in the documents referring to donations to the abbey that the monks were following the Rule of Saint Benedict.[7] In this year the *praepositus*,[8] the abbot's second-in-command in the Benedictine Rule,[9] is first mentioned in Sahagún. An interesting document from the year 1006 indicates how the monks gathered together, in accordance with the 'holy rule', to deliberate on the sale of a property that was a long way from the abbey and hardly produced any income. They thus decided to sell it and spend the money on acquiring another property, for the monks' maintenance, or for the repair of the church.[10] It is a clear example of the practical application of chapter III of the Rule of Saint Benedict, but it is, unfortunately, the only one we know of.

It is not known which interpretation of Saint Benedict's Rule the abbey followed. We do not know if the original text was their only reference or whether they knew the Carolingian and post-Carolingian benedictism.[11] At some time during the eleventh century Sahagún may have come under the influence of the Cluniac reforms which were encouraged by King Sancho III the Great of Navarre in the monasteries of his kingdom, and which spread towards Castile.[12] In any case, the fundamental reform of their monastic life took place in 1080, when

---

sarrazeni pergunt ad Domnos Sanctos ut destruerent eum: Colección Sahagún, ed. J. M. MÍNGUEZ (note 5 above), doc. 340.

[7] *ubi regit congregatio monachorum Vincentius abba sub regula Sancti Benedicti*: Colección Sahagún, ed. J. M. MÍNGUEZ (note 5 above), doc. 150; *est ibi agmina monachorum adunata serviens Deo die noctuque sub regula Sancti Benedicti* (ibid., doc. 162). Two previous documents, from 905 and 950, also mentions this rule, but they are false (ibid., docs. 8, 123).

[8] Ibid., doc. 159.

[9] G. M. COLOMBAS (ed.), San Benito. Su vida y su regla, Madrid 1968, pp. 680–685 (RSB cap. LXV). LINAGE dates it in 985, because he only consulted documents published at that time (A. LINAGE CONDE, Los orígenes del monacato benedictino en la Península Ibérica, 3 vols., León 1973, vol. 2, pp. 593–599).

[10] *concederet eam a Sancto Facundo et Primitiuo uel a fratribus ibidem Deo militantium sub regula Sancti Benedicti* […]. *Dum stante in iuri nostro atque permanente sub potestate nostra ex concessione nostra domna Gunterote et nobis longinqua et ut parbum subsidium adque prode de ea nobis ueniebat, congregatis fratribus monachis et confessoribus Deo inuocantes ab aula Sancti Facundi, secundum quod sancta regula docet in unum et dederunt totam congregationem, ut a longe nobis erat, dixerunt: emamus de ea precium et mittamus aut in alia hereditate aut in sufficientia fratrum aut in substentationem ecclesie* (Colección diplomática del Monasterio de Sahagun (857–1230), ed. M. HERRERO DE LA FUENTE, 2 vols., León 1988, vol. 2, doc. 386).

[11] These questions were dealt with in: A. LINAGE CONDE, Los orígenes (note 9 above), vol. 2, pp. 1001–1006. A review: J. MATTOSO, L'introduction de la Règle de S. Benoît dans la Péninsule ibérique, in: Revue d'Histoire Ecclésiastique 70 (1975), pp. 731–742. See also: J. MATTOSO, Le monachisme ibérique et Cluny. Les monastères de la diocèse de Porto de l'an mille 'a 1200, Louvain 1968.

[12] J. Á. GARCÍA DE CORTÁZAR, Monasterios hispanos en torno al año mil: función social y observancia regular, in: XXX Semana de Estudios Medievales. Estella 14–18 julio 2003. Ante el Milenario del reinado de Sancho el Mayor. Un rey navarro para España y Europa, Pamplona 2004, pp. 213–269, at pp. 262–266.

King Alfonso VI charged the Cluniac monk Robertus with introducing the customs of Cluny to the abbey, something which was problematic, as is stated in various documents at this time.[13] The monks' resistance to Robertus's governance led to his replacement by the abbot Bernardus, another monk who had come from Cluny. He managed to persuade Pope Gregory VII to grant them the 'Roman liberty', similar to that of Cluny, so that the abbey would be able to shine in Spain just like its counterpart in Gaul, as well as the right of the monks to freely elect their abbot (1083).[14] In the following years, the donations once more point to the monks of Sahagún following the Rule of Saint Benedict. This fact ceases to be mentioned from 1115 onwards. This could be because it was no longer deemed necessary or because it was not deemed to be sufficiently expressive.[15] Sahagún enjoyed the special protection of King Alfonso VI who had himself buried there (1109) along with two of his wives.[16]

In the second and third decades of the twelfth century the abbey had many problems arising from the civil war that swept through the realm and the rebellion of the town's burghers against the abbot's authority. Many of their possessions were taken by kings and nobles, and the observance of the Rule was weakened. The abbey was once more turned over to Cluny by King Alfonso VII in the year 1132. Pope Innocent II specified that the said donation would only be temporary, with the aim of reforming the religious life and improving the state

---

[13] *Ita uero sicut abetur Domnos Sanctos in consuetudinem Sancti Petri, ita abeatur Sancti Petri in consuetudinem Marcilinieco*: Colección Sahagun, ed. M. HERRERO (note 10 above), vol. 3, doc. 777; *per quosdam religiosos uiros ad instar Cluniacensis norme monastici ordinis sancti Benedicti docte eruditos instituere curaui* (ibid., doc. 781); *ut teneant ibi regulam et monasticum ordinem sicut docet beatus Benedictus et secundum quod fratres Sancti Petri Cluniacensis obtinent* (ibid., doc. 782). Concerning this reform of the monastery: C. M. REGLERO DE LA FUENTE, La primera reforma cluniacense de Sahagún, el concilio de Burgos y la crisis de 1080: revisión cronológica y desarrollo, in: Monarquía y sociedad en el reino de León. De Alfonso III a Alfonso VII, 2 vols., León 2007, vol. 2, pp. 689–732.

[14] *sub perpetue defensionis et Romane libertatis tutela prefatum monasterium suscipimus* […] *sancte apostolice sedi specialiter aderens ad instar et formam Cluniacensis cenobii, quod sub libertate Romana, Deo auctore, pene per omnes partes terrarum fama religionis et onestatis adque amplitudinis luce clarius resplendet, perpetua et inuiolabili securitate fruatur; ut sicut illud in Gallia ita istud in Ispania libertatis prerogatiua clarescat et quod, oppitulante Deo, consimile erit in religione, par etiam sit apostolice sedis confirmatione*: Colección Sahagun, ed. M. HERRERO (note 10 above), vol. 3, doc. 809.

[15] Later mentions: Colección diplomática del Monasterio de Sahagun (857–1300). 4, (1110–1199), ed. J. A. FERNÁNDEZ FLÓREZ, León 1991, docs. 1191, 1192. Between 1161 and 1194 there were only four mentions. It must be remembered that the Cistercians did not settle in the kingdom until the 1140s (V. Á. ÁLVAREZ PALENZUELA, Monasterios cistercienses en Castilla (siglos XII–XIII), Valladolid 1978. J. PEREZ–EMBID WAMBA, El Cister en Castilla y León: monacato y dominios rurales (siglos XII–XV), Valladolid 1986, pp. 32–58, 269–281. C. M. REGLERO DE LA FUENTE, Los reyes hispanos y la reforma monástica benedictina, in: Monasterios y monarcas: fundación, presencia y memoria regia en monasterios hispanos medievales, Aguilar de Campoo 2012, pp. 125–158).

[16] Crónicas anónimas de Sahagún, ed. A. UBIETO ARTETA, Zaragoza 1987, pp. 16–17, 26.

of the abbey's possessions.[17] The ephemeral subjection to Cluny did not detract from the efficacy of religious reform, so that Sahagún became a point of reference, comparable to Cluny, for Spain's Benedictine monastic life in the second half of the twelfth century.[18]

Pope Innocent II's papal bull linked religious reform and economic prosperity. The aim of this study is to analyse the changes in the abbey's administration and its economic management which coincide with the introduction of the customs of Cluny.

The reign of Alfonso VI, a time of change

The reform of Sahagún in 1080 occurred at the start of the reign of King Alfonso VI, when the kingdom also went through important ecclesiastical, political and economic changes. Worthy of note among the first kind is the adoption of the Roman liturgy instead of the Hispanic or Visigothic. This was done upon the order of Pope Gregory VII and also involved the acceptance of the Pope as the supreme authority in ecclesiastical matters.[19] Another important change in the ecclesiastical field was the restoration of the ecclesiastical provinces and the primacy of the seat of Toledo. This occurred in the years following the conquest of the city, the former capital of the Visigothic kingdom (1085), to which the Cluniac Bernardus, until then abbot of Sahagún, was appointed.[20]

The changes during the reign of Alfonso VI were no less important in the economic field. Following the conquest of Toledo, silver coins were minted there. Silver coinage had been known over the previous three centuries in the kingdom of León, and Visigothic, Andalusí or Carolingian pieces had been in

---

[17] *ad reformationem religionis et rerum temporalium incrementum*: Bibliotheca Cluniacensis, ed. M. MARRIER, Macon/Paris 1614, col. 1396–1397. P. SEGL, Königtum und Klosterreform in Spanien: Untersuchungen über die Cluniacenserklöster in Kastilien–León vom Beginn des 11. bis zur Mitte des 12. Jahrhunderts, Kallmünz 1974, pp. 93–102. C. M. REGLERO DE LA FUENTE, Cluny en España: los prioratos de la provincia y sus redes sociales (1073–ca. 1270), León 2008, pp. 168, 210–212.

[18] C. M. REGLERO, Los reyes hispanos (note 15 above), pp. 145–146.

[19] The chronology of support for and resistance to this issue is still in question today. Please see: B. F. REILLY, El Reino de León y Castilla bajo el rey Alfonso VI (1065–1109), Toledo 1989, pp. 113–136; L. VONES, La sustitución de la liturgia hispana por el rito romano en los reinos de la Península Ibérica, in: S. ZAPKE (ed.), Hispania vetus: manuscritos litúrgico–musicales de los orígenes visigóticos a la transición francorromana (Siglos IX–XII), Bilbao 2007, pp. 43–59; T. DESWARTE, Une chrétienté romaine sans pape. L'Espagne et Rome (586–1085), Paris 2010, pp. 403–484, or the brief chapter: C. M. Reglero de la Fuente, La Reforma Gregoriana y la introducción del rito romano, in: J. A. ESCUDERO (dir.), La Iglesia en la Historia de España, Madrid 2014, pp. 317–326.

[20] J. F. RIVERA RECIO, El Arzobispo de Toledo Don Bernardo de Cluny (1086–1124), Rome 1962; A. HOLNDONNER, Kommunikation – Jurisdiktion – Integration: Das Papsttum und das Erzbistum Toledo im 12. Jahrhundert (ca. 1085 – ca. 1185), Berlin 2014, pp. 72–268.

circulation, but the kings did not strike them. It is usual for the documents to value property and goods in terms of money, but the payments were often made in kind. The quantity of coins and species increased substantially from the mid-eleventh century onwards thanks to the money of the parias, the tributes paid by the Andalusí kings to the monarch of León, as well as through the arrival of pilgrims and traders from north of the Pyrenees along the pilgrimage route to Santiago. With Alfonso VI, a decisive step was taken towards the monetarization of society.[21]

The reign of Alfonso VI also marks the beginning of the urbanization of north-west Iberia. The few cities from Roman-Visigothic times had either disappeared or had been reduced to ecclesiastical burghs or fortresses. From the end of the eleventh century this king promoted the growth of the old centres and the foundation of new ones, granting numerous legal privileges and protecting the holding of markets. In addition he encouraged the settlement of people from the other side of the Pyrenees (*franci, francigenae*), dedicated to commerce and craftsmanship.[22]

Sahagún Abbey had first-hand experience of these economic changes from 1080 onwards. During Bernardus's time as abbot (1081–1085), a town was founded adjacent to the abbey, a constellation similar to that in Cluny. It was populated in particular by *franci*[23] dedicated to craftsmanship and commerce. They were not given agricultural land to cultivate but only a plot on which to

---

[21] C. SÁNCHEZ ALBORNOZ, Moneda de cambio y moneda de cuenta en el reino asturleonés, in: Cuadernos de Historia de España 31–32 (1960), pp. 5–31; J. J. TODESCA, What touches all: coinage and monetary policy in Leon–Castile to 1230, Ph. D. read in Fordham University, New York 1996; IDEM, The Crown Renewed: The Administration of Coinage in León–Castile c.1085–1200, in: The Emergence of León–Castile c. 1065–1500. Essays Presented to J. F. O'Callagham, Farnham 2015, pp. 9–32; J. GAUTIER DALCHÉ, L'histoire monétaire de l'Espagne septentrionale et centrale du IX au XII siècles: quelques réflexions sur divers problèmes, in: Anuario de estudios medievales 6 (1969), pp. 43–96; IDEM, Aperçus sur la monnaie et les usages monétaires dans les Asturies, d'après la documentation de San Pelayo d'Oviedo (1043–1270), in: En la España medieval 2 (1982), pp. 379–394; W. DAVIES, Sale, Price and Valuation in Galicia and Castile–León in the Tenth Century, in: Early Medieval Europe 11/2 (2002), pp. 149–174. A summary in: J. M. DE FRANCISCO OLMOS, El nacimiento de la moneda en Castilla: de la moneda prestada a la moneda propia, in: I Jornadas Científica sobre Documentación jurídico–administrativa, económico–financiera y judicial del reino castellano–leonés, siglos X–XIII, Madrid 2002, pp. 303–346.

[22] J. GAUTIER DALCHÉ, Historia urbana de León y Castilla en la Edad Media (siglos IX–XIII), Madrid 1989, pp. 67–168; P. MARTÍNEZ SOPENA, Fundavi bonam villam. La urbanización de Castilla y León en tiempos de Alfonso VI, in: J. GARCÍA TURZA / I. MARTÍNEZ NAVAS (coord.), El fuero de Logroño y su época, Logroño 1996, pp. 167–188; IDEM, El mercado en la España Cristiana de los siglos XI y XII, in: Codex aquilarensis: Cuadernos de investigación del Monasterio de Santa María la Real 13 (1998), pp. 121–142; IDEM, Las migraciones de francos en la España de los siglos XI y XII, in: J. I. RUIZ DE LA PEÑA SOLAR / M. J. SANZ FUENTES / M. CALLEJA PUERTA (coord.), Los fueros de Avilés y su época, Oviedo 2012, pp. 253–280.

[23] The *franci* refers to all those from the territory of the ancient Carolingian Empire, including Catalonia and, in general, those arriving from north of the Pyrenees, including the English.

build their houses. They had to pay the abbey a tax in coin: rent for the *suelo* (the plot of land where the house was built), to which was soon added another for the right to have an oven (1096).[24]

The abbots of Sahagún not only achieved the settlement of people in the town by the king's order, but they also got him to grant the market privilege, which a nearby royal town, Grajal (1093),[25] duly lost. In 1155 a three-week fair to celebrate Pentecost was added, though its length was later reduced to two weeks, in 1195.[26] The abbey would receive the fines imposed in the said market and fair.

This commercial activity explains why Queen Urraca, in 1116, and King Alfonso VII, in 1119, should make an agreement with the abbot to mint coins in the town under the abbot's supervision. The abbey would receive a part of the profits: in 1116 one third would go to Sahagún, another third to its feminine dependency of San Pedro and the other third to the queen; in 1119 half would go to Sahagún and the other half to the king. With the consent of the king, the abbot and the council of Sahagún, the agreement could be renewed annually.[27] In any case, on signing the agreement the abbot was very concerned to ensure his control over the town of Sahagún, given that the minting of coin was the king's prerogative.

The income generated by the market was substantial. In 1150 the monks assigned the market's weekly profits to the cellarer, from which 50 gold coins had to be given to the abbot and ten to the monks.[28] One may suppose that the cellarer's surplus which could be used for other expenses, exceeded this amount. In addition, the market and the fair would facilitate the sale of part of the rents paid in kind from the extensive domains of Sahagún.

The income from the market and the fair or the ground rents were not the abbey's only income in coin. The donations could be gold or silver (sometimes

---

[24] The original *fuero* (local law) no longer exists, only a version from the mid twelfth century with numerous additions. However, the tax (*census*) paid for the *suelo* is part of the original version, while the tax for the oven comes from an agreement of 1096 (A. M. BARRERO GARCÍA, Los Fueros de Sahagún, in: Anuario de Historia del Derecho Español 42 (1972), pp. 385–598, at pp. 500–501). Colección Sahagun, ed. M. HERRERO (note 10 above), vol. 3, docs. 823, 974. Crónicas anónimas, ed. A. UBIETO (note 16 above), pp. 19–24.

[25] Colección Sahagun, ed. M. HERRERO (note 10 above), vol. 3, doc. 911. Crónicas anónimas, ed. A. UBIETO (note 16 above), p. 23.

[26] Colección Sahagún, ed. J. A. FERNÁNDEZ FLÓREZ (note 15 above), vol. 4, docs. 1320, 1497.

[27] Ibid., docs. 1195, 1201. Concerning the minted coins: L. HERNÁNDEZ–CANUT Y FERNÁNDEZ–ESPAÑA, El Abadengo de Sahagún. Vestigios de una manifestación monetaria feudal en los reinos de Castilla y León durante el siglo XII, in: Gaceta Numismática 137 (2000), pp. 7–28.

[28] Colección Sahagún, ed. J. A. FERNÁNDEZ FLÓREZ (note 15 above), vol. 4, doc. 1310.

coin was indicated), although it was only mentioned if the donation in question included real estate.[29] Of the many other money offerings nothing is known.

Finally, the abbey took sizeable pecuniary fines from Sahagún council or other inhabitants for opposing the abbot's power. For instance, in 1152, the inhabitants of the town of Grajal had to pay 2,000 solidi (shillings) for repeated damage to a dam belonging to the abbey;[30] and in the time of abbot Iohannes (1182–1194), the burghers of Sahagún had to pay 5,000 maravedís (a gold coin) to the abbot for rebelling against him.[31] It was, however, common for part of the fine to be paid by other means, not with coin.

The use of coins

To what was this income in coin dedicated? At the moment there are no accounts which would allow us to study this aspect. A significant portion would be destined to the acquisition of goods for consumption. Thus, the 10 maravedís of the market rent that the cellarer had to give to the abbey were used for a meal in the refectory on the feast of the Circumcision (January 1st); to these were added another 10 maravedís that the abbot ceded to the abbey in 1160 for his anniversary meal; another 20 maravedís of the abbot's part were used to illuminate several altars.[32] It must be supposed that the remainder of the income received by the cellarer would also be used for the purchase of food for the abbot, the monks and the servants.

The study of MARTÍNEZ LIÉBANA concerning the estate of Sahagún in the eleventh and twelfth centuries has shown how its growth depended on donations; while the purchases made up less than one twentieth of the total amount of acquisitions.[33] This was not because there was no market for land, but

---

[29] For instance in 1049: *Post obitum uero meum medietate de omnia mea facultate uobis concedo: aurum et argentum, equos et mulos, uaccas et equas, oues et boues et omnia premiscua pecora, uel utensilia, usque ad minimam rem, ubique ea potueritis inuenire; exceptis illos atondos et illas sellas maiores que uenerunt in mea diuisa, que dono ad filios meos*: Colección Sahagun, ed. M. HERRERO (note 10 above), vol. 2, doc. 527. Other generic references from 1091 to 1092: Ibid., vol. 3, docs. 878, 888 In 1104 the hospice of Sahagún received 11 silver *solidi*, as well as wine and cereal, together with farmland (Ibid., vol. 3, doc. 1116). The scribe of the Becerro Gótico de Sahagún suppressed many of these references, considering them unnecessary for providing a legal claim to the monastic properties: J. A. FERNÁNDEZ FLÓREZ / M. HERRERO DE LA FUENTE, Libertades de los copistas en la confección de los cartularios: el caso del Becerro Gótico de Sahagún, in: Scribi e colofoni. Le sottoscrizioni di copista dalle origini all'avento della stampa, Spoleto 1995, pp. 301–320, at pp. 314–315.

[30] Colección Sahagún, ed. J. A. FERNÁNDEZ FLÓREZ (note 15 above), vol. 4, doc. 1313.

[31] Crónicas anónimas, ed. A. UBIETO (note 16 above), pp. 134–135.

[32] Colección Sahagún, ed. J. A. FERNÁNDEZ FLÓREZ (note 15 above), vol. 4, docs. 1310, 1336.

[33] E. MARTÍNEZ LIÉBANA, El dominio señorial (note 3 above), pp. 191–195, 275–280.

Years	A	B	C	D
1000–1009	16	4		
1010–1019	5		1	
1020–1029	5		3	1
1030–1039	4	1	4	
1040–1049	20	1	6	
1050–1059	24	4	5	
1060–1069	13		5	3
1070–1079	15	1	5	2
1080–1089	19		10	
1090–1099	16	8 (+7*)	19	5
1100–1109	14	7 (+24*)	10	16(+4*)
1110–1119				
1120–1129	2		3	2
1130–1139	5		2	2
1140–1149	14	1	1	
1150–1159	8			
1160–1169	8	2		
1170–1179	5	2	1	1
1180–1189	14	5		1
1190–1199	28	11	2	
1200–1209	20	9		5
1210–1219	7	4		3
1220–1229	14	9		1

Table 1: Purchases and sales in Sahagún's documentation

A. Total number of documents concerning purchases and sales (not including Sopratello)

B. Purchase documents in favour of Sahagún

C. Documents with donations to Sahagún of those properties previously bought

D. Documents concerning donations to Sahagún including *roborationes*

* Inventory of Sopratello

that the abbey was not very interested in purchasing real estate.[34] However, the growth of the abbey's domain was not completely dissociated from this aspect, as a significant part of the land or goods donated had previously been bought from a third party (Table 1).

On the other hand, donations could oblige the abbey to offer something in exchange, the *roboratio*.[35] This could be simply a good meal, but also animals suited to the donor's social status depending on whether they were nobles or peasants – a horse, a mule, a hunting dog, or an ox, valuable objects, especially textiles, or money in coin. In fact, throughout the eleventh and twelfth centuries Sahagún abbey spent more on these roborationes than on the purchases themselves. Table 2 shows the figures taken from the documentation, although it should be pointed out that part of the merchandise was not given a value, so it has not been taken into account. Similarly, neither has it been possible to calculate the amount spent by the abbey on lifelong annual pensions in coin or kind as compensation for a donation.[36]

---

[34] Of 185 bills of sale preserved from 1000 to 1160, only 27 (15%) purchases and 5 (3%) sales were made by the monastery. By 1200, the figure had increased to 240 bills of sale, of which 47 (20%) were purchases of Sahagún. The document about the manor of Sobradillo is not included here, although it records about 30 acquisitions by the monastery between 1090 and 1110 (Colección Sahagún, ed. J. A. FERNÁNDEZ FLÓREZ (note 15 above), vol. 4, doc. 1180). In the table, these purchases are marked with an asterisk.

[35] Money or goods handed over to the prior owner by those who acquired a property through purchase or donation, and which served as ratification of the sale or donation.

[36] See the section The setting–up of corrodies.

Years	Purchases		Roborationes		Total
	Solidi	Apreciatura	Solidi	Apreciatura	Solidi
1000–1009	90	86			176
1010–1019					
1020–1029				24	24
1030–1039		2			2
1040–1049	26				26
1050–1059	99				99
1060–1069			10	500	510
1070–1079		100	400		500
1080–1089					
1090–1099	533		150	230	913
1100–1109	1 130	350	1 500	2 044	5 024
1110–1119					
1120–1129			3 006		3 006
1130–1139			1 975		1 975
1140–1149				325	325
1150–1159					
1160–1169	322.5				322.5
1170–1179	97.5	33.7	772.5		903.7
1180–1189	705	270			975
1190–1199	2 253.7		112.5		2 366.2
1200–1209	2 151.7		1 700	66	3917.7
1210–1219	269.2		337.5		606.7
1220–1229	1 567.5		225		1792.5
Total	9 245.2	841.7	10 188.5	3 189	23 464.4

Table 2: The investment made, in coin and merchandise, in purchases and *roborationes*

The figures from Table 2 show a clear difference in the use of money between the eleventh and twelfth centuries. Until 1109 the abbey used money and merchandise almost equally in payment for purchases and *roborationes*,[37] but after 1120 money becomes almost completely dominant.[38] This is a clear indication of the monetarization of the economy in Sahagún, both from the abbey's point of view, which had money to spend, and from that of the surrounding area, which accepted this money.

It is interesting to compare the use of coin and merchandise by the abbey and by individuals that can be seen in the documentation of Sahagún. Until the year 1080, when the use of money was less frequent, the abbey used almost twice as much coin as the surrounding area (47% of payments as opposed to 26%). However, between 1080 and 1110, a strong monetarization of the payments in the abbey's surroundings occurs (76%), while the abbey itself maintains the traditional formulas, with only a slight increase in the use of coin (55%). The crisis created by the civil war (1110–1117) reactivated sales in exchange for cereals and grain, yet after that, coin once more dominates as the preferred form of payment, while the merchandise (mainly textiles and food) is used as *roborationes* in transactions with the main payment in coin, both by the abbey and the surrounding area.

The amount of coin used by Sahagún also tended to increase, although with strong oscillations, which may have been due more to the changes in the abbey's will to buy or to the need to pay roborationes for donations, privileges or judicial agreements, than to the volume of coin circulating in the kingdom. Before 1070, the amounts used were limited, and even between 1010 and 1039, there was no registration of money being handed over by the monks. This does not, however, mean that they did not sell land in the first quarter of the century in exchange for money.[39]

In the reign of king Alfonso VI (1067–1109), a considerable growth in the use of money can be noticed, reaching its maximum in the first decade of the twelfth century. From the mid-eleventh century, the kings of Leon were paid tribute by the Muslim rulers in exchange for military aid, protection or simply to buy peace. Some Christian knights also served as mercenaries to the Muslim kings for money. All this money was then redistributed by the kings of Leon among the aristocracy and the knights for their aid and loyalty, or donated to monasteries and cathedrals as alms in exchange for their prayers. The conquest of al-Andalus by the Almoravids in the 1090s put an end to these tributes and therefore to this

---

[37] Until 1079 they paid 46.7% in coin, rising to 55.8% between 1080 and 1109. The figures are approximate as some merchandise is not valued.

[38] About 93% of payments were made in coin, with little difference before and after 1150. The same happened between 1200 and 1229.

[39] In 1006 Sahagún sold properties for a value of 250 *solidi* [Colección Sahagun, ed. M. HERRERO (note 10 above), vol. 2, doc. 386] and another 45 *solidi* in 1022 (Ibid., doc. 410). Another sale during these years had no price (Ibid., doc. 422).

source of monetary income for the king, the aristocracy and the knights of the kingdom of Leon. It must be asked whether the nobles looked to the abbey for the money which they had before received from the king.

The civil war that devastated the kingdom during the second and third decades of the twelfth century caused the abbey to become a seller, the objective being to obtain food rather than money.[40] In addition, the abbey was at this time subjected to the demand for gold and silver by different kings. In 1126, king Alfonso VII confirmed various privileges for the abbey which had been violated in previous years, when gold and silver had also been confiscated from the abbey. The abbot, in *roboratio*, handed over to the king an enormous sum of money: 3,000 *solidi* in silver.[41] It is probably similar to another case which occurred in 1127 in Santiago de Compostela, when the king, after demanding a great sum from the bishop, confirmed several of his privileges.[42] On the other hand, the first of the *Crónicas anónimas* of Sahagún denounced Sahagún's governors, put in place by Alfonso I 'the Battler', for selling the abbey's agricultural lands and forests to the burghers in order to obtain money. It also condemned the abbot imposed by the king, his brother Ramiro, for having taken part of the abbey's treasure for himself.[43]

The second reform of Sahagún in 1132 substantially reduced this expense in coin over the middle decades of the twelfth century. We have to wait until the last third of the century for the abbey to recuperate its normal level of purchases and roborationess, reaching a new peak around the year 1200. The main use for money from the 1180s onwards may also be related to the start of minting gold coins (maravedís) by king Alfonso VIII., in 1172.[44]

The *palatium* of Sobradillo

A third of the entire amount invested in purchases or *roborationes* was concentrated in only two decades, between 1090–1110, coinciding with the time that Didacus was abbot. These are the years following the foundation of the town,

---

[40] In 1111, the monks sold a garden for 200 *solidi* paid in wheat and rye (Colección Sahagún, ed. J. A. FERNÁNDEZ FLÓREZ (note 15 above), vol. 4, doc. 1183). In 1113 a house was sold for 615 *solidi*, of which 315 were paid in wine and the rest in silver *solidi* (Ibid., doc. 1190).

[41] Ibid., doc. 1226. Soon after, in 1130, the abbey gave 250 maravedis, that is 1875 *solidi*, to the *infanta* Sancha, sister of Alfonso VII, as *roboratio* for the *post mortem* donation of the church of Santervás (Ibid., doc. 1239).

[42] C. M. REGLERO DE LA FUENTE, Reyes y obispos en los reinos de León y Castilla (c. 1050–c. 1200): oración, servicio y memoria, in: M. D. TEIJEIRA / M. V. HERRÁEZ / M. C. COSMEN (eds.), Reyes y prelados. La creación artística en los reinos de León y Castilla (1050–1500), Madrid 2014, pp. 45–66, at pp. 45–48.

[43] Crónicas anónimas, ed. A. UBIETO (note 16 above), pp. 56–57.

[44] J. M. DE FRANCISCO DE OLMOS, El nacimiento de la moneda (note 21 above), p. 335.

the creation of the market and also the start of the minting of coin by king Alfonso VI. It was at this time that the manor (*palatium*) of Sopratello was created within Sahagún's *cautum* (*banleuca*, landed immunity). An exceptional document has been preserved which includes all the acquisitions made there. This provides information on the extent of the use of coinage as well as a comparison of the relative importance of purchases, donations and exchanges.[45]

In 1092, Gonzalo Núñez,[46] to whom the abbot Didacus had given responsibility for all the abbey's farms and villages (*super omnes uillas ipsius monasterii*), decided to build a *palatium* next to a church, to which end he began to acquire the surrounding land over a period of 17 years. The operation meant assigning four plots of land, which already belonged to the abbey but which were ascribed to other obedientiaries (including 3 to the cellarer), to the *palatium*. In addition, 69 plots of land and 33 vineyards were also acquired. Almost half the land (30 plots) were bought, for a total payment of 236 *solidi*, as well as boots and spurs to the value of 60 solidi and, in one case, wheat and wine. The amounts paid oscillated between 3 and 35 *solidi*, but half of them were under 10 solidi. Nevertheless, only two vineyards were bought for a total of 35 *solidi*.

The second most important means of acquiring land was by exchange (16 cases), on one occasion completed with the additional payment of a small amount of money. Exchanging lands did not necessarily mean that the abbey had no money to buy it, since it could have been a condition imposed by the other party, who did not want money but other plots of land. It was so in one case, in which the land exchanged by Gonzalo had previously been bought. In the case of the vineyards, exchange was used only three times.

There was also a third method of acquisition which, overall, was more important than the exchange: this was *mañería*, a term which meant the abbey's right as lord to inherit the goods of those who died without legitimate children. It was in this way that the abbey got hold of no less than 15 plots of land and 28 vineyards, from six different deceased persons. In a similar way, the laws allowed the abbey to gain possession of land belonging to a woman who had not been a virgin at the time of her matrimony. On the other hand, the donations, which at this time was the principal means of acquiring goods for Sahagún, were reduced,

---

[45] Colección Sahagún, ed. J. A. FERNÁNDEZ FLÓREZ (note 15 above), vol. 4, IV, doc. 1180.

[46] In 1110 Gonzalo Núñez became prior of Sahagún (Colección Sahagún, ed. J. A. FERNÁNDEZ FLÓREZ (note 15 above), vol. 4, docs. 1180, 1182). Between 1098 and 1106 he received some donations for the monastery and its abbot Didacus: Colección Sahagun, ed. M. HERRERO (note 10 above), vol. 3, docs. 1024, 1051, 1066, 1104, 1140, 1144). In 1095 Gonzalo Núñez, together with his wife Goto, offered their daugther Teresa to the monastery of San Pedro de los Molinos, a dependence of Sahagún, along with some properties (Ibid., doc. 950). In 1100 Gonzalo Núñez and his brothers and sisters made some donations to Sahagún and San Pedro (Ibid., docs. 1063, 1064). It is possible that the said donations were made by a local noble, Gonzalo Núñez, who finally became a monk.

in this particular case, to four plots of land, which is logical, given the limitations of both time and space.

The palace of Sopratello belonged to the abbot of Sahagún's portion, although it had been administered by Gonzalo Núñez, who became the abbey's prior and then proposed an exchange to the abbot: the monks of Sahagún would receive this manor for their kitchen in exchange for another property they had (1110). This internal reassignment of properties is the result of a previous division of the abbey's properties, itself another consequence of the reform in 1080.

Abbey administration: offices, obediencies, *decaniae*

The administrative organisation of the abbey of Sahagún before 1080 is little known. Apart from the abbot, references to the abbey's officials only appear in a document of 1022, confirmed by the abbot and 20 monks.[47] The majority are defined as presbyters (6), deacons (5) or simply monks (*fratres*) (5). Among the offices mentioned are the abbot and the cellarer, both present in the Rule of Saint Benedict.[48] The *decanus Legione* is not one of the deacons of the Rule,[49] but the administrator of one of the abbey's *decaniae*, of the properties that Sahagún had in León and the surrounding area. In addition, there is mention of a treasurer, a *stabulario*, an *orriario*, a *super uillas* monk, and a *super sarrazes* monk.

Thus, we have the two fundamental offices of the Rule together with others that arise from different traditions or from within the abbey itself. The expression *frater et super uillas* reminds us of that used in 1110 to define Gonzalo Núñez, *super omnes uillas ipsius monasterii*,[50] that is, the monk in charge of administering the abbey's dependent villages, in particular those within the abbey's *cautum*. As for the *frater super sarrazes*, it should be understood as the monk in charge of the abbey's muslim serfs.

The organisation into *decaniae* of the properties which were far away from the abbey has been documented in Sahagún since the tenth century, although the term is hardly used in this abbey,[51] as the usual thing is to speak of *monasteria*,

---

[47] Colección Sahagun, ed. M. Herrero (note 10 above), vol. 2, doc. 410.
[48] G. M. Colombas, San Benito (note 9 above), pp. 680–685 (R.B. 65) and pp. 516–521 (R.B. 31).
[49] Ibid., pp. 480–483 (R.B. 21).
[50] Colección Sahagún, ed. J. A. Fernández Flórez (note 15 above), vol. 4, doc. 1180.
[51] Colección Sahagún, ed. J. M. Mínguez (note 5 above), doc. 287; Colección Sahagun, ed. M. Herrero (note 10 above), vol. 2, doc. 630. Most of the references to deaneries concern the monastery of Saelices de Mayorga, given to Sahagún around 1070: Colección Sahagún, ed. J. M. Mínguez (note 5 above), doc. 23; Colección Sahagun, ed. M. Herrero (note 10 above), vol. 2, docs. 531, 532, 637, 640, 681, 683, 687, 691; or to the monastery of San Mancio (Ibid., doc. 693), which was donated to Sahagún in 1195. As for the deaneries of Abellar, another monastery in Leon that followed the Rule of Saint Benedict in the tenth century, see: M. J.

ecclesiae or *villae* to define these management units. Even so, monks from Sahagún do appear in the documentation as being responsible for sets of properties around a church.[52] Although the Benedictine Rule refers to *de fratribus qui longe ab oratorio laborant*,[53] in that case, it refers to a temporary and not a permanent situation.

The Cluniac reform of Sahagún in 1080 brought a fundamental change from the administrative point of view: the appearance of the obedientiaries, each of whom had properties assigned to him. Their first appearance is in the last decade of the eleventh century, and the different monastic obedientiaries appear in the documentation throughout the first decades of the twelfth century. It is not possible to know whether this is due to the fact that they took time to create or just through a lack of news.

The first office (*obedientia*) to be documented was the almonership (1091).[54] It was controlled by a (senior) monk, but the designation as almoner does not occur until 1125.[55] The almonry received a donation and its administrator was charged with defending its properties.

The abbey's 'kitchen' is mentioned in 1102, when the abbot Didacus handed over some ruined mills to the monks *ad opus uestre quoquine*, after the prior and the cellarer had asked him for them. It would seem logical to assume that the mills were for milling the necessary grain for feeding the monks. Their repair cost 300 *solidis denariorum*, which came out of the 'kitchen' money provided by the prior and the cellarer. The abbot, for his part, ceded the ruined buildings that housed the mills as well as the necessary wood for their repair. Finally, Didacus ordered that no-one should remove the mills from this office.[56] This document shows

---

CARBAJO SERRANO, El monasterio de los Santos Cosme y Damián de Abellar. Monacato y sociedad en la época astur–leonesa, León 1988, pp. 78–80.

[52] Fernando and Miguel in San Salvador de Boñar and San Juan de Corniero at the beginning of the tenth century (Colección Sahagun, ed. M. HERRERO (note 10 above), vol. 2, docs. 389, 390, 393, 394). The priest Froilán of San Vicente de Tolia (Ibid., doc. 466) or Petro Vellitiz in Villalobos (Ibid., doc. 577).

[53] G. M. COLOMBAS, San Benito (note 9 above), p. 600 (R.B. 50).

[54] This concerns a dispute about a vineyard donated to San Salvador in Tejadillo, that some laymen maintained: *cum seniore domno Petro, qui regebat elemosinam Sancti Facundi* (Colección Sahagún, ed. M. HERRERO (note 10 above), vol. 3, doc. 884).

[55] Colección Sahagún, ed. J. A. FERNÁNDEZ FLÓREZ (note 15 above), vol. 4, doc. 1219.

[56] *Quia necessitudo uictui cogebat uos, placuit michi ut ad opus uestre quoquine darem uobis, spontanea mea uoluntate, illos molinos de Quadrones, qui modo sunt destructi, in quibus olim fuerunt due domus ex quibus una tenebant sanctimoniales Sancti Petri, alteram uero possidebat ille qui tenebat Medianos. Utrique uero non tenebant de hereditate sed ex prestamo de Sancto Facundo. Sed petente michi eos prior domnus Gotinus et domnus Uistremirus, qui erat tunc cellararius, annui peticioni eorum cuncteque congregationi; uidensque ego Diacus abbas iam prefatus hanc necessitudinem uestre quoquine, precepi priori domno Gotino, quatinus uestris denariis, illos hedificarent. In quorum dispendiis expensi sunt CCC^{ti} solidis denariorum ex sumptu quoquine per manus Gotini prioris et cellararii qui tunc erat nomine Arias. Et in adiutorium expense do ego uobis tres ulmos necnon etiam et pedes quinque molendinorum et insuper ramos ad claudendum portum. Constituoque*

that the abbey's 'kitchen' was organised as an *obedientia* and that it had both properties and money to cover expenses.

Some years later (1109–1110), came the first reference to the monk in charge of the 'kitchen'. He had taken his vows four years before, on seeing himself in danger of dying, donating all his possessions to the abbey. Some years later, this monk's creditors demanded the payment of his liabilities from the abbey. The prior and the said monk in charge of the kitchen, then redeemed the debts by paying 75 *solidi* of the monks' money. It was for this reason that the abbot assigned the property donated by this monk to the abbey's kitchen.[57]

Everything seems to indicate that the kitchen was controlled by the cellarer, under the supervision of the prior, although a document of 1125 does mention a *coquine prepositus* in addition to the cellarer.[58] The income assigned to the latter included the profits from the weekly market, at least following the agreement reached between the monks on the death of the abbot Dominicus II, which was then ratified by the new abbot Dominicus III after his election (1150).[59] The number of officials related to the monks' food was increasing: in 1150 a keeper of the wine cellar (*apotecarius*) was mentioned, but from 1157 onwards, they spoke of both a *cellerarius maior* and the *apotecarius maior*, adding a *refectorarius maior*, which would indicate that they had assistants in their functions.[60]

The cost of the monks' dress and footwear was covered by the chamber (*camara*), which, in 1117, received a generous donation of properties in the town of Sahagún and the surrounding area.[61] The official in charge was the chamberlain (*camerarius*), who was not mentioned until 1157.[62] He should not be confused with the abbot's chamberlain, who was the principal official in the administration of the abbey's possessions and who was mentioned in the second decade of the

---

uobis ut omnibus annis uel temporibus licentiam habeatis aprehendere ex ramis arborum uel de spinis aut ex salicibus quot necessarium fuerit ad portum claudendum. Ita ut amodo et deinceps ipsi molini seruiant ad ipsam quoquinam cunctis diebus uel temporibus. Nullusque ausus sit auferre illos ab hac obedientia [...]: Colección Sahagun, ed. M. HERRERO (note 10 above), vol. 3, doc. 1081.

[57] Colección Sahagún, ed. J. A. FERNÁNDEZ FLÓREZ (note 15 above), vol. 4, doc. 1182.

[58] In a list of 37 monks, the *coquine prepositus* Martinus appears in the middle, and the cellarer Iohannes at the end (Ibid., doc. 1219). Two years earlier a cellarer named Martinus was mentioned (Ibid., doc. 1214).

[59] Ibid., doc. 1310. Ten years later this abbot assigned new properties to the monks' kitchen. Using this rent, the cellarer had to give a feast to the monks on the octave of the Nativity of the Virgin Mary (Ibid., doc. 1337).

[60] Ibid., docs. 1310, 1327, 1329, 1330, 1336, 1337, 1351.

[61] ut ipsa hereditas sit semper in obsequium monacorum ibidem Deo seruientium et seruiat semper ad illa camara, ut illi seniores habeant inde uestimenta uel calciamenta [...] ut omnia supradicta seruiant ad illa camara de illis senioribus, quatinus inde uestimenta uel calciamenta habere possint (Ibid., doc. 1199).

[62] Ibid., doc. 1236. Again in 1160 and 1164 as *camerarius maior* (Ibid. docs. 1336, 1337, 1351). This must not be confused with the *camerarius abbatis,* who also appears in 1164.

twelfth century.[63] Other offices that appeared and received goods for their expenses were the guest quarters or *albergaria* (1104),[64] and the abbey works or *opera* (1134).[65] In 1160, the abbot assigned an amount of 20 maravedís and a church to illuminate several altars, yet no obedientiary or particular official to administer it was mentioned.[66]

In reality, only four documents from the archives of Sahagún use the term *obedientia* between 1096 and 1123.[67] In three of them, it designates only one of the abbey's local domains, organised around a church or a monastery, and controlled by a monk appointed by the abbot. This is what, in other documents, is called *decania*[68] or, in the most important cases, 'priory'. The first of the *Crónicas anónimas* of Sahagún, whose first version can be traced back to the second decade of the twelfth century, refers several times to the villages, priories (*obediencia*) and abbey farms as places from which the domain's properties were administered and where the monks resided.[69]

Debts and loans

The abbey of Sahagún also lent its money to third parties, although little evidence of this activity has survived to the present day, since we have no accounting documents. The only remaining written evidence comes from creditors' defaults, when bad loans resulted in the incorporation of property into the abbey's domains.

---

[63] Crónicas anónimas, ed. A. UBIETO (note 16 above), pp. 55, 69. He appears in a document of 1164 together with the *camerarius maior* (Colección Sahagún, ed. J. A. FERNÁNDEZ FLÓREZ (note 15 above), vol. 4, doc. 1351).

[64] Colección Sahagun, ed. M. HERRERO (note 10 above), vol. 3, doc. 1115. The hospitaler (*hospitalarius, hostarius*) is mentioned from 1125 onwards (Colección Sahagún, ed. J. A. FERNÁNDEZ FLÓREZ (note 15 above), vol. 4, docs. 1219, 1310, 1327, 1337, 1351. The hospital of Sahagún was endowed by Alfonso VI in 1078 (Colección Sahagun, ed. M. HERRERO (note 10 above), vol. 3, doc. 765).

[65] Colección Sahagún, ed. J. A. FERNÁNDEZ FLÓREZ (note 15 above), vol. 4, 1253. *Petrus Stefani, regens operam Domnis Sanctis, scripsit et conf.* is mentioned in 1157 (Ibid., doc. 1326).

[66] Ibid., doc. 1336.

[67] Colección Sahagun, ed. M. HERRERO (note 10 above), vol. 3, docs. 977 (1096), 1081 (1102). Colección Sahagún, ed. J. A. FERNÁNDEZ FLÓREZ (note 15 above), vol. 4, docs. 1180 (1110), 1216 (1123). It reappears in a papal document of 1260 (Colección diplomática del Monasterio de Sahagun (857–1300). 5, (1200–1300), ed. J. A. FERNÁNDEZ FLÓREZ, León 1994, doc. 1778).

[68] The donation of Alfonso VI to Sahagún of the monastery of San Salvador de Villaverde is a good example. He ordered the *monacos Sancti Facundi qui ibi quesierint habitare uolo habere talem consuetudinem et foro quomodo alii monachi eiusdem monasterii habent, qui licentia abbatis in omnibus decaniis suis undique sunt dispertiti, hoc est, ut nullus ibi ubi quisquam eorum fuerit non audeat pignorare aut aliquam uiolentiam inferre* (Colección Sahagun, ed. M. HERRERO (note 10 above), vol. 3, doc. 1045).

[69] Crónicas anónimas, ed. A. UBIETO (note 16 above), pp. 54, 55, 56, 60, 65.

The oldest evidence comes from the end of the eleventh century. Romanus Petri received 100 silver *solidi* from Sahagún, paying them back over a year later (1097). It would seem that Romanus paid off the loan using the money that the abbey gave him as *roboratio* for a donation he made to the abbey itself, partly giving a small monastery while still alive and partly giving other properties *post mortem*, unless he died with legitimate children, who would obtain possession of the goods.[70] The donation thus seems to be an agreement to resolve an unpaid loan, in which the debtor retains certain rights over the properties handed over. The donation was the confirmation of another made a decade before, at that time with his relatives, in which he also confirmed an endowment for a monastery by his father or grandfather.[71]

On the other hand, Munius Petri's journey to Jerusalem justifies a loan of 1,000 *solidi* that the monks gave him in the year 1100. The abbot Didacus lent him 500 silver *solidi* measured by the Mark of Saint Peter of Cologne and another 500 *solidi* in coin. Munius gave the abbey his properties in three places as security. The abbey would retain control of the properties for five years, and by this we understand that the abbey would receive the income from the properties in lieu of interest. If, within this period of time, Munius returned and paid back the money to the abbey, he would then recuperate his properties, but if he died, the properties would remain with the abbey. The document of the loan was preceded by the donation that Munius Petri made to the abbey of his estates in 19 different places, including the three in question, *pro remedio animae*.[72] The loan was a modification of a post mortem donation made some months before. In the new document, Munius excluded his properties in one place,[73] which he had sold for a mule valued at 400 *solidi*. Thus, on lending the money, Sahagún now received a part of the goods while the donor still lived. This type of loan to knights who went on crusade has been widely documented in Cluny by DUBY;[74] but in Sahagún, this is the only known case.

---

[70] *Et ad confirmandam hanc cartulam accepi de uos C^m solidos de argento, quod tenui per unum annum et plus quod postea uobis tornaui quia in prestatum acceperam* (Colección Sahagun, ed. M. HERRERO (note 10 above), vol. 3, doc. 1017).

[71] Ibid., vol. 3, doc. 831. Something similar happened in 1097 when Isidoro Vellitiz and his wife gave a property to San Salvador de Villacete in lieu of 200 silver *solidi* loaned to them by the monastery: *pro remedio anime mee et pro CC^s solidos de argento que michi inprestastis, que uobis debeo dare. Do uobis proinde ipsa hereditate* (Ibid., doc. 998). A property donated to Sahagún in 1104 had been acquired in lieu of an unpaid loan of 1000 *solidi* (Ibid. doc. 1119).

[72] Ibid., doc. 1053.

[73] Ibid., doc. 1049.

[74] G. DUBY, Le budget de l'abbaye de Cluny entre 1080 et 1155. Économie domaniale et économie monétaire, in: G. DUBY, Hommes et structures du Moyen Âge, Paris 1984, p. 67.

Some years later, it was the abbey that had to pay 75 *solidi* to the creditors of one of the monks, to pay off the debts contracted before his entry into the community (1110). This allowed Sahagún abbey to retain the properties that the said monk had donated on taking his vows.[75]

After many years without news, the abbey once more entered the loan market at the end of the twelfth century. In 1182, the abbey lent 120 maravedís (i.e., 900 *solidi*) to a married couple, taking their properties in two places as security. The creditors would recuperate their goods in accordance with the repayment of the entire amount, a half or a third of the money.[76] Thus, the income produced by the estates became the loan's interest payments.

When the debtors or heirs could not recuperate the pawned goods, they could try to reach an agreement with the abbey. Thus, in 1190, three brothers sold their properties in one place to the chamberlain of Sahagún for 25.5 maravedís. The same properties had already been pawned by a fourth brother, with their consent, to the current chamberlain's predecessor for 12 maravedís.[77]

It is probable that it was also the monks of Sahagún who lent money to Didacus Alvari to buy a property, which he then pawned. His son later sold it to the abbey for 10.5 maravedís, probably because he could not pay the debt (1192).[78] On the other hand, when the abbey received or bought a pawned estate (1187–1214), the debt then had to be paid if they wanted to retain this estate.[79]

The chronology of the loans made by the abbey: 1097–1110 and 1182–1192, coincides with the times at which the abbey made the most purchases. We must, therefore, assume that this activity reflects the availability of the necessary liquidity. A personal component must be added to this; the abbacies of Didacus (1088–1110) and Iohannes (1182–1194). Another important element is the social condition of the creditors, who were usually members of the nobility, the *mediocri*, of which a text from the beginning of the twelfth century speaks.

The first news of Sahagún abbey being in debt appears in the first third of the thirteenth century, but this does not mean that the abbey was free of debt before that date. On the one hand, debt was the result of its expansive policy, yet it was also a symptom of their lack of liquidity. Thus, in 1201, the abbey handed over

---

[75] Colección Sahagún, ed. J. A. Fernández Flórez (note 15 above), vol. 4, doc. 1182.

[76] Ibid., doc. 1406.

[77] Ibid., doc. 1454. In 1190, the chamberlain was Petrus Michaelis. His predecessor, Dominicus, is mentioned from 1182 to 1188 (Ibid., docs. 1406, 1417, 1424, 1441).

[78] Ibid., doc. 1470: *ego Garsias Didaci, filius Didaci Albari, uendo uobis Iohanni abbati Sancti Facundi totam meam hereditatem de Uillella, scilicet, nonam partem tocius medietatis quam hemit pater meus et suppignorauit; et uendo eam uobis pro X morabetinis et dimidio, inter precium et aluaroc; et sum iam paccatus.*

[79] Colección Sahagún, ed. J. A. Fernández Flórez (note 15 above), vol. 4, doc. 1434. The properties given by the donors in a village were mortgaged for 22 maravedis: Colección Sahagún, ed. J. A. Fernández Flórez (note 67 above), vol. 5, cocs. 1553, 1554, 1596.

some properties in Valladolid for a period of nine years to a married couple. The abbey was forced to do so in order to pay 270 maravedís they owed the couple from whom they had bought another property. In fact, if the monks paid the debt after only four of the nine years, they could recuperate the ceded property.[80]

In 1212, the abbey once more had to cede the possession of another property to pay the 700 maravedís it owed. The origin of the debt is not specified. The creditors would apply half the income from the said property to pay the principal debt, which means that the other half would be computed as interest. The property would be returned when the debt had been satisfied. Nevertheless, the abbey could recuperate it earlier if they paid what remained of the principal debt.[81] In 1227, there is further news of a property ceded due to a debt.[82]

These cessions are similar to those made to different nobles who donated properties to the abbey and who received other properties from the abbey during their lifetime as precarial estates (*prestimonium, beneficium*).[83] In one case, in addition to the property, the donors, members of the high nobility, should receive 200 maravedís annually, a high amount.[84]

The setting-up of corrodies

Some donations had, as compensation, the payment by the abbey to the donors of a corrody, an annual lifelong income, either in kind or in coin. It is not exceptional in the practice of monasteries, or indeed laymen.[85] In practice it was like a life pension or life insurance, 'avant la lettre'. Thus, Mayor, her sons, daughters and sons-in-law, in four different documents, donated their rights in Matilla to the abbot Didacus (1097). In addition to being able to retain usufruct, they and their heirs, the donors would receive during their life 10, or in some cases 20, silver *solidi* annually. The amount spent by Sahagún had to be substantial, given that they were paying 50 *solidi* annually.[86]

---

[80] Ibid., doc. 1542.
[81] Ibid., doc. 1585.
[82] Ibid., doc. 1644.
[83] Ibid., docs. 1548, 1563, 1595, 1603, 1619.
[84] Ibid., doc. 1545.
[85] Colección Sahagun, ed. M. HERRERO (note 10 above), vol. 3, doc. 954. For the economic meaning of this practice see: A. BELL / C. SUTCLIFFE, Valuing Medieval Annuities: Were corrodies underpriced?, in: Explorations in Economic History 47/2 (2010), pp. 142–157, [https://doi.org/10.1016/j.eeh.2009.07.002].
[86] Colección Sahagun, ed. M. HERRERO (note 10 above), vol. 3, docs. 997, 1001, 1006, 1014.

Petrus Gutierri, who donated his properties before leaving on pilgrimage to Jerusalem, would receive sustenance from the monks if he returned alive (1100).[87] Gundisalvus Ermegíldiz, besides the horse handed over as *roboratio* in his donation, would receive, each year, cereals (an amount that would be sufficient to feed him), clothes and footwear (1093).[88] Another five similar agreements were reached throughout the second half of the twelfth century (1156, 1157, 1181, 1195, 1199) with two men and three women who donated their properties in exchange for an annual quantity of wheat, grapes or grapejuice, as well as money or meat and clothes.[89] In two of the cases, the principal asset handed over was a house in Sahagún, which probably meant they were burghers of the town.

Conclusion

The abbey of Sahagún went through a double change between 1080 and 1110. On the one hand, the Cluniac reform transformed its internal administration system, which gave rise to the appearance of the monastic obedientiaries. On the other, it took advantage of the economic changes occurring in the kingdom, becoming immersed in a monetarized economy. Its income thenceforward came from both its landed wealth and the town's crafts and commerce. With the money it received as donations and rents, it could acquire land (through purchases or encouraging donations with *roborationes*, loans, the setting-up of corrodies…), but also food for the monks.

Its relation to this monetarized economy had a sweet side (when they received donations or income in coin, bought or loaned), as well as a bitter side (when the abbey itself went into debt at the start of the thirteenth century). This double-edged sword can also be seen in the social dynamics of the town of Sahagún. In the second decade of the twelfth century, a monk wrote about the abbot's conflicts with the inhabitants of the town:

"And given that the burghers of Sahagún used their merchandise peacefully and negotiated with great tranquillity, merchandise arrived and was brought from many parts, both gold and silver, and many clothes of diverse fabrication, so the said burghers and inhabitants were very rich and enjoyed many pleasures. Yet, as the abundance and multiplication of temporal things usually gives rise to a damaging alteration and to great arrogance and pride, pride began to grow in the hearts of the said burghers, as many times happens among the sons of lowly

---

[87] Ibid., doc. 1060.
[88] Ibid., doc. 904.
[89] Colección Sahagún, ed. J. A. FERNÁNDEZ FLÓREZ (note 15 above), vol. 4, docs. 1324, 1326, 1404, 1501, 1523.

origin and vile condition if they should have abundance of temporal things" (First of the *Crónicas anónimas* of Sahagún).[90]

Money was also seen as the origin of the sin of pride among the *laboratores*, who had to work.

---

[90] E por quanto los burgeses de San Fagum usavan paçificamente de sus mercadurías e negoçiavan en gran tranquilidad, por eso benían e traían de todas las partes mercadurías, así de oro como de plata, y aún muchas bestiduras de diversas façiones, en manera que los dichos burgeses e moradores eran muchos ricos e de muchos deleites abastados. Pero como suele reinar en la abundançia e multiplicaçion de las cosas tenporales enpeçible e dañosa alteraçion e gran arrogancia e soberbia, el coraçon de los dichos burgueses començose a creçér e levantar en sobervia, como muchas beçes se acostumbra a los fijos de pequeño suelo e vil condiçion si tengan abastança de las cosas tenporales: Crónicas anónimas, ed. A. UBIETO (note 16 above), p. 24.

English Benedictine Finance and the Crown Between the Norman Conquest and the Hundred Years War

Jens Röhrkasten

In the decades following the Norman Conquest of 1066 the English kingdom developed into a centralised state, its government based on the royal court, an efficient financial administration and a judicial system focused on the king. This evolution resulted in the creation of a modern central administration which affected all parts of society. The new branches of central government worked closely with older administrative and judicial structures which continued to exist in the shires into which royal authority was projected in two ways, through the appointment of permanent royal officials at the level of the shire and the hundred and through itinerant royal representatives.[1] Liberties outside this structure were forced to participate in this central machinery while the emerging palatinates developed corresponding features of their own. As far as its estates and most of its revenues were concerned, the Church was integrated into this system and although the ecclesiastical and secular sphere began to separate in the second half of the twelfth century, the secular and regular clergy were affected, even controlled, by the central royal institutions. Royal involvement in ecclesiastical appointments and the role of ecclesiastics in all branches of central government established close links which continued up to the Reformation and beyond.

All religious houses in existence at the time of the Norman Conquest came under the control of this centralised state and they were integrated into its judicial and financial structures, even though English kings did not create a 'monastic system' comparable to that of the Carolingians.[2] Such a homogenous system was not required because beginning with William I., the kings began to exert an increasing degree of control over the English Church and they had the tools to exert complete control over the secular affairs of all religious houses in their kingdom. From the late thirteenth century onwards, in times of external conflict when alien houses, mostly priories dependent on mother houses in the French kingdom, became suspect, these could be supervised or even abolished.[3] When

---

[1] S. C. F. MILSOM, Historical Foundations of the Common Law, London ²1981, pp. 25–36; A. L. POOLE, From Domesday Book to Magna Carta 1087–1216, Oxford ²1955, pp. 201–208, 385–413; J. A. GREEN, The Government of England Under Henry I, Cambridge 1986, pp. 51–117.

[2] H. LAWRENCE, Medieval Monasticism, Abingdon ⁴2015, pp. 68–72; G. MELVILLE, Die Welt der mittelalterlichen Klöster. Geschichte und Lebensformen, Munich 2012, pp. 42–49.

[3] C. NEW, History of the Alien Priories in England to the Confiscation of Henry V., Chicago 1916; B. THOMPSON, The Statute of Carlisle, 1307, and the Alien Priories, in: Journal of Ecclesiastical History 41 (1990), pp. 543–583.

it became politically expedient to remove monasticism altogether at the time of the Reformation, this also could be achieved in a relatively short period of time. Seen from this perspective, all English religious houses, irrespective of the rules followed by their inmates, shared the important feature of being subject to secular external control to a high degree.

A significant change in England's monastic landscape occurred with the establishment of Cluniac priories, and the arrival of the Cistercians, the Premonstratensians, the Carthusians, the foundation of the Gilbertines and the proliferation of the Augustinian Canons in the twelfth century. All of them, together with the English properties of the military orders, had to accept and abide by the financial and legal procedures of the royal administration. They were subject to royal law as far as their real estate and the related income was concerned and they were also under political control since the appointment of heads of houses was in most cases controlled by the Crown. Royal power extended to access to monastic wealth, leaving monasteries as objects of royal support on the one hand but also as economic centres whose wealth could be tapped. This was not necessarily an antagonistic relationship, in fact, harmony and co-operation predominated. However, there were also confrontations. The ambivalent relationship between king John and the English Cistercians may serve as an example. John was on the one hand founder and generous supporter of Beaulieu Abbey in Hampshire but he refused to accept the Cistercians' privileges, burdening the convents in his English kingdom with high demands for fiscal support.[4]

---

[4] A. L. POOLE, From Domesday Book to Magna Carta (note 1 above), pp. 448–449; S. CHURCH, King John. England, Magna Carta and the Making of a Tyrant, London 2016, p. 184.

The large English Benedictine monasteries will be at the centre of this article, irrespective of whether they were founded before the Norman Conquest of England[5] or founded or restored after 1066 like Battle[6], Selby[7], Shrewsbury[8], Chester[9], Colchester[10], Reading, Faversham[11], the Priory of Great Malvern, Whitby, Tewkesbury[12], St. Mary's, York[13], Godstow nunnery[14] or Hyde Abbey near Winchester. The Benedictine cathedral priories of Canterbury, Winchester and Worcester and the post-1066 creations of Bath, Coventry, Durham, Norwich, Ely and Rochester will also be included.[15] The aim is to assess the links between the monasteries living under the rule of St. Benedict and individual English monarchs in the context of the emerging state between the eleventh and fourteenth centuries. The focus will be on the interaction between royal government and the

---

5   The male houses of Abbotsbury, Abingdon, Burton, Bury St. Edmunds, St. Augustine, Canterbury, Cerne, Chertsey, Crowland, Ely, Evesham, Eynsham, Glastonbury, Gloucester, Malmesbury, Milton, Muchelney, Pershore, Peterborough, Ramsey, St. Albans, St. Benet Holme, Tavistock, Thorney, Westminster, Winchcombe and the nunneries Amesbury, Barking, Romsey, Shaftesbury.

6   E. SEARLE, Battle Abbey and Exemption: the Forged Charters, in: English Historical Review 83 (1968), pp. 449–480; EADEM, Lordship and Community: Battle Abbey and its Banlieu 1066–1538 (Pontifical Institute of Mediaeval Studies, Studies and Texts 26), Toronto 1974.

7   J. D. HASS, Medieval Selby: a New Study of the Abbey and Town, 1069–1408 (Yorkshire Archaeological Society, Occasional Paper 4), Leeds 2006, pp. 41–52.

8   The Cartulary of Shrewsbury Abbey, ed. U. REES, 2 vols., Aberystwyth 1975, vol. 1, pp. x–xxii.

9   E. K. MCCONNELL, The Abbey of St. Werburgh, Chester, in the Thirteenth Century, in: Transactions of the Historic Society of Lancashire and Cheshire 55 (1903/04), pp. 42–66; A. NIGHTINGALE, The 'Red Book' of the Abbey of St. Werburgh, Chester, in: Transactions of the Historic Society of Lancashire and Cheshire 104 (1952), pp. 159–162.

10 G. RICKWORD, The Abbey of St John the Baptist, Colchester, in: Journal of the British Archaeological Association n.s. 25 (1919), pp. 203–212.

11 Reading, founded in 1121 by Henry I., as well as Faversham, founded in 1147 by king Stephen and Matilda, were influenced, even initially headed, by Cluniacs but did become abbeys in their own right, C. W. HOLLISTER, Henry I, New Haven/London 2001, p. 434; A. SALTMAN, Theobald Archbishop of Canterbury, London 1956, p. 82; E. KING, King Stephen, Yale 2012, pp. 248–249.

12 J. P. MCALEER, Tewkesbury Abbey in the Later Twelfth and Thirteenth Centuries, in: Transactions of the Bristol and Gloucestershire Archaeological Society 110 (1992), pp. 77–86. R. B. DOBSON, Tewkesbury, in: Lexikon des Mittelalters, vol. 8, Munich 1997, col. 594. E. R. DOWDESWELL, The Monks of the Monastery of St. Mary at Tewkesbury, in: Transactions of the Bristol and Gloucestershire Archaeological Society 25 (1902), pp. 77–93.

13 A. J. MAINMAN, Monasticism in York, in: M. GLÄSER (ed.), Lübecker Kolloquium zur Stadtarchäologie im Hanseraum IX: die Klöster (Lübecker Kolloquium zur Stadtarchäologie im Hanseraum 9), Lübeck 2014, pp. 63–74.

14 The Latin Cartulary of Godstow Abbey, ed. E. AMT, Oxford 2014.

15 J. GREATREX, The English Benedictine Cathedral Priories: Rule and Practice, c. 1270–1420, Oxford 2011; E. MILLER, The Abbey and Bishopric of Ely. The Social History of an Ecclesiastical Estate from the Tenth Century to the Early Fourteenth Century, Cambridge 1951. This article will not include the smaller Benedictine priories and cells, the Cluniacs or the Cistercians. The English property of Norman abbeys will also be excluded.

monastic economy with a specific reference to their financial relations. This will include a brief survey of different forms of taxation and the fiscal implications of royal justice.

In previous research it was asked whether external events and demands had any impact at all on the monasteries. In 1934 Frances PAGE found it "surprising how little national politics and crises were reflected in the records of the Crowland estates" and Reginald SMITH found stability lasting through the upheavals of war and natural desaster – including the Black Death – in the finances of Christ Church Priory, Canterbury, due to the reforms of archbishop John Pecham (1279–1292) and prior Henry of Eastry (1285–1331).[16] This may suggest that the monasteries in question were largely independent of their political and economic context, a view which needs to be questioned.

Much attention has been given to the more general economic evolution and structure of English monastic estates in the context of phases of expansion and inflation as well as during years of crisis. The economic model underlying the financial situation of medieval English Benedictine monasteries was provided by Dom David KNOWLES between the 1930s and the 1950s. According to him, the transition of a land-based economy to a monetarized system occurred in the thirteenth century, in a period of inflation in England.[17] As a response to rising prices and the fall in the value of rents derived from long-term leases, lands which had been leased out were recovered by their monastic lords to be directly managed by the religious houses in order to produce cash crops and wool.[18] This was the beginning of a period of 'high farming' when monasteries could benefit from rising prices by producing goods which were then marketed by themselves. This policy had clear advantages over an approach centred on relying on fixed annual rents whose value was declining over time.

This research indicated that long-term economic planning based on a close observation of the markets and the monitoring of economic change was very common in the religious communities. Planning permitted the communities to find structured responses to economic change, it involved negotiations with tenants, the acquisition of further land which could then be directly managed, as at Ramsey Abbey, the assarting of woodland as at Peterborough Abbey[19] or the enforcement of services from unfree tenants who had to work on the demesne. Long-term planning did not merely involve the estate and its tenants but also its

---

[16] F. M. PAGE, The Estates of Crowland Abbey: A Study in Manorial Organisation, Cambridge 1934, p. 59.

[17] P. D. A. HARVEY, The English Inflation of 1180–1220, in: Past and Present 61 (1973), pp. 3–30.

[18] D. KNOWLES, The Religious Orders in England, 3 vols., Cambridge 1948–1959, vol. 1, pp. 32–37.

[19] J. BOLTON, The Medieval English Economy 1150–1500, London 1980, p. 88.

administration. Older systems of obedientiaries, where cellarer and sacrist were the key officials responsible for supply and finances, were replaced by a much wider distribution of responsibilities including the use of professional lay administrators who were entrusted with estate management at different levels. These highly mobile and largely independent agents whose accounts were audited by monastic officials dealt directly with tenants and collected rents.

According to older historiography the large Benedictine houses participated in the economic prosperity of the twelfth and thirteenth centuries. This experience was shared by the religious communities of other orders which appeared in England in the eleventh and twelfth centuries, the Cluniacs and Augustinians and then the Cistercians and Premonstratensians. This was a time of demesne farming. Leased land was returned to the demesnes so that the convents could benefit from improved methods of agriculture and a modern internal administration. However, the beneficial economic climate began to change in the second half of the thirteenth century. It became more difficult to balance the monastic economy and from the fourteenth century onwards there was a trend to rely on the fixed income provided by the rents due from tenants who held long-term leases of monastic land. The demographic crisis caused by the arrival of the Black Death in the middle of the fourteenth century exacerbated the situation and it is not surprising to find that the English Benedictines were affected by the economic downturn from the second half of the fourteenth century onwards. In a time characterised by rising costs and falling prices, demesne lands were leased, labour services were commuted, marginal lands were abandoned and religious houses tended to rely increasingly on rent income. This apparent symmetry – high farming and a period of prosperity and a restructuring of the demesne with a reversion to rent income based on long-term leases in a period of crisis – presents a plausible model of the Benedictine economy in late-medieval England.

Studies of individual religious houses and of specific monastic estates produced since the publication of the pioneering works by KNOWLES present a much more differentiated picture.[20] Much attention has been given to the separation of economic assets between a portion set aside for the head of the community and a share set aside for the religious, a structure which can be found in

---

[20] KNOWLES was only able to draw on a few studies: R. H. SNAPE, English Monastic Finances in the Later Middle Ages, Cambridge 1926; F. M. PAGE, Estates of Crowland Abbey (note 16 above). Later research was based on his work: J. A. RAFTIS, The Estates of Ramsay Abbey: A Study in Economic Growth and Organization, Toronto 1957; F. R. H. DuBOULAY, The Lordship of Canterbury. An Essay in Medieval Society, London 1966; R. B. DOBSON, Durham Priory 1400–1450, Cambridge 1973; M. BONNEY, Lordship and the Urban Community: Durham and its Overlords 1250–1540, Cambridge 1990; M. THRELFALL–HOLMES, Monks and Markets: Durham Cathedral Priory 1460–1520, Oxford 2005; B. HARVEY, Westminster Abbey and its Estates in the Middle Ages, Oxford 1977; EADEM, The Obedientiaries of Westminster Abbey and Their Financial Records, c. 1275–1540, Rochester (USA) 2002; E. KING, Peterborough Abbey 1086–1310. A Study in the Land Market, Cambridge 1973.

many Benedictine abbeys and priories, most clearly in the monastic cathedral chapters. This division took place between the eleventh and early thirteenth century and its purpose was to protect the religious community during a vacancy when the estates could be managed by royal agents. The division into two portions could lead to the creation of two administrative systems with officials in the abbot's household on the one hand and the obedientiaries, e.g. cellarer, sacrist, almoner, who each administered a defined portion of the community's estates, on the other. Historians analysing the structure of individual monastic estates have emphasized their diversity. This was caused by the varying proportions of different economic segments, represented by firstly the demesne economy consisting of arable, pasture and perhaps woodland, land use being determined by factors like soil quality, location in relation to the monastery and the proximity of markets, secondly rents and leases, a type of income depending on the legal relationship between the religious houses and their tenants or vassals, thirdly income from appropriated churches and tithes, fourthly income from urban property and finally the proceeds of proto-industrial activity like mining, salt-production, the fulling of textiles, a segment estimated by KNOWLES to have represented slightly over 10% of the monastic economy in the later Middle Ages.[21] In some cases, e.g. Bury St. Edmunds, there was also income from sources normally controlled by the crown, i.e. the mint and the control of several hundreds in Suffolk. The management of such structures of varying complexity needed constant attention. Decisions had to be taken as to the way in which individual estates were used, the type of farming most suitable to the situation, the choice of crops to be grown in the coming season, the collection of rents, necessary investments and financial requirements. Of a different nature were long-term decisions concerning structural change, i.e. attempts to adapt to a shift in the economic context. These included the purchase, sale, amelioration or exchange of land, the enforcement or commutation of labour services from unfree tenants, the policy towards new lease agreements and the identification of commodities which were in demand in the markets.[22]

Even though the picture presented by David KNOWLES is likely to indicate the general trend, an increasing amount of detailed information relating to individual houses reveals a much higher degree of diversity. The monks of Westminster Abbey had held on to many of their demesne estates in the period before 1200 and the transition from food rents to money payments on their estates took

---

[21] D. KNOWLES, Religious Orders (note 18 above), vol. 3, p. 249; E. MILLER / J. HATCHER, Medieval England. Towns, Commerce and Crafts 1086–1348, Harlow 1995, pp. 56–57.

[22] J. N. HARE, The Monks as Landlords: the Leasing of the Demesnes in Southern England, in: C. M. BARRON / C. HARPER–BILL (eds.), The Church in Pre–Reformation Society, Woodbridge 1985, pp. 82–94; B. HARVEY, Westminster Abbey and its Estates (note 20 above), ch. 3.

place already in the first half of the twelfth century.[23] The nuns of Chatteris in Cambridgeshire did purchase land in the thirteenth century, however, in the same period they also sold much of their property for a fixed income, indicating that they were not aware of or not concerned about inflationary tendencies. At the same time there are signs of demesne farming.[24] In the later Middle Ages and even in the decades prior to the Dissolution – at the time of the monastic rent-collection economy – many monasteries were holding on to large flocks of sheep which produced an essential portion of their revenue.[25] Studies with a focus on the economic structures of individual houses will inevitably reveal a great variety of economic systems.

Within this diversity certain patterns can be recognised. Wool production played an important role in many houses throughout the later Middle Ages. The majority of tenants on Benedictine estates tended to be unfree, owing labour services and rents. In the twelfth century a significant part of the income was paid in kind, in the form of fixed amounts of grain, livestock and other commodities due from each estate. This was complemented by fixed cash rents because the transition to a money economy was under way. The period of rising prices, beginning in c. 1180, brought difficulties for the religious houses because their costs changed while their income remained fixed. Although many monastic estates were restructured, through the increase of the demesne and the acquisition of land and other sources of income, as mentioned above, some of the large Benedictine monasteries sank into debt, liabilities which went beyond the 'normal' level of debt in an economy insufficiently supplied with species.

The majority of the older monasteries were subject to different royal taxes and to a variety of other material demands. It would be desirable to assess their impact on monastic finances. A long-term survey of the Crown's fiscal demands might provide additional information on the context of the picture presented in earlier research. It might also help to clarify the relationship between monarchs who could impose material burdens on the abbeys on a regular basis but who could also enter into agreements with the religious who could offer spiritual services in return for royal patronage. Monasteries could benefit from royal material support in different ways, through donations, awards of privileges, the granting of subsidies and patronage in return for prayers and the benefits of confraternity. The commitment shown by individual English kings in the foundation or evolution of a specific monastery, William I.'s foundation of Battle Abbey, Henry I.'s foundation of Reading and Henry II.'s support for the new abbey or Henry III.'s rebuilding of Westminster Abbey were expressions of personal piety, motivated by the desire for atonement in the case of Battle or the creation of a necropolis

---

[23] Ibid., pp. 78, 80.
[24] The Cartulary of Chatteris Abbey, ed. C. BREAY, Woodbridge 1999, pp. 58–59, 64–65.
[25] D. KNOWLES, Religious Orders (note 18 above), vol. 3, pp. 250–252.

in the case of Westminster. They demonstrated the kings' understanding of the importance of the work of devotion done by the religious.[26] Such links to specific religious communities were part of a king's wider performance of piety which extended in many different directions. They existed in parallel to a very different relationship, the connections between the monasteries as subordinate institutions and the central government, primarily the royal household, the exchequer and the law courts.

The administration of complex economic entities could only be achieved on the basis of processes of control and planning which relied on written information. Although a wide variety of sources were created, they can be broadly grouped into two classes, firstly those providing written proof to legal claims and secondly those which recorded economic – including financial – data. The first type needed to be carefully archived, the second form of documentation was relevant only for a limited period of time. However, even if this broad classification suggests a form of homogeneity, this was not the case. Although all the religious communities in question lived according to the Benedictine rule, their administrative processes differed. There was not even consistency in the economic administration of a single convent because adjustments had to be made in line with changing circumstances, new economic conditions, a change in personnel or an attempt to introduce innovative practices. It is true that from the twelfth century onwards the financial administration of the larger Benedictine houses in England came to be modelled on that of the royal Exchequer but this was a structural similarity due to the evolution of a medieval state with ever more sophisticated systems of royal taxation and justice to which the religious had to adapt.[27] Despite such similarities, significant variations remained in the economic

---

[26] D. C. DOUGLAS, William the Conqueror, London 1964, p. 328; E. SEARLE, Lordship and Community: Battle Abbey (note 6 above), pp. 21–23; J. PELTZER, 1066. Der Kampf um Englands Krone, Munich ²2019, pp. 244–246; C. W. HOLLISTER, Henry I (note 11 above), pp. 282–287; W. L. WARREN, Henry II, London 1973, p. 212; Reading Abbey Cartularies. British Library Manuscripts: Egerton 3031, Harley 1708 and Cotton Vespasian E XXV, ed. B. R. KEMP, 2 vols. (Camden Fourth Series 31), London 1986, vol. 1, pp. 13–15; Eulogium Historiarum sive Temporis. Chronicon ab Orbe Condito usque ad Annum Domini MCCCLXVI, ed. F. S. HAYDON, 3 vols. (Rerum Britannicarum medii aevi scriptores 9), London 1858–1863, vol. 1, p. 274; The Great Roll of the Pipe for the Eighth Year of the Reign of King Henry the Second, A.D. 1161–1162 (Publications of the Pipe Roll Society 5), London 1885, pp. 2, 13, 16, 28, 31, 43, 44, 60, 72; The Great Roll of the Pipe for the Fifteenth Year of the Reign of King Henry the Second, A.D. 1168–1169 (Publications of the Pipe Roll Society 13), London 1890, p. 161; The Great Roll of the Pipe for the Sixteenth Year of the Reign of King Henry the Second, A.D. 1169–1170 (Publications of the Pipe Roll Society 15), London 1892, p. 157; The Great Roll of the Pipe for the Seventeenth Year of the Reign of King Henry the Second A.D. 1170–1171 (Publications of the Pipe Roll Society 16), London 1893, p. 138; The Great Roll of the Pipe for the Twenty–First Year of the Reign of King Henry the Second, A.D. 1174–1175 (Publications of the Pipe Roll Society 22), London 1897, p. 214; D. CARPENTER, Henry III. The Rise to Power and Personal Rule 1207–1258, New Haven/London 2020, pp. 330–348.

[27] R. A. L. SMITH, Canterbury Cathedral Priory: A Study in Monastic Administration, Cambridge 1943, p. 20.

and financial organisation of abbeys which differed in their size, in their type of income, in the nature of their estates and in the ways in which they organised their properties. Repeated attempts by visitors and by the English Benedictine general chapter, an institution created after the IV. Lateran Council, could not bring about a standardisation of procedures.

Many monastic records were lost at the time of the Dissolution of the English and Welsh monasteries. However, cartularies with collections of title deeds and related documents of legal relevance as well as information about the structure of the monastic economy, extents, recent rent rolls, account rolls of monastic manors, income assigned to obedientiaries or inventories, were confiscated and preserved or even copied, together with anything of material value, because they were the basis for the future exploitation of the estates. This is the reason for the survival of extensive and detailed sources on the monasteries' estates and their finances. They have enabled historians to study procedures of financial management and to observe in what ways officials in monasteries and priories responded to economic change and how they interacted with their secular and ecclesiastical environment.[28] This information was kept in different formats. Apart from original charters and copies, there are cartularies, mostly in book form, rolls and miscellaneous hybrid material. This is perhaps in line with the origins of this kind of enrolment. Titles to property were initially entered into Gospel books, as at St. Augustine and at Christ Church, Canterbury[29], into a copy of the Rule of St. Benedict, as at Bury St. Edmunds[30] or into the convent's 'Liber Vitae', as at Durham and Hyde Abbey.[31] The revised version of DAVIS's 'Medieval Cartularies of Great Britain' prepared by Claire BREAY, Julian HARRISON and David M. SMITH is exemplary in its approach and seems to be complete as far as the first category of sources is concerned – legal titles and privileges – while it also contains valuable information on a number of surviving surveys and accounts.[32] However, even though some of the business records are included, it was not

---

[28] Sacrist Rolls of Ely, ed. F. R. CHAPMAN, 2 vols., Cambridge 1907, vol. 1, p. vi; P. D. A. HARVEY, Mid–13th–Century Accounts from Bury St Edmunds Abbey, in: A. GRANSDEN (ed.), Bury St Edmunds. Medieval Art, Architecture, Archaeology and Economy (The British Archaeological Association Conference Transactions 20), Leeds 1998, pp. 128–138; C. BEAUMONT, Monastic Autonomy, Episcopal Authority and the Norman Conquest: The Records of Barking Abbey, in: Anglo–Norman Studies 38 (2016), pp. 35–50.

[29] G. R. C. DAVIS, Medieval Cartularies of Great Britain, revised by C. BREAY / J. HARRISON / D. M. SMITH, London 2010, pp. 38–39 (London, Lambeth Palace, MS 1370; BL MS Royal 1 D IX), 42 (Cambridge, Corpus Christi College MS 286).

[30] Ibid., p. 28 (Oxford, Corpus Christi College, MS 197).

[31] Ibid., p. 71 (London, BL Cotton Domitian A VII), 213 (London, BL Stowe 944).

[32] References to cartularies of the major Benedictine abbeys are in: ibid., pp. 1–2, 5, 7–10, 22–29, 36, 39–43, 46, 48, 54, 57, 61–62, 68–71, 77–79, 81, 87–92, 99, 111, 127, 133–134, 137, 141–142, 146, 152–155, 158–162, 164, 167, 169–170, 177–180, 185–186, 191, 193, 195, 199–200, 203, 206–213, 217, 219, 223–225.

possible to list all of them. Accounts, the records prepared by the heads of department or obedientiaries, manorial extents, courts rolls, rentals giving the names of tenants and the amounts of money due from them and other material of a similar nature, are not covered by the volume.[33] There is a good reason for this. The financial sources survive in different collections, among the public records, in local record offices as well as in private collections.[34] The sources, e.g. those relating to individual manors, may also not always be readily attributable to a specific monastery even if there is a complete list of estates because in times of vacancy much of the income was managed by royal officials who acted as caretakers. In such cases the monastic community may not have been the recipient of the income. Narrative sources are also not completely included in the list produced by DAVIS although many of them contain copies of documents or even records of legal proceedings. In some cases their purpose seems to have been to document the convents' titles to properties and privileges.[35] Whether records of legal titles or pools of information for the daily administration of the monastic economy, the material was an indispensable tool for obedientiaries and other officials.[36]

---

[33] Examples of such records are in: Cartulary of Chatteris Abbey, ed. C. BREAY (note 24 above), p. 7.

[34] Glastonbury Abbey Records at Longleat House: A Summary List, ed. K. HARRIS (Somerset Record Society Publications 81), Taunton 1991; S. KEYNES, The Cartulary of Athelney Abbey Rediscovered, in: Monastic Research Bulletin 7 (2001), pp. 2–5. IDEM, A Lost Cartulary of St Albans Abbey, in: Anglo–Saxon England 22 (1993), pp. 253–279.

[35] Examples are the chronicles of Ramsey, Chronicon Abbatiae Ramesiensis, a saec. X. usque ad An. Circiter 1200: in quatuor partibus, ed. W. D. MACRAY (Rerum Britannicarum medii aevi scriptores 83), London 1886, pp. 48–51, 151–152, 181–189, 200–207, 214–232, 276–293, 296–301, 320–324 which gives the texts of documents as well as stories of land acquisitions or the Chronicon Petroburgense, ed. T. STAPLETON (Camden Society, o. s. 47), London 1849, pp. 11–13, 35–36, 38–39, 47–52, 55, 66–69, 95, 103, 118.

[36] D. M. GERRARD, Jocelin of Brakelond and the Power of Abbot Samson, in: Journal of Medieval History 40 (2014), pp. 1–23, at p. 18. A work of reference for the records preserved in monastic archives does not exist but a list of the more important monastic estates has been established: M. JURKOWSKI / N. RAMSEY / S. RENTON (eds.), English Monastic Estates, 1066–1540: a List of Manors, Churches and Chapels, 3 vols. (List and Index Society SO40–SO42), Kew 2007. Some sets of administrative records have been described in detail: H. W. SAUNDERS, Introduction to the Obedientiary and Manor Rolls of Norwich Cathedral Priory, Norwich 1930, ch. 2 (with a comparison of Norwich Cathedral Priory to other Benedictine archives on pp. 18–19). There are numerous stray references to surviving records from monastic archives. M. BAILEY, Sheep Accounts of Norwich Cathedral Priory, 1484 to 1534, in: Poverty and Wealth. Sheep, Taxation and Charity in Late Medieval Norfolk (Norfolk Record Society 71), Norwich 2007, pp. 1–97; H. H. E. CASTER, The Red Book of Durham, in: English Historical Review 40 (1925), pp. 512–513; H. B. CLARKE, Condensing and Abbreviating the Data: Evesham C, Evesham M, and the Breviate, in: D. ROFFE / K. KEATS–ROHAN (eds.), Domesday Now. New Approaches to the Inquest and the Book, Woodbridge 2016, pp. 247–275; H. DEWEZ, The Writing of Obedientiary Account Rolls at Norwich Cathedral Priory (1256–1344), in: S. BARRET / D. STUTZMANN / G. VOGELER (eds.), Ruling the Script in the Middle Ages: Formal Aspects of Written Communication (Books, Charters, and Inscriptions), Turn-

Historical research into English monasticism began in the seventeenth century with the 'Monasticon' by William DUGDALE who also collected and edited numerous documents.[37] While DUGDALE had structured the material in his three volumes according to the convents' religious affiliation, beginning with the Benedictines, Cluniacs, Cistercians and Carthusians, Thomas TANNER, whose work is based on extracts from DUGDALE, arranged his short notes on each house by county.[38] A significant further development occurred in the nineteenth century after a new interest in medieval records had also led to a new edition by a group of record specialists of the volumes produced by DUGDALE and his successors.[39] In the middle of the century two important serial publications began, firstly the volumes of the Camden Society in 1838 which included sources related to the monastic economy[40] and secondly the decision to publish significant narrative

---

hout 2016, pp. 197–226; H. P. R. FINBERG, Some Early Tavistock Charters, in: English Historical Review 62 (1947), pp. 352–377; C. T. FLOWER, Obedientiars' Accounts of Glastonbury and Other Religious Houses, in: Transactions of the St. Paul's Ecclesiological Society 7 (1912), pp. 50–62; R. FLOWER, The Last Pre–Dissolution Survey of Glastonbury Lands, in: British Museum Quarterly 10 (1935–1936), pp. 69–72; B. HARVEY, The Obedientiaries of Westminster Abbey (note 20 above); R. HILTON, A Rare Evesham Abbey Estate Document, in: Vale of Evesham Research Papers 2 (1969), pp. 5–10; J. R. HUNN, A Medieval Cartulary of St Albans Abbey, in: Medieval Archaeology 27 (1983), pp. 151–152; N. R. KER, Hemming's Cartulary, in: R. W. HUNT / W. A. PANTIN / R. W. SOUTHERN (eds.), Studies in Medieval History Presented to F. M. Powicke, Oxford 1948, pp. 49–75; S. KEYNES, The Lost Cartulary of Abbotsbury, in: Anglo Saxon England 18 (1989), pp. 207–243; E. KING, The Peterborough *Descriptio Militum* (Henry I), in: English Historical Review 84 (1969), pp. 84–101; H. G. D. LIVING, The Records of Romsey Abbey: An Account of the Benedictine House of Nuns with Notes on the Parish Church and Town (A.D. 907–1558), Winchester 1906; J. D. MARTIN, The Court and Account Rolls of Peterborough Abbey: A Handlist (University of Leicester, History Department. Occasional Publication 2), Leicester 1980; W. A. PANTIN, English Monastic Letter–Books, in: J. G. EDWARDS / V. H. GALBRAITH / E. F. JACOB (eds.), Historical Essays presented to James Tait, Manchester 1933, pp. 215–217; N. VINCENT, Medieval Cartularies, in: Monastic Research Bulletin 3 (1997), pp. 7–38; 4 (1998), pp. 6–12; 5 (1999), pp. 26–28.

[37] W. DUGDALE, Monasticon Anglicanum, 3 vols., London 1655–1673. Two additional volumes were added by John STEVENS in 1772–1773. This is more substantial than the section on English abbeys in the sixth volume of T. FULLER, The Church History of Britain, 6 vols., London 1655.

[38] T. TANNER, Notitia Monastica, Oxford 1695.

[39] J. CALEY / H. ELLIS / B. BANDINEL (eds.), William Dugdale, Monasticon Anglicanum, 6 vols., London 1817–1830.

[40] Chronica Jocelini de Brakelonda, de rebus gestis Samsonis abbatis monasterii sancti Edmundi, ed. J. G. ROKEWODE (Camden Society 13), London 1840; Chronicon Petroburgense, ed. T. STAPLETON (note 35 above); Registrum sive liber irrotularius et consuetudinarius prioratus beatae Mariae Wigorniensis, ed. W. HALE (Camden Society 91), London 1865; Custumals of Battle Abbey in the Reigns of Edward I and Edward II, 1282–1312, ed. S. R. SCARGILL–BIRD (Camden Society, new series 41), London 1887; Accounts of the Obedientars of Abingdon Abbey, ed. R. KIRK (Camden Society, new series 52), London 1894; Documents Illustrating the Activities of the General and Provincial Chapters of the English Black Monks, 1215–1540, ed. W. A. PANTIN, 3 vols. (Camden Society, 3rd series 45, 47, 54), London 1931–1937; The Kalendar of Abbot Samson of Bury St. Edmunds and Related Documents, ed. R. H. C. DAVIES

sources in a national series, the 'Rerum Britannicarum Medii Aevi Scriptores' (Rolls Series) which is only being superseded today. Despite its focus on narrative sources, the series included a number of cartularies and a letter book from Benedictine houses.[41] By their nature the sources also contained economic data and legal documents.[42] Of great significance was the rise of antiquarian societies and of county record societies whose editions made local and regional sources available to a wide audience and who over the years have published the bulk of monastic economic data which can be found in print today.[43] In conjunction with the central government souces of the royal Exchequer, the Chancery and the different royal law courts this material provides a sound basis for a study of the relationship between the English kings and the Benedictine houses in their kingdom from the middle of the eleventh century onwards.

The monastic economy already featured in the first studies of individual monasteries which were published in the early twentieth century.[44] The focus was on the wool trade as well as on the economic state of the monasteries at the time of

---

(Camden Society, 3rd series 84), London 1954; Liber Eliensis, ed. E. O. BLAKE (Camden Society, 3rd series 92), London 1962; Documents Illustrating the Rule of Walter de Wenlok, abbot of Westminster, 1283–1307, ed. B. F. HARVEY (Camden Society, 4th series 2), London 1965.

[41] Historia et Cartularium Monasterii Sancti Petri Gloucestriae, ed. W. H. HART, 3 vols. (Rerum Britannicarum medii aevi scriptores 33), London 1863–1867; Registrum Malmesburiense. The Register of Malmesbury Abbey, eds. J. S. BREWER / C. T. MARTIN, 2 vols. (Rerum Britannicarum medii aevi scriptores 72), London 1879–1880; Cartularium Monasterii de Rameseia, eds. W. H. HART / P. A. LYONS, 3 vols. (Rerum Britannicarum medii aevi scriptores 79), London 1884–1893; Litterae Cantuarienses. The Letter Books of the Monastery of Christ Church, Canterbury, ed. J. B. SHEPPARD, 3 vols. (Rerum Britannicarum medii aevi scriptores 85), London 1887–1889.

[42] In addition some editors contributed documentation of economic relevance to the appendices of their volumes: e.g. Registrum Malmesburiense, eds. J. S. BREWER / C. T. MARTIN (note 41 above), vol. 2, pp. 364, 392–393; Johannes de Oxenedes, Chronica, ed. H. ELLIS (Rerum Britannicarum medii aevi scriptores 13), London 1859, p. 326; Annales Monastici, ed. H. R. LUARD, 5 vols. (Rerum Britannicarum medii aevi scriptores 36), London 1864–1869, vol. 1, pp. 511, 515; Chronicon Abbatiae de Evesham ad annum 1418, ed. W. D. MACRAY (Rerum Britannicarum medii aevi scriptores 29), London 1863, p. 340; Chronicon Monasterii de Abingdon, ed. J. STEVENSON, 2 vols. (Rerum Britannicarum medii aevi scriptores 2), London 1858, vol. 2, pp. 288–289, 297–312, 324–332.

[43] P. CROOT, Bedfordshire, in: C. CURRIE / C. P. LEWIS (eds.), A Guide to English County Histories, Stroud 1994, pp. 32–41, at p. 39; D. BOLTON, Buckinghamshire, in: ibid., pp. 54–61, at p. 56; J. BETTEY, Dorset, in: ibid., pp. 125–131, at p. 128; H. SMITH / R. VIRGOE, Norfolk, in: ibid., pp. 280–290, at p. 286; D. COX, Worcestershire, in: ibid., pp. 423–432, at p. 429.

[44] J. B. HURRY, Reading Abbey, London 1901; E. K. MCCONNELL, The Abbey of St. Werburgh, Chester (note 9 above); H. G. D. LIVING, The Records of Romsey Abbey (note 36 above); J. A. ROBINSON, Gilbert Crispin Abbot of Westminster. A Study of the Abbey under Norman Rule, Cambridge 1911; F. M. STENTON, The Early History of the Abbey of Abingdon, Oxford 1913; G. RICKWORD, The Abbey of St John the Baptist, Colchester (note 10 above). Chronologically this coincided with the publication of the first volumes of the Victoria County History which gave prominent attention to the religious institutions.

the Dissolution.⁴⁵ This approach led historians to move from the research into the history of a single convent to the study of the monastic economy in general.⁴⁶ The extensive historiography into the economic history of the English Benedictines begins with Robert Hugh SNAPE's book on English monastic finance, published in 1926. SNAPE pursued his aim, to discover new facets of religious life, through an analysis of the monastic organisation and the identification of income and expenditure. He also studied levels of debt and pointed to some of the financial burdens imposed on the religious houses by the papacy and by the English Crown, including royal presentations to corrodies and loans demanded by the king.⁴⁷

Economic and financial matters constituted a significant element in the classic studies of English medieval monasticism by David KNOWLES who related the economic side of monastic life to the ambition of individual abbots and priors to rebuild churches and acquire suitable ornaments for them, to accumulate treasures and to establish libraries.⁴⁸ However, the female houses did not feature prominently in the volumes, probably because by the time of the publication of KNOWLES's first major study, a first general history of the English nunneries had already been published by Eileen POWER.⁴⁹ The continuation of this work up to the Reformation is less specific about the Benedictines but still remains the basic work until today.⁵⁰ This research inspired others and from the 1940s onwards a number of studies into the economic, financial and administrative history of English Benedictine houses was published. It can be divided into four broad categories, firstly work focused on the economic and financial state or on the administrative structures of specific religious houses, beginning with Frances Mary PAGE's work on Crowland and Reginald SMITH's study of Canterbury Cathedral

---

⁴⁵ R. J. WHITWELL, English Monasteries and the Wool Trade in the Thirteenth Century, in: Vierteljahresschrift für Sozial– und Wirtschaftsgeschichte 2 (1904), pp. 1–33; A. SAVINE, English Monasteries on the Eve of the Dissolution, Oxford 1909. Relevant are also the case studies in G. G. COULTON, Five Centuries of Religion, 4 vols., Cambridge 1923–1950, vol. 3, pp. 65–86, 149–197, 232–247. G. W. BERNARD, The King's Reformation. Henry VIII and the Remaking of the English Church, New Haven/London 2015, pp. 245, 250, 270.

⁴⁶ C. NEW, History of the Alien Priories in England (note 3 above); E. POWER, Medieval English Nunneries, c. 1257 to 1535, Cambridge 1922.

⁴⁷ R. H. SNAPE, English Monastic Finances (note 20), pp. 95, 127, 139–143.

⁴⁸ D. KNOWLES, The Monastic Order in England, Cambridge 1949, pp. 86, 101–104, 172–177, 431–443, 598–600, 612–615.

⁴⁹ A study on the female Franciscan houses in England appeared only four years after E. POWER, Medieval English Nunneries (note 46 above): A. F. C. BOURDILLON, The Order of Minoresses in England (British Society of Franciscan Studies 12), Manchester 1926. Later studies: J. BURTON, The Yorkshire Nunneries in the Twelfth and Thirteenth Centuries (Borthwick Paper 56), York 1979. Based on an Oxford PhD: K. COOKE, Donors and Daughters: Shaftesbury Abbey's Benefactors, Endowments and Nuns c. 1086–1130, in: Anglo–Norman Studies XII. Proceedings of the Battle Conference 1989, Woodbridge 1990, pp. 29–45.

⁵⁰ D. KNOWLES, Religious Orders (note 18 above), vol. 1, pp. 32–63; vol. 2, pp. 309–330; vol. 3, pp. 241–259.

Priory,[51] secondly histories of individual abbeys which also cover the economic side of the Vita religiosa[52] and thirdly more general, sometimes regional, surveys of monastic history.[53] The fourth category differs from the previous three because the authors are interested in general economic structures or agricultural techniques and output rather than in the history of monasticism or the monastic economy. Their use of material from medieval abbeys is merely incidental and the authors tend to give little attention to the original purpose of monasticism and to the different forms of religious life.[54] Monasteries tended to be seen as aristocratic institutions and the context – the different normative preconditions, the affiliation to a specific religious order – is often not seen as significant.[55] Much of this research has highlighted the significance of the monasteries in the wider English economy, even though not all sources relating to the monastic economy have yet even been identified.

The Norman Conquest of England changed the kingdom's monastic landscape through the new emphasis on the Cluniacs and the attempt to reform the established religious houses. Relations between the monasteries and the English kings also changed fundamentally. DOUGLAS identified the strength of the Norman duchy firstly as the aristocracy which had aligned its interests to those of the duke and secondly as the well organised Church, especially the monasteries. The

---

[51] F. M. PAGE, Estates of Crowland Abbey (note 16 above); R. A. L. SMITH, Canterbury Cathedral Priory (note 27 above); E. SEARLE, Lordship and Community: Battle Abbey (note 6 above). E. MILLER, The Abbey and Bishopric of Ely (note 15 above).

[52] Examples are: E. KING, Peterborough Abbey (note 20 above); F. R. H. DUBOULAY, The Lordship of Canterbury (note 20 above); E. GORDON, Eynsham Abbey: 1005–1228. A Small Window Into a Large Room, Chichester 1990; B. HARVEY, Westminster Abbey and its Estates (note 20 above); J. D. HASS, Medieval Selby (note 7 above); N. SUMNER, The Countess Lucy's Priory? The Early History of Spalding Priory and Its Estates, in: Reading Medieval Studies 13 (1987), pp. 81–105.

[53] J. N. HARE, The Monks as Landlords (note 22 above); M. HEALE, The Dependent Priories of Medieval English Monasteries, Woodbridge 2004, pp. 229–250; IDEM, Monasticism in Late Medieval England, c. 1300–1535, Manchester 2009; T. PESTELL, Landscapes of Monastic Foundation. The Establishment of Religious Houses in East Anglia c. 650–1200, Woodbridge 2004; H. G. RICHARDSON, Some Norman Monastic Foundations in Ireland, in: J. A. WATT / J. B. MORRALL / F. X. MARTIN (eds.), Medieval Studies Presented to Aubrey Gwynn S.J., Dublin 1961, pp. 29–41.

[54] R. HILTON, Winchcombe Abbey and the Manor of Sherborne, in: University of Birmingham Historical Journal 2 (1949/50), pp. 31–52, at p. 32, wanted to write an economic history of the Cotswolds. C. DYER, Lords and Peasants in a Changing Society. The Estates of the Bishopric of Worcester, 680–1540, Cambridge 1980; R. H. BRITNELL, The Proliferation of Markets in England, 1200–1201, in: Economic History Review 2nd ser. 34 (1981), pp. 209–221; J. A. RAFTIS, Peasants and the Collapse of the Manorial Economy on some Ramsey Abbey Estates, in: R. BRITNELL / J. HATCHER (eds.), Progress and Problems in Medieval England. Essays in Honour of Edward Miller, Cambridge 1996, pp. 191–206; IDEM, Western Monasticism and Economic Organization, in: Comparative Studies in Society and History 3 (1961), pp. 452–469.

[55] K. ELM, Vorwort, in: K. ELM (ed.), Erwerbspolitik und Wirtschaftsweise mittelalterlicher Orden und Klöster (Berliner Historische Studien 17; Ordensstudien VII), Berlin 1992, p. 7.

abbeys had been re-established by the dukes and their aristocracy from the 1030s onwards and they contributed to political unity.[56] The new king of England was confronted with a monastic leadership which was largely hostile. Two of the thirty-five heads of Benedictine houses in England had died or been wounded on the battlefield at Hastings, others organised or supported the resistance against his rule. His response was decisive. With the help of archbishop Lanfranc he began a reform of the English Church which extended to the monasteries and saw a gradual replacement of almost all abbots who had been in office before the Conquest. He also made most prelates of the English Church tenants-in-chief who owed him knight service. According to Matthew Paris these services had been defined by 1070.[57] The abbeys confronted with this requirement had to contribute a certain number of knights towards the royal army or for garrison duty in the king's castles. The alternative to service was the payment of scutage. Even though the duty to perform the services or to make the payments rested with the monastic chief vassals, the abbots were responsible for the organisation or alternatively for the collection and for the transfer of the money. If not enough land had been subinfeudated to military tenants to perform the service demanded by the king, the abbey had to find and finance the remaining number of knights directly.[58] This responsibility had an economic and a legal component; it established a link between the monastic economy and royal finance which had not existed before.

The duty to perform knight service rested only on abbeys which were already in existence at the time of the Conquest. No monastery founded after 1066 was liable to perform knight service and of the older houses only twenty-four abbeys, located mostly in the south and east of England, had this obligation.[59] It is not clear why some older houses which were listed as tenants-in-chief in Domesday Book were not settled with these duties although they as well as later Benedictine foundations did receive summons to perform their services in the thirteenth and fourteenth centuries.[60] The cause for the discrepancies in the amount of service demanded is equally uncertain. The burden was not always related to the size and

---

[56] D. C. DOUGLAS, William the Conqueror (note 26), pp. 105–112, 117.

[57] Matthaei Parisiensis, monachi Sancti Albani Historia Anglorum, ed. F. MADDEN, 3 vols. (Rerum britannicarum medii aevi scriptores 44), London 1864–1869, vol. 1, p. 13; H. M. CHEW, Ecclesiastical Tenants–in–Chief and Knight Service, Oxford 1932, p. 3.

[58] J. H. ROUND, The Introduction of Knight Service into England, in: ID., Feudal England. Historical Studies on the XIth and XIIth Centuries, London 1909, pp. 225–314, at p. 241.

[59] Abbotsbury, Abingdon, Bury St. Edmunds, Cerne, Chertsey, Coventry, Evesham, Glastonbury, Hyde, Milton, Malmesbury, Muchelney, Pershore, Peterborough, Ramsey, St. Albans, St. Augustine Canterbury, St. Benet Holm, Shaftesbury, Sherborne, Tavistock, Westminster, Wilton, Winchcombe, H. M. CHEW, Ecclesiastical Tenants–in–Chief (note 57 above), p. 5.

[60] Athelney, Burton, Gloucester, the nunneries of Barking and St. Mary's Winchester, in: ibid., pp. 8, 11.

capacity of the abbeys' economies. The wealthy abbey of St. Albans had to provide the service of six knights while the much more modestly endowed Tavistock had to supply fifteen.[61] Abingdon and Peterborough, were both on the scale of an annual income of between £200 and £500, had to provide the service of thirty and sixty knights respectively.[62] There have been speculations about the reasons for these discrepancies. CHEW thought that hostility towards the first Norman king might have resulted in an increased burden, citing Peterborough as an example because here hostility to the new regime was combined with a heavy demand for service. However, Peterborough was not the only religious house which was initially hostile to the new rule.[63] It is more likely that the quantity of service is related to the number of knights which were garrisoned in the monasteries in the years immediately after the Conquest when William I.'s authority had to be consolidated. These armed servants were gradually enfeoffed with land of the demesne to remove them from the vicinity of the main church and cloister. Their duties remained but it was the role of the abbot, their lord, to ensure that they delivered, otherwise he and the community were liable.

In the years immediately after the Norman Conquest when the new king was still faced with internal resistance and the threat of invasion, the loyalty of the monasteries was of great significance. William the Conqueror made full use of the practice – already common under Edward the Confessor – of making appointments in the case of abbatial vacancies and he also removed opponents among the heads of religious houses. This policy was a mixture of political expediency to ensure loyalty of the great monastic landholders and of introducing ecclesiastical reform. The appointment of the Benedictine monk Lanfranc as archbishop of Canterbury was an important move although the examples of Odo of Bayeux and – in the case of the religions houses – of the scandal-ridden abbot Thurstan, show that not all new appointments were successful.[64] A process of 'Normanization' of religious houses ensued, a policy based on the external interference in the senior appointments in religious houses which continued into the twelfth century. Royal involvement in abbatial elections – though not unique to England – became a characteristic feature of English monasticism. Drastic measures were taken against those religious who gave assistance to the opponents of the new regime. The abbot of Ely, who had given support to king William's opponents in the Isle of Ely, was only granted a royal pardon upon payment of

---

[61] H. R. P. FINBERG, Tavistock Abbey. A Study in the Social and Economic History of Devon (Cambridge Studies in Medieval Life and Thought, n.s. 2), Cambridge 1951, p. 8; D. KNOWLES, The Monastic Order in England (note 48 above), p. 610.

[62] S. HARVEY, Domesday England, in: H. E. HALLAM, (ed.), The Agrarian History of England and Wales. Volume II 1042–1350, Cambridge 1988, pp. 45–135, at p. 95; H. M. CHEW, Ecclesiastical Tenants–in–Chief (note 57 above), p. 5.

[63] Ibid., p. 8; D. C. DOUGLAS, William the Conqueror (note 26), pp. 324–325.

[64] Johannes de Oxenedes, Chronica, ed. H. ELLIS (note 42 above), p. 35.

£1000.⁶⁵ Here was a clear distinction between the monastery as a religious house on the one hand and the institution as a political and economic unit on the other. This dual perception was to pervade the relationship between the monarchs and the monasteries for centuries. In the case of William the Conqueror the enforcement of his authority and the demand of loyalty are in contrast with his support which extended to the foundation of a new Benedictine abbey on the battlefield near Hastings. He and his successors made extensive donations of properties in England to convents in Normandy while they also planted Cluniac monasticism in the newly conquered kingdom. On the other hand there were royal claims to a high degree of control, especially the control of monastic income.

The changes in landholding which affected the Benedictine monasteries in the three decades before 1100 may not always have led to a reduction of their estates although it was reported that the Conqueror's half-brother bishop Odo of Bayeux deprived Evesham of twenty-eight villages.⁶⁶ The efforts to have their possessions as well as their genuine as well as their desired liberties and privileges confirmed by William I. and his successors, so well documented in monastic cartularies, reveal the uncertainty of the religious about their future. A new political elite was making its own contributions to the monastic landscape and a new episcopate was determined to extend its authority over the religious houses in their dioceses. Selby and Eynsham became bishops' monasteries. Malmesbury was controlled by bishop Roger of Salisbury for a time and Glastonbury, the wealthiest house at the time of the Norman Conquest, came under temporary control of Henry of Blois, bishop of Winchester (1129–1171).⁶⁷

Some chroniclers complained of the depredations inflicted on monastic treasures and estates after 1066. The Abingdon chronicler reported that many valuables, books, vestments as well as items made of silver and gold were carried away and a similar story is told by Florence of Worcester.⁶⁸ However, it appears that royal action was mostly focused on the deposits left in the convents by William I.'s opponents and that the king's action was not directed against the monasteries as such. It is not likely that all religious houses suffered a general material loss and it needs to be taken into account that property transfers and losses were not

---

⁶⁵ D. KNOWLES, The Monastic Order in England (note 48 above), p. 105.
⁶⁶ Chronicon Abbatiae de Evesham, ed. W. D. MACRAY (note 42 above), p. 97.
⁶⁷ D. KNOWLES, The Monastic Order in England (note 48 above), pp. 180, 270, 313–324, 402; Chronicon Abbatiae Ramesiensis, ed. W. D. MACRAY (note 35 above), pp. 152–153: land at Hemmingford belonging to Ramsey given by William I to Alberic de Vere.
⁶⁸ Chronicon Monasterii de Abingdon, ed. J. STEVENSON (note 42 above), vol. 1, p. 486; Florentii Wigorniensis monachi Chronicon ex Chronicis, ed. B. THORPE, 2 vols. (English Historical Society), London 1848–1849, vol. 2, p. 5: *rex Willelmus monasteria totius Angliae perscrutari, et pecuniam, quam ditiores Angli, propter illius austeritatem et depopulationem, in eis deposuerant, auferri et in aerarium suum jussit deferri*. Johannes de Oxenedes, Chronica, ed. H. ELLIS (note 42 above), p. 33: *Rex Willelmus monasteria totius Angliae perscrutari, et pecuniam, quam ditiores Angliae in eis deposuerant auferri, et ad aerarium suum jussit deferri.*

necessarily due to royal action because pressure was also exerted by the new local landholders as e.g. at Peterborough.[69] Another argument against Benedictine decline is the fact that Benedictine monasticism expanded to the north of England in his reign, with the foundation or refoundation of Whitby, Selby, St. Mary's, York and the cathedral priory of Durham.[70] Nevertheless the new king could and did depose hostile heads of religious houses and he also made demands on the economic assets of the religious. There was no large-scale depredation of the monasteries although in the years immediately after the Conquest some monastic treasures were robbed and estates devastated, especially in areas of resistance to the new government although overall monastic income remained high.[71] In the years after the Norman Conquest the Benedictines found themselves confronted by different forces, all of which had an interest to exert control over them: the ecclesiastical reformers and the episcopate, the king and local landholders. Another party has to be added to this group of powers: the papacy. Even if it is true that pope Alexander II.'s support for the duke of Normandy's claim is a post-invasion fiction, there was an affinity between the Normans, who were important papal allies, and the pope.

The Conqueror's successor is regarded as a ruler who treated the monasteries as his private property.[72] However, he began his reign by depositing his treasure in English churches, leaving the larger shares of his wealth in the more important monasteries, some of which were also given grants of land and revenues.[73] His generosity to the Church and to religious houses, in particular during a serious illness 1093, was noted and the chronicler of Abingdon mentioned the high esteem in which the king held their abbot. This coincided with building activity in the abbey.[74] Three centuries later Thomas Walsingham reported building activity also at St. Albans extending into the reign of William Rufus.[75] The urban Benedictine houses of Chester and Colchester were founded in his reign, in Winchester the monks moved into the New Monastery and the dedication of the abbey

---

[69] R. HUSCROFT, The Norman Conquest. A New Introduction, Harlow 2009, p. 301; E. KING, Peterborough Abbey (note 20 above), p. 19.

[70] J. D. HASS, Medieval Selby (note 7 above), p. 4.

[71] Chronicon Abbatiae Ramesiensis, ed. W. D. MACRAY (note 35 above), pp. 152–153: *in tempore Normannorum eandem terram de Hemmingforde et quinque hidas quas rex Hardecnut nobis dederat amisimus*. D. KNOWLES, The Monastic Order in England (note 48 above), pp. 117, 119.

[72] Ibid., p. 397.

[73] F. BARLOW, William Rufus, London 1983, p. 63; Florentii Wigorniensis monachi Chronicon ex Chronicis, ed. B. THORPE (note 68 above), vol. 2, p. 21.

[74] Chronicon Monasterii de Abingdon, ed. J. STEVENSON (note 42 above), vol. 2, pp. 23–24, 41; M. SWANTON, The Anglo–Saxon Chronicles, London 2000, p. 227; The Life of St Anselm Archbishop of Canterbury by Eadmer, ed. R. W. SOUTHERN, Oxford 1962, p. 64.

[75] Chronica Monasterii S. Albani, Thomas Walsingham, Gesta Abbatum Monasterii Sancti Albani, ed. H. T. RILEY, 3 vols. (Rerum britannicarum medii aevi scriptores 28), London 1867–1869, vol. 1, p. 53.

church at Gloucester in 1099 indicates that a certain point in the construction of the building had been reached.[76] However, the king's generosity faded when he recovered from his sickness and the land grants were withdrawn. Abingdon Abbey was placed under royal administration when the abbot lost the king's friendship and its properties were granted to royal favourites. The Annals of Winchester identify Ranulph Flambard as the chief culprit, who is said to have despoiled the churches entrusted to him. This period is also associated with high tax demands addressed to the monasteries.[77] Monastic property was used for the royal fisc during vacancies and it was said that three bishoprics and eleven abbacies were vacant at the time of the king's death in 1100.[78] William II. showed no great interest in the crusade and his willingness to assist his brother Robert to raise the funds for this venture was clearly caused by self-interest because the duke had to give Normandy as security for the loan. If it is true that the proceeds collected during the vacancies were used by William II. to provide the funds for the journey of his brother Robert of Normandy to the Holy Land, it would have been the first occasion on which the English Benedictines provided material contributions to the crusades.[79]

From the late eleventh century three sources of authority exerted control over monastic affairs in England: the king and the royal government, the English bishops and the papacy. These three forces could project their power in different constellations. Papal provision to monasteries continued to be a factor into the later middle ages when it became a cause for concern and led to legislation[80] and despite the occasional involvement of papal legates in the appointment or in the deposition of heads of religious houses, papal control was at best secondary to that of the king. There were only a few instances of greater ecclesiastical autonomy, e.g. in the early years of Henry I.'s reign when in 1102 the council of Lon-

---

[76] Florentii Wigorniensis monachi Chronicon ex Chronicis, ed. B. THORPE (note 68 above), vol. 2, p. 44.

[77] Annales Monastici, ed. H. R. LUARD, 5 vols. (Rerum britannicarum medii aevi scriptores 36), London 1864–1869, vol. 2, p. 37. Under the year 1097: *Hoc anno transfretavit rex, et regnum Walkelino et Radulfo Passeflaberc commisit. Radulfus xvi ecclesias carentes pastoribus sub tutela sua habebat, episcopatus, et abbatias, quas ad extremam paupertatem perduxit. Ecclesiae quibus pastores praeerant, dabant singulis annis regi ccc. vel cccc. marcas, aliae plus, aliae vero minus.*

[78] D. KNOWLES, The Monastic Order in England (note 48 above), p. 612; Chronicon Monasterii de Abingdon, ed. J. STEVENSON (note 42 above), vol. 1, pp. 41–43; M. SWANTON, The Anglo–Saxon Chronicles (note 74 above), p. 235; C. N. L. BROOKE, Kings and Princes as Patrons of Monasteries, in: Il Monachesimo e la riforma ecclesiastica (1049–1122), Settimana di studio, Quarto passo della Mendola, 1968 (Miscellanea del Centro di studi medioevali 6), Milan 1971, pp. 125–144, at p. 135.

[79] Florentii Wigorniensis monachi Chronicon ex Chronicis, ed. B. THORPE (note 68 above), vol. 2, p. 40; C. TYERMAN, God's War, A New History of the Crusades, London 2007, p. 76.

[80] Stat. Provisors, The Statutes of the Realm, eds. T. E. TOMLINS / J. FRANCE / W. E. TAUNTON / J. RAITHBY, 12 vols., London 1810–1828, vol. 1, p. 316.

don, called by archbishop Anselm, deposed abbots who had obtained their position through simony, an occasion which led to an immediate rift between the metropolitan and the king, or the deposition of abbot Roger Norreys of Evesham by the papal legate Pandulf in 1213. The latter event was followed by the drafting of new constitutions in which the administration of the abbey's revenues was organised.[81] In the 1250s there was close co-operation between the English king and the papacy while in the late thirteenth century the relationship between Edward I. and Boniface VIII. had become difficult. In the early phase of the Hundred Years War the relations between the popes, then residing in Avignon, and the English ruler deteriorated again. Measures were taken to curb papal influence. An early example is a royal writ sent to Shrewsbury Abbey, forbidding the abbot "to make inquiry into the revenues of the monasteries, on behalf of the Pope" and there was also resistance from English monastic communities who were facing demands by cardinals for the payment of financial stipends.[82] This was already indicative of an atmosphere in which the legislation against papal provisions and the Statute of Praemunire were passed.[83] The attempt by Edmund Bramfield to become abbot of Bury St. Edmunds by papal provision in 1379 was noted by Benedictine chroniclers and led to proceedings before the royal council, to litigation in the King's Bench and eventually to his imprisonment. Government action did not stop there but extended to the investigation and prosecution of his supporters, even among the townsmen of Bury St. Edmunds.[84]

Even though a systematic study of English Benedictine cartularies from the twelfth to fourteenth century has not yet been conducted, one might speculate that the pre-emince of royal authority becomes visible even in the structure and in the contents of these text collections and the same is true for some monastic chronicles. Royal grants of land, royal privileges and the confirmations of such documents tend to take a more prominent place than even papal documents. Royal authority was more immediate and kings could be supporters, protectors against episcopal attempts to encroach upon monastic privileges, they could be founders or powerful patrons, even of religious houses founded by others.[85] In violent altercations between burgesses and their local monastic lords the monarchs and their judicial machinery could be powerful protectors or at least avengers, as at Bury St. Edmunds, Coventry, St. Albans or Norwich where urban

---

[81] Johannes de Oxenedes, Chronica, ed. H. ELLIS (note 42 above), pp. 41–42. Chronicon Abbatiae de Evesham, ed. W. D. MACRAY (note 42 above), pp. 205–221, 241–250.

[82] Documents, ed. W. A. PANTIN (note 40 above), vol. 3, pp. 18, 19.

[83] Statutes of the Realm, eds. T. E. TOMLINS / J. FRANCE / W. E. TAUNTON / J. RAITHBY (note 80 above), vol. 1, p. 329; W. M. ORMROD, Edward III, New Haven/London 2011, p. 368.

[84] R. L. STOREY, Papal Provision to English Monasteries, in: Nottingham Medieval Studies 35 (1991), pp. 77–91, at pp. 83–88.

[85] The Cartulary of Shrewsbury Abbey, ed. U. REES (note 8 above), vol. 1, p. 12.

protest against monastic rule led to violence against the religious.[86] On the other hand, royal demands for taxes and for other forms of material support could also become a burden and the loss of the king's favour could force the institution to provide protection for itself at great cost, as the monks of Ramsey Abbey discovered in 1251, when Henry III. annulled some of their liberties, as the monks of St. Albans experienced when a suspected thief was tried and convicted in their court, allegedly in violation of royal authority, and as Bury St. Edmunds learned when the Franciscans arrived to settle in their liberty in 1257.[87] It is true that charismatic prelates could also act as protectors. In the dispute between Evesham Abbey and Mauger, bishop of Worcester, about visitation rights Hubert Walter, archbishop of Canterbury acted as the monks' proctector and the dispute was eventually decided in Rome. It is not surprising that the episode took the place of prominence in the account produced by one of the protagonists in this longstanding, costly and complicated dispute, Thomas of Marlborough. He also made sure to insert the texts of key documents into his account.[88] When the dispute between the monks of St. Swithun's, Winchester, and the bishop-elect about the auditing of the priory's accounts escalated in 1255, Henry III. intervened: *sed conventus sperabat meliorem pacem consequi per dominum Papam, renuit pacem, et inde deceptus fuit.*[89] It is not surprising that the religious mostly turned the focus of their attention to the political leadership of the English kingdom. Texts of royal charters and privileges take a prominent place in the chronicles of Ramsey and Abingdon,

---

[86] N. M. TRENHOLME, The Risings in the English Monastic Towns in 1327, in: American Historical Review 6 (1900/1901), pp. 560–670; J. RÖHRKASTEN, Conflict in a Monastic Borough: Coventry in the Reign of Edward II, in: Midland History 18 (1993), pp. 1–18; Norwich 1272, e.g. Annales Monastici, ed. H. R. LUARD (note 77 above), vol. 2, p. 111.

[87] Johannes de Oxenedes, Chronica, ed. H. ELLIS (note 42 above), p. 187; Annales Monastici, ed. H. R. LUARD (note 77 above), vol. 1, p. 134: *Magna turbatio orta est apud Sanctum Albanum pro suspensione cujusdam pueri minus caute judicati et suspensi per ballivos abbatiae. Similiter apud Radinges propter occisionem quorundam hominum, cui, ut dicitur, interfuerunt quidam servientes abbatiae, unde dominus rex graviter utrique domui commotus est.*

[88] Chronicon Abbatiae de Evesham, ed. W. D. MACRAY (note 42 above), pp. 171–197. C. CHENEY, Episcopal Visitations of Monasteries in the Thirteenth Century (Publications of the University of Manchester, Historical Series 58), Manchester 1931, p. 90.

[89] Annales Monastici, ed. H. R. LUARD (note 77 above), vol. 2, p. 95.

where a significant amount of space is devoted to them, or in cartularies of Athelney[90], Reading[91] and Peterborough.[92]

A similar picture emerges when the contents of many English cartularies and monastic chronicles are analysed more closely in order to identify the importance given by their authors or scribes to English common law, to the activities of the royal courts of law, to parliamentary legislation and to the procedures of the royal administration. Many of them contain copies of legislation, of royal ordinances and even extensive extracts from legal records, detailing cases in which religious houses were involved. This does not merely apply to the chronicle of Battle Abbey with its account of the dispute between the monastery and bishop Hilary of Chichester, culminating in the dramatic description of the scene in Henry II.'s court when the bishop is confronted by a furious king.[93] Apart from such regulations as the assizes of bread and beer, the register of Malmesbury contains the information that fines for beaupleader have been abolished, the texts of the writ *ad quod damnum*, the Statutes of Westminster I (1275), Gloucester (1278) as well as Winchester and Westminster II (1285), information on the *Quo warranto* proceedings, and extracts from plea rolls including lists of jurors' names.[94] The compilers of the fourteenth-century cartulary of Winchester cathedral paid similar attention to the statutes of Edward III.[95] John de Oxenedes' Chronicle refers to the Statute of Mortmain (1279) and it also contains a section on the 1286 Norfolk Eyre when the legal claims of the author's abbey, St. Benet of Holme, were scrutinized in the *Quo warranto* proceedings[96]. The arrival of royal itinerant justices, texts of statutes and litigation involving the religious house also feature prominently in other Benedictine collections and historical narratives, the Annals of

---

[90] Chronicon Monasterii de Abingdon, ed. J. STEVENSON (note 42 above), vol. 1, pp. 10–13, 24–25, 29–35, 41–43, 51–69, 73–76, 79–87, 91–119, 131, 134, 145–197, 204–217, 219–244, 255–343, 352–354, 358–428, 434–442, 446–450, 452–455, 488–489; vol. 2, pp. 2, 8, 79–79, 82, 86–87, 90, 92–95, 115, 173, 182. Chronicon Abbatiae Ramesiensis, ed. W. D. MACRAY (note 35 above), pp. 151–152, 181–232, 276–293, 296–301, 320–324; Two Cartularies of the Benedictine Abbeys Muchelney and Athelney in the County of Somerset, ed. E. H. BATES (Somerset Record Society 14), Taunton 1899, pp. 1–112; 113–201, at pp. 118–123.

[91] Reading Abbey Cartularies, ed. B. R. KEMP (note 26 above), vol. 1, pp. 3, 33–109; papal acts follow on folio 64v, p. 129.

[92] E. KING, Peterborough Abbey (note 20 above), p. 3.

[93] The Chronicle Battle Abbey, ed. E. SEARLE, Oxford 1980, p. 11: the author "was a common law man to the bone."

[94] Registrum Malmesburiense, eds. J. S. BREWER / C. T. MARTIN (note 41 above), vol. 1, pp. 45, 64, 65, 113–117, 134, 135, 207–245, 251–264; vol. 2, pp. 309–310.

[95] Chartulary of Winchester Cathedral, ed. A. W. GOODMAN, Winchester 1927, p. xxx.

[96] Johannes de Oxenedes, Chronica, ed. H. ELLIS (note 42 above), pp. 255, 266–267.

Burton[97], the Annals of Tewkesbury[98], the *Annales de Wintonia*[99] or the Annals of Worcester.[100] Collections of royal statutes could also be found in the cartularies of Ramsey Abbey or in the library of St. Peter, Gloucester, where the abbey's cartulary contained a reference to the activities of justices of Trailbaston at Gloucester in 1305, had the texts of Magna Carta and the Charter of the Forest as well as extracts from a plea from the 1221 Gloucester Eyre.[101] This preoccupation with royal justice could extend to reports on individual cases, to the copying of the texts of final concords or to the inclusion of extracts from plea rolls. This was done e.g. in the chronicle of Peterborough which contains accounts of litigation from the early years of Edward I.'s reign onwards as well as extracts from plea rolls.[102] Volumes with copies of royal statutes, registers of writs or, in the case of Shrewsbury Abbey, a copy of the *Liber Rubeus Scaccarii*, can still be identified as parts of monastic libraries, at Abbotsbury, St. Augustine, Canterbury, Cerne, Crowland, Gloucester, Malmesbury or Thorney, even though often only small parts of the collections survive.[103]

This pre-eminence of texts from the royal law courts, of statutes and related material highlights the dominance of royal authority in a functioning centalised medieval state. The presence of royal officials in the counties and in the hundreds was much more immediate than the occasional appearance of papal representatives in the kingdom, even though their decisions and actions could have far-reaching repercussions. The papal *Curia* was of importance for those few Benedictine houses who wanted to obtain exemption from episcopal control. This affected at most six English abbeys, St. Augustine's Canterbury, Westminster Abbey, Bury St. Edmunds, St. Albans, Evesham and Malmesbury.[104] The confirmation of such privileges was expensive, not counting the costs of travel and of retaining proctors at the Roman *Curia*. The expenses of the monks of Spalding who began litigation in Rome for the right to elect their own prior in 1230 were considerable. By the time they obtained their privilege, in 1245, the costs

---

[97] Annales Monastici, ed. H. R. LUARD (note 77 above), vol. 1, pp. 252, 254, 256, 329–330.

[98] Ibid., vol. 1, pp. 64, 65, 97–99, 107, 119, 137–138, 156–157.

[99] Ibid., vol. 2, p. 107.

[100] Ibid., vol. 4, pp. 413, 427, 432, 348, 447, 464, 511.

[101] Historia et Cartularium Monasterii Sancti Petri Gloucestriae, ed. W. H. HART (note 41 above), vol. 1, pp. 38, 225, 322; vol. 2, pp. 276–280; vol. 3, pp. xiv–xv; Cartularium Monasterii de Rameseia, eds. W. H. HART / P. A. LYONS (note 41 above), vol. 1, p. x.

[102] Chronicon Petroburgense, ed. T. STAPLETON (note 35 above), pp. 66–69.

[103] G. R. C. DAVIS, Medieval Cartularies (note 29 above), pp. 1, 43–45, 49, 54, 56, 92, 128, 179, 189.

[104] D. KNOWLES, The Monastic Order in England (note 48 above), pp. 576, 580–581, 589; C. CHENEY, Episcopal Visitations (note 88 above), p. 39.

amounted to 1000 marks.[105] However, on occasion even these claims to privileged status could be challenged. In such cases the royal government could be a potential ally for the religious in the occasional disputes about episcopal control of the Benedictine abbeys. The example of Evesham shows the difficulties that could be caused by the lack of such support. The dispute about the right of visitation between the bishop of Worcester and Evesham led to costly litigation in Rome at the turn from the twelfth to the thirteenth century. The originals of the abbey's precious legal titles had to be given to Roman merchants as security for loans and it is quite possible that the 400 marks mentioned by Thomas of Marlborough were only a part of the monastery's liabilities in this episode.[106] The timing of the quarrel was an additional complication because it occurred when the community was headed by a notoriously corrupt abbot who was on good personal terms with the royal justiciar, Geoffrey Fitz Peter, and who used this government protection against his own monastery; it permitted him to interfere arbitrarily with the obedientiaries' estates. The abbot's cronies and relatives were the beneficiaries of this policy. An attempt by the monks to defend themselves led to a confrontation with the secular authorities.[107] Up to the Statutes of *Praemunire* in the fourteenth century there remained the possibility to use both royal and papal jurisdiction for certain types of cases. In some narratives legal disputes in the royal courts are given the same imporance as litigation about monastic parish churches conducted – often at greater cost – in the papal curia.[108]

Apart from the question of their status in their dioceses, a number of Benedictine abbeys also had obtained royal privileges, including franchises and liberties. This could include the devolution of royal government authority to the abbot, famously in the cases of Bury St. Edmunds, where the abbot controlled seven of the hundreds of the county of Suffolk[109], of Ely, Gloucester or Tavistock. Here the abbots could appoint officials who held the hundred courts and collected the perquisites. As tenants-in-chief, abbots could also exercise their own jurisdiction in baronial courts.[110] Liberties could include an abbey's control

---

[105] N. SUMNER, The Countess Lucy's Priory? (note 52 above), p. 93.

[106] Chronicon Abbatiae de Evesham, ed. W. D. MACRAY (note 42 above), pp. 130–138, 151–201.

[107] Ibid., p. 125: *Sed nos non ferentes tantam iniquitatem licet circumdedissent nos undique angustiae, quoddam assartum quod dederat senescallo nostro ad tuitionem aliorum, quod ipse seminaverat, non veriti sumus metere, pro quo facto et regis iram contra nos excitavimus et indignationem archiepiscopi incurrimus.*

[108] Thomas Walsingham, Gesta Abbatum Monasterii Sancti Albani, ed. H. T. RILEY (note 75 above), vol. 1, pp. 335–337.

[109] Regesta Willelmi Conquestoris et Willelmi Rufi 1066–1100, ed. H. W. C. DAVIS, Oxford 1913, p. 12 nos. 41 (vii); 42 (v); M. HOWELL, Regalian Right in Medieval England, London 1962, pp. 13–18.

[110] E. MILLER, The Abbey and Bishopric of Ely (note 15 above), p. 30; H. R. P. FINBERG, Tavistock Abbey (note 61 above), p. 17; F. BARLOW, William Rufus (note 73 above), p. 178; Historia et Cartularium Monasterii Sancti Petri Gloucestriae, ed. W. H. HART (note 41 above), vol. 1, pp. 149–151.

of its own prison, the exclusion of a convent's subsistence supplies from demands for tolls and other payments, or the management of a royal mint.[111] Henry I. granted Battle Abbey the right to exclude royal itinerant justices from its land, other houses obtained exemptions from being summoned to forest eyres or even from the summons to the general eyres.[112] The abbot of Ramsey had the right to hold common pleas arising from his estates.[113] In many cases such privileges and liberties were accumulated over time, giving the abbeys a dual character, not only as spiritual centres but also as centres of secular local government.[114] This status could be combined with their role as powerful economic units. The privileges brought prestige and an additional income of fines and perquisites, even though the profits were not always very considerable. In the mid-fourteenth century Crowland Abbey generating an annual income from these sources amounting to £6 6 shillings 9 pence.[115]

Originally royal privileges seem to have been granted free of charge because a monarch wanted to support the religious in their regular worship. When Henry I. granted extensive liberties to Ramsey Abbey for some of its estates, he gave a standard reason: *pro Dei amore, et animabus patris et matris meae, et pro remissione peccatorum meorum, et pro pace et stabilitate regni mei*.[116] The confirmation or extension of such grants and privileges by the original patron's successor was not so straightforward, even if the abbot of the monastery in question had direct access to the king. The original document had to be scrutinised formally – there was an awareness of the skills of monastic forgers – and its contents analysed, an investigation might have to be conducted into the convent's customs and practices and royal advisers had to be consulted. This could be a lengthy process and the confirmation might not be free of charge. In 1203 the abbot of Selby had to pay king John 100 marks Sterling for the confirmation of a grant.[117] When Henry III. obtained a new seal in 1227, all regular religious were forced to have their royal privileges validated under the new seal, an expensive and highly unwelcome requirement.[118]

---

[111] Cartulary of Chatteris Abbey, ed. C. BREAY (note 24 above), pp. 74–75.

[112] J. A. GREEN, The Government of England Under Henry I (note 1 above), p. 114; Registrum Malmesburiense, eds. J. S. BREWER / C. T. MARTIN (note 41 above), vol. 1, p. xxxviii.

[113] D. W. SUTHERLAND, Quo Warranto Proceedings in the Reign of Edward I: 1278–1294, Oxford 1963, p. 3.

[114] H. R. P. FINBERG, Tavistock Abbey (note 61 above), pp. 192–214.

[115] F. M. PAGE, Estates of Crowland Abbey (note 16 above), p. 124; H. W. SAUNDERS, Introduction (note 36 above), p. 9; D. KNOWLES, The Monastic Order in England (note 48 above), p. 73.

[116] Cartularium Monasterii de Rameseia, eds. W. H. HART / P. A. LYONS (note 41 above), vol. 1, p. 241.

[117] W. L. WARREN, Henry II (note 26 above), pp. 303–304; J. D HASS, Medieval Selby (note 7 above), p. 15.

[118] Johannes de Oxenedes, Chronica, ed. H. ELLIS (note 42 above) p. 155: *Tunc denunciatum est viris religiosis et aliis qui suis volebant gaudere privilegiis et libertatibus ut innovarent cartas suas de novo regis sigillo scientes quod rex cartas antiquas nullius esse momenti reputabat, pro quarum innovatione non juxta singulorum*

The sum of 100 marks *exceptis aliis ponderosis expensis foris* had to be paid to Edward II's treasury by Ramsey Abbey in 1320, *pro carta ipsius Regis obtinenda de diversis libertatibus*.[119] In 1338 Edward III. issued a confirmation of the charters granted by his predecessors to Reading Abbey, mentioning the monastery's earlier grant of jewels and valuables to the royal fisc. In this case the abbey's provision of valuables predated the confirmation.[120] The royal confirmation of the liberties and earlier grants was a matter of great importance and noted by monastic chroniclers.[121] Still in the reign of Henry V the abbot and the monks of Evesham paid the king a sum of 24 marks for such a confirmation.[122]

The claim to liberties and royal privileges did not necessarily mean that their use went unchallenged and they also entailed responsibilities. Revenues from the liberties belonging to the king had to be accounted for at the Exchequer.[123] Furthermore, a liberty, e.g. the control of a hundred or a royal mint, brought obligations and subjected the owner to regular control by royal justices and other officials. The same is true for legal privileges. The royal Exchequer made sure that the abbot of Bury St. Edmunds would answer for the chattels of a felon executed in his liberty.[124] There were other controls. The exercise of the rights embodied in the franchises could not be taken for granted. In January 1233 the abbot was given a return day in the Exchequer *ad ostendendum cartam per quem clamat habere libertates suas*.[125] These were challenges every holder of a franchise had to face. Any perceived abuse could be punished by the withdrawal of the franchise. In a dispute about the royal mint in Bury St. Edmunds in 1237 the abbot had to pay a fine of £200 for trespass and for the return of the mint: *pro transgressione quam homines sui fecerunt de cuneo suo apud sanctum Eadmundum et pro cuneo suo rehabendo*[126] Whenever the head of a religious house had the right to exercise royal authority, the use of this liberty was strictly controlled. Any perceived mismanagement usually resulted in a financial penalty which could consist of a substantial slice of the abbey's annual income.

In 1255 the holders of franchises were challenged to show upon demand, by what right (*Quo warranto*) they claimed to hold their liberty. At that time it was a

---

facultatem taxatio facta est sed quicquid justiciarius aestimabat solvere sunt coacti; et sic diatim odium omnium et maledictiones in caput suum coacervavit.

[119] Chronicon Abbatiae Ramesiensis, ed. W. D. MACRAY (note 35 above), p. 350.

[120] Reading Abbey Cartularies, ed. B. R. KEMP (note 26 above), vol. 1, pp. 103–104, no. 109.

[121] Annals of Burton, in: Annales Monastici, ed. H. R. LUARD (note 77 above), vol. 1, pp. 236, 246.

[122] Chronicon Abbatiae de Evesham, ed. W. D. MACRAY (note 42 above), p. 306.

[123] E. KING, Peterborough Abbey (note 20 above), p. 95.

[124] TNA E159/8 m 1.

[125] TNA E159/12 m 16d.

[126] TNA E159/15 m 24. Restoration of the franchise of Reading Abbey in 1244: Reading Abbey Cartularies, ed. B. R. KEMP (note 26 above), p. 84, no. 66.

country-wide inquest but not yet a general policy. This changed in 1278 when eyre justices were instructed to conduct investigations into the claims of franchise holders.[127] The systematic introduction of the *Quo Warranto* process affected the Benedictine houses who either had to relinquish some of their privileges or re-negotiate their status.

Royal licences which allowed an abbey to improve its estates, e.g. the permit to hold a weekly market, the acquisition of a royal charter to found a borough or the right to assart, were separate from the franchises which allowed the exercise of royal rights in a defined area. They were seen as commodities which were sold for a fee. Examples are easy to find in the royal records. In December 1219 the abbot of Bury St. Edmunds had to promise the young Henry III. a light saddle horse for the grant of a weekly market on one of his manors and the same was demanded in September 1221 from the abbess of Barking.[128] The abbot of Buckfast had to pay 5 marks for a similar privilege and at about the same time the grant to hold a weekly market cost the abbot of Burton two horses.[129] When the royal government granted a weekly market to the abbey of St. Werburgh in Chester in January 1223, a payment of a horse had to be made.[130] Two grants of two markets for Tavistock Abbey cost two horses and 5 marks respectively and the right to hold a market and an annual fair cost the abbey of St. Peter of Gloucester 100 shillings.[131] In the same way the improvement of monastic estates, e.g. by assarting or through the draining of moorland, required royal permission and was possible only after the payment of a fee set by the administration. Peterborough Abbey paid 200 marks for disafforestation on some of its estates.[132] Privileges or licences which entailed an obvious economic benefit for the recipient were sold by the crown. In such transactions the monasteries were not regarded as religious houses but as economic enterprises which had to pay for the right to have a fair[133], to hold assets at farm[134], to have custody of a manor[135] or even to improve their own estates by assarting or by building a mill.[136]

---

[127] D. W. SUTHERLAND, Quo Warranto Proceedings (note 113 above), pp. 22–23; H. R. P. FINBERG, Tavistock Abbey (note 61 above), pp. 17–18.

[128] Calendar of the Fine Rolls of the Reign of Henry III, Volume 1, 1 to 8 Henry III 1216–1224, eds. P. DRYBURGH / B. HARTLAND, Woodbridge 2007, p. 130 no. 4/401, p. 216; no. 5/301.

[129] Ibid., p. 144 no. 4/129; p. 203 no. 5/213.

[130] Ibid., p. 178 no. 5/48.

[131] Ibid., p. 163 no. 4/258; p. 194 no. 5/152; pp. 128–129 no. 4/26.

[132] J. BOLTON, The Medieval English Economy (note 19 above), pp. 12, 88.

[133] E.g. Ramsey, TNA E159/48 m 71.

[134] E.g. Cerne, TNA E159/49 m 28.

[135] E.g. Westminster Abbey, TNA E159/8 m 5d; prior of Coventry Cathedral Priory, TNA E159/20 m 16d.

[136] TNA E159/5 m 2, 14; E159/6 m 5, 12; E159/16 m 14d.

Both the control of the old liberties and franchises through *Quo warranto*, as well as the policy to turn royal grants into a commodity which could be obtained for a price, demonstrate the level of power wielded by the centralised state. This power was underpinned by the fact that the heads of religious houses were normally appointed by the Crown. It is true that this was not invariably the case because firstly kings could grant free elections and their influence was reduced in times of political crisis. In addition, papal influence and the activities of papal legates have to be taken into account although papal support was expensive.[137] Furthermore it seems that in the control of abbatial elections a deliberate royal policy was not always pursued because in many cases consent was given to the candidate proposed by the community. However, this influence on abbatial elections also had an important economic component because the monarch could determine the duration of the vacancy and in this period the bulk of the monastic income went into the royal treasure.

As major landholders the heads of the large religious houses became crown vassals after the Norman Conquest for the lands held directly from the king and they were burdened with the feudal services belonging to this status. This included the monarchs' claim to control the monastic estates during vacancies and to derive the income from them, just as feudal lords obtained the revenues from their vassals' estates during a minority. Although the supply of the religious with food and clothing was safeguarded, a substantial part of a monastery's income could be given to royal favourites or was simply paid into the Exchequer for the duration of the vacancy. In the reigns of William II. and Henry I. vacancies could last for years, by the thirteenth century their duration was often much shorter.[138] A custodian was appointed for the vacant abbey of Crowland on 20 September 1236, royal assent to the election of a new abbot followed on 28 September; an administrator for the vacant abbey of Thorney was appointed on 18 August 1237, the royal licence to elect a new abbot has the date of the same day. On 10 June 1256 Abingdon was described as 'now void' and royal assent to an election followed six weeks later, on 24 July.[139]

Even though it became unusual to extend vacancies over years, they could still generate substantial payments in cash and in kind for the Crown. Between 1168 and 1175 the priest Wimar, accounting for revenue from St. Benet Holme, paid more than £260 into the royal Exchequer.[140] At the same time, between

---

[137] N. SUMNER, The Countess Lucy's Priory? (note 52 above), p. 93; D. KNOWLES, The Monastic Order in England (note 48 above), pp. 398, 400–401; R. L. STOREY, Papal Provision (note 84 above), p. 82.

[138] D. KNOWLES, The Monastic Order in England (note 48 above), pp. 612–615.

[139] Calendar of Patent Rolls 1232–1247, London 1906, pp. 158–159. Calendar of Patent Rolls 1247–1258, London 1908, pp. 193, 480.

[140] The Great Roll of the Pipe for the Fourteenth Year of the Reign of King Henry the Second, A.D. 1167–1168 (Publications of the Pipe Roll Society 12), London 1890, p. 33; Great Roll of

1169 and 1172, when Malmesbury Abbey was *in manu domini regis*, the sheriff of Wiltshire accounted for more than £103 of the revenues, not counting the payments for the monks' supply.[141] The administrator of Abingdon had to account for more than £87 for half a year in 1165 when he paid more than £10 into the Exchequer and used a further £23 to serve some of the monastery's old debts.[142] Between 1171 and 1175 two administrators accounted for £190 of the revenue of Battle Abbey and they were declared quit at the Exchequer in 1176.[143] Two royal caretakers paid £108 of the revenues of Hyde Abbey into the treasury in 1171, a further £351 6 shillings and 8 pence follwing in the years 1172 to 1174.[144] The first vacancy account from Westminster Abbey for the years 1173 to 1175 records various payments amounting to £435 from the monastery.[145] At Barking more than £219 were collected by the royal keeper of the estates during a vacancy lasting six months.[146] The cartulary of Ramsey Abbey contains extracts from Pipe Rolls, noting the payment of more than £336 from the monastery's income for

---

the Pipe for the Fifteenth Year of the Reign of King Henry the Second (note 26 above), p. 106; Great Roll of the Pipe for the Sixteenth Year of the Reign of King Henry the Second (note 26 above), p. 13; Great Roll of the Pipe for the Seventeenth Year of the Reign of King Henry the Second (note 26 above), p. 10; The Great Roll of the Pipe for the Eighteenth Year of the Reign of King Henry the Second, A.D. 1171–1172 (Publications of the Pipe Roll Society 18), London 1894, p. 32; The Great Roll of the Pipe for the Nineteenth Year of the Reign of King Henry the Second, A.D. 1172–1173 (Publications of the Pipe Roll Society 19), London 1895, p. 131; The Great Roll of the Pipe for the Twentieth Year of the Reign of King Henry the Second, A.D. 1173–1174 (Publications of the Pipe Roll Society 21), London 1896, p. 48.

[141] Great Roll of the Pipe for the Fifteenth Year of the Reign of King Henry the Second (note 26 above), pp. 22, 24; Great Roll of the Pipe for the Sixteenth Year of the Reign of King Henry the Second (note 26 above), p. 65; Great Roll of the Pipe for the Seventeenth Year of the Reign of King Henry the Second (note 26 above), p. 24; Great Roll of the Pipe for the Eighteenth Year of the Reign of King Henry the Second (note 140 above), p. 128.

[142] The Great Roll of the Pipe for the Eleventh Year of the Reign of King Henry the Second, A.D. 1164–1165 (Publications of the Pipe Roll Society 8), London 1887, pp. 74, 77.

[143] Great Roll of the Pipe for the Seventeenth Year of the Reign of King Henry the Second (note 26 above), p. 130; Great Roll of the Pipe for the Eighteenth Year of the Reign of King Henry the Second (note 140 above), p. 133; Great Roll of the Pipe for the Nineteenth Year of the Reign of King Henry the Second (note 140 above), p. 29; Great Roll of the Pipe for the Twentieth Year of the Reign of King Henry the Second (note 140 above), p. 120; Great Roll of the Pipe for the Twenty–First Year of the Reign of King Henry the Second (note 26 above), p. 84; The Great Roll of the Pipe for the Twenty–Second Year of the Reign of King Henry the Second, A.D. 1175–1176 (Publications of the Pipe Roll Society 25), London 1904, p. 203.

[144] Great Roll of the Pipe for the Seventeenth Year of the Reign of King Henry the Second (note 26 above), p. 42; Great Roll of the Pipe for the Eighteenth Year of the Reign of King Henry the Second (note 140 above), p. 4; Great Roll of the Pipe for the Nineteenth Year of the Reign of King Henry the Second (note 140 above), p. 56; Great Roll of the Pipe for the Twentieth Year of the Reign of King Henry the Second (note 140 above), p. 136.

[145] B. HARVEY, Westminster Abbey and its Estates (note 20 above), p. 56.

[146] Cartulary of Chatteris Abbey, ed. C. BREAY (note 24 above), p. 22.

the period 24 June 1201 to 25 December 1202.[147] The same period in the years 1207 to 1208 yielded more than £581.[148] Surviving accounts from the abbey of Peterborough show payments of more than £394 for a vacancy lasting for a year in 1176, of more than £1000 for a vacancy of six months in 1210 and of more than £808 for another vacancy lasting a year in 1211.[149] Following the deposition of the abbot of Peterborough in 1177 the administrator accounted for more than £342 at the Exchequer.[150] A vacancy of Peterborough and Ramsey in the first years of the thirteenth century had raised revenue of more than £2241.[151] For the three years between the death of abbot Samson in 1211 and the accession of abbot Hugh of Northwold, the prior of Bury St. Edmunds owed £145, £237 10 shillings, and £500 respectively.[152] Not all income from vacant monasteries had these proportions. In the years 1170 to 1176 the administrators of Thorney accounted for £57[153] and the small abbey of Muchelney yielded not much more than £10 in 1172–1173.[154] Nevertheless one may assume that these payments made up a significant portion of the royal income in these years.

The larger Benedictine communities – the more recent foundations of Battle and Reading excepted – tried to protect themselves by separating the abbot's estate from that of the convent, a measure designed to protect the latter's portion of the income from being put under administration.[155] During a vacancy the two had to be clearly separated. This arrangement became more complicated when the convent's income was subdivided among the obedientiaries' departments, sacrist, chamberlain, almoner and the others deriving a fixed income from clearly defined manors and estates. There could also be disputes between the monastic

---

[147] Cartularium Monasterii de Rameseia, eds. W. H. HART / P. A. LYONS (note 41 above), vol. 1, p. 227.

[148] Ibid., vol. 1, pp. 228–231.

[149] E. KING, Peterborough Abbey (note 20 above), p. 145.

[150] The Great Roll of the Pipe for the Twenty–Third Year of the Reign of King Henry the Second, A.D. 1176–1177 (Publications of the Pipe Roll Society 26), London 1905, p. 104.

[151] S. K. MITCHELL, Taxation in Medieval England (Yale Historical Publications 15), New Haven 1951, p. 18.

[152] TNA E159/3 m 11.

[153] Great Roll of the Pipe for the Sixteenth Year of the Reign of King Henry the Second (note 26 above), p. 95; Great Roll of the Pipe for the Seventeenth Year of the Reign of King Henry the Second (note 26 above), p. 115; Great Roll of the Pipe for the Nineteenth Year of the Reign of King Henry the Second (note 140 above), p. 161; Great Roll of the Pipe for the Twentieth Year of the Reign of King Henry the Second (note 140 above), p. 66; Great Roll of the Pipe for the Twenty–First Year of the Reign of King Henry the Second (note 26 above), p. 143; Great Roll of the Pipe for the Twenty–Second Year of the Reign of King Henry the Second (note 143 above), p. 76.

[154] Great Roll of the Pipe for the Eighteenth Year of the Reign of King Henry the Second (note 140 above), p. 78; Great Roll of the Pipe for the Nineteenth Year of the Reign of King Henry the Second (note 140 above), p. 197.

[155] Ibid., pp. 404–405; B. HARVEY, Westminster Abbey and its Estates (note 20 above), p. 64.

community and the royal administration about the king's rights during a vacancy because the separation of the estates was regarded as a ploy to evade payments due to the king. Such a dispute arose in 1279 during a vacancy in Bury St. Edmunds when the convent's as well as the abbot's portion were claimed by the king. Edward I. accepted the separation of the two in the following year – for a payment of more than £1000.[156] In June 1287 such a dispute involving the abbey of St. Peter, Gloucester, was resolved by a jury verdict heard before the escheator and a royal justice. The result was duly recorded in the monastery's cartulary: *qui dicunt per sacramentum suum quod tempore vacationis dictae abbatiae nullus eschaetor domini regis maneria dictorum obedientiariorum ingredi, seu exitus aliquos de dictis maneriis ad opus ejusdem domini regis percipere consuevit*.[157]

The prospect of administration by royal agents during a vacancy was an incentive for some monasteries to offer substantial fines for the privilege to retain control of its economy and finances in such a situation. Not all administrators were entirely reliable in the execution of their duties. In 1243 horses and other valuables were unlawfully taken at Evesham, and monastic income could become freely disposable in the royal financial system when it was assigned to third parties in payment of royal debts.[158] Conversely the administrator could take out a loan on behalf of the monastery during a vacancy, as happened at St. Swithun's, Winchester, early in the reign of Edward I., where a sequence of loans from Italian bankers was initiated in 1278.[159]

There were other potential problems. The effects of the administrators' work was not predictable; Westminster Abbey had the livestock of one of its manors taken away in 1284 after Edward I. had granted the animals to his wife.[160] The administration had to communicate the commands coming from the centre and this took time although such delays were expected. But unexpected delays might occur, e.g. because of the death of an administrator whose executors had to receive appropriate instructions[161], or through the delay in an important land transaction because the manor about to be transferred was retained in the king's hand.[162] A different problem occurred at the nunnery of Shaftesbury in 1242

---

[156] Johannes de Oxenedes, Chronica, ed. H. ELLIS (note 42 above), pp. 254, 257.

[157] Historia et Cartularium Monasterii Sancti Petri Gloucestriae, ed. W. H. HART (note 41 above), vol. 3, pp. 19–20.

[158] Close Rolls 1242–1247, London 1916, pp. 24, 33; Close Rolls 1247–1251, London 1922, p. 422: 40 marks assigned out of the revenue of Pershore. Other examples are the payment of 200 marks and 50 marks out of the revenues of Glastonbury in 1275, Calendar of Close Rolls 1272–1279, London 1900, pp. 143, 159.

[159] R. W. KAEUPER, Bankers to the Crown. The Riccardi of Lucca and Edward I, Princeton 1973, p. 38.

[160] Calendar of Close Rolls 1279–1288, London 1902, p. 254.

[161] Calendar of Close Rolls 1272–1279 (note 158 above), p. 270

[162] Close Rolls 1242–1247 (note 158 above), p. 88.

when the election of an abbess, licensed by the king, could not take place because the convent's prioress had died, causing further delay in the process.[163] The payment of a negotiated and fixed amount offered voluntarily to the king could avoid these and other problems. In 1273 Selby Abbey paid a fine of 50 marks to avoid the intrusion of royal agents into its financial management, the same amount was paid by the abbey of St. John, Colchester; for the same reason Hyde Abbey paid 120 marks in the following decade.[164] The larger houses could offer much more substantial payments. In the 1280s Ramsey Abbey offered Edward I. 2000 marks Sterling *pro habenda custodia domus suae*. This sum was paid in instalments and immediately assigned to Italian bankers who were financing the king's policies.[165] The monks of Westminster Abbey offered king Richard II. an annual payment of more than £533 during a vacancy and this arrangement was still valid in 1420.[166] When queen Eleanor of Castile, wife of king Edward I., was indebted to Shaftesbury abbey in 1285 this sum was deducted from the amount owed by the abbey to the king for having been granted the custody of its temporalities during the last vacancy.[167] A different problem arose in the abbey of St. Werburgh in Chester. Although nothing had been taken away during vacancies in 1241 and 1249, there was a dispute about external intrusion into the abbey in 1265 and this may have caused a quarrel in the reign of Edward I. The abbey made a successful claim in 1292, saying that although the justices of Chester could appoint an official during a vacancy, who could stay within the monastery, the king would receive nothing from its estates. The monks were able to argue that they held of the earls of Chester just as the Benedictines of Shrewsbury could point to the fact that their monastery had been founded by the earls of Shrewsbury.[168] When the sometimes extensive English properties of alien houses, often priories of monasteries located in areas which were controlled by the French kings, were confiscated during the Hundred Years War, the priors negotiated in a similar manner with the Exchequer in order to retain the administration of their estates.[169]

---

[163] Ibid., pp. 28, 75, 77.

[164] Calendar of Close Rolls 1272–1279 (note 158 above), pp. 34, 159; Calendar of Close Rolls 1279–1288 (note 160 above), p. 199.

[165] Cartularium Monasterii de Rameseia, eds. W. H. HART / P. A. LYONS (note 41 above), vol. 3, pp. 13–15.

[166] B. HARVEY, Westminster Abbey and its Estates (note 20 above), p. 60.

[167] Calendar of Close Rolls 1279–1288 (note 160 above), pp. 338, 383.

[168] Calendar of Close Rolls, 1288–1296, London 1904, p. 216. A. P. BAGGS / A. J. KETTLE / S. LANDER / A. THACKER / D. WARDLE, Houses of Benedictine Monks: The Abbey of Chester, in: C. ELRINGTON / B. E. HARRIS (eds.), A History of the County of Chester, vol. 3, London 1980, pp. 132–146.

[169] R. GRAHAM, Four Alien Priories in Monmouthshire, in: Journal of the British Archaeological Association n.s. 35 (1929), pp. 102–121, at p. 113.

Apart from the claim to control the estates of a crown vassal, during a vacancy, or during the heir's minority in the case of a secular tenant, the king could also demand services, either in the form of direct military support or – if service was not provided – in the form of scutage payments. The collection of the money was not always straightforward. Monasteries were in arrears and some heads of religious houses with a good link to the royal household seem to have conducted informal negotiations. In the period 1159 to 1165, fourteen of twenty-three religious houses liable to pay scutage paid the full amount while nine were in arrears for at least part of the time.[170] In 1166 the abbot of Westminster Abbey owed £60 of the old scutage. However, the abbey adjacent to the main royal residence was a special case and some of these debts were put *in respectu donec rex inde loquatur*.[171] Arrears of scutage were not necessarily due to resistance from the heads of the religious communities because they themselves could encounter resistance from their own tenants. In such cases the royal administration could provide assistance to the abbey in levying the payment.[172]

The collection of scutage was complicated and there were other problems. Some convents were not confronted with a claim for military service or the demand for scutage even though they held land directly from the king: Gloucester, Burton, Athelney, Barking and St. Mary Winchester. In the thirteenth century some heads of houses, e.g. those of Barking, Burton and Gloucester, as well as those of some smaller convents like Eynsham or Whitby and Selby, received summons, between 1244 and 1285.[173] It has already been mentioned above that the distribution of this burden did not necessarily relate to the potential of the monastic economy, although the convents in turn had the right to demand the payments from those of their tenants who held by military service if these tenants

---

[170] The houses in arrears were: Abingdon, Chertsey, Coventry Cathedral Priory, Evesham, Gloucester, Peterborough, Ramsey, St. Albans and Westminster. Acquitted were: Abbotsbury, St. Augustine, Canterbury, Cerne, Crowland, Glastonbury, Malmesbury, Milton, St. Benet of Holme, Shaftesbury, Sherborne, Tavistock, Tewkesbury, Wilton and Hyde Abbey. Based on The Great Roll of the Pipe for the Seventh Year of the Reign of King Henry the Second, A.D. 1160–1161 (Publications of the Pipe Roll Society 4), London 1885; Great Roll of the Pipe for the Eighth Year of the Reign of King Henry the Second (note 26 above); The Great Roll of the Pipe for the Ninth Year of the Reign of King Henry the Second, A.D. 1162–1163 (Publications of the Pipe Roll Society 6), London 1886; The Great Roll of the Pipe for the Tenth Year of the Reign of King Henry the Second, A.D. 1163–1164 (Publications of the Pipe Roll Society 7), London 1886; Great Roll of the Pipe for the Eleventh Year of the Reign of King Henry the Second (note 142 above).

[171] The Great Roll of the Pipe for the Twelfth Year of the Reign of King Henry the Second, A.D. 1165–1166 (Publications of the Pipe Roll Society 9), London 1888, pp. 78, 81, 123.

[172] An example is a writ to the sheriff of Somerset and Dorset from 1242: *Mandatum est vicecomiti quod sit in auxilium Abbati Glastonie ad distringendum milites et libere tenentes suos qui de eo tenent per servicium militare ad reddendum eidem Abbati scutagia sua Regi debita pro exercitu Regis ad transfretationem Regis in Wascon'. Ita quod pro defectu sui non remaneat quin de scutagio predicto possit Regi sufficienter responderi.* TNA E159/21 m 19d.

[173] H. M. CHEW, Ecclesiastical Tenants–in–Chief (note 57 above), pp. 8, 11, 13.

did not perform this service in person when called upon to do so. There was another issue which complicated assessment and collection: changes in the tenurial relationship. In the twelfth century disputes arose about service and scutage payments because economic activity led to subinfeudation and to the subdivision of larger estates. In addition there were changes to the monastic demesnes. Despite the arrival of the Savignacs and the Cistercians who elicited substantial material support from the royal family and the aristocracy, land donations were still received by the old Benedictine houses in the twelfth century. As a result of theses changes Henry II.'s government conducted an investigation into the scope of the obligations in 1166, distinguishing between enfeoffments made before the death of Henry I. (1135) and those made after that time.[174] The result was a modification of the demands but the Exchequer still demanded payment for knights' fees even when the obligation was not recognized by the religious.

In the second half of the twelfth century the payments seem to have fallen into arrears in many cases. Between 1168 and 1178 seven abbeys were declared quit for their scutage payments or for the corresponding *auxilium* for the marriage of Henry II.'s daughter to the duke of Saxony[175], while another four delayed payment or paid in part. They were Abingdon, where a debt of 8 shillings 11 pence, recorded in 1168, was carried over to 1173 when it was finally paid and where the aid for the marriage of the king's daughter remained on the books until 1178[176], Cerne, where one payment was made in 1172 while a debt of 8 marks

---

[174] Ibid., pp. 18, 20. G. L. HARRISS, King, Parliament and Public Finance in Medieval England to 1369, Oxford 1975, p. 11.

[175] They were Evesham, Great Roll of the Pipe for the Eighteenth Year of the Reign of King Henry the Second (note 140 above), p. 22; Milton, in: ibid., p. 77; Pershore, in: ibid., p. 23; St. Albans, Great Roll of the Pipe for the Fourteenth Year of the Reign of King Henry the Second (note 140 above), p. 39, Great Roll of the Pipe for the Eighteenth Year of the Reign of King Henry the Second (note 140 above), p. 44; St. Benet Holme, Great Roll of the Pipe for the Fourteenth Year of the Reign of King Henry the Second (note 140 above), p. 21; Great Roll of the Pipe for the Twenty–Second Year of the Reign of King Henry the Second (note 143 above), p. 65; Wilton, Great Roll of the Pipe for the Fourteenth Year of the Reign of King Henry the Second (note 140 above), p. 160; Winchcombe, Great Roll of the Pipe for the Fourteenth Year of the Reign of King Henry the Second (note 140 above), p. 123; Great Roll of the Pipe for the Eighteenth Year of the Reign of King Henry the Second (note 140 above), p. 122.

[176] Great Roll of the Pipe for the Fourteenth Year of the Reign of King Henry the Second (note 140 above), p. 203; Great Roll of the Pipe for the Fifteenth Year of the Reign of King Henry the Second (note 26 above), p. 79; Great Roll of the Pipe for the Sixteenth Year of the Reign of King Henry the Second (note 26 above), p. 71; Great Roll of the Pipe for the Seventeenth Year of the Reign of King Henry the Second (note 26 above), p. 90; Great Roll of the Pipe for the Eighteenth Year of the Reign of King Henry the Second (note 140 above), p. 14; Great Roll of the Pipe for the Nineteenth Year of the Reign of King Henry the Second (note 140 above), p. 65. For the aid see: Great Roll of the Pipe for the Twentieth Year of the Reign of King Henry the Second (note 140 above), p. 113; Great Roll of the Pipe for the Twenty–First Year of the Reign of King Henry the Second (note 26 above), p. 134; Great Roll of the Pipe for the Twenty–Second Year of the Reign of King Henry the Second (note 143 above), p. 132; Great Roll of the Pipe for the Twenty–Third Year of the Reign of King Henry the Second

was carried from 1169 to 1178[177], Sherborne, which was acquitted on two occasions but did not meet the demands for 1174 and 1175[178] and Ramsey, whose abbot made a commitment to pay 80 marks Sterling *pro habendo respectum* in 1175.[179] Eight monasteries appear to have defaulted altogether in this period. These included rich houses like Bury St. Edmunds[180], Glastonbury, in this period

---

(note 150 above), p. 47; The Great Roll of the Pipe for the Twenty–Fourth Year of the Reign of King Henry the Second, A.D. 1177–1178 (Publications of the Pipe Roll Society 27), London 1906, p. 103.

[177] Great Roll of the Pipe for the Fifteenth Year of the Reign of King Henry the Second (note 26 above), p. 4; Great Roll of the Pipe for the Sixteenth Year of the Reign of King Henry the Second (note 26 above), p. 114; Great Roll of the Pipe for the Seventeenth Year of the Reign of King Henry the Second (note 26 above), p. 14; Great Roll of the Pipe for the Eighteenth Year of the Reign of King Henry the Second (note 140 above), p. 73; Great Roll of the Pipe for the Nineteenth Year of the Reign of King Henry the Second (note 140 above), p. 192; Great Roll of the Pipe for the Twentieth Year of the Reign of King Henry the Second (note 140 above), p. 17; Great Roll of the Pipe for the Twenty–First Year of the Reign of King Henry the Second (note 26 above), p. 23; Great Roll of the Pipe for the Twenty–Third Year of the Reign of King Henry the Second (note 150 above), p. 155; Great Roll of the Pipe for the Twenty–Fourth Year of the Reign of King Henry the Second (note 176 above), p. 39.

[178] Great Roll of the Pipe for the Fourteenth Year of the Reign of King Henry the Second (note 140 above), p. 145; Great Roll of the Pipe for the Fifteenth Year of the Reign of King Henry the Second (note 26 above), p. 4; Great Roll of the Pipe for the Eighteenth Year of the Reign of King Henry the Second (note 140 above), p. 76; Great Roll of the Pipe for the Twentieth Year of the Reign of King Henry the Second (note 140 above), p. 18; Great Roll of the Pipe for the Twenty–First Year of the Reign of King Henry the Second (note 26 above), p. 24.

[179] Great Roll of the Pipe for the Twenty–First Year of the Reign of King Henry the Second (note 26 above), p. 14; paid in the following year, Great Roll of the Pipe for the Twenty–Second Year of the Reign of King Henry the Second (note 143 above), p. 73.

[180] Great Roll of the Pipe for the Fourteenth Year of the Reign of King Henry the Second (note 140 above), p. 22; Great Roll of the Pipe for the Fifteenth Year of the Reign of King Henry the Second (note 26 above), p. 99; Great Roll of the Pipe for the Sixteenth Year of the Reign of King Henry the Second (note 26 above), p. 7; Great Roll of the Pipe for the Seventeenth Year of the Reign of King Henry the Second (note 26 above), p. 6; Great Roll of the Pipe for the Eighteenth Year of the Reign of King Henry the Second (note 140 above), p. 27; Great Roll of the Pipe for the Nineteenth Year of the Reign of King Henry the Second (note 140 above), pp. 123, 127; Great Roll of the Pipe for the Twentieth Year of the Reign of King Henry the Second (note 140 above), pp. 42, 45; Great Roll of the Pipe for the Twenty–First Year of the Reign of King Henry the Second (note 26 above), p. 116; Great Roll of the Pipe for the Twenty–Second Year of the Reign of King Henry the Second (note 143 above), pp. 63, 65; Great Roll of the Pipe for the Twenty–Third Year of the Reign of King Henry the Second (note 150 above), pp. 127, 128; Great Roll of the Pipe for the Twenty–Fourth Year of the Reign of King Henry the Second (note 176 above), pp. 21, 27.

closely linked to the bishop of Bath and Wells[181], Peterborough[182], Hyde[183] and Westminster Abbey, which did make some scutage payments but carried debts over years with impunity, protected by its physical proximity to the centre of royal government and the close links with most of the English monarchs.[184]

---

[181] Great Roll of the Pipe for the Fifteenth Year of the Reign of King Henry the Second (note 26 above), p. 3; Great Roll of the Pipe for the Sixteenth Year of the Reign of King Henry the Second (note 26 above), p. 113; Great Roll of the Pipe for the Seventeenth Year of the Reign of King Henry the Second (note 26 above), p. 13; Great Roll of the Pipe for the Eighteenth Year of the Reign of King Henry the Second (note 140 above), p. 73; Great Roll of the Pipe for the Twentieth Year of the Reign of King Henry the Second (note 140 above), p. 17; Great Roll of the Pipe for the Twenty–First Year of the Reign of King Henry the Second (note 26 above), p. 23; Great Roll of the Pipe for the Twenty–Second Year of the Reign of King Henry the Second (note 143 above), p. 155; Great Roll of the Pipe for the Twenty–Third Year of the Reign of King Henry the Second (note 150 above), p. 18; Great Roll of the Pipe for the Twenty–Fourth Year of the Reign of King Henry the Second (note 176 above), p. 39.

[182] Great Roll of the Pipe for the Fifteenth Year of the Reign of King Henry the Second (note 26 above), p. 74; Great Roll of the Pipe for the Nineteenth Year of the Reign of King Henry the Second (note 140 above), p. 35; Great Roll of the Pipe for the Twentieth Year of the Reign of King Henry the Second (note 140 above), p. 53; Great Roll of the Pipe for the Twenty–First Year of the Reign of King Henry the Second (note 26 above), p. 42; Great Roll of the Pipe for the Twenty–Second Year of the Reign of King Henry the Second (note 143 above), p. 48; Great Roll of the Pipe for the Twenty–Third Year of the Reign of King Henry the Second (note 150 above), p. 89.

[183] Great Roll of the Pipe for the Fifteenth Year of the Reign of King Henry the Second (note 26 above), p. 154; Great Roll of the Pipe for the Sixteenth Year of the Reign of King Henry the Second (note 26 above), p. 122; Great Roll of the Pipe for the Seventeenth Year of the Reign of King Henry the Second (note 26 above), p. 36.

[184] Until the vacancy of 1175: Great Roll of the Pipe for the Fourteenth Year of the Reign of King Henry the Second (note 140 above), pp. 36, 111, 122; Great Roll of the Pipe for the Fifteenth Year of the Reign of King Henry the Second (note 26 above), pp. 113, 124, 137; Great Roll of the Pipe for the Sixteenth Year of the Reign of King Henry the Second (note 26 above), pp. 56, 75, 105; Great Roll of the Pipe for the Seventeenth Year of the Reign of King Henry the Second (note 26 above), pp. 85, 97, 119; Great Roll of the Pipe for the Eighteenth Year of the Reign of King Henry the Second (note 140 above), pp. 22, 40, 120; Great Roll of the Pipe for the Nineteenth Year of the Reign of King Henry the Second (note 140 above), pp. 14, 152, 164; Great Roll of the Pipe for the Twentieth Year of the Reign of King Henry the Second (note 140 above), pp. 22, 27, 68; Great Roll of the Pipe for the Twenty–Second Year of the Reign of King Henry the Second (note 143 above), pp. 2, 35, 124. The other convents were Chertsey, Great Roll of the Pipe for the Fifteenth Year of the Reign of King Henry the Second (note 26 above), p. 168; Great Roll of the Pipe for the Seventeenth Year of the Reign of King Henry the Second (note 26 above), p. 163; Great Roll of the Pipe for the Eighteenth Year of the Reign of King Henry the Second (note 140 above), p. 142; Great Roll of the Pipe for the Nineteenth Year of the Reign of King Henry the Second (note 140 above), pp. 92, 94; Great Roll of the Pipe for the Twentieth Year of the Reign of King Henry the Second (note 140 above), pp. 4, 5; Great Roll of the Pipe for the Twenty–First Year of the Reign of King Henry the Second (note 26 above), pp. 204, 205; Great Roll of the Pipe for the Twenty–Fourth Year of the Reign of King Henry the Second (note 176 above), p. 133; Coventry Cathedral Priory, Great Roll of the Pipe for the Eighteenth Year of the Reign of King Henry the Second (note 140 above), p. 109; Great Roll of the Pipe for the Nineteenth Year of the Reign of King Henry the Second (note 140 above), p. 180; Great Roll of the Pipe for the Twentieth Year of the Reign of King Henry the Second (note 140 above), p. 142 and Tavistock, Great Roll of the Pipe for the Eighteenth Year of the Reign of King Henry the Second (note 140 above), p. 102;

In the thirteenth century the administration of the scutage became ever more difficult to control. While attempts in earlier decades had included an effort to identify the legal background for the claim to scutage, the Exchequer only managed to keep track of the amount owed. In 1217, during the crisis of the first years of Henry III.'s reign, a servant of Abbotsbury delivered 6 marks *de fine quem idem abbas fecit nobiscum pro servicio unius militis*. Cerne, another Benedictine house in Dorset, contributed 12 marks.[185] In 1243 the abbot of Chertsey owed 32 marks *de pluribus scutagiis* but it was not quite clear whether payment was due or whether it had been postponed by the king.[186] Payments were delayed or had been postponed, the collection of the money was complicated and it is not surprising to find that at least nineteen abbeys were in arrears over long periods of time between 1219 and 1243.[187] Even though some monasteries continued to send knights and armed servants to participate in royal campaigns, Ramsey Abbey in 1240 to Wales, in 1242 to Poitou, in 1244 to Scotland, and in 1245 and 1257 again to Wales[188], the payment of scutage continued and its nature began to change. It seems that negotiations between the religious house and royal government about the payment of a fine instead of the scutage began to play a greater role. The negotiations between king Richard I. and the abbot of Bury St. Edmunds in 1198 may be indicative of a transition. Faced with royal demands for military service on the one hand and a refusal of his tenants to provide assistance on the other, the abbot offered the king scutage which, however, was rejected

---

Great Roll of the Pipe for the Twentieth Year of the Reign of King Henry the Second (note 140 above), p. 93; Great Roll of the Pipe for the Twenty–First Year of the Reign of King Henry the Second (note 26 above), p. 62; Great Roll of the Pipe for the Twenty–Second Year of the Reign of King Henry the Second (note 143 above), p. 143; Great Roll of the Pipe for the Twenty–Third Year of the Reign of King Henry the Second (note 150 above), p. 3; Great Roll of the Pipe for the Twenty–Fourth Year of the Reign of King Henry the Second (note 176 above), p. 12.

[185] Patent Rolls 1216–1225, London 1901, pp. 60–61.

[186] TNA E159/21 m 27d, and ibid. m 3.

[187] Bury St. Edmunds, TNA E159/5 m 9, E159/6 m 7d, E159/10 m 3d; Cerne, E159/6 m 17, E159/8 m 9, E159/10 m 9d, E159/15 m 1, E159/16 m 15d, E159/19 m 14d; Chertsey, E159/5 m 11d, E159/9 m 3d, 4d, E159/10 m 1, E159/15 m 1d, E159/16 m 17d; Coventry Cathedral Priory, E159/12 m 6d, E159/15 m 6d, 19; Evesham, E159/12 m 2d; Glastonbury, E159/21 m 19d; Hyde, E159/10 m 3d; Malmesbury, E159/21 m 11; Pershore, E159/10 m 3d, E159/12 m 2d, E159/15 m 4d; Peterborough, E159/9 m 3, 10, E159/10 m 5d; Ramsey, E159/8 m 8, 12d, E159/10 m 4d, E159/12 m 7d, E159/16 m 14, E159/21 m 24; Reading, E159/21 m 12, 14d; Shaftesbury, E159/5 m 4d, E159/6 m 9d, 17, E159/7 m 10, E159/8 m 3, 9, E159/10 m 1, E159/12 m 5, E159/15 m 1, E159/16 m 8, 15d, E159/19 m 14d, E159/21 m 20d; Sherborne, E159/6 m 17, 19d; St. Albans, E159/3 m 8, 9, E159/8 m 3; St. Augustine Canterbury, E159/5 m 17, E159/6 m 18d, E159/12 m 2, 9; St. Benet, E159/8 m 6; E159/10 m 3d; Tavistock, E159/6 m 16d, E159/12 m 5; Westminster, E159/3 m 3, E159/5 m 16, E159/6 m 8d, 11, E159/10 m 3d, E159/12 m 2, E159/15 m 4d, E159/16 m 13, E159/19 m 17, E159/20 m 18d, E159/21 m 20; Winchcombe, E159/10 m 4d, E159/12 m 6d.

[188] Cartularium Monasterii de Rameseia, eds. W. H. HART / P. A. LYONS (note 41 above), vol. 3, pp. 48–52; Reading Abbey Cartularies, ed. B. R. KEMP (note 26 above), vol. 1, p. 83.

because Richard wanted fighters for his army. Consequently the abbot had to hire the required number of knights and undertook to pay for their maintenance. However, since the duration of the campaign and consequently the overall costs were unknown, a payment of £100 was offered in return for being released from all further responsibilities, a combination of direct service and a negotiated payment.[189] When Henry III. was about to cross to Poitou in 1242, the abbot of Hyde paid 50 marks in aid of the king's crossing, and the abbot of Tewkesbury met the monarch at Portsmouth and 'pacified' him with a payment of 20 marks. In return for the payment the abbot of Hyde was released of five knights' fees for which he owed scutage and it is very likely that the abbot of Tewkesbury was also released from scutage obligations.[190] Given the overall financial volume of a costly campaign these sums may appear small but the sum of the funds provided by the Benedictines was a valuable addition to the royal treasure. Worcester Cathedral Priory paid 30 marks, Abingdon and Bury St. Edmunds added a further 100 marks each and the prior of St. Swithin's, Winchester, contributed a further 200 marks.[191] The keeper of the royal wardrobe received £40 in July 1244 from the abbot of Abingdon instead of his military service, on this occasion for the king's campaign to Scotland.[192] Abbot and convent of Tewkesbury paid another 20 marks in 1253 when the king again planned to recover lost territories overseas. On this occasion the Benedictine priory of Worcester cathedral contributed 40 marks.[193] In the reign of Edward I. the payment of fines became even more common, as the examples of Abbotsbury, Malmesbury, Sherborne, Shaftesbury, Bury St. Edmunds or Ramsey show.[194] However, at the end of the thirteenth century, when these payments had become merely part of a system of financial exaction by the crown, two significant changes had occurred. The first change was political and consisted of the creation of political and administrative mechanisms which allowed the government to raise different types of taxes. Secondly, the government was at least partly financed by Italian banks which accepted the king's sources of income as collateral for their loans. In 1289 the Exchequer was informed that the abbot of Bury St. Edmunds had paid fines for two scutages, one

---

[189] H. M. CHEW, Ecclesiastical Tenants–in–Chief (note 57 above), pp. 42–43.

[190] Annals of Tewkesbury, in: Annales Monastici, ed. H. R. LUARD (note 77 above), vol. 1, p. 122. H. M. CHEW, Ecclesiastical Tenants–in–Chief (note 57 above), p. 26. Calendar Patent Rolls 1232–1247 (note 139 above), p. 284.

[191] Ibid., pp. 278, 281.

[192] Close Rolls 1242–1247 (note 158 above), pp. 210–211.

[193] Annals of Tewkesbury, in: Annales Monastici, ed. H. R. LUARD (note 77 above), vol. 1, p. 152; vol. 4, p. 442.

[194] Calendar of Close Rolls 1279–1288 (note 160 above), pp. 92, 102, 169, 383, 518; Calendar of Close Rolls, 1288–1296 (note 168 above), pp. 2, 4, 348; Cartularium Monasterii de Rameseia, eds. W. H. HART / P. A. LYONS (note 41 above), vol. 3, p. 5.

of £200 the other of 200 marks, and that the sums had been paid directly to Edward I.'s Italian bankers.[195]

With the exception of privileged institutions like the military orders or the mendicants, all English monasteries were expected to contribute to one-off demands by the Crown or to the more regular taxation and this included the English Benedictine houses. They were liable to contribute to feudal aids, e.g. for the marriage of the king's daughter, and to participate in other taxes. The ransom paid for the release of king Richard I. in 1194 belonged to the former category. In the spring of 1193 the king sent a letter to the English clergy, including the heads of religious houses, as well as to the laity, with a request for financial aid (*auxilium*) although a specific sum was not yet mentioned. This request was supported by the pope in a separate letter to the English clergy.[196] Following instructions by the captive monarch, the government levied 20 shillings for each knight's fee and 25% of the annual income of the laity and the clergy. In addition all ecclesiastical ornaments of gold and silver had to be surrendered.[197] In later chronicles sums of 100,000 marks or even of £100,000 are mentioned.[198] This hybrid levy was unusual; more common were taxes on revenue, on movable property or on land, the carucage.

The administration of these taxes and the political processes surrounding their imposition have been analysed in some detail although the burden they imposed on the finances of England's great Benedictine houses or the contribution made by the Black Monks remains to be assessed in future research.[199] However, it seems very likely that fiscal demands by the Crown were key factors in monastic finance. Following the last collection of the Danegeld in 1162 the main types of taxes – apart from the payments due to the monarch as feudal lord and as lord of his demesne – were imposed on movables, on income and on land. Although the main economic burden was certainly financial, many religious houses were also involved in the administration of such taxes. This affected their abbots or priors who acted on occasion as sub-collectors in their region and it also had an impact on the routine activities of the religious community because central convent buildings were sometimes used as depositories for cash which had been

---

[195] Calendar of Close Rolls, 1288–1296 (note 168 above), pp. 2–3.

[196] Chronica Magistri Rogeri de Houeden, ed. W. STUBBS, 4 vols. (Rerum britannicarum medii aevi scriptores 51), London, 1868–1871, vol. 3, p. 208.

[197] Ibid., vol. 3, pp. 210–211.

[198] Annals of Margam, in: Annales Monastici, ed. H. R. LUARD (note 77 above), vol. 1, p. 22; Eulogium Historiarum, ed. F. S. HAYDON (note 26 above), vol. 3, p. 83.

[199] S. K. MITCHELL, Taxation in Medieval England (note 151 above); W. LUNT, Financial Relations of the Papacy with England to 1327, Cambridge/MA 1939; G. L. HARRISS, King, Parliament and Public Finance (note 174 above); M. JURKOWSKI / C. L. SMITH / D. CROOK, Lay Taxes in England and Wales 1188–1688 (Public Record Office Handbook 31), Richmond 1998, pp. xvi–xli.

levied by the collectors. It also needs to be taken into account that royal taxation was only one type of the levies to which the religious community had to respond. They also had financial obligations towards the Church. During their visists to Rome the abbots of wealthy houses were expected to bring gifts to the pope, to cardinals and officials. Some of the houses, among them Bury St. Edmunds, Chertsey, Faversham, Malmesbury, Great Malvern, St. Albans, St. Augustine's, Canterbury and Tavistock, had to pay the census to Rome, an acknowledgment of their status as owned by the Church.[200] In crisis situations extra payments, subsidies, could be demanded from the clergy by the papacy. The chronicler of Peterborough records the demands made by pope Gregory IX. in 1229, at the time of the first dispute between emperor Frederick II. and the papacy and adds that his house paid 210 marks Sterling, *exceptis donis*.[201]

Given the status of the English kingdom as a papal fief, the collected tax could also be designated to relieve financial problems of the English king. A subsidy called by pope Honorius III. in 1217 was meant to help the government of the young king Henry III. at a time when the English financial administration had broken down as a consequence of the armed confrontation between king John and the baronial opposition. Another subsidy granted to Henry III. by papal mandate followed in 1226.[202] Even though much of the tax was to be levied from parishes, the monasteries were also involved because a substantial part of their revenue was derived from the churches and chapels they had appropriated. These first instances of a hybrid form of taxation were followed by other papal tax demands where the proceeds were either split between pope and king or designated for a specific purpose, most commonly the crusade.[203] English funds were also provided in support of the papal policy in Sicily following the death of Frederick II. After king Henry III. had been persuaded to fund the military conquest of the Sicilian kingdom in return for the transfer of its crown to his younger son Edmund, he was forced to levy new taxes. The payments demanded in 1256 from monasteries like Malmesbury, Bury St. Edmunds, Durham, Eynsham or Peterborough represented three or even five times the normal tax burden and Bury St. Edmunds as well as St. Albans had to borrow money on the market at exorbitant cost to fulfil their obligations.[204]

The significance of these external demands on the religious communities is reflected in a number of monastic chronicles and cartularies where reference is made either to the levying of the tax as an event or to the amounts contributed

---

[200] W. LUNT, Financial Relations of the Papacy with England to 1327 (note 199 above), pp. 91–123, 640, Appendix V.

[201] Chronicon Petroburgense, ed. T. STAPLETON (note 35 above), p. 10.

[202] Ibid., p. 187.

[203] Ibid., pp. 177–178.

[204] Ibid., pp. 285–286.

by the respective religious house. The monks of Malmesbury even copied the text of Edward I.'s writ of summons to the royal host which the royal chancery sent in 1294 at the start of the war with Philip IV. of France into their register.[205] John of Oxenedes, monk of St. Benet of Holme, did not merely think of the burden imposed on his community when he recorded the tax demands made by king John after the treaty of Le Goulet (1200) but thought of the English population as a whole and set the financial burden in the wider context of other royal demands.[206] The same chronicler is even more hostile in his reference to the next great rounds of taxation in 1203 and in 1205, the year under which he mentioned the resentment caused by royal policy *cunctis murmurantibus, sed contradicere non audentibus*.[207] The decision by king John's government in 1207 to impose a new tax, a thirteenth on moveables and on income, was seen as an event worth recording by the monks of Gloucester.[208] Gloucester Abbey cartulary also records the next royal tax demand under the year 1210, when the monastery's chalices had to be sold in order to raise 500 marks, as well as carts and horses. Centuries later Thomas Walsingham remembered the payment of 500 marks by St. Albans to king John. The Burton annlist noted the burden carried by the monasteries and the general annoyance caused by the demands.[209] Under the year 1225 the annalist of Tewkesbury recorded that the king had been granted a fifteenth from laymen as well as clerics and John de Oxenedes added: *Compulsi sunt etiam viri religiosi et clerici hanc quintam decimam dare omnium bonorum suorum*.[210] The fortieth of 1232 was also recorded by him as well as by the Annals of Worcester and by those of

---

[205] Registrum Malmesburiense, eds. J. S. BREWER / C. T. MARTIN (note 41 above), vol. 2, p. 391. The writ with the king's demand for military service against Scotland in 1306: ibid., vol. 2, p. 404. Similar writs sent by Edward II for service against King Robert of Scotland, ibid., vol. 2, pp. 407, 416–417.

[206] Johannes de Oxenedes, Chronica, ed. H. ELLIS (note 42 above), p. 111: *Quae nimirum gravis exactio valde populum terrae extenuavit cum antea gravis exactio scutagii praecessisset*.

[207] For 1203: *Videns rex Johannes defectum suum seseque omni militari subsidio destitutum, in Angliam veniens, maximam pecuniam a viris religiosis et magnatibus regni extorsit. Cepit etiam ab omnibus septimam partem omnium mobilium suorum. Habuitque hujus rapinae executores, in ecclesiasticis rebus Hubertum Cantuariensem archiepiscopum, in laicis Galfridum filium Petri, justiciarium, qui in executione jam dicta nulli pepercerunt.*, ibid., p. 117. For 1205: ibid., p. 119.

[208] Historia et Cartularium Monasterii Sancti Petri Gloucestriae, ed. W. H. HART (note 41 above), vol. 1, p. 23: *Johannes, rex Angliae, concilio suorum fidelium, decimam tertiam partem substantiae tam cleri quam populi per totam Angliam exegit, ad manutenendum guerram suam contra regem Franciae*. also ibid., pp. 145–148.

[209] *De quingentis marcis per Episcopum Dunelmensem, ad usum Regis Angliae, a memorato Abbate violenter extortis*. Thomas Walsingham, Gesta Abbatum Monasterii Sancti Albani, ed. H. T. RILEY (note 75 above), vol. 1, p. 242; Historia et Cartularium Monasterii Sancti Petri Gloucestriae, ed. W. H. HART (note 41 above), vol. 1, p. 24; Annals Burton, in: Annales Monastici, ed. H. R. LUARD (note 77 above), vol. 2, p. 81: *Ecclesiae et domus religiosorum maximis exactionibus vexatae fiscum non sine gravi dispendio ampliaverunt*.

[210] Ibid., vol. 1, p. 64; Johannes de Oxenedes, Chronica, ed. H. ELLIS (note 42 above), p. 154.

Tewkesbury.[211] In 1235 Tewkesbury paid a further 30 marks in tallage and the exaction of the thirtieth in 1237 was also duly noticed by the annalist.[212]

While the feudal aids of 1245 and 1253, for marrying the king's eldest daughter and for knighting the king's eldest son, did not provoke monastic chroniclers to hostile comments, this was different in the case of the payments which were demanded in the context of the 'Sicilian business', Henry III.'s political and financial assistance to the popes Innocent IV. and Alexander IV. in their attempt to topple Manfred, Frederick II.'s son who succeeded his father as ruler of Sicily, in return for the coronation of his second son Edmund as king of Sicily. As far as the English Church and its monasteries were concerned this venture resulted in a co-operation between papacy and royal government. In 1254 the pope granted the English king the tax of a tenth from his kingdom's clergy. Attempts by abbots to invoke their convents' privileges were met with papal threats of excommunication. Ramsey Abbey had to pay 680 marks Sterling, St. Albans added a further 500 marks.[213] The scale and the quick succession of the tax demands led to a political crisis in England which lasted for a decade.

For the chronicler of St. Benet of Holme the culprit responsible for the crisis was easily identified: it was Peter of Aigueblanche, bishop of Hereford (1240–1268), Henry III.'s negotiator in Rome: *Hujus quoque injuriosae extorsionis machinator fuit ille proditor, episcopus Hertfordensis*.[214] This is not surprising because it has long been known that bishoprics as well as canonries and other ecclesiastical benefices were to a degree reserved for members of the royal administration.[215] Peter of Aigueblanche had been keeper of the king's Wardrobe. Even in his new role as prelate he, like many other administrators, continued in royal service. Even some of the chief justiciars and most of the medieval English royal chancellors were members of the episcopate. But not only secular clergy were involved in the administration of royal finances, in negotiating taxes and organising their collection, the Benedictines themselves often played an important role. John of Caux, abbot of Peterborough, was one of Henry III.'s treasurers between 1260 and 1263 and in the next reign, Richard Ware, abbot of Westminster, held a similar position.[216] Nicholas of Litlyngton, abbot of Westminster, was sent to Rome as royal ambassador and later held the office of royal treasurer.[217] Simon Langham, abbot of the

---

[211] Ibid., p. 161; Annales Monastici, ed. H. R. LUARD (note 77 above), vol. 1, p. 87; vol. 4, p. 423.

[212] Ibid., vol. 1, pp. 97, 102, 105.

[213] Chronicon Abbatiae Ramesiensis, ed. W. D. MACRAY (note 35 above), p. 343; Johannes de Oxenedes, Chronica, ed. H. ELLIS (note 42 above), p. 205.

[214] Ibid., p. 206.

[215] W.A. PANTIN, The English Church in the Fourteenth Century, Cambridge 1955, pp. 30–46.

[216] Johannes de Oxenedes, Chronica, ed. H. ELLIS (note 42 above), p. 326.

[217] TNA 403/30 m 4: *Abbati Westmonasterii eunti in nuncium regis ad curiam romanam centum marcas ad expensas suas*. See also: E403/45 m 1.

same house in the middle of the fourteenth century, also headed the treasury. In 1240 a Benedictine monk, Richard le Gras, abbot of Evesham, even became chancellor.[218] Abbots and obedientiaries of Benedictine houses could act as tax collectors.[219] As royal agents the religious could pay tax revenue directly to the king's Italian creditors, as the abbot of Burton-on-Trent did in 1294 and in 1317.[220] The abbot of St. Mary's, York, received £2000 from an Italian bank which was providing funds for the king's plans in Scotland, *pro expeditione quorundam magnorum et arduorum negociorum domini regis versus partes boriales inde expediendorum*.[221]

As important local and regional centres the Benedictine monasteries were also important for the fabric of the royal administration in other ways. They were often involved in the administration of taxes. Abbots and other heads of religious houses who acted as tax collectors could use their own monasteries as depositories for the funds raised.[222] Taxes collected in cash could be stored in relative safety in monastic precincts until their transfer was ordered by royal command. On such occasions some monasteries became extended parts of the royal financial administration. The significance of their contribution remains to be assessed, but examples from 1272, when the abbot of St. Werburgh of Chester was to act as recipient for money to be delivered by the Prince of Wales, or from 1276, when the abbeys of St. Peter at Gloucester and Sherborne acted as depositories for the fifteenth granted in 1275, underline their importance on these occasions.[223] In addition to securing the cash, the convents also held on to the related documentation. In 1243 the prior of Evesham received a royal command to hand over *quedam scripta nos et scaccarium nostrum tangentia* which the abbot had deposited in the monastery before his journey abroad as part of the king's entourage on the expedition to Gascony.[224] In the fourteenth century heads of religious houses

---

[218] Annales Monasterii de Theokesberia, in: Annales Monastici, ed. H. R. LUARD (note 77 above), vol. 1, p. 121; D. CARPENTER, Henry III (note 26 above), p. 322.

[219] Annales Monastici, ed. H. R. LUARD (note 77 above), vol. 3, p. 372; Johannes de Oxenedes, Chronica, ed. H. ELLIS (note 42 above), p. 258. TNA E403/155 m 5: the abbot of Hyde in 1310. E403/180 m 8: the abbot and convent of Reading in 1317.

[220] TNA E403/90 m 1; E403/180 m 4.

[221] TNA E403/265 m 23.

[222] E.g. the abbot of Shrewsbury as collector in Shropshire in 1272, TNA E159/47 m 21.

[223] M. JURKOWSKI / C. L. SMITH / D. CROOK, Lay Taxes (note 199 above), p. 20; Calendar of Close Rolls 1272–1279 (note 158 above), pp. 2, 351, 366. J. H. DENTON, Robert Winchelsey and the Crown 1294–1313, Cambridge 1980, pp. 65, 197.

[224] TNA E159/21 m 18.

appear to have been systematically entrusted with the collection of clerical subsidies.[225]

Such participation in the royal administration could bring a reward, just as other services or *curialitates*, perhaps in the form of the reduction of an amercement owed by the monastery, or by the grant of an economic asset at favourable conditions or simply through a personal reward for the abbot.[226] This was also true for those occasions when monarchs visited a shrine or when the royal household or another part of the administration made use of the buildings within the abbey precinct.[227] Their facilities and their capacity to store food for large numbers of people and animals also made them ideal stage posts for an itinerant royal household. It was a memorable occasion when Edward II.'s queen Isabella staid at Ramsey in 1309 but the chronicler noted that the costs were exorbitant, amounting to more than £256. However, there was an awareness of the economic burden which could be imposed by such visits and it was not uncommon for the royal visitor to allocate compensation. On this occasion an annual income of £10 was assigned.[228] The situation was slightly different when the royal presence was primarily caused by religious motives, the desire to visit a shrine, or to express a request for prayers, although at such times it was even more likely that donations would be offered.[229] Use could also be made of the king's physical presence. When king Henry II. visited St. Albans he became directly involved in a dispute between the abbey and the bishop of Lincoln who demanded control over the monastery. The king was well received by the monks and sided with them.[230] Despite such advantages, hospitality on this scale could become an economic threat. The initial section of Edward I.'s first major piece of legislation,

---

[225] W. LUNT, The Collectors of Clerical Subsidies, in: W. A. MORRIS / J. R. STRAYER (eds.), The English Government at Work, 1327–1336, 3 vols. (The Mediaeval Academy of America Publication 37, 48, 56), Cambridge/MA 1940–1950, vol. 2, pp. 227–280, at p. 232. ID., Financial Relations of the Papacy with England to 1327 (note 199 above), pp. 632–638.

[226] TNA E159/48 m 5: *Postea thesaurarius et barones propter diversas curialitates quas idem Abbas fecit domino Regi sicut testificatum est per dominum R. Burnell et alios de consilio domini Regis remiserunt ei predictas £50 usque ad 10 marcas solvendas ad scaccarium*. Calendar of the Fine Rolle of the Reign of Henry III, Volume 1 1 to 8 Henry III 1216–1224, eds. P. DRYBURGH / B. HARTLAND, Woodbridge 2007, p. 125 no. 4/2.

[227] Cartularium Monasterii de Rameseia, eds. W. H. HART / P. A. LYONS (note 41 above), vol. 1, p. 263. On Edward II's visit to St. Peter, Gloucester, in 1318, see: Historia et Cartularium Monasterii Sancti Petri Gloucestriae, ed. W. H. HART (note 41 above), vol. 1, p. 44; F. M. PAGE, Estates of Crowland Abbey (note 16 above), p. 59.

[228] Chronicon Abbatiae Ramesiensis, ed. W. D. MACRAY (note 35 above), pp. 344–345; *ad magnos sumptus ipsius abbatis*. Ibid., p. 354.

[229] Johannes de Oxenedes, Chronica, ed. H. ELLIS (note 42 above), p. 107; Annals of Worcester, in: Annales Monastici, ed. H. R. LUARD (note 77 above), vol. 4, pp. 514, 516.

[230] Thomas Walsingham, Gesta Abbatum Monasterii Sancti Albani, ed. H. T. RILEY (note 75 above), vol. 1, p. 197.

the Statute of Westminster I (1275), contains a warning to founders of monasteries and their families not to burden religious houses by demands for hospitality. This king only spent short periods of time in monasteries, four days in Abingdon in March 1281, eight days in Pershore in January 1282, followed by another eight in Sherborne in March of the same year, seventeen days in St. Albans from December 1295 to January 1296, three weeks in Bury St. Edmunds in November 1296, another seven days in St. Albans in April 1298 and another ten days there in April 1300.[231] Most of his other visits to English monasteries lasted only two to three days in line with the principles laid down in the 1275 statute.

A more important cost factor was the law. The abbeys and priories were subject to the fast-developing papal legislation which time and again required most of them to launch costly appeals to the Curia, to pay for proctors and defray travel costs.[232] In addition they were involved in legal proceedings in different roles and at different levels of English law. The larger houses which had their own areas of jurisdiction like Bury St. Edmunds, could enjoy the perquisites of their courts although such liberties also entailed responsibilities and the scale of the income was difficult to predict. In addition their full integration into the medieval English state had far-reaching financial consequences. Firstly this could entail personal involvement of the heads of religious houses.[233] In the twelfth and thirteenth centuries it was not uncommon to find heads of religious houses temporarily appointed as itinerant royal justices. The abbots Samson of Bury St. Edmunds, Robert of Malmesbury and John of Hyde were appointed as justices of the 1194–1195 eyre visitation. Alan, abbot of Tewkesbury, had a similar role in the visitation of 1198–1199. Hugh, abbot of Ramsey, Simon, abbot of Reading and Ranulf, abbot of Evesham, participated in the visitation of 1218–1222 and other Benedictine dignitaries can be found as justices in eyre in 1226, 1234–1236, 1239–1241, 1250–1252, 1254–1258 and still in the visitation of 1278–1289. However, this activity came to be reserved for the emerging legal profession. By the last quarter of the thirteenth century the appointment of abbots and priors had become exceptional.[234]

The economic effects of such activities were probably not as significant as the monasteries' constant involvement in litigation in the royal courts. The Ramsey

---

[231] Statutes of the Realm, eds. T. E. TOMLINS / J. FRANCE / W. E. TAUNTON / J. RAITHBY (note 80 above), vol. 1, p. 26; H. GOUGH, Itinerary of King Edward the First, 2 vols., Paisley 1900, vol. 1, pp. 117, 127, vol. 2, pp. 136, 164; R. H. SNAPE, English Monastic Finances (note 20 above), p. 111.

[232] For English examples see: A. BOUREAU, How Law Came to the Monks: The Use of Law in English Society at the Beginning of the Thirteenth Century, in: Past and Present 167 (2002), pp. 29–74, at pp. 29–39, 48.

[233] S. K. MITCHELL, Taxation in Medieval England (note 151 above), p. 76.

[234] D. CROOK, Records of the General Eyre (Public Record Office Handbooks 20), London 1982, pp. 57–58, 62, 71, 76, 79, 91, 93, 97, 100, 104, 116, 119, 121, 123, 156.

chronicler expresses his admiration for abbot Simon Eye (1316–1343) not only because of his good governance but also because he defended the convent in the courts: *contra persecutiones, insultus et placita omnium adversantium sibi et ecclesiae suae omni strenuitate et austeritate valida, sumptibus et numerosis expensis, infra monasterium et extra viriliter munivit*. The catalogue of legal disputes in which he was involved and the list of costs fills several pages in the chronicle.[235]

As major landholders the monasteries were all subject to royal jurisdiction. It is rare to find a plea roll of the royal courts without the record of cases involving one or the other of the Benedictine houses or their cells. Litigation was not only caused by disputes with neighbours and tenants about land or related rights but also by the necessity to defend the claims to liberties and privileges which could be challenged by lay landholders, other religious institutions or by royal officials. In the twelfth century the monks of Abingdon discovered that the royal officials in Berkshire did not respect their tax privileges and levied an excessive rate on their properties in that county. The abbey had to turn to royal justices and the dispute was only settled after an inquest by a commission in the county court.[236] In 1230 the abbot of Battle complained that royal justices had taken 5 marks as an amercement from him because he had taken the chattels of fugitives without involving the royal coroner even though he had the right to act in such capacity on his own estates even in the absence of royal officials.[237] In the following year the prior of Spalding had to enforce his claim to amercements pronounced in eyre levied from his own lands.[238] Examples like these show that monastic privileges were not automatically accepted by royal representatives, that they could be challenged and that they had to be constantly defended. Royal commands to officials to respect the privileges, apparently elicited at the request of a religious community, go back as far as the eleventh century.[239]

The involvement in the kingdom's legal system had different financial implications. The expenses on writs, final concords, the payments of amercements, fines or even damages were a routine cost factor for all major landholders. In addition there were the costs of legal advisers who were often retained for an annual fee and who were sometimes even provided with a corrody.[240] These specialists were in a different category from the attorneys who represented the heads

---

[235] Chronicon Abbatiae Ramesiensis, ed. W. D. MACRAY (note 35 above), pp. 349, 350–355.

[236] Chronicon Monasterii de Abingdon, ed. J. STEVENSON (note 42 above), vol. 2, p. 160.

[237] TNA E159/10 m 5d; E159/16 m 6.

[238] TNA E159/11 m 12.

[239] Regesta Willelmi Conquestoris et Willelmi Rufi, ed. H. W. C. DAVIS (note 109 above), p. 51 no. 189 (Canterbury Cathedral Priory); p. 54 no. 201; p. 76 no. 289; p. 99 nos. 390, 391 (Abingdon); p. 100 no. 394 (Bury St. Edmunds); p. 51 no. 189 (St. Augustine, Canterbury); p. 106 no. 426; p. 116 no. 481 (Durham).

[240] N. RAMSAY, Retained Legal Counsel, c. 1275–c.1475, in: Transactions of the Royal Historical Society 5th ser. 35 (1985), pp. 95–112; J. R. MADDICOTT, Law and Lordship: Royal Justices as

of the houses in the trials and who were often members of the religious community. A number of them were active as royal justices, some were canon lawyers. Their advice could relate to individual lawsuits but their links to the royal courts and to other branches of the administration put them in an excellent position to act as advisers when negotiations had to be conducted about the control of temporalities during vacancies, the payment of taxes or fines. They received regular pensions which provided preferential access to their services. It seems to have been common to augment these pensions with an additional remuneration when they were actually called upon to act for their client. At first sight the payments appear small, often between 20 shillings and £3-6-8, however, the accumulated costs were much higher. An abbey like Peterborough retained more than twenty legal advisers, all of whom received annual stipends.[241] A separate type of cost was the hospitality awarded to justices in eyre and to other itinerant justices and their retinues. These were voluntary offers of food and accommodation which had the purpose to ensure good will. The itinerant justices were only present for limited periods of time and the costs were only temporary.[242] Nevertheless, even these expenses could be regarded as noteworthy by a monastic chronicler, as in Gloucester in 1305 when the arrival of the justices in trailbaston was celebrated with a big meal.[243] Sweeteners paid to royal officials could become a problem when they came to be regarded as regular payments which could be enforced by law.[244]

The costs of litigation and the amounts of money demanded by the Crown or by the courts for transgressions or simply *pro habenda gratia* could be considerable.[245] Cerne Abbey owed three palfreys for the mere transfer of a plea from the eyre to the King's Bench in 1238.[246] The Evesham chronicler mentions the sum of £360 in the second half of the fourteenth century, which had to be borrowed for the purpose of obtaining royal assistance; two lawsuits cost Ramsey Abbey

---

Retainers in Thirteenth and Courteenth–Century England, in: Past and Present, Supplement 4 (1978); S. RABAN, Lawyers Retained by Peterborough Abbey in the Late Thirteenth and Early Fourteenth Centuries, in: S. JENKS / J. ROSE / C. WHITTICK (eds.), Laws, Lawyers and Texts. Studies in Medieval Legal History in Honour of Paul Brand (Medieval Law and Its Practice 13), Leiden/Boston 2012, pp. 201–225.

[241] Ibid., pp. 202–204.

[242] Liber Ecclesiae Wigorniensis: a Letter Book of the Priors of Worcester, ed. J. H. BLOOM (Worcestershire Historical Society), Worcester 1912, p. xi.

[243] *Circa lxx fuerunt in dicto festo, xxx. milites, priores Lantoniae et Sancti Oswaldi, et aliae personae ecclesiasticae et alii multi, et totius comitatus personae honorabiliores quae in praedicta justiciaria extiterunt, qui omnes in convenienti ordinatione aulae et servitii in omnibus placati, et ad vota abundantissime procurati, sine strepitu et defectu quocumque, tam justiciarii quam alii barones qui huic festo interfuerunt praeconizantes dixerunt eos a magnis temporibus retroactis tale festum et tanti honoris in partibus istis minime vidisse.*, Historia et Cartularium Monasterii Sancti Petri Gloucestriae, ed. W. H. HART (note 41 above), vol. 1, p. 38.

[244] Chronicon Monasterii de Abingdon, ed. J. STEVENSON (note 42 above), vol. 2, p. 230.

[245] TNA E159/47 m 20, prior of St. Swithun, Winchester.

[246] TNA E159/16 m 15d.

more than £213 and £278 respectively and the abbot of St. Albans spent 2000 marks on a lawsuit about a warren – admittedly against the relative of John Mansel, a high-ranking official in Henry III.'s administration.[247] Even for wealthy religious houses such sums represented a substantial part of their annual income. In addition there were the costs caused by formal errors or other transgressions, some of them caused by mistakes made in the administration of a liberty. In 1221 the abbot of Chertsey owed 5 marks for a false essoin, the abbot of Ramsey owed 80 marks imposed as a murder fine in 1222 while Pershore Abbey was held to pay 2½ marks for the same in 1226.[248] The abbot of St. Albans was recorded in 1224 as owing 300 marks for a forest offence, a debt which was carried as a debt to the Crown for several years.[249] Four years later the abbot of Ramsey owed 100 marks, apparently because he had arraigned a jury of attaint without proper authority.[250] Westminster Abbey owed 100 shillings for unjust imprisonment in 1233, Holy Trinity, Canterbury, owed 100 marks for the trespass alleged to have been committed by one of its monks and the abbot of Malmesbury had to pay 40 marks for treasure trove in the reign of Edward I.[251] In addition the monasteries were responsible for their servants and secular officials and they often had to pay amercements on their behalf.[252] The economic burden caused by the frequent involvement in litigation was mitigated by the possibility to negotiate the conditions for payment or even to be pardoned by the king.

Although there is a report from Abingdon about high annual tax payments already in the first half of the twelfth century and despite the fact that the contributions for Richard I.'s ransom as well as the demands in the reign of king John were considerable, the king's financial requirements in the 1250s, when Henry III. tried to intervene in the politics of the Mediterranean after the death of emperor Frederick II. led to demands on a new scale.[253] The contribution of 680 marks by Ramsey Abbey in 1254, a substantial part of the annual income, is very likely representative.[254] Combined with payments to the Curia and contributions

---

[247] Chronicon Abbatiae de Evesham, ed. W. D. MACRAY (note 42 above), pp. 309–310; Chronicon Abbatiae Ramesiensis, ed. W. D. MACRAY (note 35 above), p. 355; Thomas Walsingham, Gesta Abbatum Monasterii Sancti Albani, ed. H. T. RILEY (note 75 above), vol. 1, pp. 315–320.

[248] TNA E159/4 m 12; E159/5 m 2; E159/8 m 9.

[249] TNA E159/6 m 10; E159/8 m 3; E159/9 m 10d; E159/10 m 3; E159/11 m 6.

[250] TNA E159/9 m 14d.

[251] TNA E159/12 m 3d; E159/48 m 75: *Prior sancte Trinitatis Cantuarie .C. marcas pro transgressione Roberti monachi sui.*; Registrum Malmesburiense, eds. J. S. BREWER / C. T. MARTIN (note 41 above), vol. 2, pp. 385–386, 415.

[252] *Abbas de Redinges debet misericordias hominum suorum de Itinere Justiciariorum*. TNA E159/6 m 8. Spalding Priory: E159/12 m 12d.

[253] After the death of abbot Faritius: *omnes res sive redditus hujus ecclesiae mox describuntur, ac trecentis libris fisco regali per singulos annos deputatis*, Chronicon Monasterii de Abingdon, ed. J. STEVENSON (note 42 above), vol. 2, pp. 158–159.

[254] Chronicon Abbatiae Ramesiensis, ed. W. D. MACRAY (note 35 above), p. 343.

to new crusade ventures this was the beginning of a new era for the old monasteries. The wars of Edward I. in Wales, Scotland and France led to new demands for taxation in the last quarter of the thirteenth century. This resulted in national taxation on an unprecedented scale in the 1290s and culminated in a political crisis.[255] While the abbeys' duties as tenants-in-chief remained, they were expected to make a full contribution to the new taxes on movable goods. In addition they had to meet their liabilities towards the Church. Under pope Nicholas IV. an attempt was made to establish the scale of the monasteries' annual income and the levy in the fourteenth century came to be based on the assessment of their annual revenue made in 1291.[256]

Despite the impressive studies of the different forms of taxation in medieval England, the impact of the tax burden on the monastic economy remains to be established by future research. Monastic chroniclers refer to the payments but they rarely specify the amounts that were actually paid.[257] The £120 disbursed by the abbot of Glastonbury in 1276 do not even appear to have been part of the contribution for the fifteenth raised in 1275.[258] Worcester Cathedral Priory made a voluntary payment of 30 marks in the expectation of escaping demands on a larger scale in 1283, while Peterborough contributed 275 marks in the Welsh wars, including queen's gold.[259] In 1289 Bury St. Edmunds received the confirmation of payments for different purposes, £200 for the king's Welsh campaign, a further 200 marks assigned to the king's Italian creditors as a repayment, and a further £50 as a part-payment of a fine.[260] After 1295 Ramsey Abbey was confronted with a demand for £1000 to be paid into the royal Exchequer.[261] Further demands were made in 1305–1306, when 80 marks were paid for the Scottish campaign, to be followed by a fine of 60 marks for Edward II.'s military venture

---

[255] G. L. HARRISS, King, Parliament and Public Finance (note 174 above), pp. 49–53, 59–70; M. JURKOWSKI / C. L. SMITH / D. CROOK, Lay Taxes (note 199 above), pp. 20–29; S. JENKS, The Lay Subsidies and the State of the English Economy 1275–1334, in: Vierteljahresschrift für Sozial– und Wirtschaftsgeschichte 85 (1998), pp. 1–39, at pp. 4–5.

[256] R. H. SNAPE, English Monastic Finances (note 20 above), p. 71; W. LUNT, Financial Relations of the Papacy with England to 1327 (note 199 above), pp. 340–347; Taxatio Ecclesiastica Angliae et Walliae, auctoritate P. Nicholai IV. Circa A.D. 1291, eds. T. ASTLE / S. AYSCOUGH / J. CALEY (Record Commission), London 1801; I. R. ABBOT, Taxation of Personal Property and of Clerical Incomes, 1399 to 1407, in: Speculum 17 (1942), pp. 471–498, at p. 471.

[257] Registrum Malmesburiense, eds. J. S. BREWER / C. T. MARTIN (note 41 above), vol. 1, pp. 268–277; Cartularium Monasterii de Rameseia, eds. W. H. HART / P. A. LYONS (note 41 above), vol. 1, p. 71.

[258] Calendar of Close Rolls 1272–1279 (note 158 above), p. 291.

[259] Annales Monastici, ed. H. R. LUARD (note 77 above), vol. 4, pp. 486–488; Chronicon Petroburgense, ed. T. STAPLETON (note 35 above), p. 56.

[260] Calendar of Close Rolls, 1288–1296 (note 168 above), pp. 2–4.

[261] Chronicon Abbatiae Ramesiensis, ed. W. D. MACRAY (note 35 above), pp. 390–391.

in 1313–1314.²⁶² According to the Evesham chronicle abbot John of Brokhampton (1282–1316) paid 1000 marks towards the kings' wars and taxes on movables amouting to 250 marks while a single fine for a forest offence amounted to 100 marks.²⁶³

Many abbeys made even further contributions to royal finances. This could take very different forms, ranging from providing surety for royal debts to sending supplies, carts, horses or men as direct support for the king's military campaigns. A thirteenth-century attempt to force the abbot of St. Albans to take out a debt of 2500 marks on behalf of the king, leading to the abbot's resistance, was still remembered by Thomas Walsingham a century later.²⁶⁴ Westminster Abbey, Henry III.'s great construction project, had to underwrite a royal loan of 1000 marks.²⁶⁵ In 1287 the Benedictine general chapter in England decided to prohibit the heads of religious houses to provide financial security for the loans taken out by third parties. However, an exception was made if the refusal would lead to damaging irritations. Refusing a royal request could do just that.²⁶⁶ The political crisis of the mid-thirteenth century cost Peterborough more than £4324.²⁶⁷ Evesham and two non-Benedictine houses had to underwrite a liability of £11000 owed to the king by the earl of Gloucester before his marriage into the Plantagenet family.²⁶⁸ Peterborough was forced to take out a loan of £100 on behalf of the king, a sum eventually allocated to the convent in the royal Exchequer.²⁶⁹ Gloucester Abbey offered security for an English prisoner in French captivity in 1298.²⁷⁰ Following the English defeat in the Scottish campaign of 1314, the abbey of St. Peter, Gloucester, made a list of the carts, horses and men lost on this occasion.²⁷¹

---

²⁶² Cartularium Monasterii de Rameseia, eds. W. H. HART / P. A. LYONS (note 41 above), vol. 3, pp. 3–5.

²⁶³ Chronicon Abbatiae de Evesham, ed. W. D. MACRAY (note 42 above), p. 288.

²⁶⁴ Thomas Walsingham, Gesta Abbatum Monasterii Sancti Albani, ed. H. T. RILEY (note 75 above), vol. 1, pp. 373–376, 379.

²⁶⁵ W.C. JORDAN, A Tale of Two Monasteries: Westminster and Saint–Denis in the Thirteenth Century, Princeton 2009, pp. 52–53.

²⁶⁶ *Quia multa incommoda et enormia eveniunt domibus religiosis per instrumenta obligacionum facta pro personis extraneis, decretum est sub pena deposicionis et officii privacionis, ut nullus abbas aut prior abbatem non habens de cetero presumat obligare domum suam aut ecclesiam pro quacumque alia persona aut magnate in regno Anglie vel extra, ne forte pro huiusmodi factis obligationibus domus aliqua seu ecclesia iacturas graviores seu importunas inquietaciones incurrat.* Documents, ed. W. A. PANTIN (note 40 above), vol. 1, p. 254.

²⁶⁷ J. BRUCE, Introduction, in: Chronicon Petroburgense, ed. T. STAPLETON (note 35 above), p. xi.

²⁶⁸ M. PRESTWICH, Edward I, London 1988, pp. 348–349; Annals of Tewkesbury, in: Annales Monastici, ed. H. R. LUARD (note 77 above), vol. 1, p. 151.

²⁶⁹ Chronicon Petroburgense, ed. T. STAPLETON (note 35 above), p. 33.

²⁷⁰ Historia et Cartularium Monasterii Sancti Petri Gloucestriae, ed. W. H. HART (note 41 above), vol. 1, p. lxxxii.

²⁷¹ Ibid., vol. 3, p. 276.

An additional burden to monastic finance was the imposition of corrodies, life pensions given to royal officials or royal favourites who often were also provided with accommodation in the monastery. It is true that corrodies had been sold against down payments by the convents themselves and as such they were a tool to raise funds. They had also been awarded to the servants of the monastery, however, there was no concrete compensation for the corrodies imposed by the king, apart, perhaps, in the form of the king's good will.[272] In its standard form the corrody consisted of a room or a suite of rooms in the monastery for the recipient, possibly also for a servant, stabling for one or more horses, as well as an allocated daily or weekly quantity of food and drink. Related to the corrody was the annual pension, e.g. the 80 marks per annum owed by Shrewsbury Abbey in 1273 and acknowledged by the abbot in the royal Exchequer.[273] People earmarked for a monastic corrody by the king were given a letter of request directed to the head of the respective religious house and presented themselves to the abbot. In the period 1290 to 1296 such letters were directed to Crowland (1290), to Eynsham, Gloucester, Faversham and Malmesbury (1293), to St. Werburgh, Chester, Abbotsbury and Christ Church, Canterbury, (1294) as well as to Abingdon, where the recipient was only to remain for nine months, with two servants and two horses.[274] The maintenance of these pensioners was expensive and it is not surprising to find that there were attempts to avoid the obligation. When Edward I. requested a corrody for his personal surgeon, who was also to bring his servant and his horse, in Ramsey Abbey in May 1303, the abbot immediately sent a reply, pointing out that the house was already supporting two of the king's infirm servants. The abbey's attempt to find an ally in the royal chancellor failed. Another royal letter with a repetition of the request arrived in June, already slightly less cordial in tone, reminding the abbot that royal favour could not only increase but also diminish.[275] In the same month a letter from the chancellor arrived with the advice not to provoke the king. This advice was not heeded as abbot and community tried to find other supporters, writing to the queen and to

---

[272] Registrum Malmesburiense, eds. J. S. BREWER / C. T. MARTIN (note 41 above), vol. 1, pp. 427–429.

[273] E159/47 m 21: *Recognicio Luce abbatis Salopie. Idem venit coram Baronibus et recognovit pro se et successoribus suis se teneri Radulpho Dungun in quaterviginti marcis annuis quamdiu vixerit. De quibus reddet eidem Radulpho unam medietatem ad festum Purificationis beate Marie. Et aliam medietatem ad festum Nativitatis sancti Johannis Baptiste proximum futurum apud Novum Templum London. Et nisi fecerit concessit pro se et successoribus suis quod Barones de Scaccario predictos denarios de bonis terris tenementis et catallis suis in quorumcumque manibus existant fieri faciant ad opus eiusdem Radulphi.*

[274] Calendar of Close Rolls, 1288–1296 (note 168 above), pp. 144, 279, 383

[275] Chronicon Abbatiae Ramesiensis, ed. W. D. MACRAY (note 35 above), pp. 381–385; ibid. p. 383: *vos, preces nostras, ut accepimus, minime ponderantes, quin potius parvipendentes in hac parte, dictum magistrum W. statim vacuis manibus remisistis, excusationem insufficientem minus provide cancellario nostro rescribentes, de quo plurimum non inmerito admiramus: Quocirca devotionem vestra iteratis precibus excitamus quatinus id quod alias ommissum est in praemissis ad hanc nostram instantiam taliter supplere velitis quod gratiam et benevolentiam regiam erga vos augere potius debeamus quam minuere.*

the king's daughter Elizabeth, still in the hope of avoiding the responsibility for the payment of another life pension. In reply the king sent another letter in August 1303 with a request for a further corrody for one of his servants. This dispute coincided with the abbey's struggle to pay royal as well as papal taxes and with a demand to provide financial security for the ransom of an English knight. The abbot of Ramsey and those of his obedientiaries responsible for financial control were well aware of the risks involved in taking on too many commitments and they will also have known the ruling made by the English Benedictine general chapter in 1287 which prohibited monastic office holders from selling corrodies without higher authorisation.[276] This regulation was related to a constitution made by cardinal Ottobuono, who had arrived in England as papal legate in the autumn of 1265. Among the reforms introduced by the legate and his advisers, among whom were two future popes, Tedaldo Visconti (Gregory X.) and Benedetto Gaetani (Boniface VIII.), was also a clause addressed to the heads of religious houses not to overburden their communities by the excessive sales of corrodies, a measure still remembered a hundred years later.[277]

An important tranche of monastic wealth often taken for granted were the appropriated churches. Religious houses sometimes felt that these had to be protected from the intrusion of the local bishop. This asset of monastic patronage also came to be tapped by the royal government. During vacancies the royal administrators could grant a void benefice to a candidate presented by the king. The procedure could involve a prelate, as in a case concerning Shaftesbury in 1242, or the demand for a benefice in an appropriated parish church could become part of the conditions for the appointment of the new abbot.[278] In 1300 Edward I. requested the benefice from a church belonging to Ramsey for one of his clerks. In the following year the queen added another request.[279] As in the case of an imposed corrody the monastery lost the material benefits which it would normally have obtained.

The increase of the financial burdens on religious houses in the last quarter of the thirteenth century, consisting of royal and papal taxation as well as the financial provision for future crusades and current wars, coincided with the gradual end of the long phase of economic expansion.[280] The large Benedictine houses were wealthy and they were able to adapt to a changing environment. Many had tried to develop their estates throughout the thirteenth century, enabling them to maintain their status as formidable economic entities, allowing

---

[276] Documents, ed. W. A. PANTIN (note 40 above), vol. 1, p. 255.

[277] Ibid., vol. 2, p. 88; M. POWICKE, The Thirteenth Century, 1216–1307, Oxford 1953, pp. 206–218, 472–474; D. KNOWLES, Religious Orders (note 18 above), vol. 1, p. 14.

[278] Calendar of Patent Rolls 1232–1247 (note 139 above), pp. 324, 351.

[279] Chronicon Abbatiae Ramesiensis, ed. W. D. MACRAY (note 35 above), pp. 371–372.

[280] J. H. DENTON, Robert Winchelsey (note 223 above), p. 63.

them to meet the king's expectations and demands and also to develop, e.g. to defray the costs of their gradual appearance at the English universities which required the purchase of town houses, the maintenance of these properties and the support of their students. Despite the changing economic context, the level of their wealth remained high. Peterborough Abbey received more than £1000 in cash plus another £700 worth of grain in 1300. Canterbury Cathedral Priory had c. 10000 sheep on its estates in Kent and Gloucester Abbey is thought to have possessed a similar number.[281] In 1291 the annual income of Westminster Abbey amounted to almost £1300 and in the years before the dissolution of the monasteries the net income was in the region of £2800. At that time the annual income of Selby Abbey stood at over £730, which made it one of the smaller Benedictine houses.[282] Romsey, one of the larger Benedictine nunneries, had an income of more than £400 from its temporalities in 1412–1413.[283] Tavistock had an estimated income of just over £200 in the early fifteenth century.[284]

Despite this wealth many abbeys were in financial difficulties in the second half of the thirteenth century. The period of demesne farming was coming to an end because the direct cultivation of large estates became unprofitable. It was gradually replaced by economic structures in which leases and fixed rents came to predominate, a process accelerated by the demographic crisis beginning with the Black Death.[285] Martin HEALE has pointed out that it became more difficult to attract lay patronage and that pious donations were gradually replaced by the purchase of the estates which were to be integrated into the convents' property portfolios.[286]

There were signs of crisis. The nuns of Barking began to neglect the anniversaries of former abbesses and of lay patrons in order to save costs.[287] Attempts

---

[281] J. BOLTON, The Medieval English Economy (note 19 above), pp. 94, 96.

[282] The total annual income in 1535 was assessed as follows: Glastonbury: £3311; Canterbury, Christ Church: £2349; St. Albans: £2102; Reading: £1938; Abingdon: £1876; Ramsey: £1715; Peterborough: £1679; Bury St. Edmunds: £1656; York St. Mary: £1650; Tewkesbury: £1598; Winchester St. Swithun: £1507; Gloucester St. Peter: £1430; Canterbury St. Augustine: £1413; Durham Cathedral Priory: £1366; Worcester Cathedral Priory: £1299; Evesham: £1183; Crowland £1093.

[283] B. HARVEY, Westminster Abbey and its Estates (note 20 above), pp. 26, 58, 62–63; J. D. HASS, Medieval Selby (note 7 above), p. 50; J. MOUNTAIN, Nunnery Finances in the Early Fifteenth Century, in: J. LOADES (ed.), Monastic Studies II, Bangor 1991, pp. 263–272, at p. 263.

[284] H. R. P. FINBERG, Tavistock Abbey (note 61 above), p. 27.

[285] M. POSTAN, The Trade of Medieval Europe: the North, ch. VI, in: M. POSTAN / E. MILLER (eds.), Cambridge Economic History of Europe Volume II: Trade and Industry in the Middle Ages, Cambridge ²1987, p. 244.

[286] M. HEALE, Monasticism in Late Medieval England (note 53 above), p. 6. See also: M. HICKS, The Rising Price of Piety in the Later Middle Ages, in: J. BURTON / K. STÖBER (eds.), Monasteries and Society in the British Isles in the Later Middle Ages (Studies in the History of Medieval Religion 35), Woodbridge 2008, pp. 95–109, at p. 95.

[287] G. G. COULTON, Five Centuries of Religion (note 45 above), vol. 3, p. 71.

were made to resist taxation and to avoid the imposition of corrodies. The abbot and convent of Ramsey sent a letter to Edward I. *de penuria* and the monastery had to pawn one of its manors. The abbot of Reading sold an annual grant of 10 marks Sterling, originally received from king John in the form of 1 mark of gold and converted to silver by Henry III., for a one-off payment of £100 in 1291.[288] In 1305 the abbey made a part-repayment of a debt to the royal justice Sir William Bereford who was owed £240. By 1349 the abbey's debts had increased by a further 2500 marks.[289]

It is true that the Benedictines were not the only religious encountering financial difficulties in this period and it is well known that they had encountered economic crisis before. The existence of economic problems at Bury St. Edmunds became apparent before the death of abbot Hugh in 1180. The abbey's chronicler, Jocelin of Brakelond, describes Hugh as a devout man who lacked ability in business matters. He drew on external financial resources without any attempt to control the abbey's debts. In the years between 1173 and 1180, these debts rose annually by between £100 and £200 and the interest accumulated. The convent's obedientiaries had their own seals and they took on separate loans from Christian as well as Jewish creditors. Jocelin of Brakelond mentions sums of £880 and even £1040. Since Jewish money transactions were controlled by the Crown, the state of affairs at Bury St. Edmunds came to be known to king Henry II. who sent his almoner to investigate. However, the community – though internally divided – managed to placate the royal household official. The seriousness of the situation emerged when creditors refused further funds during abbot Hugh's final illness. At this time the abbey's estates were already divided between the abbot and the community and the abbot's portion was immediately taken under the control of royal officials. During the two-year vacancy the situation seems to have deteriorated even though the future abbot, Samson, was already trying to introduce reforms in his role as sub-sacrist. After his election, abbot Samson instituted a reform consisting of the collection of information, especially on the rents and services due from each manor. He controlled the expenses of hospitality, reduced the costs of the abbot's household, acquired new churches and advowsons, invested in new buildings and appointed new officials who were responsible for specific estates. He also reallocated responsibilities within the abbey. The information relating to the estates was collected in a book, his *Kalendar* which became his chief instrument for economic control, exerted by him personally, usually in

---

[288] TNA E403/15A m 1; E403/72 m 2: *Abbati Rading' .C. libras pro remissione et quieta clamatione quas idem abbas pro se et conventu suo ac successoribus suis fecit domino regi nunc et heredibus suis de illis decem marcis annuis quas ipse et predecessores sui percipere consueverunt ad scaccarium regis ex concessione celebris memorie domini .H. quondam regis Anglie patris domini regis nunc pro illa marca annua quam Johannes quondam rex Anglie avus domini regis nunc eis concessit per cartam suam ad idem scaccarium percipiendam in puram et perpetuam elemosinam quam pro remissione et quieta clamatione omnium arreragiorum earundem.*

[289] Cartularium Monasterii de Rameseia, eds. W. H. HART / P. A. LYONS (note 41 above), vol. 1, pp. 13, 64; Chronicon Abbatiae Ramesiensis, ed. W. D. MACRAY (note 35 above), p. 374.

the form of visits to the individual estates.²⁹⁰ In addition he pursued a policy of increasing the demesne, trying to return abbey property to direct control instead of having it farmed for a fixed rent. Within a year of his election he reduced the abbey's debts by more than £3000.²⁹¹

It is possible that difficulties at Glastonbury already began in 1184 when the church and most of the buildings were destroyed by fire, an event which – according to the abbey's fourteenth-century chronicler John of Glastonbury – also led to the destruction of relics and a *confusio thesauri tam in auro et argento quam in pannis, cericis, libris et ceteris ecclesiasticis ornamentis direpcio*.²⁹² Although the fire occurred during a vacancy and king Henry II. instructed his chamberlain to assist with the reconstruction by handing over funds provided by the monarch and despite the fact that abbot Henry of Sully tried to consolidate the abbey's income from its churches, generating additional annual revenues of more than £32, economic difficulties ensued.²⁹³ In 1193, when abbot Henry of Sully became bishop of Worcester, a dispute began about his succession, which led to a conflict with the bishop of Bath about the abbey's exemption from episcopal control and this eventually resulted in numerous costly embassies to the Roman Curia. This was the background to the difficult abbacy of Robert of Bath (1223–1234), who – despite some minor reallocation of funds to the convent – let the abbey sink heavily into debt.²⁹⁴ John of Glastonbury reports that abbot Robert wanted to lead the monks to the pinnacle of piety. Instead he divided the monastic community and entrusted its economic fate to outsiders. His successor, Michael of Amesbury, who found the abbey burdened with debts of 500 Marks Sterling, instituted a programme of economic reform. He recovered alienated properties by purchase or legal process, he assarted woodland, invested in new ploughs and is credited with the construction of mills as well as other buildings.²⁹⁵

The Benedictines constituted a part of the financial market already in the twelfth century, when e.g. Abingdon gave land as collateral for a debt.²⁹⁶ Evesham, which owed Italian bankers 1000 marks, benefited from royal policies in the early thirteenth century when king John turned against the *Romanos*. However, the monastery suffered after the raprochement between the king and pope Innocent III. in 1213 which allowed the creditors to press home their demands. The

---

[290] D. M. GERRARD, Jocelin of Brakelond (note 36 above), p. 18.

[291] Ibid., p. 13.

[292] The Chronicle of Glastonbury Abbey, ed. J. P. CARLEY, Bury St. Edmunds 1985, p. 172.

[293] Ibid, p. 178.

[294] Ibid., p. 210: *sese domusque negocia libencius secularibus quam monachis committebat. Et sic monasterium in se diuisum continuo desollacionis incurrit dispendium. In rebus necessariis egens est effectum alienoque uehementer ere gravatum.*

[295] Ibid., pp. 210–214.

[296] Chronicon Monasterii de Abingdon, ed. J. STEVENSON (note 42 above), vol. 2, p. 21.

buildings in the precinct could not be properly maintained and other properties also fell into disrepair.[297] There is even a claim that monks died of hunger.[298] Canterbury Cathedral Priory borrowed from Italian and Jewish bankers at interest rates of between c. 20% and c. 40%.[299] In 1241–1242 Evesham and Westminster undertook to pay £20 and 20 marks to the queen which two Jewish bankers owed to her as queen's gold. Since the two houses stood surety with their property it is likely that they were indebted to the two bankers.[300] Italian merchants were an important source of credit. A visitation of Glastonbury found the house in debt in 1281 and it was determined that the abbot should reduce the size of his *familia* and that efficient financial procedures should be introduced. In 1288 the abbot of Glastonbury acknowledged debts of respectively 250 marks and of 906 marks to an association of Italian bankers, in 1291 he had another debt of 380 marks recorded to the same group.[301] A loan taken out by Westminster Abbey from Italian bankers led to litigation at the Curia in the 1260s which added further costs.[302] The monks of St. Swithun, Winchester, encountered other difficulties in their dealings with Italian merchants. In 1285 they made a contract with the Riccardi firm to provide 40 sacks of wool over six years from 1287 in return for ready cash. Problems arose when the monks were unable to meet the stipulated quantity and renegotiated further loans for further deliveries of wool. When the Riccardi lost Edward I.'s favour in 1294, the monks' debts were transferred to the king.[303] At the time of the Dissolution Bury St. Edmunds had a net income of more than £1600 and the monks of Glastonbury could even draw on £3300. Canterbury Cathedral Priory had c. 10.000 sheep on its Kentish estates alone and yet the house was in debt to the tune of £5000 in 1285, twice its annual income.[304] Reading Abbey, with an annual income of £1938 in 1535, was heavily in debt in 1275 and required external intervention in 1281.[305] The situation in Canterbury was turned around completely during the long term in office of prior

---

[297] Ibid., pp. 224, 230, 264–265.

[298] Ibid., p. 240.

[299] J. BOLTON, The Medieval English Economy (note 19 above), p. 341.

[300] TNA E159/20 m 12d.

[301] Registrum Epistolarum Fratris Johannis Peckham, archiepiscopi Cantuariensis, ed. C. T. MARTIN (Rerum britannicarum medii aevi scriptores 77), London 1882–1885, vol. 1, no. ccxiii, pp. 259–264. Calendar of Close Rolls 1279–1288 (note 160 above), pp. 540–541; Calendar of Close Rolls, 1288–1296 (note 168 above), p. 195.

[302] W. C. JORDAN, Westminster Abbey and its Italian Bankers During the Abbacy of Richard de Ware, 1258–1283, in: Revue Bénédictine 118 (2008), pp. 334–354, at pp. 336–340.

[303] R. W. KAEUPER, Bankers to the Crown (note 159 above), pp. 39–41.

[304] D. KNOWLES, Religious Orders (note 18 above), vol. 1, p. 49; J. BOLTON, The Medieval English Economy (note 19 above), p. 96.

[305] D. KNOWLES, Religious Orders (note 18 above), vol. 1, pp. 99, 109.

Henry of Eastry. Reading Abbey was still (or again?) in debt with a sum of 450 marks in 1290.[306]

Despite the occasional grant of a royal pardon for a debt or deferments of payment, many of the old abbeys were sliding into debt in the second half of the thirteenth century. The situation had been similar a hundred years earlier, however, the context had been different.[307] The complexity of financial structures had increased, the taxation system had developed and the general economic conditions had deteriorated. Furthermore, although the English Benedictines had organised themselves into a legislative body which, among other things, also facilitated the economic reorganisation of the monasteries and the reform of financial management after the IV. Lateran Council, and despite the attempts to find efficient procedures of financial control, there were no universal reforms but each monastery continued to pursue its own policy.[308] This leads to two questions which need to be briefly addressed, even though a full discussion needs to be reserved for future research. Firstly: what were the causes of the problem? Secondly: how serious was the monastic debt crisis?

It is not easy to find an answer to the first question because the conditions in the monasteries differed in terms of the size and the nature of their economies. Perhaps it was impossible to harmonise the financial management of the Benedictine abbeys because this simply did not and could not exist due to the different conditions of each monastery. For Edmund KING the fragmentation of financial control between the obedientiaries was a key weakness in Peterborough and Ramsey at a time when external economic conditions were changing.[309] There is no doubt that internal mismanagement was an important factor in the crisis of Benedictine houses in the late twelfth and early thirteenth centuries, e.g. by abbot Hugh at Bury St. Edmunds or Roger Norreys at Evesham, just as good management, e.g. by abbot Sampson at Bury St. Edmunds or by Henry of Eastry at Christ Church, Canterbury, was decisive in turning around failing economies. Financial control was tightened by regulating the drafting of the obedientiaries' accounts and by regular audits. Important sources of income, notably the wool production, were reorganised to become more efficient. In addition the English Benedictine general chapter tried to establish standard procedures of financial management, however, the attempt was not successful.[310] It needs to be added that this task was not made easier by some of the royal legislation passed in the last quarter of the thirteenth century. The Statute of Westminster II (1285) contained a clause in effect prohibiting the alienation of property donated to religious

---

[306] Calendar of Close Rolls, 1288–1296 (note 168 above), p. 141.
[307] D. KNOWLES, The Monastic Order in England (note 48 above), p. 302.
[308] D. KNOWLES, Religious Orders (note 18 above), vol. 1, pp. 10–14.
[309] E. KING, Peterborough Abbey (note 20 above), p. 98.
[310] D. KNOWLES, Religious Orders (note 18 above), vol. 1, p. 61.

houses. If such property had been donated by the king or one of his ancestors, it could be confiscated and other founders or patrons of monasteries were given a legal remedy to recover such land if an attempt was made to sell it.[311] This legislation hampered the reorganisation of monastic estates. The statute *De viris religiosis* (1279) prohibited alienation in mortmain and this was developed further in 1285 when fraudulent transfers, possible through collusion between the parties, was also prohibited.[312] Five years later it was included in the statute *Quia emptores* although it had become possible to alienate land to a religious house after a royal licence had been obtained.[313] The 1306 Statute of Carlisle, which prohibited the export of money by religious houses also had economic consequences, because it restricted access to financial markets. It furthermore ordered that convent seals were to be kept in a way which prevented a superior from making any legally binding contracts without the convent's knowledge.[314]

In the assessment of the causes for the financial difficulties affecting a number of English monasteries in the late thirteenth century it is difficult to bridge the gap between identifying the effect created by the particular conditions of each specific house on the one hand and the factors which affected all of the older religious houses. Royal favour often brought significant financial advantages, not merely in terms of pardons or delayed payments. It is sufficient to point to Westminster Abbey, turned into the royal necropolis in the thirteenth century or to the royal foundation of Reading Abbey, where Edward I. took care to relieve the abbey of its debts while it was in his custody in the 1280s.[315] Another place in the immediate royal orbit for a time was Amesbury, where the king's mother resided from 1276 onwards and where his daughter Mary became a nun in 1285.[316] She received generous royal stipends *ad sustentationem camere sue* at first of £100, later

---

[311] Statutes of the Realm, eds. T. E. TOMLINS / J. FRANCE / W. E. TAUNTON / J. RAITHBY (note 80 above), vol. 1, pp. 71–95, at p. 91.

[312] Statute *De viris religiosis: quo nullus religiosus aut alius quicumque terras aut tenementa aliqua emere vel vendere, aut sub colore donationis aut termini vel alterius tituli cujuscumque, ab aliquo recipere, aut alio quovismodo arte vel ingenio sibi appropriare presumat, sub forisfactura eorundem, per quod ad manum mortuam terre et tenementa hujusmodi deveniant quoquo modo*, Statutes of the Realm, eds. T. E. TOMLINS / J. FRANCE / W. E. TAUNTON / J. RAITHBY (note 80 above), vol. 1, p. 51. Ibid., vol. 1, p. 87, c.xxxii. J. RÖHRKASTEN, Amortisationsgesetze und Wahrnehmung religiöser Orden im Spätmittelalter, in: F. FELTEN / A. KEHNEL / S. WEINFURTER (eds.), Institution und Charisma. Festschrift für Gert Melville zum 65. Geburtstag, Cologne 2009, pp. 149–158.

[313] Statutes of the Realm, eds. T. E. TOMLINS / J. FRANCE / W. E. TAUNTON / J. RAITHBY (note 80 above), vol. 1, pp. 106, 111.

[314] Ibid., vol. 1, pp. 151–152.

[315] Reading Abbey Cartularies, ed. B. R. KEMP (note 26 above), vol. 1, nos. 93, 94, 95, 98, pp. 96–98; D. KNOWLES, Religious Orders (note 18 above), vol. 1, p. 99.

[316] M. PRESTWICH, Edward I (note 268 above), pp. 123, 128.

of £200 per annum.³¹⁷ It is not possible to say to what extent these payments which are recorded fairly regularly between 1285 and 1298, contributed to the nunnery's finances. In the reign of her brother, Edward II., the annual payments were reduced to 100 marks and later an additional 50 marks were paid per annum for the maintenance of Eleanor de Bohun, the king's niece. At this time sister Mary also received 25 tuns of wine from her family.³¹⁸ Royal intervention could be a decisive factor for the improvement or for the deterioration of a monastery's financial situation. It could cause high levels of debt just as it could alter conditions for repayment, pardon debts or provide material support, thus enabling the religious community to resolve the problem.

Despite the concern shown and the benefits granted in these particular cases, the royal government made full use of the economic power wielded by the abbeys and priories and many convents were in debt. Tax demands increased while incomes stagnated at a time when the larger houses had close links to the royal financial machine. In some cases, e.g. at Romsey, taxation may have been responsible for monastic debt.³¹⁹ Legislation, on the one hand protecting religious houses from undue burdens in hosting founders' families but on the other hand preventing the easy transfer of donations and restricting the houses' ability to participate in the land market will also have been a factor. Corrodies imposed by the monarch, additional contributions to the wars of Edward I. will have played a role. Royal policy was not consistent. On the one hand there were donations and other signs of favour or even the pardoning of debts, on the other hand it was quite possible for the government to take out a loan in the institution's name during a vacancy, as happened with St. Swithun, Winchester, in 1278.³²⁰ This could lead to a spiral of new loans and defaults.

The fiscal demands by the state continued during the wars with Scotland and France in the fourteenth century. In times of financial difficulties emergency measures were taken by drawing on the treasures and the cash reserves kept in the monastic churches and treasuries.³²¹ In the first years of the Hundred Years War when the English financial administration faced a serious crisis partly due to bad management and because the expected profits from the monopoly on wool sales did not materialise, the religious houses, among them the Benedictines, once

---

317 TNA E403/52 m 1; E403/53 m 1; E403/54 m 1; E403/56 m 1; E403/62 m 1; E403/64 m 1; E403/72 m 1; E403/74 m 1; E403/77 m 1; E403/80 m 1; E403/83 m 1; E403/86 m 1; E403/93 m 1; E403/100 m 1; E403/101 m 1; E403/102 m 1; E403/104 m 1.

318 TNA E403/155 m 4; E403/178 m 9; E403/207 m 10; E403/219 m 4; E403/240 m 1.

319 J. MOUNTAIN, Nunnery Finances (note 283 above), p. 271; V. SPEAR, Leadership in Medieval English Nunneries, Woodbridge 2005, p. 101.

320 R. W. KAEUPER, Bankers to the Crown (note 159 above), p. 38.

321 W. M. ORMROD, The Reign of Edward III. Crown and Political Society in England 1327–1377, New Haven/London 1990, p. 134.

again became a source of credit.[322] When Edward III. left England to begin his campaign against Philip VI. of France in July 1338, the monks of Ramsey provided a loan consisting of four chalices, assessed at £74 2 shillings 2 pence as well as a *capa* worth 40 marks while Reading gave jewels from its treasure.[323] St. Augustine, Canterbury, contributed a loan of £33 6 shillings 8 pence *pro passagio regis versus partes transmarinas*, a sum that was repaid in October 1339. On 30 March 1340 further loans were raised from the Benedictines, £200 from the prior of Holy Trinity, Norwich and £133 6 shillings 8 pence from the abbot of St. Benet of Holme. Both sums were repaid within a fortnight.[324] This policy of raising loans from the monasteries continued into the last phase of the reign, Worcester Cathedral Priory providing a loan of 600 marks in 1370, after the renewed outbreak of the war.[325] The sum was not repaid in full during the reign and it seems that creditors could not always be sure of the date or the method of repayment, because they were given instalments or simply assignments on royal revenues in the form of tallies.[326]

The answer to the second question – related to the seriousness of the monastic financial crisis – is even more difficult to find.[327] The revenue of the major Benedictine houses declined and some appear to have been unable to recover.[328] The number of nuns declined at Chatteris, and Selby, while managing to reduce its debts before the arrival of the Black Death, was settled with large debts in the early fifteenth century. Chertsey received £20 as royal alms in 1354 and a further £100 in the following year and the economy of Ramsey was in a long-term decline from the second half of the fourteenth century onwards.[329] On the other hand it has been doubted that the debt level of English Benedictine houses was much above an annual income. Furthermore administrative reforms in some

---

[322] J. BOLTON, The Medieval English Economy (note 19 above), p. 338.

[323] Cartularium Monasterii de Rameseia, eds. W. H. HART / P. A. LYONS (note 41 above), vol. 1, pp. 21–23, 264; Reading Abbey Cartularies, ed. B. R. KEMP (note 26 above), vol. 1, no. 109, pp. 103–104.

[324] TNA E403/307 m 6, 41 (repayment of the loan on 11 April 1340).

[325] Liber Ecclesiae Wigorniensis, ed. J. H. BLOOM (note 242 above), p. xi; R. H. SNAPE, English Monastic Finances (note 20 above), p. 127.

[326] W. M. ORMROD, Edward III (note 83 above), p. 112.

[327] D. KNOWLES, Religious Orders (note 18 above), vol. 3, p. 255: "the whole question of monastic solvency requires more careful treatment than it has received."

[328] J. BOLTON, The Medieval English Economy (note 19 above), pp. 210, 218–220. M. M. POSTAN, The Medieval Economy and Society. An Economic History of Britain in the Middle Ages, London 1972, p. 36; B. HARVEY, Westminster Abbey and its Estates (note 20 above), p. 53; M. HEALE, Monasticism in Late Medieval England (note 53 above), p. 10.

[329] Cartulary of Chatteris Abbey, ed. C. BREAY (note 24 above), p. 96; J. D. HASS, Medieval Selby (note 7 above), pp. 50, 52; J. A. RAFTIS, Peasants and the Collapse of the Manorial Economy (note 54 above), p. 196. TNA E403/374 m 14; E403/377 m 18.

houses were so successful that the decades before the Black Death could be described as "the golden age of monastic high farming".[330] A reduction in income may have been temporal in many cases and the figures produced by R.A.L. SMITH for Canterbury Cathedral Priory show that monastic income could fluctuate wildly and was not predictable.[331] Not only the larger monasteries but also a smaller convent like Tavistock was able to recover. In this context it is important to remember that monasteries, their heads or their obedientiaries could also act as creditors. Some of those monasteries involved in the financial markets were also lending money, e.g. Westminster Abbey, St. John, Colchester, St. Peter, Gloucester and even the smaller house of Tavistock, although the sums involved in the loans tended to be smaller than those mentioned in the context of debts.[332] The severity of the crisis has also been questioned by BOLTON who pointed out that e.g. Durham was able to embark on an extensive building programme despite a reduction of income.[333] Construction costs and the maintenance of monastic buildings – which included town houses as well as all argricultural and commercial structures like mills and workshops – were a significant and regular cost factor. In addition there were the occasional requirements to repair damage caused by war or natural disaster.

It is remarkable that quite a number of religious houses were able to complete ambitious construction projects to furnish their churches even in crisis periods or at times when the state's financial demands were high. Ramsey Abbey, which had been plundered in the civil war in 1140s, had begun a building programme about a decade later.[334] When Henry III. required urgent funds for his plans concerning the kingdom of Sicily, abbot Hugh was beginning the construction of a new refectory, built a new altar and a new shrine for St. Ivo and acquired new houses and lands.[335] Despite the financial demands by king John, a new west front was built for the abbey church of St. Albans in his reign and this work was completed even though the fabric was severely damaged in winter. A new refectory and a new dormitory were added at the same time. Financial difficulties were overcome by fundraising preachers who carried relics of St. Alban through the countryside, collecting alms earmarked for the project.[336] The abbey was also able

---

[330] D. KNOWLES, Religious Orders (note 18 above), vol. 1, p. 47; R. H. SNAPE, English Monastic Finances (note 20 above), pp. 119–120.

[331] R. A. L. SMITH, Canterbury Cathedral Priory (note 27 above), p. 13.

[332] TNA, E159/47 m 14; Calendar of Close Rolls 1279–1288 (note 160 above), pp. 535, 550; Calendar of Close Rolls, 1288–1296 (note 168 above), p. 54.

[333] J. BOLTON, The Medieval English Economy (note 19 above), pp. 221, 274; J. MOUNTAIN, Nunnery Finances (note 283 above), p. 263.

[334] Johannes de Oxenedes, Chronica, ed. H. ELLIS (note 42 above), p. 52; Chronicon Abbatiae Ramesiensis, ed. W. D. MACRAY (note 35 above), pp. 335–336.

[335] Ibid., p. 344.

[336] Thomas Walsingham, Gesta Abbatum Monasterii Sancti Albani, ed. H. T. RILEY (note 75 above), vol. 1, pp. 218–220; R. H. SNAPE, English Monastic Finances (note 20 above), p. 146.

to fund an extensive building programme in the first decades of Henry III.'s reign, including the acquisition of town houses in London and Yarmouth and the construction of a palatial hall with adjacent buildings.[337] In 1239, at a time of high demands for scutage and taxation, the churches of Great Malvern, Winchcombe, Tewkesbury, St. Peter, Gloucester, Pershore and Alcester, a priory belonging to Evesham, were dedicated. Evesham Abbey, despoiled by its abbot Roger Norreys and involved in expensive litigation with the bishop of Worcester at the turn from the twelfth to the thirteenth centuries, suffered the collapse of the main tower of its church in 1207 and Thomas of Marlborough made great efforts to repair the building *licet redditus ad hoc non haberet assignatos*. At Gloucester this followed serious fires in 1190, 1214, 1222 and 1223 which partly also affected the abbey.[338] Despite the damage caused by fire, the great eastern tower of the church was built in 1222 and a new vault in the ceiling of the nave was completed in 1242.[339] Pershore Abbey had also been destroyed by fire in 1223 and was apparently able to rebuild much of the fabric over the next sixteen years.[340] Construction work in the church of Tewkesbury had begun in 1230 and was sufficiently advanced for a new dedication in 1239 despite a bad harvest and although a serious fire in 1234 had destroyed the main gate and two stables.[341] Donations for repairs after natural disasters sometimes came from the king, a fourteenth-century example is Amesbury, where the sum of £20 was paid in 1354 *in auxilium domorum eiusdem prioriatus reparandarum nuper subito combustarum*.[342]

The case of Amesbury is indicative of the dual nature of the religious houses. As prominent places of worship the nuns were recipients of royal alms and donations while as economic entities they were liable to taxation. The relationship between the monarch and the monasteries was even more complex. The English Benedictine abbeys were largely controlled by the king, they formed part of the political, administrative, legal and financial system. Heads of religious houses were normally appointed by the monarch, who had wide-ranging access to monastic wealth during vacancies. At other times the houses were subject to different types of taxation, the tenure of monastic real estate was subject to royal law and the king's administration had extensive control over the use made of the properties. All plans for improvement – assarting, draining of marshland, the

---

[337] Thomas Walsingham, Gesta Abbatum Monasterii Sancti Albani, ed. H. T. RILEY (note 75 above), vol. 1, pp. 280–281, 285–286, 289–292, 294–295, 299, 314.

[338] Chronicon Abbatiae de Evesham, ed. W. D. MACRAY (note 42 above), p. 265. Historia et Cartularium Monasterii Sancti Petri Gloucestriae, ed. W. H. HART (note 41 above), vol. 1, pp. 22, 25, 26, 28; Annales Monastici, ed. H. R. LUARD (note 77 above), vol. 1, p. 112, vol. 4, p. 430.

[339] Historia et Cartularium Monasterii Sancti Petri Gloucestriae, ed. W. H. HART (note 41 above), vol. 1, pp. 25, 29.

[340] Annales Monastici, ed. H. R. LUARD (note 77 above), vol. 4, p. 415.

[341] Ibid., vol. 1, pp. 76, 95.

[342] TNA E403/362 m 14.

foundation of settlements, the creation of markets and eventually even the acquisition of property – had to be licensed and such licences normally had to be purchased. Often the leading religious were given administrative tasks and monastic precincts were used as depositories for royal taxes. In addition monastic precincts could be used as royal residences and as accommodation for the king's administration. Furthermore there were demands to appoint royal servants to monastic churches or to provide corrodies for them. One has to conclude that in this respect religious houses were entirely regarded as secular economic entities. However, religious houses also needed to be spiritual centres, especially in the eye of the king. They had a dual nature and there needed to be a balance between their physical presence and their spiritual significance. The duality of religious life and economic activity provided the model for the relationship between the kings and the monasteries. In the eyes of the government their secular wealth did not raise them beyond the level of other significant providers of taxes and loans, the great landholders or the towns. It was the charisma of the religious and the abbeys' role as spiritual centres which gave them their exceptional status. The Plantagenets entrusted the task of interceding for the deceased members of their family to specific religious houses, prominently Fontevraud and Westminster Abbey. The king was willing to pay for the *memoria* and for the prayers imploring God to ensure the welfare of the realm. The monks of Chertsey, who prayed for the soul of queen Isabel in 1358 for a payment of £40, received a royal visit in 1361 and in preparation of this occasion the indebted monastery had its houses repaired at the king's costs.[343] As centres of worship religious houses had received privileges and wealth from English rulers. The abbess of Godstow had received material support from Henry II. who also paid for construction costs and royal support is also documented more than a century later.[344] As royal support for the crusades the military orders were paid cash stipends. Occasionally this even included the Teutonic Knights.[345]

---

[343] TNA E403/394 m 22; E403/408 m 2.

[344] Great Roll of the Pipe for the Seventh Year of the Reign of King Henry the Second (note 170 above), p. 25; Great Roll of the Pipe for the Eighth Year of the Reign of King Henry the Second (note 26 above), p. 26; Great Roll of the Pipe for the Twenty–Fourth Year of the Reign of King Henry the Second (note 176 above), pp. 118, 119. TNA E403/180 m 3.

[345] P. WEBSTER, King John and Religion (Studies in the History of Medieval Religion 43), Woodbridge 2015; D. CARPENTER, Henry III (note 26 above), ch. 6; M. PRESTWICH, The Piety of Edward I, in: W. M. ORMROD (ed.), England in the Thirteenth Century, Stamford 1985, pp. 120–128; ID., The Personal Religion of Edward III, in: Speculum 64 (1989), pp. 11–20. Almost all of the surviving issue rolls in the National Archives, London, record the monarch's pious donations. For the Teutonic Knights, e.g. TNA E403/47 m 1: *Magistro et fratribus hospitalis beate Marie Theutonicorum in Jerusalem .xl. marcas de termino Pasche anno regni regis .E. .xiiii°. de illis xl. marcis annuis quas dominus .H. rex pater domini regis nunc concessit eis per cartam suam ad scaccarium suum percipiendas quousque eisdem magistro et fratribus per predictum patrem regis nunc vel heredes suos in aliqua certa terra in Anglia provisum fuerit competenter. Lib. fratri Willelmo de Aunderstat fratri eiusdem domus.* E403/56 m 1; E403/61 m 1.

For abbots, priors and obedientiaries this meant that they were not only expected to manage the conventual estates and control income and expenses but that they also had to have detailed knowledge of the functioning of the law and of the royal administration. The superiors had to possess skills which went beyond the mere administration of their estates. They had to market their products in international trade networks and they came to be integrated into an international financial system. This range of skills needed to be combined with those of the pious and charismatic religious leader. There was no room for those who only possessed the skills of the *athletis Christi*; they had failed time and again.[346] In contrast, the abbot who was a manager, a lawyer, a politician who increased the convent's income, who acted as builder, who added to the abbey's possessions and treasures was regarded as a success by the monastic authors of historical narratives.

---

[346] Cassianus. De institutis coenobiorum. De incarnatione contra Nestorium, ed. M. PETSCHENIG (new edition by G. KREUZ) (Corpus Scriptorum Ecclesiasticorum Latinorum xvii), Vienna 2004, p. 79.

The Administration of the Castilian Benedictine Monasteries in the First Half of the Fourteenth Century

Carlos Manuel Reglero de la Fuente[1]

This article focuses on the study of the administration of the Benedictine monasteries in Castile in the first half of the fourteenth century, in particular the aspects related to their management.[2] I use the accounts of the monasteries from the province of Toledo in 1338 to get a more general view, and the monastery of Sahagún for a more detailed analysis.[3]

In the Rule of Saint Benedict, it is the abbot who has the responsibility for taking decisions in the monastery with the advice of the monks. As for the administration of the properties, the abbot delegated responsibility to the cellarer (*cellararius*), who acted under orders from the abbot and who could be assisted by other monks (R.B. 33; R.B. 2–3).[4] In practice, the abbot was the main administrator of the monastery's properties and rents. During the Central Middle Ages, the monks' protests against the abbot for not providing them with sufficient food or clothing was resolved by creating the offices or obediences, that is, by assigning some properties and rents to a specific end, such as acquiring the monks' habits.

It should be remembered that in June 1336 Pope Benedict XII issued the papal bull *Summi Magistri* or *Benedictine* to reform the monasteries of the Black Monks. This bull aimed to restore the observance of the rule and improve their administration, limiting the power of the abbot. On the other hand, it contained notable concessions in such aspects as the consumption of meat. The bull dealt with numerous topics related to the organisation and administration of the monasteries. They were ordered to send some monks to study canon law or theology, to organise themselves into provinces and to celebrate provincial

---

[1] Universidad de Valladolid. https://orcid.org/0000–0002–3361–1815. This paper forms part of the research project "El ejercicio del poder: espacios, agentes y escrituras (siglos XI–XV)" (HAR2017–84718–P), funded by the MICINN, AEI, UE–FEDER.

[2] An overview of the literature concerning monastic accounts in: L. Maté Sadornil / M. B. Prieto Moreno / A. Santidrián Arroyo, El papel de la contabilidad monástica a lo largo de la historia en el orbe cristiano. Una revisión in: Revista de Contabilidad 20/2 (2017), pp. 143–156.

[3] The documents of Sahagún are summarised in: Colección diplomática del monasterio de Sahagún. 7, (1300–1500), eds. V. Á. Álvarez Palenzuela / M. Sánchez Martín / F. Suárez Bilbao / P. Romero Portilla, León 1997. The references to the documents corresponds with said work, even though the complete original text has been used.

[4] Benedicti Regvla, ed. R. Hanslik (Corpus Scriptorum Ecclesiasticorum Latinorum 75), Vienna 1960, pp. 19–29, 90–91.

chapters every two years. This chapter had to designate monks to visit the monasteries of the province. In the administrative field, the abbot's ability to take decisions was limited and the role played by the convent was reinforced. Thus, loans, long-term rents, the concession of corrodies in exchange for cash, had to be approved by the convent after consideration along with the abbot for at least two days. The reason for the loan or the rent and the conditions had to be very clear and they had to be put in writing. Those who favoured family members at the expense of the monastery's properties should be punished. The abbot had to swear not to dispose of the monastery's assets. If an important property was to be alienated, a papal licence was necessary. Written inventories of the administered assets had to be made. All of this was open to different spiritual and ecclesiatic sanctions.[5]

The importance of this bull in monastic life is evident from the words of Francisco de Berganza, chronicler of the Abbey of Cardeña. The bull was bound following the Rule of Saint Benedict "so that, on certain days, it could be read to the monks after coming out from the celebration of the prime."[6] The bull completed and modified the Rule in such aspects of daily life as meals and clothing, but it also did so with respect to the administration of the monastery. Both texts became the general framework by which decisions of an economic nature were taken. In any case, the Benedictine monks of Castile did not create a corpus of statutes to regulate the administration of their domains in this century. This contrasts with what happened in the cathedral chapters, such as those of Palencia or León,[7] even though these chapters were made up of secular canons who had no monastic life per se.

---

[5] Bullarium diplomatum et privilegiorum sanctorum romanorum pontificum Taurinensis editio, tomus IV. A Gregorio X (an. MCCLXXI) ad Martinum V (an. MCCCCXXXI), ed. A. TOMASSETTI, Turín 1859, pp. 366–373; D. KNOWLES, The Religious Orders in England, 3 vols., Cambridge 1948–1959, vol. 2, pp. 3–8.

[6] F. BERGANZA, Antigüedades de España, propugnadas en las noticias de sus reyes en la coronica del real monasterio de San Pedro de Cardeña, en historias, chronicones y otros intrumentos manuscritos, que hasta aora no han visto la luz publica, 2 vols., Madrid 1719–1721 (reprint: Burgos 1992), vol. 2, p. 193.

[7] T. VILLACORTA RODRÍGUEZ, El cabildo catedral de León. Estudio histórico–jurídico, siglos XII–XIX, León 1974, see pp. 65–75, 352–385; C. M. REGLERO DE LA FUENTE, La iglesia catedral de Palencia en el siglo XIV: crisis y reformas (1313–1397), in: Edad Media. Revista de Historia 7 (2006), pp. 121–158.

1. The accounts of the monasteries of the province of Toledo in 1338
1.1. The document

The bull *Summi Magistri* established that the costs of the chapter meetings, visitations and studies should be met by the monasteries according to their income. To this end, in March and April of 1338, the abbots of Silos and Cardeña created an accounts book for nine monasteries of the monastic province of Castile. Thus, they fulfilled the task given them by pope Benedict XII. in December 1336. It was a balance book of income and expenses, not the real accounts of the previous year.[8] The document has survived in a copy from 1639, but with some errors.[9] It has been studied in detail by Juan José GARCÍA GONZÁLEZ and Salustiano MORETA in two studies.[10] Here, I will focus only on the questions most closely linked to the administration.

These accounts refer to six abbeys and three priories of varying importance with respect to the income and number of monks.[11] The priory of Hornillos only

---

[8] M. FÉROTIN, Histoire de l'abbaye de Silos, Paris 1897, pp. 119–121; S. MORETA VELAYOS, Rentas monásticas en Castilla: Problemas de método, Salamanca 1974, pp. 24–25.

[9] There are arithmetic errors in some quantities: S. MORETA, Rentas monásticas, pp. 25–26 (note 8 above). It also seems that the order of the accounts of Santo Domingo de Silos were altered, so that part of the accounts of the office of the chamberlain were copied in those of the steward, which are also incomplete.

[10] J. J. GARCÍA GONZÁLEZ, Vida económica de los monasterios benedictinos en el siglo XIV, Valladolid 1972; S. MORETA, Rentas monásticas (note 8 above).

[11] The abbeys of San Salvador de Oña, San Pedro de Arlanza, Santo Domingo de Silos, San Pedro de Cardeña, Sahagún, Obarenes, and the priories of San Zoilo de Carrión, San Juan de Burgos and Hornillos. Several of these monasteries are at the centre of studies that focus differently on administrative and economic questions in general. BERGANZA was the first to summarise the contents of the accounts book of 1338, for all the monasteries, not only for Cardeña (F. BERGANZA, Antigüedades de España (note 6 above), vol. 2, pp. 193–201). The studies on Sahagún have not focused especially on the the monastery's administration: R. ESCALONA, Historia del real monasterio de Sahagún, Madrid 1782 (reprint: León 1982); J. PUYOL Y ALONSO, El abadengo de Sahagún (Contribución al estudio del feudalismo en España). Discurso leído en la recepción en la R.A.H., Madrid 1915; E. MARTÍNEZ LIÉBANA, El dominio señorial del monasterio de San Benito de Sahagún en la baja Edad Media (siglos XIII–XV), Madrid 1990. FEROTIN already includes references to the accounts notebook of 1338 (M. FÉROTIN, Histoire de l'abbaye (note 8 above)). The studies of monastic estates are numerous, as for instance that of Santo Toribio de Liébana, which was a priory of Oña, mentioned in the accounts of 1338: J. GAUTIER–DALCHÉ, Le domaine du monastère de Santo Toribio de Liébana: formation, structure et modes d'exploitation, in: Anuario de Estudios Medievales 2 (1965), pp. 63–117, at pp. 103–108. Also: M. BONAUDO DE MAGNANI, El monasterio de S. Salvador de Oña. Economía agraria, sociedad rural (1011–1399), in: Cuadernos de Historia de España, 51–52 (1970), pp. 42–122; S. MORETA VELAYOS, El monasterio de San Pedro de Cardeña. Historia de un dominio monástico castellano (902–1338), Salamanca 1971, vid. pp. 213–241; F. J. PEÑA PEREZ, El monasterio de San Juan de Burgos (1091–1436). Dinámica de un modelo cultural feudal, Burgos 1990, pp. 319–366; J. A. PÉREZ CELADA, El monasterio de San Zoilo de Carrión. Formación, estructura y decurso histórico de un señorío castellano–leonés (siglos XI al XVI), Burgos 1997, pp. 250–269.

had one monk, while there were 63 in Oña and 58 in Sahagún, the other six having between 22 and 33, with an average of about 25. The declared income of each monastery also varied greatly, so that of Sahagún was 14 times greater than that of Hornillos. On the other hand, the quality of the information given in each monastery was of a diverse nature: in Sahagún only the largest economic allocations (only the office of chamberlain had detailed expenses), while others were much more detailed (the income from each place and the main expenses).

1.2. The organisation into offices

The accounts of each monastery reflect the division between the abbacy, the offices and the priories. This was the typical administrative organisation of the monasteries of the Black Monks. The abbot, the monastic office-holders and the priors were assigned a series of properties and rents with which they had to cover certain expenses. The number of priories varies from one monastery to another. Sahagún had eleven, while Oña only had three. In Carrión, the dependent priories were included as part of the prior's rents.[12] In total, the accounts mention 22 priories, but in the copy of the manuscript some folios containing various priories of Silos have been lost.

The organisation of the offices was different in each monastery, with up to eight offices each in Sahagún and Silos, while there were none in Hornillos. San Juan de Burgos only had one, the sacrist. The rest oscillated between four and seven. The most common were the sacrist (in 8 monasteries), the infirmarian (7), the chamberlain (6), the steward (*mayordomo*) (5), the cellarer and the almoner (4). The Master or Prior of the Works or Fabric appears in two monasteries and another seven offices in only one. For instance, in Sahagún, there was an office of the Hosteler (guest-master) and another of the "Charities", and in Cardeña one of the "Anniversaries" or in Silos that of the Subprior. In general, the number of offices was conditioned by the volume of the income, but there was no proportional relation. The customs of the monastery and the conflicts and agreements between the abbot and the monks were decisive elements.[13]

---

[12] Two analyses of the accounts of San Zoilo de Carrión in: J. A. Pérez Celada, Documentación del monasterio de San Zoilo de Carrión, 2 vols., Burgos 1986–1987, vol. 2, pp. XLI–LIX; C. M. Reglero de la Fuente, Amigos exigentes, servidores infieles: la crisis de la Orden de Cluny en España (1270–1379), Madrid 2014, pp. 228–240.

[13] On the organisation into offices in the Cluniac and Benedictine monasteries: D. Knowles, The Monastic Order in England. A History of its Development from the Times of St Dunstan to the Fourth Lateran Council, 940–1216, Cambridge 1963, pp. 427–439; D. Knowles, The Religious Orders (note 5 above), vol. 2, pp. 309–330; G. de Valous, Le monachisme clunisien des origines au XVe siècle. Vie intérieure des monastères et organisation de l'Ordre. Tome Ier. L'abbaye de Cluny. Les monastères clunisiens, Paris 1970, pp. 124–186; J. Greatrex, The English Benedictine Cathedral Priories: Rule and Practice, c. 1270–1420, Oxford 2011, pp. 160–235. For Spain: C. M. Reglero de la Fuente, Cluny en España. Los prioratos de la

The Rule of Saint Benedict refers to some assistants of the abbot in the monastery's economic administration, in particular the cellarer, but it does not establish an organisation into offices. This depends on the customs of each monastery, on the conflicts and agreements between the successive abbots and the monks. In 1150, the monks of Sahagún took advantage of the death of Abbot Dominicus II. to assign certain rents to the cellarer before electing a new abbot, who then ratified it.[14] In Santo Domingo de Silos, in 1158, an agreement was reached by the mediation of the Archbishop of Toledo. This agreement specified the rents assigned to almonry, infirmary, fabric, refectory and chamber (clothing), but not the duties; the sacrist is also mentioned, but the rents assigned are not detailed; in 1278, an exchange of rents was carried out between the abbot and the monks, which affected the properties of the infirmarian, the steward (*mayordomo*) and the chamberlain.[15] A similar agreement was reached in San Pedro de Arlanza in 1266, assigning monastery rents for the refectory, "clothing" and infirmary; in addition, it was decided what the abbot should give to the monks and their servants, how the offerings for the dead were to be divided up, or how the abbot was to receive the wax from the beehives and the monks the honey[16].

Comparing these agreements with the situation in the fourteenth century, it can be seen that the organisation into offices changed gradually. In Silos, the office of the "Fabric" existed in the twelfth century, but it had disappeared by the fourteenth century. The almoner became the hosteler and the refectioner turned into the steward. In San Zoilo de Carrión, the office of "Eating and Dressing" of 1338 brought together the "Kitchen" and the "Chamber" that figure in the accounts of 1213.[17]

The evolution of each monastery explains the differences in the rents attributed to each office within each monastery. In Silos, there were between 140 maravedís for the subprior and 5425 maravedís for the Kitchen (38 times more); while in Carrión, there were between 337 maravedís for the Infirmary and 5241 maravedís for "Eating and Dressing" (15 times more). Similar contrasts are evident in the provision of the same office between one monastery and another:

---

provincia y sus redes sociales (1073–ca. 1270), León 2008, pp. 508–529; C. M. REGLERO, Amigos exigentes (note 12 above), pp. 193–201; A. I. LAPEÑA PAÚL, La distribución y las funciones de los oficios monásticos, in: J. A. García de Cortázar / R. Teja (eds.), Las edades del monje: jerarquía y función en el monasterio medieval, Aguilar de Campoo 2019, pp. 99–131.

[14] Colección diplomática del Monasterio de Sahagun (857–1300). 4, (1110–1199), ed. J. A. FERNÁNDEZ FLÓREZ, León 1991, doc. 1311, pp. 228–229.

[15] Documentación del monasterio de Santo Domingo de Silos (954–1254), ed. M. C. VIVANCOS GÓMEZ, Burgos 1988, doc. 63. Documentación del monasterio de Santo Domingo de Silos (1255–1300), ed. M. C. VIVANCOS GÓMEZ, Santo Domingo de Silos 1995, doc. 250.

[16] Cartulario de San Pedro de Arlanza: antiguo monasterio benedictino, ed. L. SERRANO, Madrid 1925, doc. 157.

[17] C. M. REGLERO, Amigos exigentes (note 12 above), p. 237.

thus, the sacrist of Sahagún had twelve times more than his colleague in Arlanza, in absolute terms.[18]

The volume of income and the duties of each office were different, depending on the monastery. The cellarer, one of the most classic offices in the benedictine monasteries, was present in four of the nine monasteries. In Silos and Arlanza, he only had to pay part of the expenses of growing corn on the land, so his rents supposed, respectively, the twentieth or the ninth part of the abbot's rents. However, in Oña, he was in charge of supplying the monks, the servants and the guests of the monastery with bread; thus, his rents were greater than those of the abbot (60% more). What normally happened was that the supply of bread and wine should be paid for by the abbot or the prior, except in Oña, where the bread was paid for by the cellarer and the wine by the steward.

The purchase of the meat, fish, fat and other condiments was the steward's responsibility who also had to bear the costs. In contrast, in Oña, the prior had to pay for the fish of 22 days; in Silos, the office of kitchener, and in Cardeña, the office of the "Anniversaries" should take responsibility for meat or fish three days in the week; or that, in Carrión, where there was no steward, the responsibility had been conferred on the office of "Eating and Dressing".

The wages due to the servants of the abbot and the officials (bread, wine, other food, clothing or salaries) could be assumed by the abbot in their entirety or shared between the offices, so the abbot would be responsible for the bread and wine and the office-holders for the rest.

1.3. The accounting

The accounts of 1338 are not the accounts books of a particular monastery, but the way in which the abbots of Silos and Cardeña interpreted them according to their necessities. There were, of course, accounts books: in the infirmary of Sahagún reference is made to one that contained detailed expenses (*libro de la despensa*).[19]

The general structure of the accounts reflects the organisation of accounting procedures in the monasteries themselves. The incomes and expenses were divided between the abbacy, the offices and the priories. Within each section, the income and expenses in cereals (wheat, barley and rye), wine and cash were dealt with separately. It seems certain that the accounting of each was done separately, irrespective of whether all the incomes came first and all the expenses came after, or whether the incomes and expenses of each were recorded together. In those

---

[18] 4771 maravedis in Sahagún (4.6% of the monastery's total income), as opposed to 383.5 maravedis in Arlanza (1.6%).

[19] J. J. GARCÍA GONZÁLEZ, Vida económica (note 10 above), p. 186.

monasteries that offer more information, the incomes are detailed according to place of origin within each budget item (corn, wine, cash). In the case of the expenses, there is not necessarily any order as such, but in some cases, it can be seen how expenses of a similar nature are grouped together: the expenses of transporting the corn to the monastery or of collecting the rents. The costs of crop farming in the fields or of working the vineyards and the labourers' wages, the payments to the king, the convent's expenses, etc., are also recorded together. The amounts under each rubric vary greatly, which indicates that there were individualised accounts for some of them. Sometimes the expenses of the previous year are recorded, while in other cases it is only an estimate.

The accounts of 1338 use accounting conventions, such as recording the monetary value of corn and wine produced on the monastic estates and consumed from their own harvest. The price is not that of a concrete purchase or sale, nor does it take into account the fluctuations throughout the year. In the same way, the consumption of food by the monks and servants is estimated as an annual quantity and is only an approximation of the real consumption. When there was a transfer between two offices, which happened frequently, transactions were accounted for as an expense in one and as income in the other, a method which slightly increased the monastery's overall income. The same effect was achieved by counting the theoretical profits from properties as income, including those that were mortgaged and thus gave no profit. The reduction in the rents for the peasants for different reasons, such as storms, was accounted for as an expense and not as a minor income.

The expenses caused by crop cultivation or transport were not discounted from the incomes in kind. The same practice was followed for collecting the tithes from the peasants. So the incomes of the monasteries pursuing a policy of demesne farming, i.e. managing the estates directly, were theoretically larger than those that charged rent in kind (and thus pay for transport themselves),[20] and the latter in turn had larger incomes than those that rented them for cash. The theoretically superior income meant that they had to pay more in contributions to the common expenses of the province, in particular the maintenance of the monks'

---

[20] The cost of collecting and transporting the corn to the monastery or a market town varied considerably. In the monastery of Oña, for example, it varied between 4% and 21% depending on the office. The cost amounted to around 15% of the abbot's rents when collected in corn, while it only cost 4% for those collected in coin (J. J. GARCÍA GONZÁLEZ, Vida económica (note 10 above), pp. 140–158). These percentages are estimated using the price of corn indicated in the accounts, which is not the real sale price. The theoretical accounting price would correspond to the weeks immediately following the harvest. If the corn was sold in April or May, the price was higher, so the percentage spent on collection and transport would be lower. In any case, an important part of the corn was consumed by the monks and their servants. If we consider the costs as a whole, they varied beween 7% in San Zoilo de Carrión, where almost all the rents were collected in coin, and 34% in Oña, a monastery which cultivated the demesne and collected many rents in corn or wine. The average cost was 19% (S. MORETA, Rentas monásticas (note 8 above), p. 136).

study, as well as the tenth collected with the authorisation of the popes. This was a stimulus to abandon direct farming.

1.4. Self-consumption or market

The study of the accounts carried out by MORETA concluded that the monasteries maintained the direct farming of some of their lands, but that most of their income came in the form of rents.[21] In general, the rent was paid in kind. This, together with what they got from the tithes, rents from mills, etc., meant that the greater part of the monastery's estimated income was in corn or wine. There were exceptions, such as Carrión, where two thirds of their income was in cash, or Arlanza, where this type of income amounted to a little over half of the total. At the other extreme, Obarenes only collected a tenth part in coin.[22]

The fundamental use of these rents paid in kind was to feed the monks, servants and guests, or, to a much smaller extent, for distribution as alms. In the case of corn, the percentage of self-consumption was usually between 45% and 70%, except in Sahagún and Hornillos, where it was less. It was always greater for wheat than for barley. In the case of wine, the percentages varied a lot and more than half the monasteries had to buy at least a part of what they consumed.[23]

Despite the high level of self-consumption, the monasteries had considerable surplus income with which to do business. This was very high in the case of some monasteries such as Sahagún.[24] The monasteries marketed their products because they needed cash to buy food, to pay wages, to service debts or to pay tributes. Unfortunately, the accounts give no indication at all of the commercialisation policy for this surplus, not even where or when it was sold.

1.5. The debt

The monastic debts rarely appeared in the accounts. The debt declared in Arlanza was 14,000 maravedis, that is, almost 60% of the theoretical rents and greater than the real income for a year. In Oña, more than 3,000 maravedis of debt were recognised; while in Carrión it was 1,000 maravedis, which was less than 5% of the monastery's income. The quantities were, in general, small; unlike the high

---

[21] Ibid., pp. 90–95.
[22] Ibid., pp. 117–119.
[23] Ibid., pp. 120–124, 127.
[24] Ibid., pp. 123–127.

deficits shown in the monasteries' accounts.²⁵ The explanation lies in the fact that these debts were only the debts owed in cash.

The Benedictine monasteries financed their economic deficit through long-term renting of domains, collecting the rent in advance. This is reflected in the so-called "rentas empeñadas" (alienated domains), which made up 62% of the monastery's theoretical income in Arlanza, 43% in Carrión and 30% in Burgos. At the other extreme, in Cardeña, they only represented 3% and in Silos 8%.²⁶ Part of these "rentas empeñadas" were properties usurped or ceded in order to gain the protection of a member of the court or of a noble in the district. In other cases, the domains had been given over in lieu of debts, to buy bread or wine in a year of scarcity, to pay the king's tax, or to cover the expenses of a lawsuit.²⁷ The amounts obtained by this procedure could be large. For instance, the monastery of Oña rented out a priory for 14 years, collecting 10,000 maravedis in advance, and another for 12 years in exchange for 20,000 maravedis. In the first case it was to buy wine for a year in which the harvest had been lost due to hail and in the second simply because the monastery needed it (*para pro del monasterio*).²⁸ Similarly, the monastery of Silos had given eight large properties in long-term rents to pay for their court battles with the Franciscans and with the clerics of the town of Santo Domingo de Silos, obtaining in total more than 20,000 maravedis.²⁹

Renting out properties was one way to repay the debts contracted in coin, which came with high interest rates.³⁰ Urgent payments forced the monasteries to contract a debt in cash at a high rate of interest. Therefore, properties were rented over long periods in order to repay these debts.³¹ If the quantity was small, the debts could be paid by conceding a corrody (*racion*) to the creditor or the benefactor, that is, an annual amount in food and money for clothes.³² The accounts mention the presence of corrodies in the monasteries, but not the

---

²⁵ J. J. GARCÍA GONZÁLEZ, Vida económica (note 10 above), pp. 227, 144, 172.

²⁶ S. MORETA, Rentas monásticas (note 8 above), pp. 145.

²⁷ J. J. GARCÍA GONZÁLEZ, Vida económica (note 10 above), pp. 133–134, 136–137, 171–172, 220–222, 229. Burgos: Este empeño fue hecho seis años ha […] por ser el año que se empeñó el pan en Castilla muy caro e no avían pan en el dicho monasterio (Ibid., p. 133). Cardeña: Dio por ello 5000 maravedís que se despendieron en décimas y pedidos que demandó el Rey al monasterio e en vino que ovo de comprar el monasterio en aquel tiempo (Ibid., p. 229).

²⁸ Ibid., p. 144.

²⁹ Ibid., pp. 203–204.

³⁰ Arlanza: para pagar deudas que estavan muy afincados por ellas (Ibid., p. 226).

³¹ C. M. REGLERO, Amigos exigentes (note 12 above), pp. 215–219.

³² Ibid., pp. 222–226. A discussion of its economic sense in: A. BELL / C. SUTCLIFFE, Valuing medieval annuities: Were corrodies underpriced?, in: Explorations in Economic History 47/2 (2010), pp. 142–157 [https://doi.org/10.1016/j.eeh.2009.07.002].

reason why the corrody was given: a service to the monastery, an imposition by the king, or as a compensation for a donation or debt.

1.6. The management of properties and rents

The accounts include the expenses incurred for the cultivation of the land and the vineyards (seeds, wages paid to the men who work the fields and bring in the harvest), as well as the transport of the corn and wine. In addition, there were also administrative costs. Of note are the costs of journeys to collect the monastery's rents or to make a claim or lawsuit in the King's court or the territorial court. The amounts dedicated to these ends are considerable: a quarter of the expenses of the abbacy of Oña (4,000 maravedis for the abbot's journeys and the same again for lawsuits). In total, a quarter of the expenses were for management and a little more was paid for the working of the domains. The rest was divided between food and clothing for the abbot, the servants and some monks (a third of the total) and the payment of diverse royal and ecclesiastical tributes (one sixth).[33] The abbot or the officials were responsible for collecting rents, that is, the management of their part of the domains,[34] assisted by their servants, collectors[35] or stewards.[36]

The accounts mention numerous servants and employees in the monasteries, under the control of either the abbot or one of the officials. Their functions went from working the lands or looking after the flocks to washing the clothes, caring for the abbot's mules or cooking. Sometimes, tasks related to management were described, although on a clearly subordinate level, such as delivering letters and messages, accompanying monks or watching over the agricultural work.[37] The lawyers and procurators had a more relevant role, as they were paid for taking charge of the monastery's lawsuits and were contracted either temporarily or permanently. Thus, in San Juan de Burgos, there was a register of payments in wheat and coin "to the lawyers and advisers and to the scribes".[38] Similar expenses were noted in the priory of Mave and in Arlanza.[39] In the latter monastery, the lawyer was given an inheritance for life, "for assistance to the monastery in lawsuits", while in Cardeña, 12 bushels of wheat annually were paid to another lawyer for

---

[33] J. J. García González, Vida económica (note 10 above), p. 142–144.
[34] Ibid., pp. 157 (steward of Oña), 163 (priory of Santo Toribio de Liébana).
[35] Ibid., pp. 159, 174, 233. Cardeña: Espiende el mayordomo en todo el año, él y su hombre, en recabdar rentas y pleitos (Ibid., p. 237).
[36] Ibid., p. 176 (office of 'Eating and Dressing' of Carrión).
[37] Ibid., pp. 243, 245 (priories of San Babiles and Santa María de Rezmondo of Cardeña). Silos: tres omes del cillerigo que van con el e estan sobre las lavores (Ibid., p. 198).
[38] Ibid., pp. 131 y 133.
[39] Ibid., pp. 165, 219.

not acting against the monastery in lawsuits.[40] The expenses of the notaries were similarly set out, for writing rental contracts or for copying lawsuits.[41] Thus, the steward of Cardeña included 100 maravedis for the "cost of lawsuits and contracts", and the chamberlain another 100 maravedis for "collecting the rents and in lawsuits and in making contracts".[42] The sums budgeted were not decided arbitrarily but represented an estimate of the legal costs facing the monastery.

The various servants who had to manage the monastic patrimony were given very different levels of responsibility. The group of servants included some with a good economic position; the abbot of Oña owed 2,200 maravedis and 6 gold *reales* to one of their servants (*Alfonso Perez nuestro criado*),[43] which is a quantity that demonstrates that this person was well-to-do. In other cases, differences can be seen in the remuneration of the various servants. In Silos, in addition to the bread and wine, the employees received other food and clothing. Those in charge of looking after the vines were paid 115 maravedís each; 155 maravedis were paid to another 15 employees, including the cook; finally, 294 maravedis were paid to the abbot's *merino* (bailiff), his chamberlain and two men who accompanied the abbot. The fundamental difference was the expense in clothing. Better clothing meant a better personal status, but also that, on accompanying the abbot, the clothing had to reflect the abbot's social position.

2. The administration of the monastery of Sahagún in the first half of the Fourteenth century (1301–1357)
2.1. The abbot and the convent

The documentation from Sahagún highlights the importance of the abbot's role in the monastery's administration. The most important administrative decisions always required his approval. He acted alone or in accord with the convent or the officials. This did not stop the most important officials from having some autonomy to administer the properties belonging to their office, with certain exceptions, among them the alienation of properties.

The use of the abbot's and the convent's seals provide important information on the convent's role in administrative processes. A total of 38 documents have been preserved in which one of the two, or both seals were used. In two thirds of cases, letters were sealed by both the abbot and the convent; these included letters naming procurators, rental agreements for large properties or long-term

---

[40] Ibid., pp. 221, 230.
[41] Burgos (Ibid., p. 131); Silos (Ibid., p. 202); Arlanza (Ibid., p. 219).
[42] Ibid., pp. 237, 242.
[43] Ibid., pp. 144.

rentals, the ratification of legal agreements, the acceptance of donations that involved either economic or spiritual compensation or internal decisions concerning the organisation of the administration. A quarter of the letters were sealed only by the abbot. These referred to churches belonging to the abbacy, letters of empowerment to monks or servants and the ratification of some court rulings, but always with reference to the abbacy or to an office. Only on two occasions did the convent authenticate a letter with its seal without the addition of the abbot's seal: one was a letter of empowerment in favour of the abbot and the other was the ratification of an agreement in a lawsuit, which the abbot ratified with his seal some days later in a separate document.

The role of the chapter, the assemblies of the abbot with the convent, in the administration of the monastery is largely unknown. In the first three decades of the fourteenth century, the documents may mention the abbot and the convent as the granting authorities, but they rarely refer to the assembly of the chapter as such.[44] The references to the chapter are a bit more frequent after 1336, perhaps due to the influence of the papal bull *Summi Magistri*. The formulas used in these letters refer to the fact that the assembly is called according to use and custom, at the tolling of the bell, that the place of assembly is the chapterhouse, and that the abbot and the convent are present. Three documents (1342, 1348, 1357) expressly mention business conducted in accordance with the requirements of canonical law and the apostolic constitutions, in a clear reference to this bull.[45] The documents that came from a chapter are of the same type as those sealed by the abbot and the convent jointly, but not all the documents of the chapter were sealed (only 7 out of 17, or 41%). In addition, the assembly of the chapter was used to appeal to Rome concerning sentences that had gone against the monastery or to notify a letter of excommunication against the abbot and the monks.[46]

2.2. The offices and the officials

The monastery of Sahagún was the richest of all the abbeys appearing in the accounts of 1338; it also had a greater number of administrative divisions: the abbacy, eight offices and eleven priories, six of them with their own sacrist; in total, 26 for 58 monks. This implies that almost half the monks held an office

---

[44] Colección, ed. V. Á. ÁLVAREZ PALENZUELA (note 3 above), docs. 1948, 2031, 2036, 2086, 2110.
[45] Ibid., docs. 2230, 2308, 2377.
[46] Ibid., docs. 1948, 2031.

and, thus, had administrative responsibilities of a greater or lesser importance, a percentage much higher than for the other monasteries studied.[47]

This was the consequence of a policy that multiplied the number of officials as a way of rewarding the monks in the monastery. In 1357, the office of sacrist in the priory of Medina del Campo was created. The reason given was not to improve the administration, but to better serve the church and the monastery. To this end, the rents and properties annexed to the office of sacrist were set out in detail. In addition, it was stipulated how to divide the donations from the faithful between the the prior and the sacrist, in particular the donations of the deceased; the prior's obligations towards the sacrist were defined: to supply the sacrist with food and clothing and also to provide food for a servant of the sacrist. Furthermore, the economic obligations of the sacrist and the prior concerning the maintenance of the church, the chapels, the bells and their tolling, the church ornaments, were also established. In general, it was laid down that the customs existing in other priories with a sacrist should be followed.[48]

Another management unit was created in 1348, the *arca común* (common chest). Abbot Diego decided that the tithes from six parishes of Sahagún, which until that time had gone to the clerics of the town, were allocated to the monastery.[49] The rents should be destined to those expenses derived from applying the reform of Benedict XII., that is, the payment of the monastery's school (*Estudio*), the monks who studied in a University, the expenses of the provincial chapter or the defence of the rights of the Benedictine monasteries. The rents were kept in a chest with three locks, the keys to which were kept by the abbot, a monk designated by the officials and another monk designated by the convent. These three monks would collect the tithes from the town of Sahagún, change them into coin, place them in the chest and spend them.[50] In 1352, the income from the notaries of Sahagún had been added, making a total of 3000 maravedís.[51] Then, in 1357, the tithes from another parish of the town were added.[52] This office differed from the rest in that it was not managed by a single monk, but by three, who represented the monastery.

---

[47] In Arlanza, 10 of the 26 monks held office; in Oña 12 of the 63; in Silos 11 of 32; in Cardeña 12 of 33; in Obarenes 6 of 22; in Carrión 8 of 25; in Burgos 2 of 12.

[48] Colección, ed. V. Á. ÁLVAREZ PALENZUELA (note 3 above), doc. 2379.

[49] Diego II took advantage of the deaths of the parish priests in the Black Death to name his own monks as replacement parish priests. He then assigned the rents to the monastery and gave the parishes back to secular clerics.

[50] Colección, ed. V. Á. ÁLVAREZ PALENZUELA (note 3 above), doc. 2305.

[51] Á. VACA, Una manifestación de la crisis castellana del siglo XIV: la caída de las rentas de los señores feudales. El testimonio del monasterio de Sahagún, in: Studia Historica. Historia Medieval 1 (1983), pp. 157–166, vid. p. 165.

[52] Colección, ed. V. Á. ÁLVAREZ PALENZUELA (note 3 above), doc. 2377.

The high number of officials in Sahagún cannot hide the fact that many of them administered a very reduced income.[53] Only the abbot, four priors and five officials (Cellarer, Almoner, Sacrist, Chamberlain, Prior of the Fabric) had incomes over 3,000 maravedis. The abbot controlled 35% of the monastery's income, the five officials controlled 25 % and the four priors 18 %, so the other sixteen officials had to share one fifth of the income.[54]

The officials' different degrees of importance were also reflected in the documentation. I have counted the number of times the different officials and priors are mentioned in the documentation from 1300 to 1357, that is, during the time that Nicolas II. (1301–1316), Martin II. (1317–1329) and Diego II. (1329–1357) were abbots. Those appearing with greater frequency are, in descending order, the chamberlain (65 times), the cellarer (54), the almoner (42), the sacrist (32) and the prior of works (21). All of them were mentioned more than twenty times and this impression is confirmed by the fact that these were offices that had incomes of more than 3000 maravedís, although they do not appear in the same order.

The documentation also mentions other officials who had no assigned income, but did have administrative responsibilities or influence.[55] The *bodeguero* (wine-cellarer) should have been completely subordinate to the abbot.[56] On the other hand, the prior was a very influential person, since two of the three abbots during this period (Martin II. and Diego II.) were priors at the moment of their election.[57]

2.3. Administrative careers

It is not easy to discover the administrative careers within the monastery because of the duplication of names among the monks and because the lists of officials

---

[53] None of the sacrists of the priories yielded more than 650 maravedis; of the 11 priories, one did not reach 1000 maravedis and another 6 had between 1500 and 3000 maravedis; in the same way, three of the monastery's offices (the infirmary, the hostelery and the 'charities') did not exceed that quantity.

[54] The offices with the highest incomes were the Cellarer (7619 maravedis) and the Almoner, followed by the Sacrist, the Chamberlain and the Prior of Works. As for the priories, Santa María de Piasca (6283 maravedis), Nogal, Mayorga and Santervás stand out.

[55] The lists of witnesses also include the prior or *prior mayor* (16 times), the wine–cellarer or *bodeguero mayor* (12) and his assistant or *bodeguero menor* (6) and the subprior or *prior segundo* (7).

[56] In the case of the wine–cellarers, the accounts of 1338 do not define their role as an office. As to the abbacy, it only says that all the wine produced was consumed by the monks. It is reasonable to think that there was a wine–cellarer responsible for it under the abbot's authority. (J. J. GARCÍA GONZÁLEZ, Vida económica (note 10 above), p. 180).

[57] Ut per litteras Apostolicas Online, Brepols, Jean XXII, Lettres communes, doc. 3590 (25 Apr. 1317), doc. 46 822 (4 Oct. 1329).

are not complete. It is difficult to distinguish between monks with the same name when they change office, since the officials were usually identified by their name followed by their office. There was a tendency to occupy offices over long periods of time, but there were also times of instability. Thus, of the six chamberlains, three held office for at least ten years.[58] Something similar occurred with the cellarers[59] or the almoners.[60]

In some cases, their careers can be followed: Alfonso Valero of Valladolid was first prior of the fabric (1336–1342), then almoner (1346–1357), before being elected abbot in 1357.[61] Juan de Bovadilla was cellarer (1330–1342) and then prior of Nogal (1347). Juan de San Mancio went from being prior of Santervás (1341) to cellarer (1344–1347); and it may have been the very same Juan who, in 1326, being sacrist of the priory of San Mancio, acted as procurator for the monastery before the king. Mateo was prior of works (1301) and sacrist (1303–1315); Pedro became wine-cellarer (1316–1317) after being the assistant (1306–1314). The lack of data does not allow us be conclusive. There were, without doubt, administrative careers, but they were rare once they had secured an important office, which are the ones we know more about.

2.4. The delegation of functions: procurators and vicars

The abbot and the convent named monks as procurators to represent them in some businesses, in courts or before the King. The documentation has 35 references to these procurator monks which relate to a maximum of 15 persons since several of them held this position on different occasions.[62] In 71% of the references to procurators it is stated that the monk held a monastic office, in particular the chamberlain and almoner, within a total of ten offices.

Besides the abbot's and the convent's ordinary procurators, both the abbot and the officials could name a procurator to represent them. In this case, it was usually one of their servants.[63] In addition, the convent or the officials could give

---

[58] Domingo Asensio (1304–1313), Alfonso (1314–1326), Domingo Fernández (1326–1329), Gonzalo (1330–1333), Martín (1335–1336), and Alfonso de Valladolid (1340–1361).

[59] Facundo (1306–1317), Gonzalo (1318–1327), Juan de Bovadilla (1330–1342), Juan de San Mancio (1344–1347), Alfonso (1349) and Juan de Almanza (1358).

[60] Juan Pérez (1301–1309), Juan Domínguez (1312–1314), Alfonso (1316–1335), Martín (1340), Alfonso Valero de Valladolid (1346–1351, 1354–1357) and Alfonso Fernández (1353).

[61] Even so, it is not easy to distinguish him from another Alfonso of Valladolid, chamberlain (1340–1361).

[62] Don Alfonso Valero of Valladolid held this position on seven occasions (1336–1356), before being elected abbot in 1357. Domingo Asensio on four occasions (1302–1313). Both of them held the office of chamberlain.

[63] Their presence in the documentation is much rarer and appears as representing the abbot, the sacrist, the cellarer or the prior of a priory.

a monk powers or a licence to act in a particular situation.[64] A licence from the abbot was necessary to place a lawsuit in the hands of a judge and to negotiate rentals, exchanges or sales of the assets belonging to an office. Such a licence was also required for the acceptance of donations that involved the foundation of anniversaries or chapels.[65]

On the other hand, the abbots of Sahagún had ecclesiastical jurisdiction in the town and in the monastery's *coto* (*banleuca*, landed immunity). They could delegate this function to a vicar, who was usually a monk, or sometimes a cleric.[66] Their judicial functions included lawsuits over ecclesiastical properties, disputes over tithes that caused clashes between parish priests and monastic officials,[67] as well as giving legal validity to copies of documents that were necessary for defending the rights of the monastery.[68] These vicars could also judge lawsuits concerning ecclesiastical properties.[69]

2.5. The servants and their functions in the monastery's administration

Among the witnesses of the monastery's documentation there are often servants of the abbot or officials, his *criados* or 'men'.[70] Their tasks are rarely specified. We know the names of 8 'criados' of the abbot Nicolas, 14 of the abbot Diego and 26 of different officials and priors.[71]

Currently the Spanish term *criado* (servant) suggests a person with a low social status carrying out unskilled tasks. In medieval Castilian the term is more ambiguous, as it includes those who are 'brought up' in another's home, undoubtedly

---

[64] Thus, in 1306, Domingo de San Felices, resident in the priory of Villagarcía, rented some properties of the priory through the specific authority given by the abbot to this effect: Colección, ed. V. Á. ÁLVAREZ PALENZUELA (note 3 above), doc. 1946.

[65] Ibid., docs. 2024, 2114, 2139, 2178, 2231, 2261, 2321, 2349, 2373.

[66] The names of about eight of them are known, most during the time as abbot of Diego: Domingo Asensio, prior of works and chamberlain (1303, 1313), Fernando Ibáñez (1314), Gonzalo, chamberlain (1331), Alfonso Pérez, monk (1332, 1334, 1335, 1340, 1341), Martín, chamberlain (1336), Alfonso of Valladolid almoner (1341, 1346, 1347), Bartolomé monk (1346–1347), Ruy Fernández cleric (1354, 1356).

[67] Colección, ed. V. Á. ÁLVAREZ PALENZUELA (note 3 above), docs. 2012, 2119, 2168, 2185, 2270, 2282.

[68] Ibid., docs. 2117, 2286.

[69] Ibid., docs. 2283, 2286.

[70] On the servants in the English monasteries: D. KNOWLES, The Monastic Order (note 13 above), pp. 439–441.

[71] Hosteler, almoner, prior, sacrist, chamberlain, cellarer and prior of works. The priors of San Mancio, San Pedro de Dueñas, Santervás and Piasca.

at his service, but sometimes relatives or persons of a noteworthy social condition.[72] Some of them acted as procurators for their lord.[73] Among the so-called servants of the abbots, there are two clerics and a bachelor.[74] Thus, the "bachelor" Juan Fernández, *criado* of the abbot in 1342,[75] was mentioned from 1330 onwards. Until 1333, he simply testifies within the group of monks and servants in the monastery.[76] In 1340, he was the abbot's scribe;[77] then, between 1346 and 1348, he was public notary for the church of Sahagún.[78] In 1347, he was also *bachiller de la Gramática* (bachelor in grammar) in the school of the monastery of Sahagún.[79] His social status is revealed by the fact that another scribe, Alfonso Iohanes, figures as his servant in two documents (1346–1347).[80] His disappearance from the documentation coincides with the epidemic of the Black Death.

Juan Fernández was replaced in the office of public notary in the church of Sahagún by Alfonso Fernández, who held that position for the rest of Diego's time as abbot.[81] Juan Fernández was not the first to be the abbot's scribe or notary, since in 1328, under Martin II., Fernando Díaz is mentioned as holding this position.[82]

---

[72] In 1313, don Bartolomé figures as the "criado" of the prior of San Mancio: Colección, ed. V. Á. ÁLVAREZ PALENZUELA (note 3 above), doc. 2017. The use of "don", an abbreviated form of *domno* or *dominus*, indicates a position of importance within the local community. The same is to be thought of Ruy Fernández, the son of don Antón de Sahelices, "criado" to the sacrist in 1329 (Ibid., doc. 2101).

[73] In 1335, Alfonso Fernández, "criado" of the abbot Diego, acted as the abbot's procurator and as such he appeared before the abbot's vicar to claim the tithes due from the lands of a neighbour of Sahagún: E. MARTÍNEZ LIÉBANA, El dominio señorial (note 11 above), doc. 31. Between 1352 and 1354, a "criado" of the same name testified in three documents, perhaps he was the very same person. It may also have been the same Alfonso Fernández of Sahagún who, in 1347, was the procurator and *síndico* of the abbot and convent of Sahagún. The abbot had made him responsible for receiving and accepting the donation of an inheritance in Villanueva de San Mancio in order to found a chapel: Colección, ed. V. Á. ÁLVAREZ PALENZUELA (note 3 above), doc. 2285.

[74] Fernando Martínez cleric, Ruy Pérez cleric, Juan Fernández bachelor (Ibid. docs. 2033, 2111, 2232).

[75] Ibid., doc. 2232.

[76] Ibid., docs. 2111, 2131, 2146.

[77] Ibid., docs. 2203, 2204.

[78] Ibid., docs. 2255–2302.

[79] Ibid., doc. 2292. On the School of Sahagún: V. BELTRÁN DE HEREDIA, El Estudio del monasterio de Sahagún, in: La Ciencia Tomista 85 (1958), pp. 687–697.

[80] Colección, ed. V. Á. ÁLVAREZ PALENZUELA (note 3 above), docs. 2273, 2282.

[81] Ibid., doc. 2303. It is tempting to identify this Alfonso Fernández with the abbot's "criado" and procurator between 1335 and 1347, but the name is very common and we cannot be sure.

[82] Ibid., doc. 2093.

Apart from the abbot's notaries (*escribanos*), mentioned from 1328 onwards, the monastery resorted to the service of other legal experts. The lawyer Juan Alfonso appears repeatedly as a witness in documents related with lawsuits between 1335 and 1348. These are lawsuits and sentences concerning the payment of tithes, an agreement about the water falling from the roof of some houses of the cellarer, a dispute over a payment that the cellarer had to make during the annual fair, and a dispute over a property ceded for life to some donors. On two occasions, the judge is expressly asked to allow Juan Alfonso to act as the monastery's lawyer.[83]

Among the lay people who held a specialised office for the abbot, the convent or the officials, we have the stewards (*mayordomos*), doorkeepers and *reposteros* (confectioners). Their function was originally domestic service, but in practice they collected and received the rents from the properties of the abbacy, the tithes or tolls (*portazgos*) due to the monastery. They could negotiate leases of the properties for limited time periods. It can be seen how the same man appears one year as a doorkeeper and in another as a steward, doorkeeper and confectioner, doorkeeper and judge of the *banleuca* (*alcalde del coto*). They sometimes acted as procurators for the abbot or an official, and even as guarantors in important contracts. This demonstrates that they were economically well off.

The stewards were in charge of managing the properties and collecting the rents of an office. Unlike in other Benedictine monasteries, in Sahagún, there was no office of steward in 1338. This, despite the reference to a steward of the abbot in 1311 and of two stewards of the "charities" (1303, 1329),[84] perhaps the same office as the prior of "charities". On the other hand, there were at least two lay stewards (1315, 1317).[85] The letter of procuration given to the abbot's steward in 1311 specified his functions: to collect and receive all the rents from the properties of the abbot and the office of hosteler and all the offices the abbot held at the time; to rent out the properties for four years. So it does not seem as if these offices were static in the monastery, neither among the monks nor the lay servants.

The gatekeeper was in principle responsible for guarding the monastery's gate. Yet his office seems to have been more important and it is possible that he assumed the tasks normally undertaken by the steward. Thus, Pedro Mínguez, gatekeeper in 1313, appears in 1315 as the steward. He must have been a wealthy man because, together with the other known steward, Domingo Fernández, they were two of the guarantors named by the monastery in an agreement with the abbot of Arbas, an important figure in the royal court.[86] Some years later, the

---

[83] Ibid., docs. 2168, 2174, 2214, 2270, 2283, 2286, 2302.
[84] Ibid., docs. 1997, 1925, 2099.
[85] Ibid., docs. 2024, 2036.
[86] Ibid., docs. 2013, 2024, 2036.

gatekeeper was a scribe, Juan Pérez (1329),[87] and Alfonso Pérez, abbot's gatekeeper between 1340 and 1346, and again in 1348, acted as procurator to the cellarer in 1346.[88] All this indicates that he was not a servant with a low status. The documents mainly refer to the abbot's gatekeeper but also mention a gatekeeper of the convent (1338, 1346).[89]

The gatekeeper was an office with a duration of one year, though Alfonso Pérez held this office for at least five years. Little is known of his activity, but he is mentioned on one occasion as having the responsibility of collecting some of the monastery's rents. To be precise, in 1331, the gatekeepers of the monastery were in charge of collecting a third of the tithes from some lands owned by the office of the kitchener.[90] Similarly, in 1338, the abbot declared before the king that his gatekeepers were responsible for collecting the king's part in the toll (*portazgo*) of the town of Sahagún.[91] This same function could explain his role as procurator for the cellarer to reclaim the payment of certain tithes from various Muslims residing in the town.[92]

Another important official in the abbot's service was the confectioner, whose functions are not specified either.[93] There exists documentation from the time of Nicolas II.,[94] but he is mentioned with less frequency than the gatekeeper, likewise changing from one year to the next. It is worth mentioning that Simón García, confectioner in 1357, had been the gatekeeper in 1348.[95]

The abbot also named the mayors (*alcaldes*) and the bailiffs (*merinos*) of the town and the "coto". In the case of the town, the intervention of the council notably conditioned the choice, and they should be considered more as officials of the council than of the abbot. Nevertheless, he still controlled the bailiff and mayor of the "coto". The abbot's bailiff in the "coto" collected the manorial rents in the villages and areas around Sahagún, which were under the abbot's jurisdiction. The mayor resolved the legal matters in this same space. Their names also appear in the documentation of the monastery as witnesses of the activities

---

[87] Ibid., doc. 2101.
[88] Ibid., docs. 2203, 2219, 2232, 2270, 2271, 2308, 2309.
[89] Ibid., docs. 2193, 2273.
[90] Ibid., doc. 2119.
[91] Ibid., doc. 2272.
[92] Ibid., doc. 2270.
[93] H. GRASSOTI, El repostero en León y Castilla (siglos XII–XIV), in: Cuadernos de Historia de España 69 (1987), pp. 41–75. This deals with the office of king's "confectioner" and his possible functions. It places him within the framework of the domestic offices of the court with public functions, such as the chamberlain. It is useful as a comparison.
[94] Colección, ed. V. Á. ÁLVAREZ PALENZUELA (note 3 above), doc. 2040.
[95] Ibid., docs. 2378, 2380, 2305, 2308.

of the abbot or the convent.⁹⁶ In 1347, Alfonso Fernández appears as mayor of the "coto", probably the same Alfonso Fernández who acted as the abbot's gatekeeper.

2.6. The relatives of the abbot and the officials

The dispositions of the bull *Summi Magistri* against the relatives of the prelates and administrators was aimed at stopping them from benefitting from the monastery's properties by negotiating fraudulent leases with advantageous rents or by appropriating the goods, rents, deeds or properties, which was a widespread practice to which Sahagún was not immune.⁹⁷

The lists of witnesses demonstrate the importance of the monks' relatives. I have counted a total of 86 references to relatives. Prominent among these are Juan Pérez, abbot Diego's brother, who testifies in 32 documents between 1330 and 1352, and the abbot's nephew Diego Álvarez, who figures in 15 documents. In addition, another two brothers are mentioned, as well as two nephews of abbot Diego and a nephew of abbot Martin.⁹⁸ It is probable that the two Juan Álvarez, nephews of abbot Diego, are also the two canons of León and Palencia who, in 1347–1352, figure in the abbot's documents, and that one of them may also be the notary with apostolic authority who testified in the years 1347–1350.⁹⁹

The brothers and nephews of the officials also appear as witnesses or procurators. Worth noting are Alfonso Díaz and Pedro Díaz of San Mancio, brothers of the cellarer Juan of San Mancio, mentioned in seven documents between 1346 and 1347. Pedro acted in 1346 as procurator for his brother in a lawsuit concerning tithes belonging to the cellarer.¹⁰⁰ These relatives of the abbot and the officials possessed properties of the monastery and, one may suppose, they administered

---

⁹⁶ Ibid., docs. 2017, 2023, 2024, 2033, 2286, 2291.

⁹⁷ Bullarium, ed. A. TOMASSETTI (note 5 above), cap. X, pp. 368–369; cap. XV, pp. 372–373.

⁹⁸ Domingo Álvarez and Juan Álvarez only appear in the said documents: Colección, ed. V. Á. ÁLVAREZ PALENZUELA (note 3 above), docs. 2166, 2274. Alfonso Martínez, nephew of the abbot Martin; Diego Álvarez and two Juan Álvarez, nephews of the abbot Diego (Ibid., docs. 2093, 2231).

⁹⁹ Ibid., docs. 2282, 2288, 2302, 2315, 2325, 2349.

¹⁰⁰ Ibid., doc. 2270. The cellarer and later chamberlain, don Gonzalo, also acted with his relatives: two brothers and two nephews, the latter two, clerics (Ibid., docs. 2055, 2067, 2131). In one of these documents, Gonzalo Fernández Cidiel donated properties to his son, Juan Fernández, to the value of 3000 maravedis, so that the abbot of Sahagún would ordain him priest; the chamberlain and his two nephews who were clerics (Gonzalo Fernández and Ferrán Martínez) act as witnesses. Given that one of the brothers of the chamberlain is called Gonzalo Fernández, we may wonder whether the donor could well be the brother (Ibid., doc. 2131). Other officials whose brothers, nephews or brothers–in–law figure in the documentation are the wine–cellarer, the almoner, the sacrist, the prior, the third prior or the prior of San Mancio (Ibid., docs. 1971, 2060, 2085, 2128, 2203, 2206, 2291).

them. A cleric, Juan Pérez, brother of the sacrist don Gonzalo, received a church belonging to this office. The problem arose after the death of his brother, or after leaving the office, when the new sacrist demanded the rent due for the said church which Juan did not pay.[101]

The family of abbot Martin also received properties from the monastery. In 1382, his nephew don Alfonso donated a vineyard to the monastery in appreciation of the benefits received from his uncle which had allowed him and his parents to appropriate monastic properties without paying the correct price for them, as the nephew acknowledged in his testament, written when he was bishop of Salamanca. Alfonso belonged to an important family of the area (Cuevas) and had risen through the church hierarchy: before being bishop of Salamanca, he had been a canon of León and archdeacon in the churches of Orense and León. Undoubtedly, the economic support from his uncle, with the resources of the monastery, helped him on the way.[102]

3. Conclusions

The economic administration of the Benedictine monasteries of Castile in the first half of the fourteenth century was the responsibility of the abbot or prior and of the monks holding the various offices, in particular the sacrist, the chamberlain, the almoner, the steward and the cellarer. The importance of the cellarer had been considerably reduced, and this obedientiary had even disappeared from some monasteries. The other monks could, on occasion, act as procurators for the abbot and the convent, sometimes concerning matters of importance. The role of the convent is not clear, although it did participate in making important decisions, at least formally.

The bull *Summi Magistri* had an influence on this administration, but it did not imply the introduction of radical changes. The preparation of the accounts of 1338 is a consequence of this same bull, as well as the creation of the *arca común* (common chest) in the monastery of Sahagún, under the supervision of three monks. In general, the abbot and the officials continued to act with great autonomy, and the number of offices even grew.

---

[101] In the document, a brother of the new sacrist testifies (Ibid., doc. 2114).

[102] The testament (Ibid., doc. 2517) mentions his sister Sancha Rodríguez, his cousin Juan García de las Cuevas and his nephew Nuño García, son of the cousin. He was promoted to the diocese of Salamanca in 1375, when he was the archdeacon of Valderas (C. EUBEL, Hierarchia catholica Medii Aevi sive Summorum Pontificum, S.R.E. Cardinalium, Ecclesiarum Antistitum series. [I], Ab anno 1198 usque ad annum 1431 perducta, Patavii 1960, p. 429). Ut per litteras Apostolicas Online, Brepols: Urbain V, Lettres communes, doc. 13664 (31 Oct. 1365), 16935 (7 Aug. 1366), 21506 (23 Nov. 1367). Ibid., Grégoire XI, Lettres secrètes et curiales (Étranger), doc. 2053 (5 Aug. 1373).

The daily management was carried out by a group of lay servants of diverse social conditions, as well as by the relatives of the abbot and the officials. Little is known about their roles but it is clear that they collected rents and acted as procurators. In the case of the relatives, it is evident that they took advantage of the properties belonging to the monastery, a practice denounced by Pope Benedict XII.

The group of literate laymen (notaries, procurators, bachelors) began to become important towards the end of the period studied here. Some were servants of the monastery, but in general they were from outside the monastic family. They provided services to the monastery on either a regular or on an occasional basis in exchange for a salary or other economic retribution, but without working exclusively for the monastery.

The accounts of 1338 indicate a structure in which management and accounting were divided between the offices, though this arrangement was not highly developed. The annual deficit was normal and this, logically, generated the debt in both loans of money and, especially, long term renting with payment in advance.

The production of the monastic estate was not especially oriented towards the market. The levels of self consumption of wheat and wine were very high. However, expenses in cash were quite high and were covered by means of rents paid in cash or by the sale of the surplus agricultural produce, which came more from the collection of rents in kind, including tithes, than from the direct exploitation of the domains.

Zur Finanzpolitik geistlicher Ritterorden im Mittelalter

Jürgen Sarnowsky

Besitz und insbesondere eigenes Kapital stellten für geistliche Orden des Mittelalters generell ein erhebliches Problem dar. Die drei monastischen Gelübde, Gehorsam, Keuschheit und eben Armut, sollten zumindest die persönliche Armut der Ordensmitglieder gewährleisten. Wenn man, was vielfach geschah, die christliche Urgemeinde in Jerusalem als Modell für alle geistlichen Orden ansah und ihr zugleich Gütergemeinschaft und (relative) Besitzlosigkeit zuschrieb,[1] lag es aber auch nahe, von den Orden zumindest eine Beschränkung auf die notwendigsten Güter zu verlangen. Diese Vorstellung führten die Bettelorden zu einem Höhepunkt, und nicht zufällig suchten insbesondere die Franziskaner jeden Umgang mit Geld zu vermeiden.[2] Das stieß dort an seine Grenzen, wo die Ordensaufgaben vielfach erhebliche Investitionen und Aufwendungen erforderten, nicht zuletzt bei den geistlichen Ritterorden, die ihren Aufgaben meist weit entfernt von ihren Herkunftsregionen nachkommen mussten.[3]

Der folgende Beitrag ist vor diesem Hintergrund insbesondere der Finanzpolitik der drei großen geistlichen Ritterorden des Mittelalters, der Templer, Johanniter und des Deutscher Ordens, gewidmet. Dabei soll unter Finanzpolitik Folgendes verstanden werden:[4] 1. der Umgang mit den Ressourcen, die die Grundlage für die Finanzen der Orden bildeten; 2. die Erschließung weiterer Einnahmequellen; 3. darauf aufbauende Finanzgeschäfte im weiteren Sinne; 4. die Ver-

---

[1] Vgl. dazu C. HOFFARTH, Urkirche als Utopie. Die Idee der Gütergemeinschaft im späteren Mittelalter von Olivi bis Wyclif (Hamburger Studien zu Gesellschaften und Kulturen der Vormoderne 1), Stuttgart 2016.

[2] S. u.a. die Beiträge in: H.–D. HEIMANN / A. HILSEBEIN / B. SCHMIES / C. STIEGEMANN (Hgg.), Gelobte Armut. Armutskonzepte der franziskanischen Ordensfamilie vom Mittelalter bis in die Gegenwart, Paderborn/München 2012.

[3] Dazu s. H. BOOCKMANN, Herkunft und Einsatzgebiet. Beobachtungen am Beispiel des Deutschen Ordens, in: Z. H. NOWAK (Hg.), Ritterorden und Region, Politische, soziale und wirtschaftliche Verbindungen im Mittelalter (Ordines Militares 8), Toruń 1995, S. 7–19.

[4] Soweit ich sehe, fehlt eine historische Begriffsbildung, ähnliche Fragen z.B. in: G. DRÖGE, Die finanziellen Grundlagen des Territorialstaates, in: Vierteljahrsschrift für Sozial– und Wirtschaftsgeschichte 53 (1966), S. 145–161; W. REICHERT, Finanzpolitik und Landesherrschaft. Zur Entwicklung der Grafschaft Katzenelnbogen vom 12. bis zum 14. Jahrhundert, Trier 1985. Die Wirtschaftswissenschaft versteht unter (betrieblicher) Finanzpolitik „die Summe aller Maßnahmen der Finanzierung einer Unternehmung zur Befriedigung des Kapitalbedarfs, unterstützt durch Finanzplanung", W. EGGERT u.a., Art.: Finanzpolitik, in: Gabler Wirtschaftslexikon online: http://wirtschaftslexikon.gabler.de/Archiv/2335/finanzpolitik–v13.html [letzter Zugriff 24.10.2019].

teilung der finanziellen Mittel im Orden; 5. Ansätze für eine geregelte Haushaltsführung, insbesondere auf zentraler Ebene. Die Aspekte sind naturgemäß eng miteinander verbunden, wie auch der bereits 1994 von Malcolm BARBER für den Templerorden insgesamt eingeführte Begriff des 'Netzwerks' deutlich macht.[5] Die Erfüllung der Stiftungsaufgabe des 'Heidenkampfes' machte erforderlich, dass innerhalb der Orden frei über Material und Gelder verfügt werden konnte, um sie sinnvoll und effektiv in den Einsatzregionen wie dem Heiligen Land, der Ägäis, dem Baltikum oder auch dem Süden der Iberischen Halbinsel verwenden zu können. Dabei entstanden gewisse Zwänge, die eine Wechselwirkung zwischen den angesprochenen Aspekten von Finanzpolitik hervorriefen, etwa wenn unzureichende Ressourcen zu einer Verschuldung im Einsatzgebiet führten. Dennoch sollen die fünf Aspekte die Leitlinie für die folgenden Überlegungen bilden.[6]

***

(1) Der Umgang mit den Ressourcen, die die Grundlage für die Finanzen bildeten, war nicht zuletzt auch durch Art und Umfang der Besitzungen bestimmt, die die Orden erworben hatten. Grundsätzlich bildeten die Einkünfte aus der Landwirtschaft die Grundlage der Ordensfinanzen. Daher mussten die Ordensleitungen darauf bedacht sein, den aus Schenkungen und Käufen erwachsenen Ordensbesitz zu vermehren und effektiv zu nutzen. Neben den Abgaben der abhängigen Bevölkerung und Erträgen aus Eigenwirtschaft kamen auch die Einkünfte aus der gewerblichen Produktion, dem Ordenshandel, dem Transport von Pilgern, Kriegsbeute und Anderem mehr dazu. Bei den Johannitern wie dem Deutschen Orden sind zudem die Einnahmen aus der Landesherrschaft auf dem Dodekanes und in Preußen und Livland zu berücksichtigen, etwa aus der Münzprägung, Zöllen und Steuern. Eine erfolgreiche Finanzpolitik war weitgehend von äußeren Faktoren wie den Folgen von Pest, Kriegen und Natureinflüssen abhängig. Nach dem Verlust der Besitzungen im Heiligen Land kam es insbesondere im 14. und 15. Jahrhundert zu massiven Zerstörungen und Wüstungen durch Kriege und Fehden, im Westen durch den Hundertjährigen Krieg, die Hussiten- und Rosenkriege, im Baltikum durch die Kriege zwischen dem Deutschen Orden und Polen-Litauen, in der Ägäis durch die Konflikte der Johanniter mit Mamluken und Osmanen.

(1.1.) Der Grundbesitz entstand anfangs aus Schenkungen, die in Komtureien / Präzeptoreien mit einem Haupthaus zusammengefasst wurden. Dies ließ bis

---

[5] M. BARBER, The New Knighthood, Cambridge 1994, bes. Kap. 7, The Templar Network, S. 229–279.

[6] Für einen Überblick über die Wirtschaftsführung der Ritterorden s. J. SARNOWSKY, Die geistlichen Ritterorden. Anfänge – Strukturen – Wirkungen, Stuttgart 2018, S. 129–141.

zum Anfang des 13. bzw. (beim Deutschen Orden) des 14. Jahrhunderts allmählich nach.[7] Dazu kamen dann mehr oder weniger systematische Erwerbungen, die den Ordensbesitz in einzelnen Regionen ergänzten und abrundeten. In Huesca im nördlichen Aragón suchten die Templer z.B. ihre Besitzungen durch Aktivitäten auf dem lokalen Immobilienmarkt zu konsolidieren und besser zu nutzen.[8] So kauften und verkauften sie vom 12. bis zum 13. Jahrhundert Weinberge, Gärten, Olivenbaumplantagen, Weideland, Mühlen und Anderes, auch um die hier besonders wichtige Wasserversorgung sicher zu stellen. Ähnlich verdichteten die Brüder ihren Besitz in der Stadt Huesca. Die Templer setzten diese Politik bis in die letzten Jahre vor ihrer Auflösung fort. Im September 1294 tauschten sie ihren Anteil an der Stadt Tortosa, in der es immer wieder Probleme mit der Abgabenerhebung gegeben hatte, mit dem König gegen ausgedehnten Landbesitz im Norden des Königreichs Valencia mit erheblichen Einkünften (1319–1320: 40.000 sol. jährlich) und kauften wenige Jahre darauf, 1303, unter erheblichem finanziellen Aufwand einen Bezirk dazu, um einen 'Gürtel' von Templerbesitz vollständig zu machen.[9] Auch bei den spanischen Ritterorden machten Käufe teilweise einen erheblichen Teil der Erwerbungen aus, wenn z.B. das Haupthaus des Santiagoordens in Ucles zwischen 1174 und 1310 49 Schenkungen erhielt, aber in derselben Zeit immerhin in 33 Fällen – wohl zumeist kleinere – Besitzungen käuflich erwarb.[10]

Die Johanniter verfolgten eine ähnliche Linie,[11] wobei die Übernahme des Templerbesitzes nach der Aufhebung dieses Ordens neue Probleme schuf. Das lässt sich z.B. im brandenburgisch-mecklenburgischen Raum beobachten, wo das von den Herren von Werle gegründete und reich ausgestattete Mirow bereits am Ende des 13. Jahrhunderts „bedeutende Besitzungen durch Kauf […] erwerben" konnte.[12] In der Neumark wurde der von den Templern erworbene Besitz nach dem Vertrag von Kremmen (1318) neu organisiert und 1350 durch den endgültigen Erwerb von Lagow ergänzt, das anstelle ehemaliger Templerbesitzungen in

---

[7] Zum Rückgang der Schenkungen bei Templern, Johannitern und dem Orden von Santiago s. A. FOREY, The Military Orders from the Twelfth to the Fourteenth Centuries, London 1992, S. 121.

[8] M. BARBER, New Knighthood (wie Anm. 5), S. 265–266.

[9] L. GARCÍA GUIJARRO, The Growth of the Order of the Temple in the Northern Area of the Kingdom of Valencia at the Close of the Thirteenth Century: A Puzzling Development?, in: N. HOUSLEY (Hg.), Knighthoods of Christ. Essays presented to Malcolm Barber, Aldershot 2007, S. 165–181, hier S. 170–171, 178–180.

[10] Nach A. FOREY, Military Orders (wie Anm. 7), S. 108.

[11] Vgl. etwa J. PFLUGK–HARTTUNG, Die Anfänge des Johanniter–Ordens in Deutschland, besonders in der Mark Brandenburg und in Mecklenburg, Berlin 1899, S. 70: „Abrundung und Vergrößerung des Besitzstandes".

[12] Ebd., S. 72.

Großendorf und Zielenzig zu einer neuen Kommende ausgebaut wurde.[13] Ähnliches galt auch in vielen anderen Regionen. In Friesland baute z.B. die Kommende Abbingwehr das durch eine Schenkung der Häuptlinge Keno tom Brok und Enno von Pilsum 1402 in ihren Besitz gekommene Miedelsum systematisch zu einem Vorwerk aus.[14] 1437 umfasste dieses 220 Grasen, von denen 120 durch Kauf erworben worden waren und weitere 20 von Konventualen beim Eintritt in das Ordenshaus 'mitgebracht' wurden. Dabei konnte weit auseinander liegender Grundbesitz durch Tauschgeschäfte allmählich um das Vorwerk herum konzentriert werden.

Auch beim Deutschen Orden in Preußen findet sich diese Politik noch im 14. und früheren 15. Jahrhundert. Der Orden suchte die direkte Kontrolle über die Böden, die mit 50 % – 60 % ohnehin schon sehr hoch lag, noch zu Lasten der kleineren Grundherren auszuweiten, indem man Güter aufkaufte und sie entweder an zinspflichtige Bevölkerung ausgab oder als Ordenshof in die eigene Bewirtschaftung übernahm. So finanzierte der Tressler 1399 den Ankauf des Guts *Damerkow* durch den Pfleger zu Bütow für immerhin 380 m. preuß. und half dem Komtur von Osterode im selben Jahr beim Kauf des Gutes *Morlyn* von Thomas von Rakowitz. Während *Damerkow* gegen Zins an Bauern ausgegeben wurde, wandelte man *Morlyn* wahrscheinlich in einen Ordenshof um.[15] Eine intensive Erwerbspolitik begann nach 1402 in der neu erworbenen Neumark, wo der Orden eine deutlich schwächere Stellung hatte als in Preußen.[16] So oder so konnten auf diese Weise die Einkünfte gesteigert werden, durch die deutlich höheren Zinsleistungen der Bauern gegenüber den eher formalen Abgaben der kleineren Grundherren und durch eine verbesserte Versorgung der Ordenshäuser, bei der Überschüsse auch verkauft werden konnten.

(1.2.) Regional standen entweder Viehzucht oder Ackerbau im Zentrum der landwirtschaftlichen Produktion, dazu kamen besondere, teilweise sehr anspruchsvolle Bewirtschaftungsformen wie der Weinbau oder die Nutzung von Mühlen.[17] Die Orden dürften aber dabei nur selten eine eigenständige 'Strategie'

---

[13] C. GAHLBECK, Lagow oder Sonnenburg, in: C. GAHLBECK / H.–D. HEIMANN / D. SCHUMANN (Hgg.), Regionalität und Transfergeschichte. Ritterordenskommenden der Templer im nordöstlichen Deutschland und in Polen, Berlin 2014, S. 271–337, hier S. 285–286.

[14] E. SCHÖNINGH, Der Johanniterorden in Ostfriesland, Aurich 1973, S. 30.

[15] Dazu und zum Folgenden: J. SARNOWSKY, Die Wirtschaftsführung des Deutschen Ordens in Preußen (1382–1454) (Veröffentlichungen aus den Archiven Preußischer Kulturbesitz 34), Köln/Weimar/Wien 1993, S. 426, 429.

[16] Ebd., S. 427, mit Anm. 6.

[17] In der Regel waren die Mühlen gegen Zins verpachtet, seltener selbst bewirtschaftet (als Ausnahme beim Deutschen Orden in Preußen), wie das für die Templer etwa aus dem Inquest von 1185 hervorgeht, vgl. u.a. M. BARBER, New Knighthood (wie Anm. 5), S. 251; H. PRUTZ, Die geistlichen Ritterorden. Ihre Stellung zu kirchlichen, politischen, gesellschaftlichen und wirtschaftlichen Entwicklungen des Mittelalters, Berlin 1908, S. 343. – Text des Inquests in: J. CALEY / H. ELLIS / B. BANDINEL (eds.), William DUGDALE, Monasticon Anglicanum. A History of the Abbies and Other Monasteries, Hospitals, Frieries, and Cathedral and Collegiate

verfolgt haben, sondern folgten wohl wesentlich den regionalen Traditionen. Bei den Templern kann vielleicht das Haus in Baugy in der Normandie als charakteristisches Beispiel für die Landwirtschaft vieler englischer oder nordfranzösischer Häuser gelten. Ackerbau und Viehzucht wurden nach der Erhebung von 1307 etwa gleichgewichtig betrieben. So wurden im eigenen Wirtschaftsbetrieb, auf der Domäne, auf rund 18 Morgen Weizen und Roggen, auf 24 Morgen Gerste und Mischfutter, auf 15 Morgen Hafer, auf 14 Morgen Erbsen und auf 6 Morgen Wicke angebaut. An Rindern gab es dort 14 Milchkühe, einige mit Kälbern und weitere Rinder, 280 Schafe und Lämmer sowie 98 Schweine und einige wenige Pferde, darunter acht, die für den Einsatz mit schwerer Rüstung geeignet waren. Daneben verfügte der Konvent über Einkünfte aus Natural- und Geldabgaben.[18]

Es gab aber auch in Frankreich Templerhäuser, wo die Bodennutzung in sehr ungleicher Weise erfolgte. So wurde im Norden teilweise auf erheblich größeren Flächen Getreide ausgesät, so in den Häusern Grand-Selve und Aimont an der Somme sogar auf 215 bzw. 380 Hektar. Im Südwesten herrschte dagegen Viehzucht vor, so z.B. in der Komturei Sainte-Eulalie-du-Larzac in Südwestfrankreich, wo die Schafherde eines einzigen Hofes 1.700 Tiere umfasst haben soll und wo auch Rinder und Pferde gezüchtet wurden.[19] In Südfrankreich spielte zudem der Weinbau eine zentrale Rolle. Dort waren die Templer im Teilbau an den Erträgen ihrer Bauern beteiligt und erhielten oft ein Viertel der Ernte. Generell, auch bei den Johannitern, fand das System des Teilbaus insbesondere bei Sonderkulturen wie Wein, Oliven und Zuckerpflanzungen Verwendung.[20]

Bei den Johannitern hingen die Bewirtschaftungsformen wie bei den Templern von den lokalen Gegebenheiten ab. Waren die Besitzungen klein und verstreut wie im englischen Essex,[21] wurden sie gegen Zins ausgegeben, bei größeren zusammenhängenden Ländereien wie teilweise in Italien übernahmen die Brüder die Verwaltung selbst. Im Zentrum stand dabei jeweils die Präzeptorei, in der die

---

Churches in England and Wales, 6 Bde., London 1817–1830, Bd. 6, 2, S. 821–831, dort S. 822, 824 zu den Mühlenzinsen.

[18] Nach dem Inventar bei L. DELISLE, Études sur la condition de la classe agricole et l'état de l'agriculture en Normandie au moyen–âge, Paris 1903, Nr. XVI, S. 721–728; übersetzt in: The Templars. Selected Sources, ed. M. BARBER / K. BATE (Manchester Medieval Sources), Manchester 2002, S. 191–201.

[19] Zu den Zahlen vgl. A. DÉMURGER, Les Templiers. Une chevalerie chrétienne au Moyen Âge, Neuaufl., Paris 2005, S. 293.

[20] J. RILEY–SMITH, The Knights of St John in Jerusalem and Cyprus, c. 1050–1310, London 1967, S. 433–434.

[21] M. GERVERS, Pro defensione Terre Sancte: the Development and Exploitation of the Hospitallers' Landed Estate in Essex, in: M. BARBER (Hg.), The Military Orders. Fighting for the Faith and Caring for the Sick, Aldershot 1994, S. 3–20.

verschiedenen Einkünfte, auch aus abhängigen Häusern, gesammelt wurden. Neben grundherrlichen Einnahmen waren dies Zehnte und weitere kirchliche Abgaben, aber auch Gerichtsgefälle und Ähnliches.[22]

Beim Deutschen Orden erreichten die Pachterträge an Getreide im Reich noch im 15. Jahrhundert ähnliche Dimensionen wie die Einkünfte aus Geldzinsen. In Eigenwirtschaft wurde vielfach Getreide angebaut, vor allem in der Nähe der großen Städte. Wenn nicht eine gewisse Konzentration des Besitzes vorlag, waren die Ländereien zumeist verpachtet, wobei im 14. und 15. Jahrhundert Erbpacht oft durch Zeitpacht abgelöst wurde. Von größerer Bedeutung war daneben die Verpachtung im Teilbau, d. h. unter Beteiligung an der Ernte, bei Sonderkulturen wie Weinbergen. Der Besitz daran erreichte in der Ballei Koblenz um die Mitte des 14. Jahrhunderts seine größte Ausdehnung; danach fielen Weinberge aufgrund klimatischer Veränderungen und einer verschlechterten Absatzlage wüst oder wurden vernachlässigt.[23]

In Preußen bildeten die Geldzinse der deutschrechtlichen Dörfer die Basis der Einkünfte, da der Orden sein Land zumeist an zinspflichtige Bauern vergeben hatte, die offenbar abhängig von der Fruchtbarkeit der Böden zu zinsen hatten. Dazu kamen Naturalabgaben wie Hühner, Honig und Pfeffer sowie das Getreide insbesondere der prußischen Dörfer. Daneben spielte für die Versorgung der Ordensbrüder gerade in Preußen die Eigenwirtschaft eine zentrale Rolle. Auf den Ordenshöfen betrieben Hofleute, Knechte und Mägde Ackerbau und Viehzucht. Die Viehhaltung erreichte schon um 1400 einen Höhepunkt, als es auf den Ordenshöfen in Preußen insgesamt rund 10.000 Rinder, 21.000 Schweine und 60.000 Schafe, aber auch Ziegen, Gänse und Bienen gab.[24] Damit wurden große Mengen Butter, Käse, Wolle und Felle produziert. So erhielt das Haus Elbing um 1386 aus den Höfen jährlich 12 Tonnen Butter, auf der Marienburg fielen vor 1410 300 Lämmerfelle für die Bekleidung der Ordensbrüder an.[25] Bei einigen Ordensburgen gab es Weinbau, so in Althaus-Kulm, das vor 1440 jährlich bis zu 15 Fass (etwa 2.800 Liter) Wein produzierte, auch wenn dieser wegen seiner minderen Qualität vor allem dem Personal vorbehalten blieb.[26]

---

[22] J. SARNOWSKY, Die Johanniter. Ein geistlicher Ritterorden in Mittelalter und Neuzeit, München 2011, S. 23; zum Eingreifen der Ordensleitung in lokale Strukturen vgl. u.a. DERS., Macht und Herrschaft im Johanniterorden des 15. Jahrhunderts. Verfassung und Verwaltung der Johanniter auf Rhodos (1421–1522) (Vita regularis 14), Münster 2001, bes. S. 131–134 (für die Generalkapitel).

[23] Dazu insbesondere K. VAN EICKELS, Die Deutschordensballei Koblenz und ihre wirtschaftliche Entwicklung im Mittelalter (Quellen und Darstellungen zur Geschichte des Deutschen Ordens 52), Marburg 1995, bes. S. 117–120.

[24] S. die Tabellen J. SARNOWSKY, Wirtschaftsführung des Deutschen Ordens in Preußen (wie Anm. 15), S. 277–280.

[25] Ebd., S. 274.

[26] Ebd., S. 275.

(1.3.) Die Einkünfte der Ordenshäuser kamen daneben auch aus anderen Erwerbszweigen. In der Komturei Douzens unterhielten die Templer zahlreiche Mühlen, die auch für die Tuchverarbeitung genutzt wurden. In Aragón sorgte der Orden im Gebiet des Rio Cinca für die Anlage eines komplexen, allgemein zugänglichen Bewässerungssystems und erhielt dafür Abgaben aus den Mühlen.[27] Oftmals waren wie z.B. im Pariser Gebiet Handwerker zu Zinszahlungen an die Templer verpflichtet.[28] Dies betraf nicht nur Geldzinsen, sondern auch die Ablieferung von gewerblichen Produkten. In Valencia besaß der Orden Backhäuser, für deren Betrieb die Bäcker jedes zwanzigste der von ihnen gebackenen Brote abliefern mussten, und in Provins vergab das Ordenshaus gegen Pacht eine Werkstatt für Ziegelherstellung, kontrollierte ein Handelshaus und Läden für Obsthändler.[29] Die Templer profitierten zudem vom Warenumschlag auf den Messen der Champagne, wo sie seit der Mitte des 12. Jahrhunderts einen Anteil an den Gebühren der Messe zu Troyes besaßen. In Provins mussten die Bürger um 1270 für das Abwiegen von Wolle Abgaben zahlen, was zu Protesten führte.[30] Anderenorts erhielten die Templer Einkünfte aus Markt- und Wegerechten. Ähnlich war das bei Johannitern und Deutschem Orden.

Die Verarbeitung der landwirtschaftlichen Erträge erfolgte vielfach in den Ordenshäusern selbst durch Handwerker, die in den Diensten der Orden standen. So wurden in den Komtureien mit intensiver Viehhaltung Häute verarbeitet oder Käse hergestellt. Überschüsse der eigenen Region wurden zudem zum Kauf gewerblicher Produktion aus anderen Regionen verwandt, sodass z.B. Tuch mit Getreideverkäufen bezahlt werden konnte. Auch gewerbliche Produkte wurden auf den Burgen selbst hergestellt. Beim Deutschen Orden arbeiteten allein auf dem Ordensschloss in Elbing um 1386 rund 150 Handwerker und Knechte.[31] Darunter fanden sich jedoch nur wenige Meister und qualifizierte Handwerker, so dass sie selten mit den städtischen Handwerkern konkurrierten. Vielmehr kam es zur Kooperation, wenn Tuchmacher Wolle beim Orden kauften oder Gerber Leder zur Weiterverarbeitung in den Burgen verkauften. Der Orden deckte sich ohnehin bei den städtischen Handwerkern ein, wenn besondere Produkte benötig wurden oder die eigenen Möglichkeiten nicht ausreichten.[32]

---

27 A. DÉMURGER, Les Templiers (wie Anm. 19), S. 308.
28 H. PRUTZ, Die geistlichen Ritterorden (wie Anm. 17). S. 377, 402.
29 M. BARBER, New Knighthood (wie Anm. 5), S. 293.
30 H. NICHOLSON, Templars, Hospitallers, and Teutonic Knights. Images of the Military Orders 1128–1291, Leicester/London/New York 1995, S. 76.
31 A. SEMRAU, Der Wirtschaftsplan des Ordenshauses Elbing aus dem Jahre 1386, in: Mitteilungen des Coppernicus–Vereins für Wissenschaft und Kunst zu Thorn 45 (1937), S. 1–74, hier S. 48.
32 R. CZAJA, Der Anteil des städtischen Handwerks an der Versorgung der Burgen des Deutschen Ordens im mittelalterlichen Preußen, in: Beiträge zur Geschichte Westpreußens 16 (1999), S. 39–54.

***

(2) Die grundherrlichen und gewerblichen Einkünfte wurden im Laufe der Zeit, sofern möglich, weiter ausgebaut und vermehrt. Dazu wurden aber auch weitere Einkünfte erschlossen, die über den Kern der Finanzierung geistlicher Institutionen hinausgehen. Das betraf neben den noch anzusprechenden Finanzgeschäften insbesondere den Aufbau eines Eigenhandels sowie die Nutzung (ritter)ordenstypischer Einnahmequellen wie der Transport von Pilgern, das Sammeln von Almosen sowie die Beute aus kriegerischen Unternehmungen.

(2.1.) Neben den Gewerben spielte auch der Handel für die Einkünfte der Orden eine Rolle. Für die Templer erleichterten die Zollbefreiungen und weiteren Rechte, die der Orden vielerorts erhielt, um seinen Aufgaben nachkommen zu können, den Handel mit seinen Produkten. Die Komtureien in den Midlands und Essex exportierten ihre Getreideüberschüsse über die Häfen an der englischen Ostküste. In England und der Champagne handelten die Templer mit Wolle und Wollprodukten, und für die Messe zu Provins durften sie jeweils 40 Fass Wein abgabenfrei einführen.[33] Die landwirtschaftlichen Erträge sicherten somit nicht nur den Unterhalt der Brüder in den Ordenshäusern im Westen, sondern verschafften dem Orden auch erhebliche Geldmittel, um die Aufgaben im Heiligen Land zu bewältigen.

Auch die Johanniter nutzten spätestens seit dem 13. Jahrhundert vielfach die auf den eigenen Ländereien erzielten Überschüsse, um aus Verkäufen Einnahmen zu erzielen. In Sizilien, das eine zentrale Rolle für die Versorgung zunächst des Heiligen Landes, später auch von Rhodos mit Lebensmitteln spielte, bewirtschaftete der Orden Weinberge und baute Getreide an, das exportiert wurde. In Aragón wie in England erwarben die Brüder Wälder und erzielten Einnahme durch erhebliche Mengen an Holz, die verkauft wurden. So wurde etwa 1240 ein Teil des Waldes von Leicester von Simon de Montfort, dem Earl von Leicester, erworben, die Bäume wurden gefällt, das Holz wurde verkauft.[34] In Aragón schloss der Kastellan von Amposta 1354 einen Vertrag, nach dem am Ordenshaus Caspe Holz im beachtlichen Wert von 156.000 Barceloneser sueldos liefern sollte. Dazu entstand teilweise auch eine eigene Infrastruktur. So erhielt der Kastellan bereits 1351 die königliche Erlaubnis, im Mündungsgebiet des Ebros bei Ulldecona zur Ausfuhr von Getreide, Wein und anderen Gütern einen eigenen kleinen Hafen einzurichten.[35] Der lokale Handel der Johanniter wurde vielfach durch Zollbefreiungen erleichtert, wie etwa in Devon in England, wo sich die

---

[33] H. PRUTZ, Die geistlichen Ritterorden (wie Anm. 17), S. 401.

[34] Zu Sizilien und England s. die Hinweise bei H. NICHOLSON, The Knights Hospitallers, Woodbridge, Sussex 2001, S. 101.

[35] A. LUTTRELL, The Economy of the Fourteenth–Century Aragonese Hospital (1994/95), ND in: The Hospitaller State on Rhodes and its Western Provinces, 1306–1462 (Collected Studies Series), Aldershot 1999, Nr. XIV, hier S. 763.

Einwohner von Plumpton und Dartmouth über die durch Zollbefreiungen geförderte Konkurrenz beklagten.[36]

Ähnliches galt im Einsatzgebiet. Aus Rhodos und aus Zypern, wo man den Templerbesitz übernahm, exportierte man Zucker, Seife und Leinentücher und aus Malta später Baumwolle, Orangen und die vom Orden aufgezogenen Falken. Gerade das Geschäft mit Zucker hatte dauerhafte Bedeutung. Schon im 14. Jahrhundert wurde in Paris und anderen Städten Frankreichs Zucker im Wert von über 6000 Florenen verkauft;[37] um 1450 wurde die Zuckerproduktion auf Zypern ertragreich verpachtet.[38] Der Handel wurde im Wesentlichen von Kaufleuten aus dem westlichen Mittelmeer getragen. Die Bürger von Narbonne und Montpellier durften sich 1356 auf Rhodos einen eigenen Fondaco einrichten und dort frei eigene und fremde Produkte umzuschlagen.[39] Die Johanniter konnten sich zudem am Tuchhandel beteiligen, da insbesondere das englische Priorat seine Responsionen in Gestalt von Tuchen übersandte. Diese wurden teilweise verkauft, etwa 1380 im Wert von über 14.000 Florenen nach Marseille und Barcelona.[40]

Auch beim Deutschen Orden erlaubten schon die Überschüsse im Reich Handelsgeschäfte. So nutzte die Ballei Koblenz schon seit dem 13. Jahrhundert ihre Zollprivilegien, um ihre Weine nach Kampen bzw. Dordrecht und von dort aus nach Antwerpen und Mecheln zu senden, und importierte mit Hilfe der Erlöse unter anderem Tuche aus Mecheln sowie Salz und Heringe aus Kampen, Dordrecht und Antwerpen.[41] Eine zentrale Rolle spielte aber vor allem der von Preußen aus betriebene Ordenshandel. Die Grundlage dafür bildeten die Privilegien Alexanders IV. und Urbans IV. von 1257 bzw. 1263,[42] die dem Orden den Handel mit Überschüssen selbst erzeugter Produkte erlaubten, um sich mit notwendigen Waren zu versorgen. Dies stand auch während der Blütezeit des Ordenshandels um 1400 im Zentrum. So hatten die beiden Großschäffer zu Marienburg und Königsberg, die den Ordenshandel leiteten, an ihre Konvente und andere Ordenshäuser ein weites Spektrum an Waren zu liefern. Gestützt auf die Überschüsse an Getreide, auf das Bernstein-Monopol des Ordens sowie auf den Export von Holz, Asche, Wachs, Teer und Flachs, führten sie Wolle, Tücher,

---

[36] H. NICHOLSON, Templars, Hospitallers, and Teutonic Knights (wie Anm. 30), S. 76.

[37] A. LUTTRELL, Actividades economicas de los Hospitalarios de Rodas en el Mediterraneo occidental durante el siglo XIV (1959), ND in: DERS., The Hospitallers in Cyprus, Rhodes, Greece and the West, 1291–1440 (Collected Studies Series), London 1978, Nr. VII, S. 178.

[38] J. SARNOWSKY, Macht und Herrschaft im Johanniterorden (wie Anm. 22), S. 425, 495–496.

[39] A. LUTTRELL, Actividades economicas de los Hospitalarios (wie Anm. 37), S. 178.

[40] Ebd., S. 179–180.

[41] Dazu K. VAN EICKELS, Die Deutschordensballei Koblenz (wie Anm. 23), bes. S. 160–167.

[42] M. HEIN, Die päpstlichen Handelsprivilegien für den Deutschen Orden von 1257 und 1263, in: Altpreußische Forschungen 15 (1938), S. 235–237; J. SARNOWSKY, Wirtschaftsführung des Deutschen Ordens in Preußen (wie Anm. 15), S. 285.

Salz, Öl, Fisch und Luxuswaren wie Gewürze, Wein, Zucker und Seide ein, die zuerst den Ordenshäusern zugutekamen, bevor weitere Waren im Land verkauft werden konnten.

Das um 1400 voll entwickelte System des Ordenshandels baute nicht auf der Konkurrenz zu, sondern auf der Kooperation mit den preußischen Kaufleuten auf.[43] Die Lieger, Wirte und Diener der Großschäffer in England, Flandern, Lübeck, Livland, Lemberg und im Ordensland waren preußische Kaufleute, die die hansischen Privilegien nicht nur für sich, sondern auch für den Orden nutzten. Die Jahre um 1400 markieren den Höhepunkt des Ordenshandels. So sind für die Marienburger Großschäfferei zum Jahr 1404 rund 52.000 Mark an sicheren Waren und Forderungen genannt, für die Königsberger zu 1406 sogar rund 77.000 Mark, bei einem Betriebskapital von 30.000 Mark.[44] Dabei handelte es sich allerdings um Schulden, die bis in die 1380er Jahre zurückreichten, nicht um Jahresumsätze. Der Handel ging zurück, als die preußischen Kaufleute ihre Unterstützung entzogen. Nach 1410 herrschten in den Schuldbüchern der Großschäffer vor allem „ungewisse Forderungen" vor, selbst die Versorgung der Konvente wurde schwieriger.[45]

(2.2.) Über die landwirtschaftlichen und grundherrlichen Einnahmequellen hinaus verfügten die Ritterorden noch über besondere Einkünfte. Gerade im 13. Jahrhundert wird die zunehmende Zahl von Pilgerreisen ins Heilige Land finanzielle Gewinne gebracht haben, wie der Vertrag von Johannitern und Templern mit Marseille von 1234 deutlich macht. Durch diesen wurden sie darauf beschränkt, „nur zwei ihrer eigenen Schiffe zweimal im Jahr im Hafen von Marseille zu halten, zu beladen oder zu entladen, nämlich zwei Schiffe im *passagium* des Augusts, und zwar eins vom Templerorden, das andere vom Hospitalorden, und im Passa- oder März-*passagium* ebenfalls zwei Schiffe, eins vom Tempel, eins vom Hospital, zur Beförderung der Angehörigen und des Eigentums der beiden Orden".[46] Die Zahl der Pilger wurde auf – schon unglaublich hohe – 1500 je Schiff

---

[43] Dazu insbesondere R. CZAJA, Der Handel des Deutschen Ordens und der preußischen Städte – Wirtschaft zwischen Zusammenarbeit und Realität, in: Z. H. NOWAK (Hg.), Ritterorden und Region (Ordines militares. Colloquia Torunensia Historica 8), Toruń 1995, S. 111–123.

[44] Übersicht bei J. SARNOWSKY, Wirtschaftsführung des Deutschen Ordens in Preußen (wie Anm. 15), Tabelle 87, S. 574.

[45] Vgl. ebd., S. 292–293.

[46] Text des Vertrags von 1233 in: Cartulaire général de l'Ordre des Hospitaliers de S. Jean de Jérusalem (1100–1310), ed. J. DELAVILLE LE ROULX, 4 Bde., Paris 1894–1905, Bd. 2, Nr. 2067, S. 462–464; übersetzt bei: Der Johanniter-Orden, der Malteser-Orden, der ritterliche Orden des hl. Johannes vom Spital zu Jerusalem. Seine Aufgaben, seine Geschichte, ed. A. WIENAND, Köln 1970, Anhang 16, S. 592–594, hier S. 593.

begrenzt, wovon die Kaufleute aber noch ausgenommen waren, welche die gewöhnlichen städtischen Abgaben entrichten sollten.[47] Bei Bedarf konnten weitere Schiffe nur für den Orden, nicht für Kaufleute oder Pilger, ausgerüstet werden. Mit dem Verlust des Heiligen Landes ging diese Einnahmequelle allerdings verloren. Nur noch die Venezianer profitierten von den Pilgern, denen sie im 15. Jahrhundert regelmäßige Dienste zwischen Venedig und Jaffa anboten, obwohl die Johanniter immer noch zahlende Gäste auf ihren Schiffen nach Rhodos mitnahmen.[48]

Im selben Kontext ist auch auf die Sammlung von Almosen und Ablassgeldern hinzuweisen, die in allen Orden eine wichtige Rolle spielte. Beim Deutschen Orden gab es zunächst umfangreiche Ablässe für die Unterstützung des Ordens insgesamt und für die Kriege gegen Prußen, Liven und Litauer, dann auch für einzelne Balleien, Ordenshäuser und -kirchen.[49] Noch im frühen 16. Jahrhundert wurden zwei Ablasskampagnen zugunsten des livländischen Ordenszweiges organisiert. Die Bedeutung der Ablässe für den Orden zeigt sich nicht zuletzt darin, dass man sie in „Ablasssummarien" zusammenstellte.[50] Bei den Johanniter gab es derartige Ablasskampagnen etwa zur Verteidigung Smyrnas in den 1390er Jahren oder zur Unterstützung für Rhodos in den 1480er Jahren.

(2.3.) Als eine Besonderheit kamen bei den geistlichen Ritterorden noch Erträge aus militärischen Unternehmungen hinzu. Im 12. Jahrhundert waren es für die Templer Gewinne aus den Auseinandersetzungen mit den islamischen Gegnern, die die Finanzen des Ordens aufbesserten. 1154 erhielten sie aus Ägypten 60.000 Dinare als Lösegeld für den gefangen genommenen Sohn des Wesirs,[51] Anfang der 1170er Jahre bekamen sie einen jährlichen Tribut von 2.000 Dinaren von den Assassinen,[52] und für die Iberische Halbinsel sind mindestens in einem

---

47 Dazu J. HASECKER, Die Johanniter und die Wallfahrt nach Jerusalem (1480–1522) (Nova Mediaevalia. Quellen und Studien zum europäischen Mittelalter 5), Göttingen 2008, S. 58.

48 Ebd., S. 60, 68–70.

49 Allgemein s. A. EHLERS, Die Ablasspraxis des Deutschen Ordens im Mittelalter (Quellen und Studien zur Geschichte des Deutschen Ordens), Marburg 2007; zu den livländischen Kampagnen s. ebd., S. 385–402; L. ARBUSOW [d.J.], Die Beziehungen des Deutschen Ordens zum Ablasshandel seit dem 15. Jahrhundert, in: Mitteilungen aus dem Gebiete der Geschichte Liv-, Est- und Kurlands 20 (1910), S. 367–478; zu den Balleien vgl. K. MILITZER, Von Akkon zur Marienburg: Verfassung, Verwaltung und Sozialstruktur des Deutschen Ordens 1190–1309 (Quellen und Studien zur Geschichte des Deutschen Ordens 56; Veröffentlichungen der Internationalen Historischen Kommission zur Erforschung des Deutschen Ordens 9), Marburg 1999, S. 211.

50 Dazu s. A. EHLERS, Ablasssummarien als Zeugnisse de Schriftlichkeit im Deutschen Orden, in: R. CZAJA / J. SARNOWSKY (Hgg.), Die Rolle der Schriftlichkeit in den geistlichen Ritterorden: innere Organisation, Sozialstruktur, Politik (Ordines Militares. Colloquia Torunensia Historica 15), Toruń 2009, S. 167–180.

51 A. FOREY, Military Orders (wie Anm. 7), S. 99.

52 M. BARBER, New Knighthood (wie Anm. 5), S. 103.

Fall hohe Zahlen von Beutetieren belegt.[53] Die Niederlagen des 13. Jahrhunderts führten allerdings dazu, dass sich die Chancen für hohe Beute verringerten.

Ähnliches galt für die Johanniter, auch wenn sich die Rahmenbedingungen nach 1291 verschoben. Einkünfte ergaben sich gelegentlich aus einzelnen militärischen Unternehmen wie etwa der Eroberung und Plünderung Alexandrias durch ein Kreuzfahrerheer 1365, an der der Orden beteiligt war, oder bei Zusammenstößen zwischen der kleinen Flotte der Johanniter und ihren muslimischen Gegnern. Generell waren die Grenzen zwischen militärischer Aktion, Kaperei und Piraterie fließend. In Kriegszeiten galten Überfälle auf die Schiffe der Gegner als legitim, aber auch sonst kam es immer wieder zu Konflikten. Die Johanniter duldeten Piraten, solange sie nicht gegen Christen vorgingen, und profitierten von ihrem Raubgut durch einen erhöhten Zoll für die Waren, die nach Rhodos gebracht wurden und dort verkauft werden sollten.[54]

Seit dem 15. Jahrhundert wurde der *corso*, die von Meister und Rat autorisierte Kaperei gegen die Gegner des Christentums, in festen Formen organisiert. So erhielten etwa im April 1413 zwei Brüder der französischen Zunge die Erlaubnis, auf eigene Kosten „gegen die ungläubigen Feinde unseres Ordens" vorzugehen und ihre Güter einzuziehen.[55] Ausgenommen davon waren die Verbündeten der Johanniter und jene Muslime, mit denen ein Waffenstillstand geschlossen war.[56] Darüber hinaus gehende Angriffe wurden auf Rhodos vor Gericht gebracht. Später verstand man diese militärischen Unternehmen vielfach als wirtschaftliche Investition, und der Orden entwickelte Regeln, um nicht die Kontrolle über die Ereignisse zu verlieren.

***

(3) Alle drei großen Orden ließen sich auf dieser Grundlage auf Finanzgeschäfte im weiteren Sinne ein. So hatten fremde, nicht eigene Gelder den wesentlichen Anteil an den finanziellen Aktivitäten der Templer. Zwei Faktoren spielten hier eine Rolle. Zum einen wurden im lateinischen Westen generell geistliche Institutionen dafür genutzt, Gelder oder Wertgegenstände von Privatpersonen zu de-

---

53 A. Forey, Military Orders (wie Anm. 7), S. 99, seien nach einem Bericht einmal 50.000 Schafe, 1.200 Ziegen und 150 Gefangene von einer Expedition in Spanien zurückgebracht worden.

54 J. Sarnowsky, Macht und Herrschaft im Johanniterorden (wie Anm. 22), S. 452.

55 Dazu s. A. Luttrell, The Earliest Documents on the Hospitaller Corso at Rhodes: 1413 and 1416 (1995), ND in: The Hospitaller State on Rhodes and its Western Provinces, 1306–1462 (Collected Studies Series), Aldershot 1999, Nr. VIII, S. 183.

56 Dazu u.a. J. Sarnowsky, Macht und Herrschaft im Johanniterorden (wie Anm. 22), S. 79, 497.

ponieren, weil man die Gefahr von Übergriffen für geringer hielt als bei weltlichen Personen und Instanzen.[57] Im Fall der Templer bot sich dies auch deshalb an, weil ihre – teilweise befestigten – Ordenshäuser besondere Sicherheit versprachen. Zum anderen waren es die Aufgaben des Ordens für das Heilige Land, die fremde Gelder in die Häuser der Templer brachten. So waren sie 1220 und 1281 an der Sammlung von Kreuzzugssteuern und -zehnten beteiligt,[58] verwalteten Testamente und Stiftungen oder erhielten im Westen Geld von Pilgern und Kreuzfahrern, das diese im Heiligen Land wieder ausgezahlt bekommen sollten. All dies machte schon früh bankähnliche Geschäfte erforderlich. Über die Deposita musste regelmäßig abgerechnet werden, da zum Teil auch Forderungen der Depositare eingezogen wurden oder die Hinterlegung von Wertgegenständen mit Pfand- und Darlehensgeschäften verbunden war. Die Gelder der Pilger und Kreuzfahrer mussten ins Heilige Land überführt oder so mit den Geldern des Ordens verrechnet werden, dass eine Auszahlung vor Ort möglich war. Teilweise war es auch erforderlich, regionale gegen überregionale Münzsorten zu wechseln. Es ist so kein Zufall, dass man in diesen Geschäften der Templer die Anfänge des europäischen Bankwesens gesehen hat. Der Orden konnte durchaus mit den aufsteigenden italienischen Bankiers aus der Lombardei bzw. aus Siena und Florenz konkurrieren, da diese zunächst noch kein Netz von 'Filialen' besaßen, das den zahlreichen Häusern des Ordens im Westen wie im Heiligen Land entsprochen hätte.

Zu den Depositaren der Templer gehörten insbesondere die westeuropäischen Herrscher,[59] die zeitweilig dem Orden ganz oder mindestens teilweise den königlichen Schatz anvertrauten. Ähnlich bedienten sich auch viele Kaufleute der Templerhäuser, um ihre Gelder sicher unterzubringen. Die Brüder hatten den Ruf, die Reichtümer nur gegen schriftliche oder persönliche Anweisung ihrer Besitzer wieder herauszugeben. Selbst in einer Notsituation wie während der Gefangennahme Ludwigs IX. auf dem Kreuzzug in Ägypten im Frühjahr 1250

---

[57] Zu den Deposita allgemein s. A. Forey, Military Orders (wie Anm. 7), S. 115–117; A. Démurger, Les Templiers (wie Anm. 19), S. 317–320; M. Barber, New Knighthood (wie Anm. 5), S. 267–268.

[58] Dazu s. das Schreiben Honorius III. an den päpstlichen Legaten vom 24. Juli 1220, gedruckt: Epistolae Saeculi XIII e Regestis Pontificum Romanorum, ed. C. Rodenberg (MGH Epistolae), 1, Berlin 1880, Nr. 24, S. 89–91; bzw. das Schreiben Martins IV. an den Abt von Cîteaux vom 21. Oktober 1281, bei L. Delisle, Mémoire sur les opérations financières des Templiers (Mémoires de l'Institut national de France. Académie des inscriptions et belles–lettres XXXIII 2), Paris 1889, Nr. xviii, S. 112–113; beides übersetzt in: The Templars. Selected Sources, ed. M. Barber / K. Bate (wie Anm. 18), S. 203–209.

[59] Dazu u.a. M.–L. Bulst-Thiele, Der Prozeß gegen den Templerorden, in: J. Fleckenstein / M. Hellmann, Die geistlichen Ritterorden Europas (Vorträge und Forschungen 26), Sigmaringen 1980, S. 375–402, hier S. 377–378.

musste der Marschall des Ordens, Renaut de Vichiers, förmlich gezwungen werden, die ihm anvertrauten Gelder herauszugeben.[60] Vor diesem Hintergrund lag es nahe, vor einer Pilgerfahrt oder einem Kreuzzug seine finanziellen Angelegenheiten mit Hilfe der Templer zu regeln und Gelder an das Ziel der Reise transferieren zu lassen. Das galt, wie das Testament des Pierre Sarrasin von 1220 belegt,[61] bereits für Pilgerfahrten innerhalb Europas, in diesem Fall nach Santiago de Compostela, vor allem aber für die Teilnahme an Unternehmen ins Heilige Land.

Die Ressourcen des Ordens ermöglichten es ihm, den Herrschern und Autoritäten immer wieder mit Anleihen zu Hilfe zu kommen. So waren die Templer schon an der Finanzierung des Zweiten Kreuzzugs durch Ludwig VII. von Frankreich 1147/1148 beteiligt, ebenso an den Lösegeldern zur Befreiung Ludwigs IX. nach seiner Gefangennahme in Ägypten 1250. 1215 erhielt König Johann von den Templern gegen eine Sicherheit sogar Gelder zur Bezahlung der gegen die englischen Barone eingesetzten Söldner, und sein Enkel Eduard I. lieh sich 1272 erhebliche Summen für seinen Kreuzzug.[62] 1260 ließ der Patriarch von Jerusalem, Guillaume d'Agen, von den Templern Gelder zur Unterstützung der durch den Mamluken-Sultan Baibars bedrohten Kreuzfahrerstaaten überweisen.[63] Neben Privatpersonen nahmen auch andere geistliche Institutionen wie der Abt von Cluny Darlehen bei den Templern auf, selbst wenn die Konditionen teilweise ungünstig waren.[64] Die Brüder gingen sogar so weit, Schulden auf dem Rechtsweg einzufordern; einmal wurde sogar Klage vor dem obersten Gerichtshof in Frankreich, dem *Parlement de Paris*, erhoben.[65] Darlehensverträge in Südfrankreich enthielten Regelungen zugunsten des Ordens, die Verluste durch eine Münzverschlechterung auffangen sollten.

Die Templer entwickelten für die von ihnen verwahrten Gelder nach und nach ein detailliertes Rechnungswesen. Dies betraf auch die Verwahrung der Gelder ranghoher Adliger. So erhielt Blanche von Kastilien, die Mutter Ludwigs IX. und lange Zeit Regentin Frankreichs, für ihre Deposita in den 1240er Jahren dreimal jährlich, zum 2. Februar, zu Christi Himmelfahrt und zum 1. November, 'Bankauszüge', die den letzten Stand, die einzelnen Ein- und Ausgänge sowie den aktuellen Stand vermerkten.[66] Die Abrechnungen aus dem Pariser Temple von

---

[60] A. DÉMURGER, Les Templiers (wie Anm. 19), S. 319; H. NICHOLSON, The Knights Templar. A New History, Stroud 2002, S. 188–189.

[61] A. DÉMURGER, Les Templiers (wie Anm. 19), S. 318.

[62] M. BARBER, New Knighthood (wie Anm. 5), S. 272, 277.

[63] Ebd., S. 266–267.

[64] D. SELWOOD, Knights of the Cloister. Templars and Hospitallers in Central–Southern Occitania 1100–1300, Woodbridge, Suffolk 1999, S. 186, spricht von "üblichen" 16–33% Zinsen.

[65] H. PRUTZ, Die geistlichen Ritterorden (wie Anm. 17), S. 414.

[66] M. BARBER, New Knighthood (wie Anm. 5), S. 269.

1295/1296 belegen rund 60 Konten der königlichen Familie, geistlicher und weltlicher Würdenträger sowie Pariser Kaufleute mitsamt der erfolgten Ein- und Auszahlungen.[67] Sie nennen zudem die diensthabenden Brüder und die Öffnungstage der 'Bankschalter'. Im November 1295 wurden an 23 Öffnungstagen 75 Geschäfte getätigt, im ruhigen August dagegen an sechs Öffnungstagen nur acht Geschäfte.[68] Eingehende Münzen verschiedener Währungen wurden am Ende des Tages mit Hilfe eines Rechenbretts in Pariser Münze umgerechnet. Insgesamt ergibt dieses Rechnungsbuch zwar keineswegs ein vollständiges Bild, doch zeigt sich bei den Finanzgeschäften der Templer eine eigene Dynamik, die so von den anderen Orden auch in den folgenden Jahrhunderten nicht erreicht wurde.

Für die Johanniter gilt dagegen immer noch die Feststellung von Hans PRUTZ, der Johanniterorden habe sich „der neuen Mittel, welche […] die […] Geldwirtschaft darbot, […] immer nur in beschränktem Maße und im Hinblick auf die durch seinen Beruf immer von neuem erzeugten besonderen Bedürfnisse" bedient.[69] Eine Ursache war zweifellos, dass das Wucherverbot im Orden immer wieder erneuert wurde. Nach einem Statut von 1428, das auch in die Statutenrevision von 1493 aufgenommen wurde, wurde Wucher mit dem Verlust des Amtes und einer zehnjährigen 'Zurückstellung' von weiteren Ämtern bestraft.[70] Im November 1450 forderte z.B. Nikolaus V. in einem Schreiben an führende Amtsträger des Ordens eine strenge Bestrafung der Brüder, die „sich vermessen, bestimmte Summen Geldes, zu denen sie sowohl durch ihre Präzeptoreien als auch auf anderem Wege gelangt sind, über Vermittlung von Kaufleuten oder anderen […] verschiedenen Personen und – was noch verdammungswürdiger ist – dem allgemeinen Schatz des genannten Hospitals unter der verbotenen Bedingung von Zinsen zu geben bzw. zu leihen, unter Gefahr für ihre Seelen".[71] Was für die einzelnen Brüder galt, die im 15. Jahrhundert durchaus ihr

---

67 A. DÉMURGER, Les Templiers (wie Anm. 19), S. 320; L. DELISLE, Mémoire sur les opérations financières des Templiers (wie Anm. 58), S. 36–37.

68 M. BARBER, New Knighthood (wie Anm. 5), S. 271.

69 H. PRUTZ, Die geistlichen Ritterorden (wie Anm. 17), S. 395.

70 Das Statut in Paris, Bibliothèque Nationale, Ms. Franç. 17255, fol. 95v, bzw. Valletta, National Library of Malta (künftig: NLM) Libr. 501, fol. 196r–v, übernommen in Libr. 244, fol. 95r; ediert in: Stabilimenta Rhodiorum militum. Die Statuten des Johanniterordens von 1489/93, eds. J. HASECKER / J. SARNOWSKY (Nova Mediaevalia. Quellen und Studien zum europäischen Mittelalter 1), Göttingen 2007, S. 218, 379. – Entsprechend findet sich das Verbot auch in einer *ordinatio* des Generalkapitels vom 17. November 1478, Arch. 283, fol. 167v.

71 Der Papst äußerte seine Entrüstung, dass sich einige Brüder dem Geiz zuwandten und ungeachtet der kirchlichen Verbote diversas pecuniarum summas que ad illos tam eorum preceptoriis quam alias pervenerunt per interpositas merchatores seu aliarum personarum manus […] sub damnata fenoris condicione diversis personis et – quod damnabilis fore dinoscitur – communi thesauro dicti Hospitalis dare seu mutuare presumpserunt in animarum suarum periculum, Archivio Segreto Vaticano, Reg. Vat. 393, fol. 102v(–103v), vom 6. November 1450; vgl. J. SARNOWSKY, Macht und Herrschaft im Johanniterorden (wie Anm. 22), S. 513 (dort auch die Übersetzung).

eigenes Vermögen verwalten – und sich untereinander oder dem Orden Geld leihen –, aber nicht testamentarisch vergeben durften, galt sicher auch für den gesamten Orden. Den Johannitern fehlte zudem im 15. Jahrhundert die wirtschaftliche Grundlage für den intensiven Verleih von Geldern.

Die Geldgeschäfte des Ordens dienten im späteren Mittelalter vor allem für Geldtransfers nach Rhodos, für die sich die Johanniter in erster Linie bestimmter Kaufleute und Bankhäuser bedienten. Gelder aus dem deutschen Priorat wurden durch venezianische oder in Venedig residierende deutsche Kaufleute nach Rhodos gebracht,[72] für die Überweisung von Geldern aus Spanien wurden vor allem Kaufleute aus Barcelona eingesetzt. Depositare, vom Orden für ihre Dienste mit jährlichen Bezügen entlohnte Kaufleute, saßen auch in Handelszentren wie Florenz und Lyon. Sie zogen Ordensgelder ein und zahlten sie wiederum für bestimmte Zwecke aus, etwa für den Kauf von Getreide.

Vielfach wurden Forderungen auf Rhodos einfach nur mit Responsionen aus den Häusern im Westen verrechnet. Dabei bedienten sich auch weltliche Personen der Hilfe des Ordens, um auf diese Weise ihre Gelder in den Westen zu transferieren bzw. bestimmten Zahlungsverpflichtungen nachzukommen. Dafür spielten wiederum die Depositare eine wichtige Rolle, wenn etwa im Oktober 1510 der Lyoner Depositar Claude Laurensin angewiesen wurde, dem Rhodeser Kaufmann Michele de Martinis bei seiner Ankunft aus den Geldern des Ordens die Summe von 600 Écus auszuzahlen, die er dem Meister auf Rhodos übergeben hatte.[73] In denselben Kontext gehören auch die Geldüberweisungen im engeren Sinne, die die Johanniter vornahmen, oft für Bürger von Rhodos, die enge Handelsbeziehungen zum Westen hatten. Im Oktober 1510 wurde z.B. Claude Laurensin ermächtigt, dem französischen Kaufmann Jean Ferrer aus Ordensgeldern 200 Écus des Rhodeser Bürgers Bernardino Ros zu übergeben.[74] Ob der Orden dafür auch Gebühren erhob, lässt sich aus den Quellen nicht erkennen.

Beim Deutschen Orden lassen sich Handel und Geldgeschäfte kaum trennen, da die Großschäffer ihre Waren vielfach auf Kredit verkauften.[75] Am Ende waren

---

[72] S. z.B. NLM Arch. 362, fol. 201(202)v, 9. Januar 1451, Zahlung des Präzeptors von Freiburg i.Ü., Johann von Ow, über einen venezianischen Kaufmann; vgl. J. SARNOWSKY, Macht und Herrschaft im Johanniterorden (wie Anm. 22), S. 523.

[73] Ebd., S. 521.

[74] Nach NLM Arch. 400, fol. 181r, vom 12. Oktober 1510, vgl. J. SARNOWSKY, Macht und Herrschaft im Johanniterorden (wie Anm. 22), S. 522; zu den Geldüberweisungen der katalanischen Kaufleute insbesondere nach Rhodos vgl. M. DEL TREPPO, I mercanti catalani e l'espansione della corona d'Aragonia nel secolo XV, Neapel 1972, S. 78–92.

[75] Erhalten sind daher auch keine Rechnungs– sondern Schuldbücher: Schuldbücher und Rechnungen der Großschäffer und Lieger des Deutschen Ordens in Preußen, 4 Bde., ed. C. FRANZKE / C. HEß / J. LACZNY / C. LINK / J. SARNOWSKY (Veröffentlichungen aus den Archiven Preußischer Kulturbesitz 62, 1–4; zugleich Quellen und Darstellungen zur Hansischen Geschichte N.F., LIX, 1–4), Köln/Weimar/Wien, 2008–2018.

allerdings viele Gelder nicht mehr einzufordern und mussten abgeschrieben werden. Obwohl der Deutsche Orden anders als die Templer keine Bankgeschäfte tätigte, vergaben die Brüder um 1400 zahlreiche größere Kredite, meist in politischer Absicht an Fürsten und Städte, um sie für ein Bündnis zu gewinnen. In Preußen selbst verliehen die Großschäffer, die seit dem Ende des 14. Jahrhunderts vom Orden gestellten Münzmeister, aber auch andere Brüder Gelder an Kaufleute und Städte. Die Zinsnahme wurde 1386 durch eine Landesordnung des Hochmeisters Konrad Zöllner von Rotenstein auf höchstens 1 Mark je 12 Mark Darlehen, d. h. auf einen Zins von 8,33 %, beschränkt,[76] doch forderte selbst der Orden teilweise höhere Zinsen. Einen Extremfall stellt allerdings der letzte Münzmeister zu Thorn, Hans von Lichtenstein, dar, der vor 1454 – allerdings nicht bei einem Darlehen, sondern für die Beschaffung von Silber für die Münze – einen Zins von immerhin 32,5 % erheben wollte.[77]

Geldtransfers wie bei Templern oder Johannitern waren die Ausnahme. Sie finden sich vor allem im 14. Jahrhundert, für die westeuropäischen Adligen, die an den Kreuzzügen in Preußen teilnahmen. Ihnen lieh der Orden teilweise erhebliche Summen, oft in Zusammenarbeit mit preußischen Kaufleuten.[78] Dabei zahlten die Brüder zwar die Summen aus, übertrugen aber die Eintreibung an Kaufleute, die als Bürgen mit dem Orden in ein Vertragsverhältnis traten. Die Rückzahlung erfolgte oft im Westen über die Ballei Koblenz oder die Lieger der Großschäffer in Brügge.[79] Auf der Ordensseite waren an diesen Geldgeschäften nicht nur Hochmeister, Tressler, Großkomtur und Großschäffer, sondern auch einzelne Komtureien beteiligt. Zinsforderungen des Ordens lassen sich dabei nicht erkennen, wohl aber die Erstattung von Kosten und Schäden.

***

(4) Ein wesentliches Moment einer sinnvollen Finanzplanung der Ritterorden war die angemessene Verteilung der finanziellen Mittel zwischen den Herkunfts-

---

[76] J. SARNOWSKY, Wirtschaftsführung des Deutschen Ordens in Preußen (wie Anm. 15), S. 133; vgl. Acten der Ständetage Preußens unter der Herrschaft des Deutschen Ordens, ed. M. TOEPPEN, 5 Bde., Leipzig 1878–1886, hier 1, Nr. 28, vom 2. Mai 1386.

[77] J. SARNOWSKY, Wirtschaftsführung des Deutschen Ordens in Preußen (wie Anm. 15), S. 66, allgemein vgl. I. JANOSZ–BISKUPOWA, Materiały do dziejów lichwy w Prusach Krzyżackich w poł. XV wieku, in: Studia i materiały do dziejów Wielkopolski i Pomorza 4 (1958), S. 355–372.

[78] W. PARAVICINI, Die Preussenreisen des europäischen Adels, 2 (Beihefte der Francia 17/2), Sigmaringen 1995, S. 244–247.

[79] Zu den Finanz–Transaktionen des Ordens und den Verbindungen mit italienischen Banken und Kaufleuten vgl. K. MILITZER, Die Einbindung des Deutschen Ordens in das europäische Finanzsystem, in: R. CZAJA / J. SARNOWSKY (Hgg.), Die Ritterorden in der europäischen Wirtschaft des Mittelalters (Ordines Militares. Colloquia Torunensia Historica 12), Toruń 2003, S. 7–17, bes. S. 10–11.

und Einsatzregionen. Dies geschah bei Templern und Johannitern durch regelmäßige Abgaben der Häuser im Westen, die Responsionen, beim Deutschen Orden nach anfänglicher intensiver Unterstützung der Eroberung Preußens zumindest durch gelegentliche bzw. durch Ausnahme geregelte Zahlungen aus den Balleien im Reich.

Bei den Templern sollten die Responsionen bei einem Drittel der Einnahmen liegen, unterlagen aber in der Praxis starken Schwankungen. So wurden sie im 13. Jahrhundert bei finanziellen Notlagen zeitweilig erhöht, beispielsweise 1260, als der Orden Sidon von seinem weltlichen Herrn kaufen wollte,[80] oder in den späteren 1290er Jahren, als die Templer einen Stützpunkt an der syrischen Küste zu erobern suchten. Die Häuser auf der Iberischen Halbinsel, die Truppen für die Reconquista stellen mussten, hatten allerdings geringere Responsionen nur von einem Zehntel der Erträge zu zahlen. Für die Provinz Aragón wurde schließlich um 1300 die Zahlung einer pauschalen Summe von 1000 Mark Silber eingeführt, die offenbar nach interner Verteilung auf die Häuser aufgebracht wurde.[81] Die tatsächlichen Eingänge waren zudem von der wirtschaftlichen Lage der Ordenshäuser abhängig. Kriege und Naturkatastrophen konnten einen erheblichen Rückgang der Responsionen zur Folge haben.

Die Responsionen werden auf den Schiffen der Templer nach Osten transportiert worden sein. Gegen Mitte des 13. Jahrhundert gab es in Aragón einen eigenen Amtsträger, der die Überweisung ins Heilige Land organisierte, während 1304 ein Kaufmann aus Barcelona mit der Überweisung der Responsionen in Höhe von 1000 Mark Silber mit Hilfe eines entsprechenden Transfers von Waren beauftragt wurde.[82] Die Ausfuhr der Responsionen dürfte häufig in Gestalt von Naturalien und Tieren erfolgt sein. 1286 erlaubte König Alfons III. von Aragón den Templern den Export von 40 Pferden aus Kastilien und Aragón sowie von Maultieren, Salzfleisch, anderen Lebensmitteln und Rüstungen.[83] Ähnliche Genehmigungen schlossen insbesondere Roggen, Weizen und Gerste ein. Am Ende des 13. Jahrhunderts gab es vermutlich regelmäßige Fahrten, die jährlich im August oder September dem Transport von Verstärkungen und der Versorgung für das Heilige Land dienten. Neben Südfrankreich spielten insbesondere die Häfen in Unteritalien und Sizilien für die Versorgung des Heiligen Landes eine zentrale Rolle, nicht zuletzt wegen der Bedeutung Siziliens als 'Kornkammer' des Mittelmeerraums und für die Pferdezucht. Die Überschüsse aus den Ordenshäusern, darunter Gemüse, Waffen und Tuch, wurden von Häfen wie Brindisi, Barletta, Trani oder Bari aus verschifft, wo die Templer über eigenen Besitz verfügten.

---

[80] M. BARBER, New Knighthood (wie Anm. 5), S. 243.
[81] A. FOREY, The Templars in the *Corona de Aragón* (University of Durham Publications), London 1973, S. 323.
[82] Ebd., S. 323–325.
[83] Ebd., S. 324.

Insbesondere Messina bildete eine wichtige Durchgangsstation für Waren aus der Provence und Katalonien. Nach der zeitweiligen Beschlagnahme des Templerbesitzes unter Friedrich II. erteilte der neue Herrscher Siziliens, Karl I., 1267 die Erlaubnis zur abgabenfreien Ausfuhr von Lebensmitteln,[84] und 1294 verfügte Karl II., der Sohn Karls I., die Waffen auf den Schiffen der Templer sollten nicht durch Zollbeamte kontrolliert werden.

Bei den Johannitern wurde die Höhe der Abgaben der Ordenshäuser durch verschiedene Statuten der Generalkapitel geregelt. Sie wurden jeweils nach von der inneren und äußeren Situation, in der sich der Orden befand, festgesetzt.[85] Lagen die Responsionen in Friedenszeiten teilweise nur bei einem Viertel oder sogar nur einem Fünftel der Einkünfte, konnten in Krisenzeiten die Hälfte oder sogar drei Viertel eingefordert werden.[86] Dabei ging man von einem festen Ansatz für die einzelnen Häuser aus, der aber angesichts wirtschaftlicher Probleme und zahlreicher kriegerischer Auseinandersetzungen immer wieder überprüft werden musste. Dazu wurden teils durch die Prioren,[87] teils durch Bevollmächtigte von Meister und Rat bzw. durch Beauftragte der Generalkapitel regelmäßig Visitationen durchgeführt.[88] Grundsätzlich galt aber nach einem Statut der Zeit Pierre d'Aubussons, dass die Verpflichtung zur Zahlung der auferlegten Abgaben selbst dann bestand, wenn die Lage in den Prioraten und für die Ämter durch Kriege, Verwüstungen und anderes ungünstig geworden war.[89] Die Zahlung hatte, unabhängig vom Termin der Provinzialkapitel, jeweils zum 24. Juni eines jeden Jahres zu erfolgen, und zwar – nach diesem Statut – in französischen Écus oder ihrem Gegenwert, ohne jede Minderung mit dem Hinweis auf Wechselkurse und Münzverschlechterungen.[90]

---

[84] M. BARBER, New Knighthood (wie Anm. 5), S. 238–239.

[85] Vgl. J. SARNOWSKY, 'The rights of the treasury': the financial administration of the Hospitallers on 15th–century Rhodes (1421–1522), in: H. NICHOLSON (Hg.), The Military Orders, Vol. 2: Welfare and Warfare, Aldershot 1998, S. 267–274, ND in: DERS., On the Military Orders in Medieval Orders in Medieval Europe. Structures and Perceptions (Variorum Collected Studies Series 992), Farnham 2011, no. VII, sowie detailliert J. SARNOWSKY, Macht und Herrschaft im Johanniterorden (wie Anm. 22), S. 725–752.

[86] Ebd., S. 482.

[87] Vgl. ebd., S. 106–107.

[88] J. SARNOWSKY, The Convent and the West. Visitations in the Order of the Hospital of St. John in the Fifteenth Century, in: K. BORCHARDT / N. JASPERT / H. NICHOLSON, The Hospitallers, the Mediterranean and Europe. Festschrift for Anthony Luttrell, Aldershot 2007, S. 151–162, ND in: DERS., On the Military Orders in Medieval Orders in Medieval Europe. Structures and Perceptions (Variorum Collected Studies Series, 992), Farnham 2011, no. IX.

[89] Dazu die Statutenversion in NLM Libr. 244, fol. 120r–121r (Statut des Kapitels von 1493), ediert in: Stabilimenta Rhodiorum militum, eds. J. HASECKER / J. SARNOWSKY (wie Anm. 70), S. 259–261.

[90] NLM Libr. 244, fol. 54r-v; Stabilimenta Rhodiorum militum, eds. J. HASECKER / J. SARNOWSKY (wie Anm. 70), S. 152.

Die Responsionen wurden aber nur in seltenen Fällen in voller Höhe an den Konvent überwiesen. So stellte der Meister Hugues Revel schon 1268 fest, dass aus Teilen Frankreichs und aus Italien nichts, aus England und Spanien nur wenig eingegangen war, und in der Folge mahnten die Generalkapitel des Ordens, etwa 1301 und 1302, immer wieder die pünktliche Zahlung der Responsionen an.[91] Zudem mussten wohl nicht nur im 15. Jahrhundert oftmals schon jene Summen von den Einkünften im Westen erstattet werden, die die Amtsträger im Auftrag des Ordens ausgelegt bzw. ausgezahlt hatten,[92] fassbar in den Zahlungsanweisungen, die sich in großer Zahl in allen *Libri bullarum* erhalten haben. Das konnte dazu führen, dass der Schatz des Ordens keine Einnahmen zu erwarten, sondern sogar noch Forderungen von Ordensbrüdern zu begleichen hatte. Gelegentlich mussten sogar für die Auszahlung der Brüder Darlehen aufgenommen werden,[93] was insbesondere in finanziellen Krisenzeiten, die nicht selten waren, zusätzliche Belastungen verursachte. Auf jeden Fall konnte durch die Zahlungsanweisungen der Unterhalt des Konvents gesichert werden.[94] Auch die Lieferungen zur Versorgung des Konvents wurden häufig vor Ort unmittelbar aus den Responsionen bezahlt, so bei Getreidelieferungen aus Unteritalien.[95] Einen Sonderfall bildeten die Responsionen aus England, die mehrfach auch in Form von Tüchern entrichtet wurden, die offenbar unter anderem über Portugal umgesetzt wurden. Als es Anfang des 16. Jahrhunderts zu Ausfuhrverboten von Gold und Silber aus England kam, entschloss sich die Ordensleitung, stattdessen Tuche und Zinn liefern zu lassen, wobei diesmal Sizilien als Umschlagplatz dienen sollte.[96]

Auch der Deutsche Orden dürfte seinen Einsatz im Heiligen Land und im Baltikum im 13. Jahrhundert wesentlich aus den Überschüssen seiner Häuser finanziert haben. Das wird z.B. an den päpstlichen Privilegien von 1257 und 1263 erkennbar, die dem Orden den Handel mit den Überschüssen aus den Kommenden erlaubten.[97] Zudem heißt es in den Gewohnheiten, dass die Balleien den Hochmeister während seiner Reisen versorgen und notwendige Gelder zumindest als Darlehen zur Verfügung stellen sollten.[98] Über regelmäßige Zahlungen

---

[91] A. FOREY, Military Orders (wie Anm. 7), S. 131.

[92] J. SARNOWSKY, Macht und Herrschaft im Johanniterorden (wie Anm. 22), S. 483.

[93] Ebd., mit einem Beispiel von 1447 zu Schulden an einen genuesischen Kaufmann.

[94] Zu den 'Techniken' von Zahlungsanweisungen und Überweisungen durch den Orden vgl. allgemein J. SARNOWSKY, Macht und Herrschaft im Johanniterorden (wie Anm. 22), bes. S. 512–524.

[95] Dazu s. u.a. ebd., S. 395, 506.

[96] Ebd., S. 483, mit einem Schreiben des Meisters von 3. November 1515.

[97] S. oben zu Anm. 38.

[98] J. SARNOWSKY, Wirtschaftsführung des Deutschen Ordens in Preußen (wie Anm. 15), S. 52; Die Statuten des Deutschen Ordens nach den ältesten Handschriften, ed. M. PERLBACH, Halle 1890, ND Hildesheim–New York 1975, S. 101 (Gw 16).

ist jedoch wenig erkennbar.[99] Eine Ausnahme bildeten die vier bzw. fünf Balleien, die der hochmeisterlichen Kammer zugewiesen waren, Böhmen, Österreich, Bozen, Koblenz und – seit dem Ausgang des 14. Jahrhunderts – Elsass-Burgund, die feste Kammerzinse leisten sollten. Die Ballei Koblenz sandte dafür z.B. jährlich eine Ladung Wein an den Hochmeister, Bozen hatte Zahlungen für den Generalprokurator des Ordens an der Kurie zu senden. Nach der Niederlage bei Tannenberg 1410 suchte Hochmeister Heinrich von Plauen auch die deutschmeisterlichen Balleien an der Finanzierung des Ordens in Preußen zu beteiligen, aber nur mit geringem Erfolg.[100] Verhandlungen zwischen dem Hoch- und dem Deutschmeister blieben auch in späteren Jahren ohne greifbares Ergebnis.[101] Vielmehr nahm der Deutschmeister bei einer Summe, die ihm der Hochmeister (für die Ballei Elsass-Burgund) nicht sofort bezahlen konnte, in den 1440er Jahren sogar Zinsen.[102]

Hochmeister und Orden konnten aber spätestens seit der (Re-)Organisation der Tresslerkasse nach 1324/25 auf geregelte Einnahmen aus Preußen zurückgreifen.[103] Zum einen hatten einige Gebietiger regelmäßige Abgaben an den Hochmeister zu leisten, um 1400 rund 4.000 m. preuß., zum anderen flossen jährlich durchschnittlich 6.000 m. preuß. bei Ämterwechseln an die zentralen Kassen. Spätestens seit 1364 wurden bei jeder Amtsübergabe Inventare angelegt, die der Ordensleitung zusammen mit Visitationsakten, Zinslisten und anderen Dokumenten die Kontrolle der Wirtschaftsführung der Gebietiger ermöglichten und auch die abgeführten Überschüsse nennen. Die von Tressler und Großkomtur verwalteten Einkünfte des Hochmeisters betrugen zumeist über 20.000 Mark.[104]

Dieses System der Ordensfinanzierung brach jedoch durch die Kriege in Preußen seit 1409 zusammen. Von den rund 37.000 Hufen waren um 1417 rund 17 %, um 1437 sogar rund 20 % wüst, leisteten also keine Abgaben. Besonders

---

[99] Wie auch K. van Eickels, Die Deutschordensballei Koblenz (wie Anm. 23), S. 205, feststellt, beteiligten sich „die deutschmeisterlichen Balleien […] an der Verteidigung des Ordenslandes nur gegen Erstattung ihrer Kosten, so daß die Hauptlast der Kriegsfinanzierung auf den Kammerballeien lag".

[100] OF 6, 81, vom 27. November 1412; vgl. R. ten Haaf, Deutschordensstaat und Deutschordensballeien. Untersuchungen über Leistung und Sonderung der Deutschordensprovinzen in Deutschland vom 13. bis zum 16. Jahrhundert, Göttingen 1951, S. 46.

[101] Ebd., S. 46–49.

[102] J. Sarnowsky, Wirtschaftsführung des Deutschen Ordens in Preußen (wie Anm. 15), S. 318.

[103] B. Jähnig, Zur Wirtschaftsführung des Deutschen Ordens in Preußen vornehmlich vom 13. bis zum frühen 15. Jahrhundert, in: U. Arnold (Hg.), Zur Wirtschaftsentwicklung des Deutschen Ordens im Mittelalter (Quellen und Studien zur Geschichte des Deutschen Ordens 38, Veröffentlichungen der Internationalen Historischen Kommission zur Erforschung des Deutschen Ordens 2) Marburg a. d. Lahn 1989, S. 113–147, hier S. 118.

[104] Zahlen hier und im Folgenden nach J. Sarnowsky, Wirtschaftsführung des Deutschen Ordens in Preußen (wie Anm. 15), bes. Tabelle 51, S. 446.

stark betroffen waren das Kulmerland und Pommerellen mit bis zu 33 % Wüstungen um 1437. Aber auch die verbliebenen Bauern konnten vielfach keine Abgaben leisten. Parallel dazu gingen die Erträge aus der Eigenwirtschaft zurück. In der Folge hatten die Amtsträger keine Überschüsse mehr, die als 'Wandelgelder' an die zentralen Kassen abgeführt werden konnten. Zugleich sanken die Zinseinnahmen des Hochmeisters auf rund 2.500 Mark und die Einkünfte aus dem Marienburger Gebiet von 8.000 auf rund 6.000 Mark. Die Ordensleitung griff deshalb immer häufiger zu Umlagezahlungen der Gebietiger, dem „Geschoss". Dieses wurde – abhängig von der Leistungsfähigkeit der Ämter – in verschiedener Höhe für konkrete Aufgaben eingefordert, eine Reaktion auf die auch in einer Klageschrift an Hochmeister Paul von Rusdorf kritisierte „Verpfründung" der Ordensämter,[105] die von den Brüdern fast nur noch zur persönlichen Versorgung verwaltet wurden. Die zentralen Kassen büßten so nach 1410 fast die Hälfte ihrer Einnahmen ein.

Noch dramatischer entwickelte sich die Lage mit dem Beginn des Dreizehnjährigen Krieges 1454/55, als man für die Soldzahlungen unter anderem die Neumark an den Kurfürsten von Brandenburg verkaufen musste und als die Marienburg und andere Ordensburgen, die an die Söldner verpfändet waren, von diese an Polen weiterverkauft wurden. Die Hochmeister versuchten erneut, Geld aus den Balleien im Reich einzuziehen, doch außer der (ebenfalls kostspieligen) Ausrüstung von Kontingenten flossen nur geringe Gelder nach Preußen. Die Soldzahlungen mussten so über die Verpfändung – und faktische Vergabe – von Ländereien in Preußen und Schuldscheine ausgeglichen werden.[106]

***

(5) Bei allen drei Orden ergaben sich nicht zuletzt vor dem Hintergrund des Austauschs zwischen regionalen und zentralen Ämtern Ansätze für eine geregelte Haushaltsführung, insbesondere auf zentraler Ebene. Aus dem weit entwickelten Rechnungswesen der Templer gibt es nur wenige Zeugnisse, die weitergehende Aussagen ermöglichen. Insbesondere fehlen zentrale Rechnungen aus dem Heiligen Land oder Zypern. Immerhin hat sich aber ein 16 Monate umfassendes

---

[105] „Wenn [ein] Gebietiger einen Pfleger, Waldmeister oder Kämmerer einsetzt, gibt man dem von der Stunde an keine Versorgung, sondern man sagt, sie sollten sich von ihren Gericht[sgefäll]en ernähren und die Kämmerer von ihrem Kammeramt. […] Wenn die Kästen gefüllt sind, so lässt man sich vom Amt ablösen; so kommt das Geld nicht in den Nutzen des Landes", aus der „Ermahnung des Kartäusers", Scriptores rerum prussicarum. Die Geschichtsquellen der preußischen Vorzeit bis zum Untergange der Ordensherrschaft, 5 Bde., ed. T. HIRSCH / M. TOEPPEN / E. STREHLKE, Leipzig 1861–1874, Bd. 4, S. 458–459.

[106] Dazu jetzt J. LACZNY, Schuldenverwaltung und Tilgung der Forderungen der Söldner des Deutschen Ordens in Preußen nach dem Zweiten Thorner Frieden. Ordensfoliant 259 und 261, Zusatzmaterial (Beihefte zum Preußischen Urkundenbuch 5) Göttingen 2019.

Fragment einer Abrechnung über den Schatz der Templer in Paris aus den Jahren 1295 und 1296 erhalten. Es erlaubt einen Eindruck davon, wie die Abgaben der Häuser im Westen organisiert wurden. Es nennt Einzahlungen von 38 Komturen sehr unterschiedlicher Stellung, von den Leitern der Provinzen Aquitanien und Normandie bis zu Vorstehern kleinerer Häuser. Offenbar wurde für Nordfrankreich nicht nach einem hierarchischen System eingezogen, sondern die Responsionen wurden nach Möglichkeit und Bedarf überwiesen. Auffällig ist allerdings, dass die meisten Zahlungen entweder zwischen Dezember und Februar oder im Juli erfolgten. Sie standen damit in zeitlicher Relation sowohl zu den Erntezeiten wie zu den beiden wichtigsten Terminen für das *passagium* ins Heilige Land im März und August.[107] Dennoch gab es immer wieder finanzielle Notlagen und Engpässe. So informierte der Templermeister seinen Vertreter in England 1260, dass die Ausgaben des Ordens im Heiligen Land so groß seien, dass die Templer ohne Hilfe aus dem Westen entweder ihre Tätigkeit im Heiligen Land einstellen oder große Teile ihres westlichen Besitzes verkaufen müssten. In ähnlicher Weise wurde 1275 der englische König Eduard I. unterrichtet.[108]

Die Johanniter hatten durchweg erhebliche Probleme, die zentralen Aufgaben zu finanzieren. Generell erwies sich eine vorausschauende Haushaltsführung als schwierig. Vielmehr wurden immer wieder Schulden gemacht, auch wenn die Amtsträger vorsichtig agierten. Das hatte oft auch mit Ernteausfällen durch Dürre und Unfruchtbarkeit der Böden, über die die Johanniter zwischen 1268 und 1282 mehrfach klagten,[109] und anderen Problemen in der Landwirtschaft zu tun, aber auch die Kosten für die Aufgaben des Ordens waren nicht leicht kalkulierbar. Nach 1200 begann der Orden im Heiligen Land mit dem Aufbau einer eigenen Flotte und erwarb trotz finanzieller Probleme umfangreiche neue Besitzungen. Dies setzte sich nach der Niederlage bei La Forbie 1244 fort, obwohl die Priorate seit 1250 immer weniger in der Lage waren, den geforderten Zahlungen nachzukommen. Trotz eines Verbots des Generalkapitels von 1262, Ordensbesitz zu entfremden, also wieder in weltliche Hände zu geben, waren selbst Verkäufe von Ländereien nicht ausgeschlossen.[110]

Nach dem Verlust des Heiligen Landes führte die Kritik an den Ritterorden zu einem Rückgang der Einnahmen, so dass der Orden auf Zypern nicht über ausreichende Mittel verfügte, um seine fortgesetzten militärischen Aktivitäten zu finanzieren. Die Eroberung von Rhodos und der Ausbau der Befestigungen führten die Johanniter ab 1306 endgültig in die Verschuldung; dazu kamen Zah-

---

[107] M. BARBER, New Knighthood (wie Anm. 5), S. 243.

[108] A. FOREY, Military Orders (wie Anm. 7), S. 131.

[109] Ebd., S. 124.

[110] J. BRONSTEIN, The Hospitallers and the Holy Land. Financing the Latin East, Woodbridge 2005, bes. S. 142–144.

lungen an die europäischen Fürsten, die Entschädigungen oder 'Verwaltungsgebühren' für die vom Papst 1312 verfügte Übergabe des ehemaligen Templerbesitzes forderten. Lange gab es offenbar keine übergreifende Finanzplanung, bis zum früheren 15. Jahrhundert. Dann aber wurde, spätestens ab Juni 1429, Meister Antoni Fluvià für drei Jahre zum Verwalter von Konvent und Schatz eingesetzt, um der Notlage besser begegnen zu können.[111] In der Folge wurde die Finanzverwaltung des Ordens komplett umgestaltet und mit den Einnahmen des Meisters auf Rhodos abgesichert.

In diesem Kontext entstand die früheste bekannte Übersicht über die Finanzen der Johanniter auf Rhodos, interessanterweise überliefert in einem Schreiben des Generalprokurators des Deutschen Ordens an der Kurie vom November 1432.[112] Sie entstammt einem Bericht an den Papst und zeichnet deshalb wohl die finanzielle Situation bewusst negativ. Danach standen jährlichen Einkünften von 46.550 Dukaten Ausgaben von 65.500 Dukaten gegenüber.[113] Etwas mehr als die Hälfte der Einnahmen stammten danach aus den westlichen Prioraten, rund 24.000 Dukaten, mit den größten Anteilen aus Frankreich und England (10.000 bzw. 7.000 Dukaten). Dazu kamen etwa zu gleichen Teilen unregelmäßige Einnahmen aus Vakanzen, Todesfällen, *spolia* und dem *passagium* der nach Rhodos kommenden Brüder, aus den Einkünften auf Rhodos und Kos sowie aus den Responsionen von Zypern. Die größten Ausgabeposten bildeten die Aufwendungen für den Lebensunterhalt der Brüder sowie die Versorgung mit Getreide, 23.000 bzw. 17.000 Dukaten. 6.000 Dukaten wurden für das Hospital und die dort beschäftigten Ärzte ausgegeben, 10.000 für den Schutz der auf dem Festland gelegenen Burg St. Peter / Bodrum.

Im Juni 1451 vereinbarten Meister, Konvent und Priorate eine neue Aufteilung der Finanzierung des Konvents. Von 54.000 Florenen jährlich sollten 20.000 von den Häusern im Westen aufgebracht werden, 18.000 aus dem östlichen Mittelmeer und der Rest aus den Einkünften des Meisters.[114] Das strukturelle Defizit wuchs dennoch in der Folge weiter an, so dass immer wieder neue Haushaltsplanungen aufgestellt wurden. Offenbar tauschten sich die Brüder darüber auch mit ihren Besuchern aus, um die Leistungen der Johanniter besonders hervorzuheben. So erfuhr der Pfalzgrafen bei Rhein, Ottheinrich, 1521, dass die Brüder auf

---

[111] J. SARNOWSKY, Macht und Herrschaft im Johanniterorden (wie Anm. 22), S. 526; dort auch allgemein zur Wirtschaftsentwicklung des 15. Jahrhunderts.

[112] J.–E. BEUTTEL, Der Generalprokurator des Deutschen Ordens an der Römischen Kurie. Amt, Funktionen, personelles Umfeld und Finanzierung (Quellen und Studien zur Geschichte des Deutschen Ordens 55), Marburg 1995, S. 614–616.

[113] Die folgenden Zahlen nach der Zusammenfassung von T. M. VANN, The Exchange of Information and Money between the Hospitallers of Rhodes and their European Priories in the Fourteenth and Fifteenth Centuries, in: J. BURGTORF / H. NICHOLSON (Hgg.), International Mobility in the Military Orders, Cardiff 2006, S. 34–47, hier S. 39–41.

[114] J. SARNOWSKY, 'The rights of the treasury' (wie Anm. 85), S. 272.

Rhodos mehr als das Doppelte vom dem ausgeben würden, was sie aus den Häusern im Westen einnehmen. Nach seinem Reisebericht müsste der Orden 97.977 Dukaten aufbringen, hätte aber nur Einnahmen von rund 47.000 Dukaten. „Das Übrige", notiert er dann auch, „müssen sie auf dem Meer holen von ihren Feinden, damit sie auskommen können".[115] Zu diesem Zeitpunkt war jedoch die Finanzverwaltung durch die Meister schon fast zur Regel geworden,[116] die mit ihren Einnahmen eine solide Grundlage auch für die Finanzierung des Konvents schufen.

Auch beim Deutschen Orden mit seiner umfangreichen, auf vielen Ebenen erhaltenen Rechnungsführung lassen sich Ansätze für eine geregelte Finanzplanung erst sehr spät erkennen. Schon die älteste Ordensregel enthält Bestimmungen zur Besitzverwaltung durch die Brüder,[117] und nach den Gewohnheiten sollten alle Amtsinhaber jährlich vor dem Kapitel Rechenschaft ablegen, mit Ausnahme des Tresslers und der Amtsträger im Haupthaus, die sogar monatlich vor dem Hochmeister zu berichten hatten.[118] Diese Regelungen wurden im Folgenden mehrfach bekräftigt, so auch durch Hochmeister Werner von Orseln (1324–30), der allerdings generell die jährliche Abrechnung einführte.[119]

Spätestens um die Mitte des 14. Jahrhunderts entstand auf dieser Grundlage in den Komtureien, Vogt- und Pflegeämtern, in den Großschäffereien und auch bei den zentralen Amtsträgern eine vielfältige, auf Dauerhaftigkeit angelegte Buchführung. Für die lokalen Ämter lässt sich das aus den Inventaren beim Ämterwechsel sowie aus den Visitationsberichten erschließen, zudem haben sich einzelne Rechnungshefte und -bücher erhalten.[120] Diese dürften meist als Kopien auf die Marienburg gelangt sein, wurden aber nicht für einen Überblick über die Ordensfinanzen genutzt. Auch auf zentraler Ebene war das nicht viel anders. Für die Jahre von 1399 bis 1409 hat sich das Tresslerbuch als zentrales Abrechnungsinstrument erhalten; von Vorläufern und möglichen Fortsetzungen der 1410er und 1420er Jahre ist wenig bekannt.[121]

---

[115] Deutsche Pilgerreisen nach dem Heiligen Lande, eds. R. Röhricht / H. Meissner, Berlin 1880, S. 575.

[116] J. Sarnowsky, Macht und Herrschaft im Johanniterorden (wie Anm. 22), S. 552.

[117] Die Statuten des Deutschen Ordens, ed. M. Perlbach (wie Anm. 98), S. 30 (R2).

[118] Ebd., S. 102 und 107 (Gw 18, 31).

[119] Ebd., S. 147 (GWe 10); vgl. J. Sarnowsky, Wirtschaftsführung des Deutschen Ordens in Preußen (wie Anm. 15), S. 29, 86.

[120] Übersicht in J. Sarnowsky, Wirtschaftsführung des Deutschen Ordens in Preußen (wie Anm. 15); vgl. u.a. Amtsbücher des Deutschen Ordens um 1450. Pflegeamt zu Seehesten und Vogtei zu Leipe, ed. C. A. Franzke / J. Sarnowsky (Beihefte zum Preußischen Urkundenbuch 3), Göttingen 2015.

[121] J. Sarnowsky, Wirtschaftsführung des Deutschen Ordens in Preußen (wie Anm. 15), S. 19–20.

Das Tresslerbuch spiegelt nicht den eigentlichen Ordensschatz, den Tressel, über den vielleicht eigenständig Buch geführt wurde, sondern die Einnahmen und Ausgaben der hochmeisterlichen Kasse wider, die mit denen des Marienburger Konvents verrechnet wurden.[122] Die Einnahmen und Ausgaben bilden auch die beiden Hauptteile der Jahresrechnungen. Erstere verzeichnen die dem Hochmeister zukommenden Zinsleistungen aus Preußen, Entnahmen aus dem Tressel, Rückzahlungen von Schulden, die Abführung von Überschüssen bei Amtswechseln und Todesfällen und weitere Einkünfte, etwa aus dem Pfundzoll oder der Münzprägung. Auch die Ausgaben waren zunächst in wiederkehrende Gruppen gegliedert, in die Ausgaben für den Hochmeister, seinen Arzt, den Ordensjuristen, den Baumeister und die Versorgung der Marienburg sowie für Bauprojekte und weitere Maßnahmen in einzelnen Ordenshäusern insbesondere an den Grenzen des Ordenslandes, so in Ragnit, Memel und Bütow, oder in der Komturei Marienburg, etwa in Dirschau, Grebin, Montau und Meselanz. Unregelmäßige Ausgaben wurden dagegen zumeist in chronologischer Reihenfolge eingetragen.

Kam man damit einem Überblick über die Ordensfinanzen schon sehr nahe, fehlt jedoch eine Bilanz. Diese wurde offenbar mit den jährlichen Abrechnungen des Tresslers vor dem Großkomtur gezogen, die in der Regel um den 22. Dezember stattfand und die Einträge des Rechnungsjahrs beschloss.[123] Das Tresslerbuch verzeichnet allerdings nur Schulden, die der Tressler noch zu erstatten hatte, verrechnet mit den Schulden vom Vorjahr. Von der finanziellen Situation des Ordens insgesamt ist jedoch nichts zu erkennen. Zumindest während der Krisenjahre nach 1410 kann man von erheblichen Defiziten ausgehen, die erst allmählich ausgeglichen wurden. Interessanterweise enthalten Rechnungen aus den 1440er Jahren aus der Zeit des Tresslers Ulrich von Eisenhofen sehr knappe, aber zunächst durchaus ausgeglichene Bilanzen.[124] So werden 1443 und 1444 für Einnahmen und Ausgaben von Hochmeister und Konvent Überschüsse von 451 m. und 35 m. preuß. verzeichnet. Das wandelt sich 1445 mit einem Defizit von 107 m., das in einem Nachtrag sogar mit dem Hinweis auf ein Defizit von 1010 m. ergänzt wird. So oder so wird hier eine Haushaltsplanung deutlich, wie sie in den späteren Jahren zum Beispiel unter dem Hochmeister Friedrich von Sachsen (1498–1510) mit Abschlüssen für einzelne Amtsjahre weitergeführt wurde.[125]

---

[122] Ebd., S. 54–55, zur Beschreibung der Buchführung im MKB; zum Aufbau: A. KLEIN, Entstehung und Komposition des Marienburger Tresslerbuchs, Ein Beitrag zur Kritik mittelalterlicher Rechnungsbücher, Offenbach 1905, ND Bremerhaven 1973, S. 14–15.

[123] Ebd., S. 14, Anm. 1–2. – Dazu und zum Folgenden vgl. meinen zweiten Beitrag in diesem Band.

[124] J. SARNOWSKY, Das Treßleramt des Deutschen Ordens in Preußen in der Zeit Ulrichs von Eisenhofen (1441–1446), Einige Dokumente zu seiner Amtsführung, in: Beiträge zur Geschichte Westpreußens 10 (1987), S. 195–222, hier S. 202–205.

[125] J. SARNOWSKY, Die Finanzpolitik des Deutschen Ordens unter Friedrich von Sachsen, in: Zapiski Historyczne 81, 4 (2016, ersch. 2017), S. 117–132; L. DRALLE, Die Ausgaben des

***

Zusammenfassend lässt sich feststellen, dass die geistlichen Ritterorden – wie übrigens auch andere geistliche Institutionen – vielfache Anstrengungen zur Vermehrung der Einnahmen unternahmen, um so eine solide finanzielle Basis für ihre Aktivitäten zu erwirtschaften. Dafür führten sie gezielt Ankäufe zur Arrondierung des Grundbesitzes durch und suchten Rationalisierung und der Region angemessene Anbauformen. Dazu kamen der Einsatz gewerblicher Methoden und der Verkauf von Überschüssen und Produkten in der Umgebung und auf internationalen Märkten, aus dem sich nicht zuletzt beim Deutschen Orden zeitweilig ein intensiver Eigenhandel entwickelte. Aber auch (ritter)ordenstypische Einnahmequellen wurden von den Orden, sofern das möglich war, intensiv genutzt. Das betrifft zum einen den Transport von Pilgern durch Templer und Johanniter, zum anderen die Sammlung von Almosen, die nicht nur bei den Johannitern gelegentlich auch aufgrund von gefälschten Urkunden betrieben wurde.[126] Weitere Einkünfte ergaben sich – im Fall erfolgreicher Unternehmen – auch aus kriegerischen Aktivitäten der Orden, zu denen auch der *corso* der Johanniter gezählt werden muss, sowie aus den Finanzgeschäften, die aber nur bei den Templern eine besondere Dynamik gewannen.

Ein wichtiges Instrument in der Finanzpolitik der geistlichen Ritterorden war zweifellos die Verschiebung von Geldern und Material zur Erfüllung der Ordensaufgaben, insbesondere in den Einsatzgebieten. Templer und Johanniter nutzten dafür als regelmäßiges Mittel die Responsionen, die die Ordenshäuser im Westen in verschiedener Höhe aus ihren Überschüssen zu zahlen hatten; beim Deutschen Orden in Preußen waren es die Wandelgelder und Geschosszahlungen, die zeitweilig denselben Zweck erfüllten. Dazu kamen immer wieder einmalige Umlagen oder die Heranziehung der Ressourcen einzelner Häuser. Dennoch entwickelten sich nur langsam Formen der Rechnungslegung und -führung, die zumindest partielle Überblicke erlaubten, bei den Templern für den Schatz in Paris, bei den Johannitern für den Konvent auf Rhodos und beim Deutschen Orden für die Rechnungsführung der auf der Marienburg residierenden Tressler. Gesamtüberblicke entstanden dabei nicht bzw. haben sich nicht erhalten. Damit war eine vorausschauende Planung nur in Ansätzen möglich und eine mehr oder weniger intensive Verschuldung häufig nicht zu verhindern, wie sie sich etwa im

---

Deutschordenshochmeisters Friedrich von Sachsen (1498–1510). Ein Beitrag zur Finanzgeschichte, in: Zeitschrift für Ostforschung 30 (1981), S. 195–228; DERS., Die Einkünfte des Deutschordenshochmeisters Friedrich von Sachsen (1498–1510), ein Beitrag zur Finanzgeschichte der ostdeutschen Territorien, in: Zeitschrift für Ostforschung 28 (1979), S. 626–640.

126 Vgl. K. BORCHARDT, Two Forged Thirteenth–Century Alms–Raising Letters used by the Hospitallers in Franconia, in: M. BARBER (Hg.), The Military Orders [1]. Fighting for the Faith and Caring for the Sick, Aldershot 1994, S. 52–56; DERS., Spendenaufrufe der Johanniter aus dem 13. Jahrhundert, in: Zeitschrift für Bayerische Landesgeschichte 56 (1993), S. 1–62, der die zwei von ihm edierten Texte als Fälschungen nachweist.

Johanniterorden im frühen 14. und in der Mitte des 15. Jahrhunderts sowie beim Deutschen Orden insbesondere nach 1454/66 ergeben hat.[127] Dennoch ist sicher eine weitere Untersuchung der Finanzpolitik der geistlichen Ritterorden ein lohnendes Thema.

---

[127] J. SARNOWSKY, Macht und Herrschaft im Johanniterorden (wie Anm. 22), bes. S. 525–552; J. LACZNY, Schuldenverwaltung (wie Anm. 106).

DIE FINANZEN DES DEUTSCHEN ORDENS IM 15. JH.

Jürgen Sarnowsky

Seit dem 19. Jahrhundert galt die Herrschaftsbildung des Deutschen Ordens in Preußen als ein 'moderner' Staat. Noch 1951 urteilte Karl Heinz Lampe: „Der Staat in Preußen wurde in jeder Beziehung ein Musterstaat, der sehr wohl den Vergleich mit einem modernen Staatsgefüge aushalten kann".[1] Diese Feststellung betraf insbesondere die Aufgaben, die die höheren Ordensämter in der Verwaltung Preußens übernahmen, und die Rationalität, mit der diese Aufgaben verteilt waren. So verglich schon der Königsberger Archivar und Historiker Johannes Voigt 1834 die fünf Großgebietiger, Großkomtur, Oberster Marschall, Oberster Spittler, Oberster Trappier und Tressler, mit einem, „wenn man in neuerer Sprache reden will, [...] hochmeisterliche[n] Ministerium".[2] Besonderes Interesse fand dabei die Organisation der Finanzverwaltung, an deren Spitze Großkomtur und Tressler standen.[3] Diese Thesen der älteren Forschung können längst als widerlegt gelten,[4] doch bleibt die Frage, wie rational die Finanzpolitik des Deutschen Ordens in Preußen tatsächlich war.

Für die Beantwortung der Frage bietet es sich an, sich auf das 15. Jahrhundert zu konzentrieren, das trotz umfangreicher Verluste vor allem für die Zeit um 1400 und dann erneut um 1500 durch eine relativ gute Quellenlage gekennzeichnet ist.[5] Die Zeit um 1400 gilt immer noch – wenn auch in mancher Hinsicht wohl doch zu Unrecht –[6] als 'Blütezeit' des Deutschen Ordens. Das für die Jahre

---

[1] Siehe: K. H. LAMPE, Die europäische Bedeutung des Deutschen Ordens, in: Blätter für deutsche Landesgeschichte 88 (1951), S. 110–149, hier S. 115.

[2] J. VOIGT, Geschichte Preußens, von den ältesten Zeiten bis zum Untergange der Herrschaft des Deutschen Ordens, 9 Bde., Königsberg 1827–1839, Bd. 6, S. 439.

[3] S. u.a. Ebd., Bd. 6, S. 442 und 454–457. Ähnlich noch A. SIELMANN, Die Verwaltung des Haupthauses Marienburg in der Zeit um 1400. Ein Beitrag zur Geschichte des Deutschen Ordens in Preußen, in: Zeitschrift des Westpreußischen Geschichtsvereins 61 (1921), S. 1–101, hier S. 24, 37, der Großkomtur als „Minister des Äußeren", der Tressler als „Finanzminister".

[4] Dazu u.a. P. G. THIELEN, Die Verwaltung des Ordensstaates Preußen vornehmlich im 15. Jahrhundert (Ost–Mitteleuropa in Vergangenheit und Gegenwart 11), Köln/Graz 1965, S. 2, 69; K. NEITMANN, Die Hochmeister des Deutschen Ordens in Preußen – ein Residenzherrscher unterwegs. Untersuchungen zu den Hochmeisteritineraren im 14. und 15. Jahrhundert (Veröffentlichungen aus den Archiven Preußischer Kulturbesitz 30), Köln/Wien 1990, S. 1.

[5] Für einen Überblick: J. SARNOWSKY, Das Historische Staatsarchiv Königsberg und die Erschließung seiner Bestände, in: M. M. RÜCKERT (Hg.), Das 'virtuelle Archiv des Deutschen Ordens'. Beiträge einer Tagung im Staatsarchiv Ludwigsburg am 11. und 12. April 2013, Stuttgart 2014, S. 93–105.

[6] Für die Außenpolitik zeigt das die Arbeit von S. KUBON, Die Außenpolitik des Deutschen Ordens unter Hochmeister Konrad von Jungingen (1393–1407) (Nova Mediaevalia 15), Göttingen 2016.

1399 bis 1409 überlieferte Tresslerbuch erlaubt interessante Einblicke in die Wirtschaftsführung und Finanzpolitik des Ordens.[7] Es enthält die Einnahmen und Ausgaben der hochmeisterlichen Kasse, die durch den Tressler verwaltet wurde.[8]

Diese 'Blütezeit' endete im Juli 1410 mit der Schlacht von Tannenberg, der Niederlage des Ordens gegen Polen-Litauen, die wirtschaftlich zu schweren Problemen und letztlich in den Konflikt mit den preußischen Ständen führte. Dennoch ist es falsch, von einem steten Niedergang zu sprechen, vielmehr gelang vor 1454 noch einmal eine Konsolidierung der wirtschaftlichen Lage.[9] Der entscheidende Einbruch kam erst durch den Dreizehnjährigen Krieg zwischen 1454 und 1466. Ein großer Teil der Stände sagte sich vom Orden los und unterstellte sich dem polnischen König, die ins Land gerufenen Söldnerverbände konnten nicht bezahlt werden und erhielten Ordensburgen und -besitzungen als Pfand. Die Situation nach dem Zweiten Thorner Frieden im Oktober 1466 glich der eines Staatsbankrotts.[10] Die Schulden blieben bis ins 16. Jahrhundert auf der Tagesordnung,[11] als mit Friedrich von Sachsen 1498 erstmals ein Mitglied einer hohen reichsfürstlichen Familie zum Hochmeister gewählt wurde. Friedrichs Amtsantritt markierte auch in der Finanzpolitik des Ordens einen Neuanfang.[12] Aus der Zeit Friedrichs haben sich ausführliche zentrale Rechnungen erhalten, die Einblicke in die Wirtschaftsführung des Hochmeisters und seiner Räte geben.[13] Zur Untersuchung der Rationalität der Finanzpolitik des Deutschen Ordens sol-

---

[7] Das Marienburger Tresslerbuch der Jahre 1399–1409, ed. E. JOACHIM, Königsberg 1896, ND Bremerhaven 1973.

[8] Dazu vgl. J. SARNOWSKY, Das Tressleramt. Aufgaben und Raumbedarf, in: A. MENTZEL–REUTERS / S. SAMERSKI (Hgg.), Castrum sanctae Mariae. Burg, Residenz und Museum (Vestigia Prussica. Forschungen zur ost– und westpreußischen Landesgeschichte 1), Göttingen 2019, S. 251–264; s. weiter DERS., Die Wirtschaftsführung des Deutschen Ordens in Preußen (1382–1454) (Veröffentlichungen aus den Archiven Preußischer Kulturbesitz 34), Köln/Weimar/Wien 1993, insbes. S. 52–61.

[9] Ebd., bes. S. 454–457.

[10] Dazu J. LACZNY, Schuldenverwaltung und Tilgung der Forderungen der Söldner des Deutschen Ordens in Preußen nach dem Zweiten Thorner Frieden. Ordensfoliant 259 und 261, Zusatzmaterial (Beihefte zum Preußischen Urkundenbuch 5) Göttingen 2019.

[11] Zu verweisen wäre etwa auf die Anlage des Ordensfolianten 261 mit Quittungen u.a. der Söldner noch 1504, vgl. J. LACZNY, Schuldenverwaltung und Tilgung der Forderungen der Söldner des Deutschen Ordens in Preußen (wie Anm. 10), S. 83.

[12] S. u.a. J. SARNOWSKY, Die Finanzpolitik des Deutschen Ordens unter Friedrich von Sachsen, in: Zapiski Historyczne 81, 4 (2016, ersch. 2017), S. 117–132.

[13] Geheimes Staatsarchiv Preußischer Kulturbesitz, Berlin, XX. Hauptabteilung (künftig GStA PK), Ordensfolianten (künftig OF) 193–198 (OF 193–194: Einnahmen und Ausgaben der Rentkammer, 1500–1502; OF 195–198: Ausgaben– und Einnahmebuch des Hochmeisters Friedrich von Sachsen 1504–1505 und 1507–1510); eine Rechnung der Rentkammer für 1499–1500 in GStA PK, Ordensbriefarchiv (künftig: OBA) 18322, vom 29. September 1500.

len hier für beide Phasen der Ordensgeschichte die relevanten Ämter, die Formen der Buchführung und die Ansätze für eine Planung und Steuerung der Einnahmen und Ausgaben behandelt werden.

Wie schon von der älteren Forschung richtig erkannt,[14] kam um 1400 Großkomtur und Tressler eine besondere Verantwortung für die Finanzen des Ordens zu. Die Aufgaben des Großkomturs werden unter anderem in den älteren Gewohnheiten formuliert: *Zu des grôzen commendures ambehte gehôret der schaz unde daz getreide [...]*.[15] Der Großkomtur war ursprünglich der Leiter des Haupthauses, der die Versorgung aller dort lebenden Brüder organisieren musste. Daraus erwuchs für die Amtsinhaber – zusammen mit Hochmeister und Tressler – die Kontrolle über den Ordensschatz. Dies äußerte sich zunächst in der Verwahrung jeweils eines der drei Schlüssel, die für den Schatz vorgesehen waren.[16] Der Großkomtur konnte den Hochmeister auch bei der am Monatsende vorgesehenen Rechnungslegung mit dem Tressler und mit den Amtsleuten vertreten, und wenn der Tressler Gold oder Silber empfing, musste er Hochmeister und Großkomtur in Kenntnis setzen.[17] Als zusätzliche Aufgabe erhielt der Großkomtur in Preußen die Kontrolle über die Schuldner des Ordens.[18] Zunächst wurden alle Schulden offenbar auf Wachstafeln eingetragen,[19] später in einem Schuldbuch des Großkomturs,[20] das auch die Buchungen von Schulden im Tresslerbuch aufnahm und das grundlegende Verzeichnis darstellte.

Der Tressler war nach den Statuten dem Großkomtur klar nachgeordnet, doch dürfte die Vielzahl seiner Aufgaben auch Freiräume für Entscheidungen ermöglicht haben. In der Regel übernahmen so nur erfahrene Brüder das Amt,[21]

---

[14] Wie Anm. 3.

[15] Die Statuten des Deutschen Ordens nach den ältesten Handschriften, ed. M. PERLBACH, Halle 1890, ND Hildesheim/New York 1975, S. 106 (Gw 28).

[16] Ebd., S. 97 (Gw 9).

[17] Ebd., S. 107, 109 (Gw 31, 36). – Diese Bestimmungen des 13. Jhs. blieben nicht zuletzt durch die Statutenrevision unter Konrad von Erlichshausen auf dem Generalkapitel von 1442 auch im 15. Jahrhundert gültig, vgl. J. SARNOWSKY, The Statutes of the Military Orders, in: DERS., On the Military Orders in Medieval Orders in Medieval Europe. Structures and Perceptions (Variorum Collected Studies Series 992), Farnham 2011, no. II, S. 8, 11.

[18] A. KLEIN, Die zentrale Finanzverwaltung im Deutschordensstaate Preussen am Anfang des 15. Jahrhunderts (Staats- und sozialwissenschaftliche Forschungen, 23, 2), Leipzig 1904, S. 131–133; J. SARNOWSKY, Die Wirtschaftsführung des Deutschen Ordens in Preußen (wie Anm. 8), S. 47–48.

[19] Ein Hinweis auf die Tafeln (zum 1. Juni 1376) bietet: Das große Ämterbuch des Deutschen Ordens, ed. W. ZIESEMER, Danzig 1921, ND Wiesbaden 1968, S. 534.

[20] Belege u.a. Das Marienburger Ämterbuch, ed. W. ZIESEMER, Danzig 1916, S. 44, 55 Anm. 1; Das Marienburger Tresslerbuch, ed. E. JOACHIM (wie Anm. 7), S. 438, 451–452, 518, Rubriken mit der Überschrift *bezalte scholt in des groskompthurs buche*.

[21] Friedrich von Wenden, Tressler 1393–1397, war z.B. zuvor Vogt von Grebin, Komtur von Engelsburg, Brandenburg und Gollub, s. künftig die Listen bei: D. HECKMANN, Amtsträger

und zwei der Tressler um 1400, Konrad von Jungingen und Paul von Rusdorf, stiegen danach unmittelbar oder mittelbar zu Hochmeistern auf. Um 1400 hatte der Tressler verschiedene Kassen zu verwalten. Ursprünglich war er nur für den Ordensschatz zuständig, dann aber führte man nach der endgültigen Übersiedlung der Hochmeister auf die Marienburg um 1325 eine eigene hochmeisterliche Kasse ein, aus der die alltäglichen Ausgaben für die Landesherrschaft finanziert wurden, die Tresslerkasse.[22] Für den Ordensschatz ist keine eigene Buchführung überliefert, vielmehr wird er nur im Zusammenhang mit der Einnahme bzw. Einlagerung von Geldern, Gold und Silber erwähnt. So ist etwa die Rede vom *grossen treszel [...] in dem keller uf dem husze* und von einer Silberkammer *uf dem husze by der treppen*.[23] Dagegen wird die Tresslerkasse nicht nur im großen Tresslerbuch der Jahre 1399 bis 1409, sondern auch in weiteren erhaltenen Rechnungen fassbar. Als drittes verwaltete der Tressler noch die Kasse des Marienburger Konvents, über die er in einem eigenen Rechnungsbuch, dem 'Konventsbuch', abrechnete.[24]

Der Tressler wurde durch weiteres Personal unterstützt. Um 1400 finden sich z.B. beim Tressler die nicht dem Orden angehörenden Schreiber Andreas und Johannes Tuwernicz.[25] Auch wenn die Ritterbrüder wahrscheinlich nicht des Schreibens mächtig waren, werden die Tressler zumindest Lesefähigkeit, zumal in der Volkssprache, besessen haben. Die Anlage der Bücher lag dennoch wesentlich in den Händen der Schreiber, wie es etwa am Beginn der Abrechnung zu 1402 heißt: *hic Johannes Thuwernicz inchoavit scribere juxta mandata domini Borghardi de Wobeke, thezaurarii*.[26] Man holte sich folglich externe Erfahrung, um die Buchführung zu organisieren.

Die Rechnungsbücher des Ordens folgen noch nicht – wie das für die Rechnungen im Hanseraum insgesamt gilt – den schon im 14. Jahrhundert in Italien

---

des Deutschen Ordens in Preußen und in den Kammerballeien des Reiches (oberste Gebietiger, Komture, Hauskomture, Kumpane, Vögte, Pfleger, Großschäffer) (Einzelschriften der Historischen Kommission für ost– und westpreußische Landesforschung 32; Towarzystwo Naukowe w Toruniu), Toruń, in Vorbereitung.

[22] Dazu s. u.a. A. SIELMANN, Die Verwaltung des Haupthauses Marienburg (wie Anm. 3), S. 42–43; P. G. THIELEN, Die Verwaltung des Ordensstaates Preußen (wie Anm. 4), S. 77–78; J. SARNOWSKY, Die Wirtschaftsführung des Deutschen Ordens in Preußen (wie Anm. 8), S. 53.

[23] Das Marienburger Tresslerbuch, ed. E. JOACHIM (wie Anm. 7), S. 44 (mit einer Verschreibung *treszeler* statt *treszel*), 46, 64, 76, 205, 598 u.a.

[24] Edition: Das Marienburger Konventsbuch der Jahre 1399–1412, ed. W. ZIESEMER, Danzig 1921. – Die Rolle des Tresslers bei den Abrechnungen wird immer wieder aus den Überschriften deutlich. So heißt es z.B. zu 1403: *Summe was der treszeler von des covents wegen entpfangen hat [...]. Do von hat der treszeler wider usgegeben [...]*, ebd., S. 114.

[25] Das Marienburger Tresslerbuch, ed. E. JOACHIM (wie Anm. 7), S. 5, 66 (Andreas) bzw. 131, 223 (Johannes Tuwernicz).

[26] Ebd., S. 131; vgl. dazu auch: A. KLEIN, Entstehung und Komposition des Marienburger Tresslerbuchs. Ein Beitrag zur Kritik mittelalterlicher Rechnungsbücher, Offenbach 1905, S. 10.

entwickelten Formen der doppelten Buchführung,[27] vielmehr legte man einzelne Listen auf Zetteln oder vielleicht auch auf Wachstafeln an, die dann in Reinschrift nacheinander in das Tresslerbuch übertragen wurden. Das lässt sich schon daran nachvollziehen, dass vielfach Posten unter einer Überschrift zusammengefasst sind, die auf die Verwaltung insbesondere der Ausgaben deutet. So heißt es etwa bei den Ausgaben zu 1401 *Dis nochgeschreben hat der huskompthur zu Danczk vor unsern homeister usgeben*,[28] und immer wieder finden sich Rubriken wie *huskompthur zu Konigisberg* oder *ken Rangnith dem steynmeister*.[29] Die Kompilation dieser Teilrechnungen war offenbar Aufgabe der Schreiber.

Anders, als man es vielleicht erwarten würde, wurden zudem die drei Kassen nicht klar voneinander getrennt. Der Ordensschatz erscheint, wie angesprochen, in der erhaltenen Rechnungsführung im Tresslerbuch nur indirekt für Entnahmen oder die Lagerung von Geldern. So wurden z.B. im Jahre 1400 unter anderem 2.400 Halbsköter,[30] 400 lübische gld., 630 ungarische gld., knapp 3.800 sch. gr., lötiges Silber und preußisches Geld aus dem Tressel entnommen. Ein Teil dieser Gelder war dem Hochmeister zuvor von Herzog Semowit von Masowien an Schulden zurückgezahlt und im Tressel deponiert worden.[31]

Einer der Schreiber hat im Marienburger Konventsbuch zu 1400 das Abrechnungsverfahren in einer Notiz näher beschrieben.[32] *Nota: Wen der herre syn ding obirlegen wil, so hebe man an czu legen das innemen der nuwen schold und ouch der alden scholt und dy scholt, dy der treszeler dem meyster noch der rechenschafft scholdig bleyb, und des homeysters czins mit enander noch deme, als her gevallen ist, und dorczu dy scholt, dy in des groskomturs buche beczalt ist*.[33] Das erste waren also die Einnahmen im jeweiligen Rechnungsjahr. Es sollte mit der Rückzahlung von Schulden begonnen werden, ebenso mit der Schuld, die der Tressler nach der Rechnungslegung des letzten Jahrs noch zu begleichen hatte, und dann mit den Zinszahlungen an den Hochmeister, wie sie eingegangen waren. Dem waren die Ausgaben gegenüber zu stellen. Ausdrücklich ist dabei sowohl von den Ausgaben des Meisters als auch von den Einnahmen und Ausgaben des Konvents die Rede, so dass Tressler- und

---

27 Vgl. F.-J. ARLINGHAUS, Art. Bookkeeping, Double-entry Bookkeeping, in: Medieval Italy. An Encyclopedia, 1, ed. C. KLEINHENZ, New York 2004, S. 147–150.

28 Das Marienburger Tresslerbuch, ed. E. JOACHIM (wie Anm. 7), S. 107.

29 Ebd., S. 109, 110, 116, 117.

30 Eine nur kurzzeitig ab 1368 neben den Schillingen geprägte große Silbermünze, vgl. O. VOLCKART, Die Münzpolitik im Ordensland und Herzogtum Preußen von 1370 bis 1550 (Deutsches Historisches Institut Warschau. Quellen und Studien 4), Wiesbaden 1996, S. 41–52.

31 Das Marienburger Tresslerbuch, ed. E. JOACHIM (wie Anm. 7), S. 44–45.

32 Gegen A. KLEIN, Die zentrale Finanzverwaltung im Deutschordensstaate Preussen (wie Anm. 18), S. 90–92, kann auf Grundlage dieser Notiz keineswegs von einer strengen Trennung der Kassen gesprochen werden.

33 Das Marienburger Konventsbuch, ed. W. ZIESEMER (wie Anm. 24), S. 36.

Konventskasse gegeneinander ausgeglichen werden sollten. Einbezogen wurden dabei sowohl die grundherrlichen Einnahmen des Ordens in der Komturei Marienburg und Bargeldbestände wie auch die Einkünfte des Hochmeisters unter anderem von Zinsen der Pfarrer (von Danzig und Thorn)[34] und von der Fähre zu Dirschau. Waren diese noch nicht eingegangen, sollten sie trotzdem unter den Einnahmen gelistet und zugleich in das Schuldbuch des Tresslers übernommen werden. Weiter heißt es: *Item so sal man denne des meysters innemen und des covents innemen czuhofe summen und off eyne syte legen und dornoch des meysters usgeben und des covents usgeben und dorczu des herren schold off die ander syte und sal denne eyns ken dem andern abenemen, so syt man denne, wy es dorumb ist.*[35] Die Bilanz sollte also noch einmal Einnahmen und Ausgaben von Hochmeister und Konvent zusammenführen.

Es überrascht wenig, dass sich dieser Ausgleich der Kassen nicht immer in den erhaltenen Rechnungsbüchern nachvollziehen lässt. Erst 1401 sind im Tresslerbuch ausdrücklich die Einkünfte des Konvents, knapp 8.800 m., mit den Einnahmen des Meister von über 14.600 m. in einer Summe zusammen gezogen.[36] Eine entsprechende Summierung findet sich am Ende des Jahres, mit Ausgaben von rund 13.300 m. für den Meister und rund 5150 m. für den Konvent,[37] ohne dass sich das in den Posten klar nachvollziehen ließe. Im Konventsbuch werden zunächst die Zinseinkünfte zu 1401 mit etwas mehr als 8.000 m. beziffert, dazu kamen rund 750 m. an Einnahmen aus Verkäufen,[38] was sich in der Summe nicht ganz mit den knapp 8.800 m. des Tresslerbuchs deckt. Die Ausgaben sind im Konventsbuch nicht summiert,[39] erreichen aber mit etwas über 1.100 m. bei weitem nicht die im Tresslerbuch genannten Ausgaben, so dass wahrscheinlich die dort gelisteten Posten mit herangezogen werden müssen. Der nächste Schreiber, Johannes Tuwernicz, hat diese Form der Abrechnung für 1402 nur teilweise übernommen. So fehlen die Summen der Einnahmen, auch wenn die Ausgaben

---

[34] Dazu: A. KLEIN, Die zentrale Finanzverwaltung im Deutschordensstaate Preussen (wie Anm. 18), S. 19–20.

[35] Wiederum: Das Marienburger Konventsbuch, ed. W. ZIESEMER (wie Anm. 24), S. 36; insgesamt vgl. J. SARNOWSKY, Die Wirtschaftsführung des Deutschen Ordens in Preußen (wie Anm. 8), S. 54.

[36] Das Marienburger Tresslerbuch, ed. E. JOACHIM (wie Anm. 7), S. 92; die Einkünfte des Konvents betrugen 8.766 m. 21½ sc. 4 d., die des Hochmeisters 14.627½ m. 3½ sc., als Summe sind genannt 23.394 m. 13 sc. 4 d.

[37] Ebd., S. 130, genauer 13.318 m. minus ½ sc., 5.149 m. 4. sc. und als Summe 18.467 m. 3½ sc.

[38] Das Marienburger Konventsbuch, ed. W. ZIESEMER (wie Anm. 24), S. 60–61; ein später aufgeklebtes Papierblatt nennt offenbar für die Einnahmen noch *summa prima 8.127 m. minus 2 d.*, ebd., S. 62.

[39] Ebd., S. 61–63.

zusammengefasst sind.⁴⁰ Ähnlich setzt sich das für die nächsten Jahre fort.⁴¹ Die 1400 von einem Schreiber formulierte Norm hatte somit keineswegs absolute Verbindlichkeit, sondern spiegelt eher die groben Linien der Buchführung.

Die Einrichtung der Tresslerkasse um 1325 lässt sich als Versuch werten, die Einnahmen und Ausgaben des Hochmeisters im Rahmen der Landesherrschaft besser zu steuern, als es mit dem etwas schwerfälligen Instrument des Ordensschatzes möglich war. Offenbar verloren bei der Einrichtung der Tresslerkasse eine Reihe von kleineren Verwaltungseinheiten des Ordens im Kulmerland ihren Status als Komturei, d.h. Sitz eines Konvents mit Brüdern unter der Leitung eines Komturs,⁴² wurden in Vogteien oder Pflegeämter umgewandelt und direkt dem Hochmeister unterstellt. Um 1400 zinsten die Vögte von Dirschau, Roggenhausen, Leipe und Brathean sowie der Pfleger von Bütow zusammen über 3.000 m. Dazu kamen 800 m. des Komturs von Tuchel sowie kleinere Zahlungen der Komture von Papau, Nessau und Schwetz.⁴³ Auch wenn das die Ausgaben des Hochmeisters in dieser Zeit bei weitem nicht deckte, bildeten diese Zinse mit 4–4.500 m. jährlich eine verlässliche Grundlage. Ihre Bedeutung zeigt sich daran, dass diese Summen unter den Einnahmen gelistet werden sollten, auch wenn sie noch nicht bezahlt waren.⁴⁴

Dazu kamen um 1400 nicht unerhebliche unregelmäßige Einnahmen aus den lokalen Ämtern. An erster Stelle sind die sogenannten „Wandelgelder" zu nennen, die Überschüsse beim Wechsel von einem Amt in ein anderes. Bei Komturen und Großgebietigern konnten die Einnahmen sehr hoch ausfallen. Als 1404 eine Reihe von Gebietigern ausgetauscht wurden, zahlten der Komtur von Tuchel 6.500 m., der Komtur von Graudenz 1.200 m. und der Komtur zu Christburg rund 4.000 m. an Wandelgeldern in die Tresslerkasse, der Tressler Burghard von Wobeke 1.000 m.⁴⁵ Daneben spielten die „Totengelder", d.h. die Nachlässe verstorbener Gebietiger, eine nicht unwichtige Rolle. 1404 zog der Tressler z.B.

---

40 Das Marienburger Tresslerbuch, ed. E. JOACHIM (wie Anm. 7), S. 203, 28.737 m. 3½ sc. für den Meister, 5123 m. 1 f. für den Konvent, insgesamt ist genannt 33.860 m. 1 f.

41 Zu 1403 findet sich z.B. am Ende der Jahresrechnung eine Summierung von Einnahmen und Ausgaben von Hochmeister und Konvent, ebd., S. 278; zu 1404 werden eingangs wieder die Einnahmen von Meister und Konvent summiert, am Ende getrennt die Ausgaben, ebd., S. 282 und 328.

42 Zu Stellung der Komture vgl. u.a. J. SARNOWSKY, Die Wirtschaftsführung des Deutschen Ordens in Preußen (wie Anm. 8), S. 116–118; P. G. THIELEN, Die Verwaltung des Ordensstaates Preußen (wie Anm. 4), S. 84–92.

43 J. SARNOWSKY, Die Wirtschaftsführung des Deutschen Ordens in Preußen (wie Anm. 8), S. 127 und 252, mit Tab. 15; zur Geschichte dieser Zinse vgl. A. SIELMANN, Die Verwaltung des Haupthauses Marienburg (wie Anm. 3), S. 88–93 und 101.

44 Dazu oben zu Anm. 38; Übersichten über die Leistungen der Gebietiger in J. SARNOWSKY, Die Wirtschaftsführung des Deutschen Ordens in Preußen (wie Anm. 8), S. 442, Tab. 50, und S. 446, Tab. 51.

45 Ebd., S. 280–281.

2.000 m. vom verstorbenen Komtur von Elbing, Johann von Rumpenheim, ein.[46] Durchschnittlich erreichten Wandel- und Totengelder um 1400 Summe zwischen 6.000 und 9.000 m. jährlich.[47] Bei jährlichen Gesamtausgaben von 21.000 bis 28.000 m. war damit schon in der Regel ein erheblicher Anteil der erforderlichen Mittel gesichert.[48]

Darüber hinaus gab es ein zusätzliches Steuerungsinstrument: die sogenannten „Ausrichtungen" bzw. „Geschosszahlungen". Dabei wurden alle oder ein Teil der Ordensämter an Maßnahmen beteiligt, die ein einzelnes Haus oder eine konkrete Belastung betrafen, entweder durch die Entsendung von Personal, Material oder finanziellen Mitteln.[49] Schon 1397 wurden z.B. die Ämter, nach der Größe differenziert (groß, mittel, klein), zu Zahlungen von insgesamt mehr als 2.600 m. herangezogen, möglicherweise im Zusammenhang mit der Vorbereitung des militärischen Unternehmens von 1398 gegen die Vitalienbrüder.[50] Auf diese Weise wurden nicht nur die Einnahmen der lokalen Ämter stärker für die Aufgaben der Zentrale herangezogen, wie schon die ältere Forschung betont hat.[51] Vielmehr konnten auf diese Weise sowohl größere Ausgaben wie auch personell aufwendige Maßnahmen, z.B. Bauten, lang- oder mittelfristig vorab geplant und abgesichert werden.

Die Ausrichtungen und Geschosszahlungen gewannen durch den dramatischen Rückgang der Wandel- und Totengelder infolge des wirtschaftlichen Niedergangs nach der Schlacht von Tannenberg 1410 noch stärkere Bedeutung und trugen zur Stabilisierung der Lage bis in die 1440er Jahre bei.[52] Dann führte aber der Dreizehnjährige Krieg zu einem völligen Zusammenbruch der bisherigen Wirtschaftsführung. Der Verlust weiter Teile des Landes und die Zahlungen an die Söldner hatten faktisch schon unmittelbar nach Kriegsbeginn den Verbrauch aller noch vorhandenen Rücklagen zur Folge, auch der Verkauf der Neumark brachte keine Entlastung.[53] Eine Folge war, dass das Amt des Tresslers nach dem Ausscheiden Eberhards von Kinsberg im Februar 1458 nicht wieder besetzt

---

[46] Ebd., S. 90 und 281.
[47] Wiederum nach ebd., S. 446, Tab. 51.
[48] Gegenüberstellung ebd., S. 451, Tab. 54.
[49] P. G. THIELEN, Die Verwaltung des Ordensstaates Preußen (wie Anm. 4), S. 93–96; J. SARNOWSKY, Die Wirtschaftsführung des Deutschen Ordens in Preußen (wie Anm. 8), S. 244–253.
[50] OBA 556, von 1397, vgl. J. SARNOWSKY, Die Wirtschaftsführung des Deutschen Ordens in Preußen (wie Anm. 8), S. 245.
[51] A. KLEIN, Die zentrale Finanzverwaltung im Deutschordensstaate Preussen (wie Anm. 18), S. 32–39.
[52] Im Überblick: J. SARNOWSKY, Die Wirtschaftsführung des Deutschen Ordens in Preußen (wie Anm. 8), S. 446 Tab. 51.
[53] Dazu J. VOIGT, Die Erwerbung der Neumark. Ziel und Erfolg der Brandenburgischen Politik unter den Kurfürsten Friedrich I. und Friedrich II. 1402–1457. Nach archivalischen Quellen, Berlin 1863, bes. S. 363–366.

wurde.⁵⁴ Nach 1466 ließ sich lange keine normale Wirtschaftsführung etablieren, auch angesichts neuer Kriegsgefahren im 'Pfaffenkrieg' der 1470er Jahre um die Besetzung des Bistums Ermland.⁵⁵

Mit der Wahl des ersten fürstlichen Hochmeisters Friedrich von Sachsen im September 1498 begann jedoch eine neue Phase. Eine der Ursachen war, dass die Gesandten, die im Namen Herzog Albrechts von Sachsen, des Vaters des künftigen Hochmeisters, und seines Bruders Herzog Georg mit dem Orden verhandelten,⁵⁶ eine angemessene Ausstattung Friedrichs forderten. Nicht nur für die persönlichen Ausgaben, sondern auch für die Politik des Ordens sollte er mindestens 20.000 rhein. gld. zu Verfügung haben, also etwa 30.000 bis 32.000 m. pr. Dafür war ausdrücklich vorgesehen, neben der dem Hochmeister nach 1466 zugewiesenen Komturei Königsberg zur finanziellen Absicherung weitere Komtureien heranzuziehen. Schon im April 1498 konnte der Vertrag zu Königsberg geschlossen werden. Er regelte die Zusatzfinanzierung, für die neben den bisherigen Ämtern die Komturei Brandenburg und eine weitere Komturei genutzt werden sollten, sondern enthielt auch die Zusage der Gebietiger, sich an der Tilgung der immer noch drückenden Schulden aus dem Dreizehnjährigen Krieg zu beteiligen.⁵⁷

Eine zentrale Rolle für die Finanzen des Ordens spielte in dieser Zeit der Pfund-, Rent- oder Kammermeister (die Bezeichnungen in den Quellen wechseln). Das Amt des Pfundmeisters war noch vor Mai 1400 für den ursprünglich

---

54 D. HECKMANN, Amtsträger des Deutschen Ordens in Preußen (wie Anm. 21), gibt als Amtsdaten Kinsbergs 1. Mai 1453– 8. Februar 1458 an; der Tressler war allerdings schon zuvor zwischenzeitig in Schivelbein gefangen und kehrte nicht nach Preußen zurück, u.a. J. VOIGT, Die Erwerbung der Neumark (wie Anm. 53), S. 366 mit Anm. 2.

55 J. VOIGT, Geschichte Preußens (wie Anm. 2), Bd. 9, S. 105–120; zur Situation nach 1466 vgl. allgemein L. DRALLE, Der Staat des Deutschen Ordens nach dem II. Thorner Frieden. Untersuchungen zur ökonomischen und ständepolitischen Geschichte Altpreußens zwischen 1466 und 1497 (Frankfurter Historische Abhandlungen 9), Wiesbaden 1975.

56 Zu den Verhandlungen vgl. allgemein die ungedruckte Dissertation von I. MATISON, Die Politik des Hochmeisters Herzog Friedrich von Sachsen (1498–1510), Diss. phil. masch. LMU München 1957, bes. S. 67–85; zu den Finanzen bes. L. DRALLE, Die Einkünfte des Deutschordenshochmeisters Friedrich von Sachsen (1498 bis 1510). Ein Beitrag zur Finanzgeschichte der ostdeutschen Territorien, in: Zeitschrift für Ostforschung 28 (1979), S. 626–640, hier S. 626; und P. OBERLÄNDER, Hochmeister Friedrich von Sachsen (1498–1510), 1. Teil: Wahl und Politik bis zum Tode König Johann Albrechts von Polen, Diss. phil. Berlin, Magdeburg 1914, S. 27.

57 Geheimes Staatsarchiv Preußischer Kulturbesitz, Berlin, XX. Hauptabteilung, Pergament–Urkunden, Schiebl. II, 9, ediert: Liv–, Est– und Kurländisches Urkundenbuch, II. Abt., Bd. 1: 1494–1500, ed. L. ARBUSOW, Riga/Moskau 1900, Nr. 661, S. 491–493; vgl. I. MATISON, Die Politik des Hochmeisters Herzog Friedrich von Sachsen (wie Anm. 56), S. 81.

hansischen, dann aber zunehmend vom Orden kontrollierten Pfundzoll eingeführt worden.[58] Nach der Aufhebung des Tressleramts wuchsen den Amtsinhabern zusätzliche Aufgaben zu. Für Hochmeister Friedrich von Sachsen wurden die Aufgaben der zentralen Ämter erstmals in einer Hofordnung festgehalten, die von einem der von Friedrich mitgebrachten Räte, Dr. Dietrich von Werther, bearbeitet und korrigiert wurde.[59] Dort heißt es zum Rentmeister: *Der sal des zcols warthenn unnd unser camern, welch ampt geldes bedarff, erholt sich an ime. Er sal auch allein unser renthen innehmenn [und berechen], unnd wo ime was gebricht, erholt er sich an uns.*[60] Als eine Einnahmequelle hatte er damit den nun in Königsberg erhobenen Pfundzoll, dazu kamen die Einkünfte der hochmeisterlichen Kammer.

Zusammen mit dem ebenfalls für wirtschaftliche Aufgaben zuständigen (Königsberger) Hauskomtur zog er die Naturalabgaben und den Bernstein ein und sorgte mit Zustimmung des Hochmeisters für deren Verkauf. Zudem sollte der Rentmeister gemeinsam mit dem Hauskomtur alle untergeordneten Ämter kontrollieren. Der Hauskomtur sollte insbesondere zusammen *mit unserm camermeister alle unser jharrentin einnheme und ausgebe und alle quatember ire rechenschafft beschlisse.*[61] Sie sollten also zusammen vierteljährlich einen Rechnungsabschluss vorlegen.

Obwohl die wirtschaftlich relevanten, untergeordneten Hausämter nur kurz angesprochen werden,[62] sollte die Hofordnung unter anderem die Finanzverwaltung neu organisieren. Es ist so vielleicht kein Zufall, dass der erste bekannte Rentmeister unter Friedrich von Sachsen, der Ordensbruder Hans von Thüngen, so etwas wie einen Haushaltsplan des Hochmeisters aufstellte, der vielleicht schon den Verhandlungen mit den sächsischen Gesandten zugrundelag. Das ursprünglich selbstständige kleine Heft von acht Seiten ist heute in das erste der

---

[58] J. SARNOWSKY, Die Wirtschaftsführung des Deutschen Ordens in Preußen (wie Anm. 8), S. 73.

[59] Hofordnung des Hochmeisters Friedrich von Sachsen, GStA PK, OBA 18215, im Findbuch datiert auf 1499 Dezember; vgl. K. FORSTREUTER, Die Hofordnungen der letzten Hochmeister in Preußen, in: Prussia 29 (1931), S. 223–231, Teil–ND (ohne Edition der Hofordnung) in: DERS., Beiträge zur preußischen Geschichte im 15. und 16. Jahrhundert, Heidelberg 1960, S. 29–34, hier S. 31. – Die Edition der Hofordnung, ebd. S. 228–231, findet sich auch online in der Datenbank des Herder–Instituts: http://www.herder–institut.de/no_cache/bestaende-digitale–angebote/e–publikationen/dokumente–und–materialien/themenmodule/quelle/1201/details/1846.html (letzte Einsichtnahme 27.11.2017).

[60] K. FORSTREUTER, Die Hofordnungen der letzten Hochmeister in Preußen (wie Anm. 59), S. 230.

[61] Ebd., S. 228.

[62] Es handelt sich daneben um die 'klassischen' Hausämter, also Schenkenmeister, Küchmeister, Kellermeister, Kornmeister, Mühlmeister, Scheunenmeister, Karwansherr und Baumeister, dazu um die beiden 'Adjutanten' des Hochmeisters, den Obersten und Untersten Kompan, ebd.

Rechnungsbücher der Zeit Friedrichs von Sachsen eingebunden,[63] mit der Überschrift: *Disz hirnachgeschriben ist die nutzung, renthe, zcinse unnd zufelle allenthalben ins herren hoemeisters cammern ierlich fellig zJ gemeynen jarn.*[64]

Die Übersicht ist zunächst geographisch organisiert. Neben dem Bistum Samland und den drei Städten Königsberg werden daher zunächst alle untergeordneten Ämter der Komturei Königsberg mit ihren Abgaben aufgelistet, dann dem Hochmeister entsprechend der Zusagen in den Verhandlungen zugeordnete Ämter in den Komtureien Brandenburg, Elbing und Neidenburg. Der Haushaltsplan trägt jedoch noch den Charakter eines unvollständigen Entwurfs, da z.B. oft konkrete Angaben zu Erträgen wie aus Jagd- und Fischereirechten sowie Wachs-, Hühner- und Honigzinsen fehlen. Ähnlich gilt das für die jährlichen Einkünfte aus dem Verkauf von Fischereirechten auf dem Haff, den Keutelbriefen, sowie insgesamt für die Komturei Brandenburg, bei der es anstelle einer Summe nur heißt, *sovil desselbigen ampts mein gnediger here genyessen mag*.[65] An Zinsen und Renten sind insgesamt rund 5.400 m. verzeichnet, dazu Gerichtsgefälle bzw. bäuerliche Zinse von 1.600 m. aus dem Samland,[66] 2.300 m. aus Verkäufen sowie Naturalabgaben. Als höchster Einzelposten erscheint jedoch der Bernsteinverkauf mit 9.000 m., ergänzt durch den Pfundzoll und weitere Zölle von insgesamt 1.100 m. Die geforderten 30.000 bis 32.000 m. wurden mit den nicht benannten Summen vielleicht so noch gerade erreicht.

Die Realität sah allerdings – soweit es die erhaltenen Rechnungen hergeben – noch einmal anders aus. Ein Problem war auch, dass Thüngen die zu erwartenden Ausgaben nicht gegen gerechnet und damit nicht strukturiert hatte. Ähnlich wie um 1400 bildeten wiederum Einzelrechnungen auf Zetteln und in Heften einen wichtigen Ausgangspunkt. Für die erste Jahresrechnung für die Zeit vom Oktober 1498 bis September 1499 sind überhaupt nur diese erhalten; sie wurden erst im 19. Jahrhundert mit dem Ausgaberegister für die Jahre 1499–1500 zusammengebunden.[67] Die Übersicht über die Einnahmen dieser Zeit ist im Ordensbriefarchiv überliefert, weicht aber teilweise von den Angaben im Register ab.[68]

---

[63] GStA PK, OF 192, S. 1–7, mit einigen Vermerken auf S. 8. Nach der Notiz des Archivdirektors Meckelburg auf dem auf der Rückseite des Vorderdeckels eingeklebten Blatt war zuvor nur das jetzt auf S. 79–260 zu findende Ausgaberegister in braunes Leder als eigener Band eingebunden. Dieses wurde dann „mit allen noch erhaltenen Registerbögen vereinigt […], welche von Hans von Thüngen seit Uebernahme des Rentamts bis Michaeli[s] 1500 angelegt worden sind". Dazu kamen noch die lose eingelegten Belegzettel und Stücke aus „zerstreuten Registern".

[64] GStA PK, OF 192, S. 1.

[65] GStA PK, OF 192, S. 6.

[66] Dazu vgl. L. DRALLE, Die Einkünfte des Deutschordenshochmeisters Friedrich von Sachsen (wie Anm. 56), S. 635.

[67] Wie Anm. 67.

[68] Nach GStA PK, OF 192, fol. 251r, lässt sich nur erschließen, dass die Ausgaben von 11.113 m. von September 1499 bis September 1500 um 622 m. höher als die Einkünfte gewesen seien; aus OBA 18322 zeigen sich bei den Einzelposten trotz ähnlicher Gesamtsumme immer wieder

Unter Hans von Thüngen wurde die Buchführung schrittweise verbessert, wie die erhaltenen Abrechnungen über Einnahmen und Ausgaben der Rentkammer für die Jahre 1500–1502 erkennen lassen.[69] Die Anlage der Rechnungsbücher wurde durch Dr. Werther, den Rat des Hochmeisters, kontrolliert und ergänzt. Nach einer Überlieferungslücke lassen sich weitere Veränderungen feststellen. Für die Jahre 1504/1505 und 1507–1510 sind jeweils jährlich geführte Ausgaben- und Einnahmebücher des Hochmeisters erhalten. Die älteren, mehr oder weniger sauber angelegten Schmalfolio-Hefte wurden dabei durchgängig durch sauber geführte, mit großen Überschriften versehene Foliobände ersetzt. Für die Jahresrechnung 1504/1505 ist erstmals ein Nicht-Ordensmitglied, Franz Busse, als Rentmeister belegt, während offenbar Thüngen daneben noch als Pfundmeister im Amt blieb und die Pfundmeister auch danach aus dem Orden kamen.[70] Wie schon um 1400 holte man also externe Kompetenz, um die wichtigen Aufgaben der Finanzverwaltung besser lösen zu können.

Die erhaltenen Rechnungen für das erste Haushaltsjahr 1498/1499 zeigen, wie wenig Thüngens Planung anfangs der realen Situation entsprach. Das betrifft zunächst zwei große Posten, die bei Thüngen mehr als 50 % der Gesamteinnahmen ausgemacht hatten, die Bernsteinverkäufe und die Einnahmen aus den Zöllen, für die – möglicherweise unvollständig – statt 9.000 m. nur knapp 1.400 m. bzw. nur ein vom alten Pfundmeister erstatteter kleiner Betrag notiert sind.[71] Aus den Zinsen und Renten der dem Hochmeister untergeordneten Ämter sowie aus den drei Städten Königsberg gingen rund 3.500 m. ein, nur aus dem Samland konnten mit knapp 2.500 m. deutlich höhere Einkünfte erzielt werden. Erträge aus den Mühlen, Verkäufe von Naturalien und von Fischereirechten auf dem Haff erbrachten knapp 1.000 m. Mit 8.400 m. blieben also die Einkünfte weit unter den Erwartungen.

In dieser Situation griff man zu einem häufig angewandten Mittel, den Geschosszahlungen der Gebietiger. So zahlten der Großkomtur, die Komture zu Balga, Preußisch-Holland, Rhein, Ragnit und Memel und andere Brüder insgesamt knapp 1.200 m. Weil auch das aber nicht reichte, wurde der neue Hochmeister offenbar im ersten Jahr noch durch den sächsischen Hof unterstützt. Dies ergibt sich aus einer Liste von Zahlungen in rheinischen und ungarischen

---

Abweichungen, vgl. L. DRALLE, Die Einkünfte des Deutschordenshochmeisters Friedrich von Sachsen (wie Anm. 56), S. 628–629.

[69] GStA PK, OF 193–194, vgl. die Übersicht oben Anm. 13.

[70] GStA PK, OF 195, fol. 1r und 4r; L. DRALLE, Die Einkünfte des Deutschordenshochmeisters Friedrich von Sachsen (wie Anm. 56), S. 631–632; J. SARNOWSKY, Die Finanzpolitik des Deutschen Ordens unter Friedrich von Sachsen (wie Anm. 12), S. 121; leider lässt sich die Reihe der Amtsträger nicht vollständig ermitteln.

[71] Dies und die folgenden Angaben nach GStA PK, OF 192, S. 13–16, 19, 21, 25, 27, 38, 48, 74; aufgenommen sind nur gerundete Mark-Beträge; die genauen Angaben bei J. SARNOWSKY, Die Finanzpolitik des Deutschen Ordens unter Friedrich von Sachsen (wie Anm. 12), S. 125, mit Tabelle.

gld., die schon ab November 1498 vor allem durch den Kanzler Dr. Paulus Watt erfolgten.[72] Diese Einnahmen summieren sich auf knapp 4.000 m. preuß., so dass die Gesamteinnahmen rund 13.400 m. betrugen. Das lag immer noch deutlich unter den Zusagen an die Familie des neuen Hochmeisters, reichte aber – soweit das aus den überlieferten Rechnungen erkennbar ist – für die Ausgaben von rund 13.000 m. im ersten Rechnungsjahr aus.[73]

Unter Hans von Thüngen blieb die Situation des Hochmeisters trotz einiger Verbesserungen fast unverändert. Die Einnahmen betrugen in den Rechnungsjahren 1499/1500–1501/1502 jeweils nur zwischen rund 10.500 und 12.400 m.,[74] nunmehr ohne zusätzliche Zahlungen der sächsischen Verwandten des Hochmeisters. Ein wesentlicher Punkt war, dass die Einkünfte aus dem Bernsteinhandel deutlich höher ausfielen, zwischen rund 3.700 und 6.900 m., und damit einen erheblichen Anteil an den Einkünften hatten. Andere Einnahmen wie die aus den Ämtern oder aus den samländischen Zinsen und Gerichtsgefällen stagnierten.

Einen zunächst qualitativen wie dann auch quantitativen Sprung gab es durch die Übernahme des Rentmeisteramts durch Franz Busse 1504. Die Gesamteinkünfte stiegen für das Haushaltsjahr 1504/1505 zunächst auf rund 15.900 m., dann von 1507/1508–1509/1510 auf rund 20.700 m. bis 25.800 m. Das lag nicht an einer besseren Buchführung, sondern an strukturellen Änderungen. Die Einnahmen aus den Ämtern lagen nunmehr bei 5.700 bis 6.800 m., weil Friedrich nunmehr alle Einkünfte aus den Komtureien Brandenburg und Preußisch-Holland erhielt, die beide durch einen Vogt verwaltet wurden, und dazu kamen Zahlungen aus der Komturei Balga sowie aus den Ämtern Seehesten, Bartenstein und Schippenbeil.[75] Zudem konnten die Erträge aus den Bernsteinverkäufen gehalten bzw. im Weiteren deutlich gesteigert werden, von rund 4.400 m. auf bis zu rund 9.500 m., während die Einnahmen aus dem Samland auf konstant hohen Niveau blieben, durchschnittlich über 2.400 m. Im Rechnungsjahr 1507/1508 wurden noch 9.000 m. mit einer außerordentlichen Steuer erhoben,[76] so dass in diesem Jahr die höchsten Einnahmen erzielt werden konnten.

---

[72] GStA PK, OF 192, S. 16. In der Umrechnung der Angaben in rheinischen und ungarischen Gulden sowie m. preuß. folge ich der Quelle, da die Summe mit einem Wechselkurs von 1:1,5 korrekt sein dürfte.

[73] Dazu wiederum J. SARNOWSKY, Die Finanzpolitik des Deutschen Ordens unter Friedrich von Sachsen (wie Anm. 12), S. 125–127; darin war mit knapp 2.200 m. noch ein relativ hoher Anteil an Zahlungen für Schulden und Leibrenten enthalten, die wesentlich noch auf den Dreizehnjährigen Krieg zurückgehen dürften.

[74] Diese und die folgenden Zahlen nach L. DRALLE, Die Einkünfte des Deutschordenshochmeisters Friedrich von Sachsen (wie Anm. 56), S. 630–637.

[75] GStA PK, OF 195, fol. 5r–8r.

[76] L. DRALLE, Die Einkünfte des Deutschordenshochmeisters Friedrich von Sachsen (wie Anm. 56), S. 637.

Vergleicht man die Einnahmen mit den Ausgaben, führt das zu einem überraschenden Ergebnis. Während der Orden noch um 1400 aus dem Vollen schöpfte und Überschüsse normal waren, würde man für die Jahre um 1500 Defizite erwarten. Das ist jedoch nur einmal, im zweiten Jahr Thüngens, 1499/1500, der Fall, als den 10.500 m. Einnahmen rund 11.000 m. an Ausgaben gegenüberstanden.[77] In allen anderen Jahren blieben die Ausgaben jeweils knapp unter den Einnahmen, zunächst bei 10.900 m. bis 11.300 m., dann im ersten Jahr Franz Busses bei rund 15.800 m., schließlich in Relation zu den Einnahmen bei 19.000 m. bis 25.600 m.

Daraus ergeben sich zwei Fragen, die sich nicht sicher beantworten lassen. Die erste Frage betrifft die Vollständigkeit und Richtigkeit der Rechnungen. Die Summenbildung der zeitgenössischen Rechnungsführer ist meist nicht ganz korrekt, und einzelne Posten könnten insgesamt vergessen worden sein. Dennoch lässt die zunehmend systematischere Buchführung kaum Lücken erkennen. Diese Frage wird sich somit nicht mehr klären lassen. Setzt man aber die Vollständigkeit und Richtigkeit der Rechnungen voraus, stellt sich als zweite Frage, warum sich die Ausgaben und die Einnahmen so weitgehend entsprechen, ob dies bereits das Ergebnis genauer Planungen oder doch eher zufällig war. Da keine weiteren Haushaltspläne neben dem Thüngens erhalten sind – und sich dieser in vieler Hinsicht als ungenau erwiesen hat –, sind auch dafür keine eindeutigen Aussagen möglich. Allerdings verfestigt sich der Eindruck, dass man im Laufe des Jahres durchaus eine Vorstellung von der Höhe der Einkünfte hatte, um die Ausgaben entsprechend steuern zu können. Bei besonderen Ausgaben dürfte vorab auf Geschossforderungen zurückgegriffen worden sein. Zudem konnte man, wie das schon 1501/1502, dann wieder 1507/1508 geschah, bei höheren Ausgaben auch Steuern der Untertanen einfordern.[78] Als langfristiges Steuerungsinstrument nutzte man weiter die Zuweisung von Einkünften aus den lokalen Ämtern, die nach den schwierigen Jahren bis 1502 noch einmal deutlich erhöht wurde.

Zusammenfassend seien die Ergebnisse für die Finanzen des Deutschen Ordens in den Jahren um 1400 und um 1500 gegenübergestellt. In beiden Phasen waren mehrere Amtsträger für die Ordensfinanzen zuständig. Während die eigentliche Abrechnung durch Tressler oder Rentmeister erfolgte, erfolgten neben dem Hochmeister noch Kontrollen durch den Großkomtur bzw. durch den Hauskomtur oder später den Pfundmeister. Um 1500 waren zudem teilweise noch die hochmeisterlichen Räte, Dr. Dietrich Werther in der Zeit Hans von

---

[77] Die Zahlen im Vergleich von L. DRALLE, Die Ausgaben des Deutschordenshochmeisters Friedrich von Sachsen (1498–1510). Ein Beitrag zur Finanzgeschichte, in: Zeitschrift für Ostforschung 30 (1981), S. 195–226, hier S. 226; und DERS., Die Einkünfte des Deutschordenshochmeisters Friedrich von Sachsen (wie Anm. 56), S. 630.

[78] Zahlen bei L. DRALLE, Die Einkünfte des Deutschordenshochmeisters Friedrich von Sachsen (wie Anm. 56), S. 637.

Thüngens als Rentmeister, beteiligt.[79] In beiden Phasen holte man zudem weltliche Personen mit besonderen Kenntnissen in die Ordensverwaltung. Um 1400 betraf dies die Schreiber Andreas und Johannes Tuwernicz, um 1500 den Rentmeister Franz Busse, unter dem sicher auch noch Schreiber beschäftigt waren.[80]

Die Buchführung folgte um 1400 wie um 1500 noch recht einfachen Formen. Die Rechnungsführung erfolgte zunächst auf Wachstafeln, Zetteln oder in kleineren Heften, um dann – mit wenigen Ausnahmen wie dem ersten Jahr Hans von Thüngens – in Reinschrift auf fertige Lagen oder in Bücher übertragen zu werden. Bei den Einnahmen war man von Anfang an auf Regelmäßigkeit bedacht, wie sich um 1400 von einem der Schreiber Hinweise auf die Anlage der gesamten Abrechnung finden.[81] Dagegen entwickelten sich bei den Ausgaben erst um 1500 festere und regelmäßig wiederkehrende Positionen, auch wenn schon die Überschriften der Abschnitte im Tresslerbuch vielfach die Zusammenhänge erkennen lassen, in denen die Teilrechnungen entstanden sind.

Generell wird ein Bemühen um Planbarkeit und Systematisierung der Einnahmen und Ausgaben erkennbar. Sowohl um 1400 wie um 1500 wurden den Hochmeistern vorab feste Einnahmen aus den lokalen Ämtern zugewiesen, die – wie in der Rechnung von 1504/1505 erkennbar – bei finanziellen Engpässen auch angepasst wurden. Ein weiterer Ansatz für eine geordnete Haushaltsführung war der Haushaltsplan Hans von Thüngens aus den Anfangsjahren des Hochmeisters Friedrich von Sachsen,[82] auch wenn er teilweise von falschen Annahmen ausging. Auffällig ist auch die weitgehend gleiche Höhe von Einnahmen und Ausgaben insbesondere in den Abrechnungen der Zeit Friedrichs von Sachsen. Es scheint, als ob man alles daransetzte, ein Defizit zu vermeiden. Das würde bereits für eine relativ gute Planung bevorstehender Ausgaben sprechen, die dann bei Bedarf durch Geschossleistungen der Gebietiger oder Steuern der Untertanen gedeckt werden konnten. Ähnlich lässt sich schon um 1400 beobachten, dass größere Ausgaben mit Entnahmen aus dem Tressel oder ebenfalls mit Geschossforderungen 'aufgefangen' wurden.

Zweifellos kann man für das 15. Jahrhundert keine Finanzplanung im modernen Sinne voraussetzen. Dennoch sollte man die Instrumente mittelalterlicher Finanzpolitik nicht geringschätzen. Sie hatten ihre eigene Rationalität, die durchaus zu den von den Zeitgenossen erwünschten Ergebnissen führten. In dieser

---

[79] Dazu ebd., S. 629.
[80] Zu den Ausgaben für Kanzleipersonal vgl. J. SARNOWSKY, Die Finanzpolitik des Deutschen Ordens unter Friedrich von Sachsen (wie Anm. 12), S. 129.
[81] Oben zu Anm. 32.
[82] Vgl. zu Anm. 64–66.

Perspektive unterscheiden sich die Planungsziele nur wenig von den gegenwärtigen staatlichen Haushaltsplanungen der 2010er Jahre, die eine 'schwarze Null' anstrebten.

The Bohemian Franciscan Observants in Their Peculiar 'Economic' Context

Petr Hlaváček

This study aims to present some aspects of the economic context in the life of the Bohemian (or Czech) Franciscan Observants, as it developed in the second half of the fifteenth century. Firstly, it should be noted that after 1419 during the Hussite Wars the majority of the Franciscan friaries in Bohemia were in ruins. Restoration of the Franciscan presence in the Czech Lands began in 1451 after the arrival of the Italian preacher John of Capistrano in Central Europe. He then began to create a new network of Bohemian Franciscan friaries. Religious communities occupied and restored the abandoned buildings of the Conventual Franciscans in the centres of Bohemian catholic cities – the only exception being Utraquist Prague. Others built new friaries *extra muros*, for various urban and spiritual reasons. The Bohemian vicariate of the Observant Franciscans was one of the most important components of the late medieval Franciscan order in Central Europe. At the birth of this vicariate in 1452 stands John of Capistrano. The original vicariate, named *Bohemia*, included the Czech, Austrian and Polish-Lithuanian territories. Only from 1469 onwards was it restricted to the territory of the Czech state by decision of the general chapter. Thus, Bohemian Franciscans could focus fully on preaching and the theological conflicts with the Czech Utraquist Church, to which most people in Bohemia belonged.[1]

Early Franciscanism was shaped in the fertile tension between the old monastic tradition with its *stabilitas loci* and the permanent mobility of the Friars Minor between cities or between town and countryside. The first Franciscans lived mostly in rural hermitages and constantly moved between the city, where they preached, and their rural 'house of prayer'. By the second half of the thirteenth century, however, they had almost abandoned this model and the Franciscans became the archetypal urban order, involved in new forms of pastoral care. The observant movement originated in the old *loci* of the Italian Franciscan provinces during the late fourteenth century, claiming the original mobility between urban and rural areas as a distinctive emblem of the Friars Minor. Reform-minded friars

---

[1] P. HLAVÁČEK, Die böhmischen Franziskaner im ausgehenden Mittelalter. Studien zur Kirchen– und Kulturgeschichte Ostmitteleuropas (Forschungen zur Geschichte und Kultur des östlichen Mitteleuropa 40), Stuttgart 2011, pp. 19–29; ID., Les ordres mendiants dans le royaume de Bohême au Moyen Âge: implantation et fonds d'archives, in: Études Franciscaines n. s., 6 (2013), pp. 9–18; ID., The Servants of Antichrist: the Denouncement of Franciscans on the Utraquist (Hussite) Pictures in Jena Codex (Bohemia, Around 1490–1510), in: IKON. Journal of Iconographic Studies 3 (2010), pp. 239–245.

left their convents *intra muros* and went forth outside the city walls. To the medieval mentality to go *extra muros* meant to be thrown into uncertainty and danger. The construction of the observant hermitages and friaries outside the city was therefore not primarily due to a lack of space in urban areas, as it is sometimes assumed *a priori*, but a specific expression of the restoration of the original Franciscan spirituality.[2]

The Bohemian context

John of Capestrano passed this mental model of the Italian Franciscan Observance on to the Bohemian Franciscans, although he sometimes pragmatically ignored it, especially when seeking the support of monarchs and nobility for his politico-religious intentions. The Central European Franciscan Observants did not call their buildings *monasterium* or *conventus*, as did the old monastic orders and Franciscan conventuals, but they used the term *locus*, which belonged to the beginnings of Franciscanism.[3]

The particular situation of confessionally-divided Bohemia in the fifteenth century forced the Observants into emergency solutions and the search for new forms of interaction between populations. The friars often took over older friaries within cities, which eliminated one of the fundamental differences between the Franciscan Observance and Conventualism. Additionally, through their royal and aristocratic founders, the sumptuousness of other Observant *loci* and churches and buildings, and their artistic activities soon levelled with Conventual friaries. The Franciscan Observance resisted, but the friaries became more and more objects to represent the status of noble families. The Observants' emphasis on the use of the term *locus* for their friaries became a mere play on words: external and internal features of their buildings were already indistinguishable from classic conventual friaries.[4]

---

[2] P. HLAVÁČEK, Die böhmischen Franziskaner (note 1 above), pp. 29–32; B. MERTENS, *Vidi quasi vias ipsorum multitudine plenas* (1 Cel 27). Die evangelische Wanderschaft in der Praxis und Debatte der Minderbrüder im 13. Jahrhundert, in: Wissenschaft und Weisheit 63 (2000), pp. 9–60.

[3] J. LE GOFF, Ordres mendiants et urbanisation dans la France médiévale. État de l'enquête, Annales, ÉSC 25 (1970), pp. 924–946; A. MINDERMANN, Bettelordenskloster und Stadttopographie. Warum lagen Bettelordensklöster am Stadtrand?, in: D. BERG (ed.), Könige, Landesherren und Bettelorden. Konflikt und Kooperation in West– und Mitteleuropa bis zur frühen Neuzeit (Saxonia Franciscana 10), Werl 1998, pp. 83–103; P. HLAVÁČEK, Al servizio dell'ordine e della cristianità: Gabriele Rangoni da Verona († 1486) e il suo operato nell'Europa centrale e in Italia, in: Frate Francesco. Rivista di cultura francescana 74 (2008), pp. 71–95.

[4] P. HLAVÁČEK, Le Coeur de l'Europe? À la recherche d'un nouveau rôle ecclésiastique et culturel pour la Bohême au Moyen Âge et au début de l'époque moderne, in: M.–M. DE CEVINS (ed.), L' Europe centrale au seuil de la modernité. Mutations sociales, religieuses et culturelles

Some of the Bohemian Observants realized that this represented a gradual deviation from the original ideal. Therefore something extraordinary happened in the area north of the Alps, in Central Europe. With the permission of the provincial vicar Peter of Hlohovec, an *eremitorium* was founded in 1470 in Silesia. This hermitage for eight or nine friars was located entirely outside the urban area, in the countryside near the village with the symbolic name of Ketzerdorf. Here was a settlement of a minority of friars, who wanted to live in the spirit of the original observant reform and depend only on the goodwill of the local villagers. Vicar Peter of Hlohovec probably intended to send friars there for spiritual renewal, in order to contribute to the reform of the Bohemian Observant Vicariate, which the Austrian and Polish friaries left in 1467. Most of the friars reacted to this establishment with widespread scepticism and the hermitage had to be closed in 1477. The Observants returned there in 1491, but it was then established as a classical *locus*, that is a friary.[5] The case of the Observant friary outside the walls of the Silesian city of Ratibor is also notable. It was built in 1491 on the right bank of the Oder, and soon a small village formed around it, named after the Franciscan Observants *Bosak* or in German *Bosatz*, i. e. "village of the discalced monks". The Observants, viewed so rarely as colonizers in the late Middle Ages, were the founders of new rural locations.[6]

The Franciscan Observant friaries in Bohemia, Moravia, Silesia and Upper Lusatia represented a significant urban phenomenon—they were linked mainly with the urban economy and only marginally with the countryside.[7] For example, the Franciscan friary of St. Ambrose, founded in 1460 in Utraquist Prague, existed due to the support of the 'heretical' King George of Poděbrady and by the charity or testamentary bequests of the Prague's burghers belonging to the Catholic minority. There was no direct economic relationship with Prague's rural surroundings. But we can at least say that this friary represented the third most popular Catholic institution in Prague, gaining more financial and material support than Prague's Cathedral Church. The second case, which I would like briefly to present, is the friary of the Virgin Mary in Pilsen, in Western Bohemia. This originally conventual friary was, from 1454, the owner of the village of Borek near

---

(Autriche, Bohême, Hongrie et Pologne, fin du xive–milieu du xvie siècle), Rennes 2010, pp. 37–56.

[5] P. HLAVÁČEK, Die böhmischen Franziskaner (note 1 above), pp. 31, 174.

[6] L. TEICHMANN, Die Franziskanerklöster in Mittel- und Ostdeutschland 1223–1993, Leipzig 1995, p. 173; P. HLAVÁČEK, Schlesien als Schlüsselland der Franziskanerprovinz 'Bohemia' im ausgehenden Mittelalter, in: L. BOBKOVÁ / J. ZDICHYNEC (eds.), Geschichte – Erinnerung – Selbstidentifikation. Die schriftliche Kultur in den Ländern der Böhmischen Krone im 14.–18. Jahrhundert, Prague/Casablanca 2011, pp. 431–437.

[7] P. HLAVÁČEK, *Extra muros*. The Bohemian Franciscans in their Mental and Economic Relations with the Countryside, in: M.-M. DE CEVINS / L. VIALLET (eds.), L'économie des couvents mendiants en Europe centrale. Bohême, Hongrie, Pologne, v. 1220–v. 1550, Rennes 2018, pp. 175–182.

Bolevec. A Pilsner burgess gave the friary ownership of the village along with all proceeds, forests, streams, pastures and a hunting area. The Observant Franciscans had already come to Pilsen in 1459. At first they lived outside the city in a country house owned by Pilsner burgher John Hladík. The Bohemian King George of Poděbrady was ordered in 1460 by Pope Pius II to request that the friary in the heart of the city be surrendered to the Observants; and that the Conventuals should either join them or leave Pilsen. In the same year, King George appointed the Pilsen aldermen to function as *procuratores et factores bonorum omnium*, i. e. as holders of the friary's property, which consisted of the village of Borek, the annual revenues of the village of Nebílovy and a few houses in Pilsen. So Franciscan Observants lived off the former urban and rural property of the Conventuals, although they did not own it. In 1495 a significant aristocratic lady, Margaret of Rožmitál, bequeathed a part of her property and rural assets to the Franciscan Observants in Western Bohemia, namely in Pilsen, Bechyně, Horažďovice and Tachov, while its use was to stay under the care of the *procurator* of monasteries, as indicated in the testament written in Czech.[8]

The situation is indeed different from that of the Bohemian Franciscan Conventuals. Unlike the Conventuals, Bohemian Observants really had no ownership or disposition rights to any property in the countryside, as evidenced by the case of a (conventual) provincial minister, Martin of Prague, who experienced problems with economic mismanagement and corruption. He was very interested in the rural property of the Moravian Conventuals, in particular their extensive vineyards in the villages near the South Moravian town of Znojmo. In 1498 he caused a scandal when, at the congregation of the Czech-Polish Conventual province in Krakow, he tried to force the definitors to transfer those vineyards and other rural property to his personal ownership. In 1515 he was convicted of manipulating the order's property and sentenced to life imprisonment in Brno friary, where he committed suicide the same year.[9]

The Franciscans in Kadaň

The royal town of Kadaň represents a rare case in Bohemia—apart from Prague. Here the friary of St. Michael had been founded in 1234. It was a community of Franciscan Conventuals, and later also an Observant friary. The Kadaň Conventuals were supported by rural farms near Kadaň. They even owned some villages, and sometimes they engaged in the pastoral care of those rural parishes. A remarkable event occurred in 1337. One of the friars, Nicholas Chrzyen, caused a

---

[8] P. Hlaváček, The Constants of Spirituality and Ecclesiastical Politics in the Family of the Bohemian King George of Poděbrady, and of the Princes of Münsterberg, in: Filosofický časopis/Journal of Philosophy 1 (2014), pp. 332–339.

[9] Die Chroniken der mährischen Minoriten, ed. A. Neumann, Olomouc 1936, p. 56.

scandal when, in the parish church in Želina near Kadaň, he publicly questioned the moral profile of the local parish priest. Outraged villagers, however, engaged him in argument and supported their pastor. Friar Nicholas countered with accusations of concubinage against the priest. The villagers then refused to send the Kadaň Conventuals their taxes and agricultural products, while Friar Nicholas was arrested for donatistic heresy by an inquisitor in a Dominican convent in Prague. He was later burned.[10]

After the conquest of the city by troops of the second Crusade *contra Hussones* in 1421, the friary rather stagnated, whilst the townspeople of Kadaň, holders of many rural farms, directed their attention to the support of the dynamic Franciscan Observant movement. The Kadaň Observant Friary of the Fourteen Holy Helpers was founded in 1473 *extra muros* in the middle of vineyards, granted directly from the Bohemian King Wladislaus Jagello. However, by 1481 he had already given his founder's rights to the aristocratic family of the Lords Hassensteiner of Lobkowicz. They funded the construction of a magnificent friary with a diamond vault and Cranach paintings from the proceeds of their rural estates in the Ore Mountains (Erzgebirge). The economic affairs of the religious community were then administered by a *syndicus*, selected from the ranks of the Kadaň townspeople. This person moderated the distribution of money and revenue granted in testaments, and was also responsible for any management issues arising from the surrounding villages. The Kadaň Observants therefore really did not own any property, and economically they were completely under the supervision of an aristocratic family of Lobkowicz and the *syndicus* from the royal city. From the city the friars received such things as cloth for religious robes, while from the countryside it was grain, flour, bread, butter, cheese, fish, wine and beer. About one third of several hundred testaments from 1473 to 1522 remembered the Observants.[11]

At the same time the Kadaň Observants had significant problems with its water suppy, because the friary well of St. John of Capistrano was not insufficient to meet their consumption requirements. As a new water supply from the city was out of the question, the burghers were forced to build a number of water supplies from the springs in the countryside to the fountains in the squares. The friars had to seek a solution in the countryside too and they looked for a spring under the Royal Hill near the village of Prunéřov. This hill was, however, part of the rural estate of Frederick of Schönburg. He finally allowed them in 1492 to

---

[10] P. HLAVÁČEK, Beginnings of Bohemian Reformation in the Northwest: The Waldensians and the Reformers in the Deanery of Kadaň at the Turn of the Fourteenth Century, in: Z. V. DAVID / D. R. HOLETON (eds.), The Bohemian Reformation and Religious Practice, vol. 4, Prague 2002, pp. 43–56.

[11] P. HLAVÁČEK, Nový Jeruzalém? Příběh františkánského kláštera Čtrnácti sv. Pomocníků v Kadani (The New Jerusalem? A Story of the Franciscan Friary of 14 Holy Helpers in Kadaň), Kadaň 2013, pp. 35–55.

build a pipeline through his land to the friary. In 1514 King Wladislaus Jagello donated some lead to the friary for the repair of the pipeline. But the Kadaň Observants still had problems with the well in the friary. For example, in 1528 a protracted conflict broke out between the Friars and the Holy Trinity mining company because the construction of a tunnel in the rock above the river Eger, below the friary, threatened the water supply from the friary well.[12]

In June 1534 the Kadaň peace was concluded between Catholics and Lutherans in the Holy Roman Empire. The main protagonists of the Catholic-Lutheran 'Peace Summit' held a formal meeting in the garden of the friary of the Fourteen Holy Helpers — a kind of feast of reconciliation. The whole festival was funded by Albrecht Schlick, the royal governor of Kadaň and a convinced Lutheran. Prominent guests included many politico-religious leaders in Central Europe: Bohemian and Roman King Ferdinand I. of Habsburg; Saxon Elector Johann Friedrich, the political leader of Luther's Wittenberg Reformation; papal legate Pier Paolo Vergerio, who belonged to the reformed wing of the Roman Church, and who in 1545 joined the Reformation himself; Cardinal Albrecht of Brandenburg, Archbishop and Elector of Mainz, a main opponent of the Reformation; and Saxon duke Georg the Bearded, the representative of the Albertin branch of the family of Wettin, a promoter of erasmianism. While the townspeople of Kadaň procured for this great feast of reconciliation wine, beer and all sorts of delicacies, the royal governor Albrecht Schlick brought in venison and other meats, commissioned from the inhabitants of the villages surrounding the friary.[13]

In 1564 the friary was dissolved, and the church was turned into a Protestant place of worship. The Bohemian King and Roman Emperor Maximilian II. of Habsburg sought the restoration of this friary, which was an important center of Central European diplomacy in the fifteenth and sixteenth centuries. In 1569 he ordered Bohuslaus Felix Hassensteiner of Lobkowicz to restore the regular contributions of his rural estates, namely sending the appropriate amount of grain, fish and firewood. The restoration of the Kadaň religious community occurred in 1571.[14]

---

[12] Prague, National Archive, Bohemian Franciscans, mss no 77, 117; P. HLAVÁČEK, Retrospektiva dějin františkánského kláštera Čtrnácti sv. Pomocníků v Kadani v 15. a 16. století: Geneze, rozkvět a úpadek (A Retrospection of History of the Franciscan Friary in Kadaň), in: J. HOMOLKA (ed.), Ústecký sborník historický 2001. Gotické umění a jeho historické souvislosti I, Ústí nad Labem 2001, pp. 79–106.

[13] P. HLAVÁČEK, Catholics, Utraquists and Lutherans in Northwestern Bohemia, or Public Space as a Medium for Declaring Confessional Identity, in: M. BARTLOVÁ / M. ŠRONĚK (eds.), Public Communication in European Reformation. Artistic and Other Media in Central Europe 1380–1620, Prague 2007, pp. 279–297.

[14] P. HLAVÁČEK, Čtrnáct svatých Pomocníků. K pozdně středověké spiritualitě elit a její christocentrické dimenzi (The Fourteen Holy Helpers), Prague 2014, pp. 178–180.

The Countryside as a danger for the Bohemian Franciscan Observants

The Bohemian countryside, inhabited by a mostly Utraquist population, was not the only area perceived as extremely dangerous by the Franciscan Observants and other religious orders. In 1468 the burghers of Nuremberg arrested the former Bohemian provincial vicar Jakob of Grossglogau in the Bavarian village of Lerrersteig. He then fled unsuccessfully to the friary of the Bohemian town of Tachov with a carriage filled with money that he had illegally gathered in Nuremberg from indulgences.[15] And this was not the only such case. In 1472 the friars went from the provincial chapter in Brno in Moravia, accompanied by mercenaries. Despite all these measures the utraquist knight Hopko captured the Observants Simon of Wrocław, Basil of Olomouc and Aegidius of Hungary somewhere in the Moravian countryside and had them imprisoned in a dungeon. Elsewhere in the Bohemian countryside, Observant clerics Alexius of Prussia and George of Kadaň, who had traveled to the Bohemian aristocratic estates, were also captured.[16] Among the consternation friar Christopher of Wittbach fled to Hungary in 1473 and went on to Livonia, where he stood at the head of a peasant rebellion. He was captured and, despite his priesthood, beheaded and quartered. His connections with villagers was considered inappropriate, especially when the vast majority of the Bohemian Franciscan Observants were recruited in an urban milieu.[17]

Such was the particular danger to Franciscans travelling between friaries and the hostility of the Utraquist villagers that they complained at the General Chapter of Urbino in Italy in 1490. The Bohemian provincial vicar was often insulted by the rural population and his carriage or horse stolen.[18] This situation continued in the Czech lands well into the sixteenth century. Foreign visitors were also affected — while travelling through Utraquist and later Lutheran countryside they were mugged, robbed and captured. The forces of nature threatened disaster too — when the General Commissioner Benedict Benchovich and the provincial minister Lukas of Grünberg travelled from Prague to Neisse in Silesia in the summer of 1522, near Glatz they had to drive through the flooded river Neisse.

---

[15] Chronica fratris Nicolai Glassberger ordinis Minorum observantium (Analecta Franciscana 2), Quaracchi 1887, p. 435.

[16] Chronica Fratrum Minorum de Observancia Provincie Bohemie, Prague, Library of the National Museum in Prague, Sign. VIII F 75, p. 114.

[17] P. HLAVÁČEK, Die böhmischen Franziskaner (note 1 above), pp. 105 and 113–114.

[18] P. HLAVÁČEK, Die deutsch–tschechischen Streitigkeiten unter den böhmischen Franziskanern auf dem Generalkapitel in Urbino (1490), in: E. BREMER (ed.), Language of Religion – Language of the People. Medieval Judaism, Christianity and Islam, Munich 2006, pp. 373–385.

Their carriage broke in the middle of the river and the Bohemian Provincial Lukas drowned in the water. The Commissioner Benedict was saved only by great luck.[19]

Pictorial representation of rural areas, very realistic from the second half of the fifteenth century onwards, appeared in the context of the communities of Bohemian Franciscan Observants. In 1469, in the Observant church of Moravian Olomouc a painting was produced depicting John of Capestrano and the Battle of Belgrade in 1456. It shows a stylized city with rural surroundings, portrayed with universal iconographic characters.[20] The real Southern Bohemian countryside from the late fifteenth century, particularly in the area of Bechyně and other Franciscan centres, appeared in the illuminations of Matthias of Retz in a manuscript on the life of St. Francis of Assisi. For friar Matthias, who was also a theologian, it was one of the expressions of the acculturation of the Franciscan phenomenon in the Bohemian environment.[21] Last but not least, I would like to mention the exclusive paintings of the Cranach School in the Observant church of the Fourteen Holy Helpers in Kadaň, which by 1520 had been commissioned by the aristocratic family of Lobkowicz. In the scenes of the Crucifixion and the Lamentation of Christ, the real vista of Kadaň Franciscan friary was incorporated into the scenes of Jerusalem, as well as the real countryside between the Lobkowicz Castle of Hassenstein and the mining town of Přísečnice in the Ore Mountains, from which, given that it was the property of the Lobkowicz family, the construction and maintenance of the Kadaň Observant friary were greatly funded.[22]

The Observant Franciscan chapters in late medieval Bohemia

In its golden age, the Bohemian vicariate of Observant Franciscans had almost thirty friaries in Bohemia, Moravia, Silesia and Upper Lusatia.[23] In those friaries lived around 800 religious brothers. As is typical for mendicant friars, communities were basically constantly on the move. The *capitulum provinciale* took place almost annually, as if the whole vicariate set off. The provincial vicar (and after

---

[19] Chronica Fratrum Minorum de Observancia Provincie Bohemie (note 14 above), pp. 299–300.

[20] P. HLAVÁČEK, Die böhmischen Franziskaner (note 1 above), p. 225.

[21] M. STUDNIČKOVÁ, Conscriptum per Fratrem Mathiam de Rehtz. Iluminované rukopisy kadaňského kláštera františkánů–observantů z konce 15. století (Conscriptum per Fratrem Mathiam de Rehtz. Decorated Manuscripts from Kadaň Franciscan Friary from the End of the Fifteenth Century), in: P. HLAVÁČEK (ed.), Františkánství v kontaktech s jiným a cizím (Europaeana Pragensia 1), Prague 2009, pp. 210–219.

[22] P. HLAVÁČEK, Čtrnáct svatých Pomocníků (note 14 above), p. 230–231.

[23] P. HLAVÁČEK, Die Oberlausitz – ein neuralgischer Punkt des spätmittelalterlichen Franziskanertums, in: T. TORBUS / M. HÖRSCH (eds.), Die Kunst im Markgraftum Oberlausitz während der Jagiellonenherrschaft (Studia Jagellonica Lipsiensia 3), Ostfildern 2006, pp. 163–171.

1517 the provincial minister and *definitores*) was elected during this event, just as new *custodes*, preachers and confessors were appointed for each friary. To attend the provincial chapter, it was often necessary to go on journeys of several hundreds of kilometres. On most occasions the assembly took place in Silesian Wrocław, which disadvantaged friars from Bohemia and Moravia: some of them had to travel up to 350 kilometres. Incompatible with the traditional monastic *stabilitas loci*, this mobility was an essential, discerning feature of the mendicant orders.[24]

A provincial chapter was also a complex event, both logistically and economically. Certainly, it could not be funded by the resources of an individual friary or a vicar. Between 1469 and 1551 (when the European Reformations subverted the Franciscan province of *Bohemia*), 56 provincial chapters were held.[25] There are brief files preserved as part of two provincial chronicles. The writing of these chronicles started in the beginning of the sixteenth century. The so-called *benefactores capituli* thus became part of the local Franciscan "pious economy". In return for this funding the friars provided certain "spiritual recompense" for them.[26]

The largest number of provincial chapters in this period were held in Wrocław, Brno, Olomouc, Opava, Nysa, Jemnice and Kadaň. Each assembly was attended by about 150 friars. The meetings lasted for approximately two weeks. It was necessary to provide food and attend to other needs. The founders or owners of the founding rights of particular friaries gave such support. But this was not always the case. Catholic burghers and nobility were greatly involved too. They publicly demonstrated their 'confessional' preference in this way. These benefactors often made use of this supreme assembly of Bohemian Observant Franciscans for their own ecclesiastical-political representation and as an ostentatious manifestation of aristocratic or patrician piety.

---

[24] P. HLAVÁČEK, Die böhmischen Franziskaner (note 1 above), pp. 29–32; ID., Les Franciscains observants de Bohême à la fin du Moyen Âge: entre particularisme national, anti–intellectualisme et non–conformisme religieux, in: Études franciscaines, n. s., 2/1 (2009), pp. 81–98.

[25] P. HLAVÁČEK, *Benefactores capituli*. The Sponsors of the Franciscan Provincial Chapters in Bohemia around 1500, in: M.–M. DE CEVINS / L. VIALLET (eds.), L'économie des couvents mendiants en Europe centrale. Bohême, Hongrie, Pologne (note 7 above), pp. 277–283.

[26] P. HLAVÁČEK, Die böhmischen Franziskaner (note 1 above), pp. 177–184.

Examples of Bohemian nobles and burghers supporting Franciscan chapters in Bohemia

In the sources of the Bohemian province, it is often simply written that the provincial chapter was provided "well and sufficiently".[27] The meaning of this 'provision' shall be illustrated with the help of a number of examples. We shall also strive to analyse the social background of these *benefactores* and their main motivations. Each provincial chapter was slightly different and had its own specificities. In 1472, for example, *fratres capitulares* had to travel to Brno accompanied by mercenaries, because a large number of thieves were active in Moravia at that time.[28] The provincial chapters in Wrocław were remarkable. The city of Wrocław founded the local friary of St. Bernardine and the burghers provided food for the gathered friars on a regular basis — often in cooperation with other ecclesiastical institutions of the town.[29] They also funded the construction of the Franciscan church significantly. Although Franciscans strenuously strove to build it in a simple architectural style, the burghers of Wrocław decided to establish an opulently decorated portal. It would have served as part of the visual representation of the town. But the provincial chapter, held in Wrocław in 1481, declared it a violation of Franciscan poverty and ordered it to be removed.[30]

Especially renowned is the 1491 provincial chapter in Silesian Nysa. Jan (John) Filipec, former bishop of Oradea (in Hungarian Nagyvárad) and administrator of the Diocese of Olomouc, came to the chapter with a huge entourage. He brought wine and gifts in the form of baize and cloths for the walls of the Franciscan churches of Silesia.[31] He also made similar gifts to the provincial chapter in Olomouc in 1492. Then Jan Filipec set off to Wrocław, where he entered the order of St. Francis.[32] The friary of St. Bernardine and the Virgin Mary in Olomouc was traditionally supported by its founders, i. e. the burghers of Olomouc. Nevertheless, as early as 1528 they refused to provide for the congregation

---

[27] P. Hlaváček, Les ordres mendiants dans le royaume de Bohême au Moyen Âge (note 1 above), pp. 9–18.

[28] Michael of Carinthia, Chronica Fratrum Minorum de Observancia Provincie Bohemie, Prague, Library of National Museum, sign. VIII F 75, pp. 113–114; Eberhard Ablauff, De novella plantatione provincie Austrie, Bohemie et Polonie quo ad fratres minores de observantia Cronica Plantatio, Prague, National Library of the Czech Republic in Prague, sign. Cheb MS 157, fo 284 vo.

[29] Ibid., pp. 431–437.

[30] Michael of Carinthia, Chronica Fratrum Minorum de Observancia Provincie Bohemie (note 28 above), pp. 169–170; Eberhard Ablauff, De novella plantatione (note 28 above), fo 292 vo.

[31] Michael of Carinthia, Chronica Fratrum Minorum de Observancia Provincie Bohemie (note 28 above), pp. 169–170; Eberhard Ablauff, De novella plantatione (note 28 above), fo 292 vo.

[32] Michael of Carinthia, Chronica Fratrum Minorum de Observancia Provincie Bohemie (note 28 above), pp. 170–171; Eberhard Ablauff, De novella plantatione (note 28 above), fo 293 ro.

of many representatives of the province: the burghers had become Lutherans and Franciscan Observance was alien to them.³³

The main supporter of the friary of Holy Trinity in Silesian Legnica was Prince Frederick I. of Legnica and Brzeg. His wife was Princess Ludmila, daughter of the 'heretical' king of Bohemia, George of Poděbrady³⁴, who took exemplary care of the Franciscans attending the chapter in Legnica. During the provincial chapter in Legnica in 1500, she brought not just food, but also cloths and *unam scatulam* with delicacies. This was rather in breach of the Franciscan ethos. Nevertheless, Franciscan chronicler Michael of Carinthia calls her gratefully *mater fratrum*, mother of the friars.³⁵

Ladislav of Sternberg, founder of the friary of the Assumption of the Virgin Mary in Bechyně and *supremus cancellarius regni Bohemiae*, was similarly generous to the chapter in Bechyně in 1513.³⁶ Henry of Schwamberg took care of the friary, when the Lutheran descendants of Ladislav of Sternberg showed no interest in it after his death in 1521. Thanks to the generous provision he made for the provincial chapter in Bechyně in 1537, he earned the appellation of *magnus ordinis nostri fautor et patronus*.³⁷ It was similar in Krupka in Northwestern Bohemia. The friary of All Saints was founded by the aristocratic family of Colditz, but its members did not show a great deal of interest in friars' needs. At a provincial chapter in Krupka in 1516, members of the aristocratic family of Colowrat (owners of the castle Rýzmburk near Krupka) provided food for the friars. Local patricians Melchior Czomer and Valentinus Gross, who became rich on mining tin, also participated in the provision of food to the friars.³⁸

The noble family of Švihov, which founded the friary of St. Angels in Bohemian Horažďovice, carried out its duties in exemplary fashion. Jindřich of Švihov sent the *capitulares* in 1519 not only a sufficient amount of food, but also wine.³⁹ The Švihov family, which remained faithfully Catholic, demonstrated its favour towards the Franciscans most extensively during the 1534 provincial chapter. Brothers Lev Zdeněk, Jindřich and Břetislav provided abundantly for the chapter

---

33 Michael of Carinthia, Chronica Fratrum Minorum de Observancia Provincie Bohemie (note 28 above), p. 323.
34 P. HLAVÁČEK, The Constants of Spirituality (note 8 above), pp. 332–339.
35 Michael of Carinthia, Chronica Fratrum Minorum de Observancia Provincie Bohemie (note 28 above), p. 185; Eberhard Ablauff, De novella plantatione (note 28 above), fo 296 ro.
36 Michael of Carinthia, Chronica Fratrum Minorum de Observancia Provincie Bohemie (note 28 above), pp. 240–241; Eberhard Ablauff, De novella plantatione (note 28 above), fo 310 ro.
37 Michael of Carinthia, Chronica Fratrum Minorum de Observancia Provincie Bohemie (note 28 above), p. 341.
38 Ibid., p. 243; Eberhard Ablauff, De novella plantatione (note 28 above), fo 312 vo.
39 Michael of Carinthia, Chronica Fratrum Minorum de Observancia Provincie Bohemie (note 28 above), p. 254; Eberhard Ablauff, De novella plantatione (note 28 above), fo 319 vo.

for twenty days. Every day they (together with other Catholic noblemen) visited the Franciscans during their debates and dined with them in the refectory.[40]

The friary of Sts. Peter and Paul and St. Bernardine in Głogów in Silesia presents a different case. Its founder was Margareta of Cilli, and her descendants held the founding rights to the friary. Yet it is Jan II. of Opole and Brzeg, prince of the adjacent territory, who is remembered as an extraordinary benefactor of the friars and their provincial assemblies. When he died in 1532, Franciscan chroniclers remembered him as someone who always provided bread, meat, salt, milk, oil, and wine for the friars.[41] Members of the aristocratic family of Hradec, who founded the friary of St. Catherine in South Bohemia, carried out their duties impeccably. They provided supplies to both the local Franciscan community and the provincial chapters and convocations gathered there. The generosity of princess Anna of Hradec was mentioned during the provincial convocation in 1536. She was called *incomparabilis omnium fratrum mater et patrona*.[42]

The provincial chapters in Kadaň

The greatest amount of information we have concerns the friary of the Fourteen Holy Helpers in Kadaň in Northwestern Bohemia. It was one of the most important friaries in the kingdom of Bohemia. There was not just a provincial school in this *monasterium*. It was a sought-after location for many politico-ecclesiastic and diplomatic meetings. The friary was founded by the Bohemian king Wladislaus Jagiello. However, as early as 1481 he handed over the founding rights to the aristocratic family of Hassensteiner of Lobkowicz: to Jan, who was the head of this noble house, a learned royal diplomat. The Lobkowicz family became involved in the construction of a sumptuous friary, as an instrument of their aristocratic representation. Yet, the relationship of the family to the Franciscan community itself seems somewhat ambivalent. It is clear from the sources that the provincial chapters held in Kadaň were supported by other neighbouring noble families and rich patricians. For the chapter in 1506, for example, Jan Hasištejnský of Lobkowicz is mentioned as a "sponsor" of the gathered friars only in the chronicle of Eberhard Ablauff,[43] who, after all, wrote parts of his chronicle of Franciscan province in the Kadaň friary. Yet, Laurentius Glatz of Starý Dvůr is listed as the main benefactor. He was a citizen who became a noble

---

[40] Michael of Carinthia, Chronica Fratrum Minorum de Observancia Provincie Bohemie (note 28 above), p. 340.

[41] Ibid., pp. 334–335.

[42] Ibid., p. 341.

[43] P. Hlaváček, Eberhard Ablauff de Rheno († 1528) im Geistesleben der böhmischen Franziskaner am Anfang der Frühen Neuzeit, in: H. Specht / T. Černušák (eds.), Leben und Alltag in böhmisch–mährischen und niederösterreichischen Klöstern in Spätmittelalter und Neuzeit (Monastica Historia 1), St. Pölten/Brno 2011, pp. 136–146.

and rich entrepreneur in the field of mining in the Ore Mountains. The lords of two neighbouring castles — Dietrich Vitzthum of Egerberg and Appel Vitzthum of Šumburk — also provided for the chapter. This is because the Vitzthum family had their necropolis in the Franciscan church, and they were rivals of the house of Lobkowicz in many ways. The chapter gained considerable material support from the patricians of the royal town of Kadaň too. At their request, a glorious public mass was held in the decanal church of Virgin Mary in Kadaň as a "satisfaction".[44]

In 1514, another chapter was held in Kadaň, lacking any support from the family of Lobkowicz, although they held the founding rights to the friary and Jan Hassensteiner of Lobkowicz resided in the castle of Kadaň, in the city. Supplies for the gathered friars were provided by Dietrich Vitzthum of Egerberg, Laurentius Glatz and Apolinarius, a citizen and mining entrepreneur.[45] Dietrich Vitzthum of Egerberg and Apolinarius are also mentioned in chronicles and records as benefactors of the provincial chapter in Kadaň in 1524.[46] Some anonymous *barones* are mentioned too. The report for 1531 is particularly interesting. Nobleman Sebastian Krabice of Weitmühle, the owner of the neighbouring domain of Chomutov, Dietrich Vitzthum of Egerberg and other *benefactores ordinis* resorted to Eusebius of Neumarkt, Minister Provincial of the Bohemian province, in order to arrange the provincial chapter in Kadaň. Lutheranism was spreading in Kadaň at the time, and they considered the chapter to be a substantial support to the Catholic Church. The Minister Provincial promised he would organise the provincial chapter in Kadaň, but he did not keep his promise. Sebastian Krabice of Weitmühle came to the chapter in Brno that year to remind the Minister Provincial of the biblical words *Verba vestra debent esse: non, non, est, est*.[47] It was not until 1533 that these Catholic noblemen achieved their goal and the provincial chapter of Bohemian Franciscans gathered in Kadaň again. Besides Sebastian Krabice of Weitmühle, Bernhardin Vitzthum of Egerberg, count Albrecht Schlick and two noble women, Ursula Glatz of Starý Dvůr and Sidonia Hassensteiner of Lobkowicz, also provided supplies for the friars. This is quite

---

[44] Michael of Carinthia, Chronica Fratrum Minorum de Observancia Provincie Bohemie (note 28 above), p. 196; Eberhard Ablauff, De novella plantatione (note 28 above), fo 300 vo.

[45] Michael of Carinthia, Chronica Fratrum Minorum de Observancia Provincie Bohemie (note 28 above), pp. 242–243; Eberhard Ablauff, De novella plantatione (note 28 above), fo 311 ro.

[46] Michael of Carinthia, Chronica Fratrum Minorum de Observancia Provincie Bohemie (note 28 above), pp. 300–301 and 308–309; Eberhard Ablauff, De novella plantatione (note 28 above), fo 326 vo.

[47] Michael of Carinthia, Chronica Fratrum Minorum de Observancia Provincie Bohemie (note 28 above), pp. 332–333.

paradoxical, as Albrecht Schlick, then royal governor of the castle of Kadaň, Ursula Glatz and Sidonia of Lobkowicz already flirted with the Wittenberg Reformation.[48]

Count Albrecht Schlick arranged the Treaty of Kadaň between Catholics and Lutherans in the Holy Roman Empire, in Kadaň in 1534. The summit of rulers took place in the Franciscan friary of the Fourteen Holy Helpers in Kadaň, where provincial chapters had been held and sponsored by neighbouring noblemen. There was a spectacular feast of reconciliation in the Franciscan garden, which was attended for example by the Roman and Bohemian king Ferdinand I., the Elector of Saxony Johann Friedrich, the Duke of Saxony George the Bearded, the Cardinal Albert of Brandenburg, the papal nuncio Pier Paolo Vergerio, and others. The feast was arranged by the local Franciscans with the help of Albrecht Schlick.[49] However, the collapse of the Bohemian Franciscan province was just around the corner: one third of the friars converted to Lutheranism or to the Czech Utraquist Church, and one by one the founders of the friaries revoked their founding rights. In the middle of the sixteenth century, the order of St. Francis was in total decline in Bohemia and in the Czech lands. Even the provincial chapters ceased to be held. The Franciscan 'pious economy' laid in ruin.[50]

Not much can be said about the context of the Bohemian Franciscan Observants' economy and the friars' relationship with the countryside, i. e. the very specific mentality of Bohemian Franciscanism. This is because the greater part of the countryside was Utraquist, especially in Bohemia, and was very hostile to the Roman Church and the Franciscan order. The Bohemian Franciscans were therefore forced to apply the original postulates of the Franciscan ethos, just as it was rehabilitated by the Observance. Indeed, the Franciscans were at the avantgarde of the Roman Church in the Czech Lands, which was in many regions the minority church only.[51] This is the specific situation of the Bohemian Franciscanism, which was, in the European context, a great anomaly.[52]

---

[48] Ibid., p. 337.

[49] Ibid., pp. 339–340.

[50] P. HLAVÁČEK, Die Franziskaner–Observanten zwischen böhmischer und europäischer Reformation. Ein Beitrag zur Religionsgeschichte Ostmitteleuropas, in: W. EBERHARD / F. MACHILEK (eds.), Kirchliche Reformimpulse des 14./15. Jahrhunderts in Ostmitteleuropa (Forschungen und Quellen zur Kirchen– und Kulturgeschichte Ostdeutschlands 36), Köln/Weimar/Wien 2006, pp. 295–326.

[51] P. HLAVÁČEK, Bohemian Franciscans Between Orthodoxy and Nonconformity at the Turn of the Middle Ages, in: Z. V. DAVID / D. R. HOLETON (eds.), The Bohemian Reformation and Religious Practice, vol. 5, Part 1, Prague 2004, pp. 167–189; P. HLAVÁČEK, Les Franciscains observants de Bohême à la fin du Moyen Âge (note 24 above), pp. 81–98.

[52] P. HLAVÁČEK, *Extra muros*. The Bohemian Franciscans in their Mental and Economic Relations with the Countryside (note 7 above); P. HLAVÁČEK, *Benefactores capituli* (note 25 above), pp. 277–283.

Alms, Preaching, Production and Property: Mendicant and Pauline Economy in Late Medieval Hungary

Beatrix F. Romhányi

When speaking about the orders founded after 1200, we traditionally classify them into two groups: the mendicant and the eremitical orders.[1] From the point of view of the economy and finances, the mendicants relied upon alms, they had no or little landed estates, and – since the well-known thesis of Jacques LeGoff[2] – historians clearly connect them with urban development. In contrast to the above, eremitical communities are considered to have adopted the monastic tradition, including the possession of landed estates and the preference for remote sites. Furthermore, in earlier Hungarian literature it was presumed that the estate management of Paulines remained feudal till the very end of the Middle Ages. However, a closer look at the sources revealed that the picture was much more complex. The analysis of differences and similarities can lead to completely different classifications. One of the most important changes that have been revealed by recent research partly done in the framework of the French-based project MARGEC,[3] is that the late medieval eremitical orders, such as the Hermits of

---

[1] The present paper is based on two books published earlier on the economy of the Pauline and of the mendicant orders in medieval Hungary. B. F. Romhányi, Koldulό barátok – gazdálkodó szerzetesek. Koldulórendi gazdálkodás a középkori Magyarországon [Mendicant economy in medieval Hungary], Budapest 2018; B. F. Romhányi, Pauline Economy in the Middle Ages. "The spiritual cannot be maintained without the temporal…", Leiden 2020 (the English translation of the book published in 2010 in Hungarian).

[2] About the thesis and its contemporary and later reception see J. LeGoff, Apostolat mendiant et fait urbain dans la France médiévale. L'implantation des ordres mendiants. Programme–questionnaire pour une enquête, in: Annales E.S.C. 23 (1968), pp. 335–352; Id., Ordres mendiants et urbanisation dans la France médiévale. État de l'enquête, in: Annales E.S.C. 4 (1970), pp. 924–947; A. Vauchez, Les ordres mendiants et la ville en Italie centrale (v.1220 – v.1350), in: Mélanges de l'École française de Rome 89 (1977), pp. 557–773; A. Vauchez, Gli ordini mendicanti e la città nell'Italia dei comuni (XIII–XV secolo). Alcune riflessioni venti'anni dopo, in: G. Chittolini / K. Elm, Ordini religiosi e società politica in Italia e Germania nei secoli XIV e XV, Bologna 2001, pp. 31–44; P. Bertrand, Commerce avec dame pauvreté: structures et fonctions des couvents mendiants à Liège (XIIIe–XIVe s.), Paris 2004. In Hungarian context see E. Fügedi, Koldulórendek és városfejlődés Magyarországon, in: Századok 106 (1972), pp. 69–95. About the role of other social groups in non–urban environments cf. M.–M. de Cevins, Les franciscains observants hongrois de l'expansion à la débâcle (vers 1450 – vers 1540), Rome 2008, pp. 132–139, and B. F. Romhányi, Mendicant Networks and Population in a European Perspective, in: G. Jaritz / K. Szende (eds.), Medieval East Central Europe in a Comparative Perspective: From Frontier Zones to Lands in Focus, Abingdon/New York 2016, pp. 99–122.

[3] About the project see http://margec.univ–bpclermont.fr [last access: 05.02.2020].

Saint Paul in Hungary, the Hermits of Saint William in the Rhineland and Tuscany, or the Hieronymites in Spain need to be seen in conjunction with the mendicant orders. After all the Austin Hermits and the Carmelites had similar roots and they preserved some of their early features even after they were transformed into mendicant communities.[4] One of the similarities was just that the possession of landed estates was not completely prohibited to the friaries of these orders. The present paper will discuss the economy and finances of the mendicant and Pauline communities in medieval Hungary, however, with an eye on the whole region of East Central Europe.

Monastic finance in a mendicant context – including the Pauline Hermits in East Central Europe – looks different. Some expressions as money-based, long-term or estate management are not always meaningful, although we should not forget them either. But the mendicants and to some extent the Pauline communities clearly preferred social networking to secure their subsistence. The material, 'temporary' element of their economic background remained secondary – it could change considerably over time. In the following article, I shall try to outline the most characteristic aspects, mainly focusing on orders other than the Franciscans – since they are discussed in another chapter of this volume.[5]

Mendicant orders, especially the Franciscans and the Dominicans – both established in the first decades of the thirteenth century – rejected landed property and postulated poverty not only on the personal, but also on the community level. Their main goal was to be more effective in pastoral care within, as well as in missions outside Latin Christianity, and this attitude also affected their ideas on economic matters. Mendicancy became the key-notion for many of the new religious orders, but alms meant a much more colourful variety of donations than we usually think. However, these new orders were soon compelled to find new techniques in dealing with economic issues partly because of the different social and economic circumstances they encountered when spreading all over Europe, partly because of the growing number of friars. Franciscans even touched upon the subject in theoretical, theological context.[6] Another, seemingly marginal, nevertheless important aspect is the chronology of the orders. 'Late-comers' as the

---

[4] The concept of the four big mendicant orders was used by Jacques LeGoff, mainly based on French, English and some other Western European sets of data. However, more recent literature, among others Paul Bertrand, Frances Andrews or the author of the present paper have argued against the exclusion of the smaller orders. See P. Bertrand, Commerce avec dame pauvreté (note 2 above), pp. 125–127; F. Andrews, The Other Friars: The Carmelite, Augustinian, Sack and Pied Friars in the Middle Ages, Woodbridge/Rochester/NY 2006; B. F. Romhányi, Mendicant Networks (note 2 above).

[5] M.–M. de Cevins, Les mécanismes de contrôle économique à l'œuvre dans la province franciscaine observante de Hongrie à la fin du Moyen Âge (v. 1450–v. 1530), in this volume.

[6] G. Todeschini, Franciscan Wealth. From Voluntary Poverty to Market Society, New York 2009. Economic principles and practices of the Dominicans were also discussed, especially in Polish historiography: M. Bukała, Mendicant Friars and medieval notions of economic life: "oeconomica dominicana" and "franciscana", and particularities in Central Europe, in:

Austin Hermits, the Carmelites – or the Paulines in Hungary and East Central Europe – had to find their way in a more or less established network dominated by the Franciscans and the Dominicans. Their adaptation can be seen both in the choice of the sites for their convents and in their economy. Furthermore, we also have to consider the eremitical roots of these orders, established in the second half of the thirteenth century. Despite some attempts to introduce the full rejection of landed property, the monasteries of the latter orders accepted such donations from the earliest period of their history on. In this context, poverty meant the conscious limitation of immovable property, as it was also expressed in one of the anecdotes recorded in the *Vitae fratrum* of the Pauline author Gregorius Gyöngyösi. The reform movements of the fifteenth century also pulled the mendicant orders in opposite directions, while the Paulines, for instance, increasingly aligned themselves to the mendicant orders. Thus, the economy of the orders mentioned above was based on a complex system of asking for alms – in their most diverse form – and on more or less regular incomes from different immovable properties, which could be temporary or long-term, sometimes in the hands of single monasteries for centuries. The whole system was very sensitive to changes of the social and/or economic environment. The strategies chosen by the different religious orders were influenced by these inner and outer factors, thus, the result was specific for both the religious community and the local society, and the fourth dimension, the time must not be left out of the analysis either.

In terms of numbers: mendicant friaries and Pauline monasteries

Because of the close links between the discussed religious communities and the surrounding society, it is necessary to say a few words about the monastic networks before speaking about their economy and estate management.[7] It is even more important, since the network of the mendicants in the Hungarian kingdom was the largest within East Central Europe, and this position was strengthened by the presence of the Pauline monasteries. In the first half of the thirteenth century East Central European countries were closely aligned, but Hungary

---

H. Specht / R. Andraschek–Holzer (eds.), Bettelorden in Mitteleuropa. Geschichte, Kunst, Spiritualität. Referate der gleichnamigen Tagung vom 19. bis 22. März in St. Pölten (Beiträge zur Kirchengeschichte Niederösterreichs 15), St. Pölten 2008, pp. 35–49; M. Bukała, "Oeconomica Mediaevalia" of Wrocław Dominicans. Library and Studies of Friars, and Ethical–Economic Ideas: The Example from Silesia, Spoleto 2010. Further relevant studies have been published by D. R. Lesnick, Dominican Preaching and the Creation of Capitalist Ideology in Late–Medieval Florence, in: Memorie Dominicane n.s. 89 (1977–1978), pp. 199–247; L. K. Little, Religious Poverty and the Profit Economy in Medieval Europe, London 1978, and B. Neidiger, Armutsbegriff und Wirtschaftsverhalten der Franziskaner im 15. Jahrhundert, in: K. Elm (ed.), Erwerbspolitik und Wirtschaftsweise mittelalterlicher Orden und Klöster (Berliner Historische Studien 17 = Ordensstudien VII.), Berlin 1992, pp. 207–230.

7   I have discussed the relation between the mendicant networks and demographic issues in an earlier paper: B. F. Romhányi, Mendicant Networks (note 2 above).

moved from this group quite early. The difference between the resulting models is striking. The Hungarian network kept growing slowly, but persistently till the early sixteenth century when it collapsed due to the parallel effect of both the Ottoman wars and the Reformation. In Bohemia the mendicant network reached its level of stabilisation relatively soon, then it was affected by the Hussite movement, resulting in the closing of friaries and the expulsion of many friars from the country. However, by the mid-fifteenth century it had been possible to stabilise the network on a lower level and even the sixteenth-century Reformation had less impact on it. Poland represents a third model: from the thirteenth century on, the mendicant network grew very slowly, but it had two ascending periods, one around 1400 and a second one in the early 1500s. Austria and Silesia were similar from the point of view of both the size and the dynamics of their mendicant networks. Like Bohemia, they reached a level of stabilisation around 1300, which they preserved till at least the mid-sixteenth century. (Table 1, Fig. 1) It seems to be clear that sustaining capacity was a decisive element in shaping the different networks, while urban development had hardly anything to do with it.[8] Since the friars wanted to be present in as many communities of the faithful as possible, one may question how they could adapt themselves to the different circumstances and to assess the – economic – barriers of their expansion.

	Austria		Bohemia		Silesia		Poland		Hungary	
	M	M+P	M	M+P	M	M+P	M	M+P	M	M+P
1240	8	8	12	12	2	2	14	14	9	12
1260	11	11	25	25	10	10	19	19	30	38
1280	19	19	37	37	13	13	29	29	40	50
1300	26	26	47	47	24	24	40	40	60	80
1320	26	26	49	49	26	26	42	42	71	100
1340	28	28	53	53	26	26	44	44	87	127
1360	29	29	61	61	27	27	56	56	96	144
1380	31	31	63	63	27	27	67	67	111	175

---

8   About demographic development in medieval Hungary see also B. F. ROMHÁNYI, A középkori magyar plébániák és a 14. századi pápai tizedjegyzék [Medieval Hungarian Parishes and the 14th–Century Papal Tithe List], in: Történelmi Szemle 61 (2019), pp. 339–360; B. F. ROMHÁNYI, És ha mégis tudtak számolni? Avagy: hány katona kell az ország védelmére? [What if they could count? Or: how many soldiers are needed for to defend the country?], in: K. M. KINCSES (ed.), Hadi és más nevezetes történetek: Tanulmányok Veszprémy László tiszteletére, Budapest 2018, pp. 106–116.

	Austria		Bohemia		Silesia		Poland		Hungary	
	M	M+P	M	M+P	M	M+P	M	M+P	M	M+P
1400	31	31	64	64	28	**30**	80	**81**	117	**179**
1420	31	32	57	57	28	30	95	97	123	189
1440	31	32	39	39	28	30	96	**100**	132	200
1460	35	36	42	42	32	**34**	105	113	146	211
1480	39	**41**	44	44	32	34	110	119	156	227
1500	39	41	44	44	32	34	112	121	177	247
1520	37	39	45	45	32	34	114	123	184	257
1540	32	34	42	42	27	29	112	121	132	185
1560	24	26	35	35	26	28	107	116	27	39
1580	23	25	30	30	26	28	105	114	9	16

Table 1: Mendicants and Paulines in East Central Europe between 1240 and 1580 (bold lines indicate the first foundation for the Pauline Order in the single regions)

There are but guesstimations about the population size of each East Central European country, however, it is worth mentioning them because it allows a comparison. Around 1500, the population of the Hungarian kingdom without Croatia was about 3.5–3.6 million, that of the countries of the Bohemian Crown about 2.3–2.4 million, that of the Polish kingdom without Lithuania about 2.9–3.0 million. In the Austrian lands, that is in Upper and Lower Austria with Styria, there were approximately 0.8 million people.

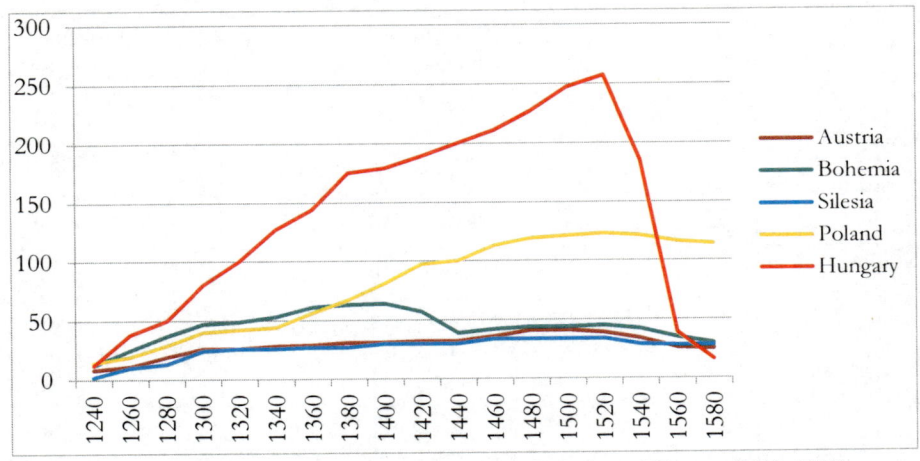

Figure 1: The development of the network of friaries in East Central Europe (1240–1580)

Non-Monastic Finance
The ways of giving alms

Paradoxically, mendicancy is the activity of the mendicant orders most difficult to grasp.[9] Since the revenue it generated was not recorded, there is no trace of it in the account books, nor can we determine from any source what proportion it represented within the friars' income. In addition, the 'technique' of begging is not an easy issue either. Mendicancy in its strict sense is mentioned very rarely in written evidence. As for the medieval Hungarian kingdom, the only source containing more details is the account book of Prince Sigismund, the younger brother of King Wladislaus II. of Hungary, who spent approximately three years in Buda in the first years of the sixteenth century. Some additional data can be taken from the account book of 1525 of King Louis II., as well. Based on these sources, there were three basic forms of getting alms: 1) asking for alms on the streets and knocking on doors, 2) addressing a supporter with a supplication letter and 3) collecting alms from the zone of quest ascribed to a particular friary. The latter was the most common for all the mendicant orders, there are even normative texts regulating the yearly collection of alms. Literally begging was mainly practiced by the Franciscans and to some extent by the Austin Hermits. In clear contrast to that, the Dominicans preferred to seek out wealthy supporters directly. There was a fourth possibility, too, namely the indulgence and the running of a pilgrimage site, however, it was used only temporarily and only by a smaller part of the monasteries.

---

[9] About the mendicancy in Western Europe, mainly in France see L. VIALLET, Pratique de la quête chez les religieux mendiants. Moyen Age – Époque Moderne, in: Revue Mabillon n.s. 23 (2012), pp. 263–271.

Mendicancy

According to the account book of Prince Sigismund of Poland, he encountered begging Franciscan friars at the gate of Buda and gave 4 deniers.[10] Similar sums were given to the Austin Hermits and Carmelites, as well as to the poor (*pauperi*) coming from one of the urban hospitals who knocked on his door. Considerably larger sums, ½ to 1 guilder were given to the friars when they came with a letter of supplication.

During his stay in Hungary Prince Sigismund of Jagiello gave the friars a total of 57 guilders and 43 deniers. Most of this (over 45 per cent) went to the Franciscans (the Observants received about twice as much as the Conventuals). The Paulines received a comparable sum, around 23 guilders (40 per cent). The Dominicans received from the prince far less: a total of 2.95 guilders (5 per cent), the Austin Hermits similarly just 3 guilders (5 per cent), while the Carmelites obtained 1.76 guilders (3 per cent).

For comparison, according to the account book of King Louis II, the Franciscans received a total of 371 guilders in the first semester of 1525, of which only one was for the alms (this was given to the Buda Observants). The king's preacher, friar Anthony, was given 10 guilders for his own use and the rest was spent for the preparation and cost of the Pentecostal Chapter. Dominicans (9 guilders) and Paulines (5 guilders) also received alms. The other two communities present in Buda, the Carmelites and the Austin Hermits, do not appear in the accounts, at least during this period. Instead, several female communities (nuns and beguines alike) were supported in Buda, Óbuda, Pest and Székesfehérvár. All in all, it appears that the average amount of the alms was slightly higher in the royal account book (1–2 guilders), but it is not clear from the records whether the subsidy was granted after supplication. The support for the Conventual Franciscans is important, since – unlike the account book of Prince Sigismund – the accounts of the King were raised after the Conventual branch of the Order embraced the observance.

Looking at the entries in the account book's records, it is quite clear that Prince Sigismund had a different relationship with each order, and this was not entirely related to the amount of alms they were given. Undoubtedly, the Franciscans, including the Observants, received most support, and they also performed various diplomatic assignments for the Prince. However, the Carmelites were the closest to Sigismund's heart, especially during his stay in Buda in 1505,

---

[10] For the detailed analysis of the sources see B. F. ROMHÁNYI, Quête et collecte des aumônes chez les frères mendiants de Hongrie à la fin du moyen âge, in: Moyen Âge 122 (2016), pp. 301–323. The publication of the sources discussed in this part of the paper: P. KOZÁK (ed.), Rationes curiae Sigismundi Iagellonici, ducis Glogoviensis et Opaviensis, Silesiae et Lusatiarum summi capitanei, de annis (1493) 1500–1507, Prague/Opava 2014; V. FRAKNÓI (ed.), II. Lajos király számadási könyve 1525-ből [The account book of King Louis II from 1525] (Magyar Történelmi Tár XXII.), Budapest 1877.

when he invited the friars six times in a little over a month, each time giving them some alms. The Dominicans' relations with Sigismund, though they received larger sums, appear to be much more formal than this, and neither did he establish close relations the Austin Hermits. The latter were almost in a business relationship with him, as they were often given alms when they offered a special gift (grapes) to the distinguished guest.[11]

The Paulines should be specifically mentioned here. Overall, they received the second highest amount (8 guilders 25 deniers) behind the Franciscans, but there was a clear downwards trend over the years. While in 1500 they regularly contacted the prince with various fruits produced by themselves, and received a total of 4 guilders, this amount was halved in the next two years, and there were no more fruit gifts either. In 1505, Sigismund probably did not meet them at all, nor did he visit the tomb of St. Paul or the church of Fehéregyháza.[12] We do not know what caused the fracture. Maybe after his arrival, Sigismund wanted to meet the Hungarian public, or he might have supported the Paulines on the advice of his brother, the king. Later, however, he followed his own path, and the Carmelites were better than the Paulines in winning his sympathy. It is also noteworthy that, although both monastic communities were present in Poland, there was a significant difference in the level of support. While the Carmelites were unequivocally supported by the king and his family, the Paulines were mainly assisted by the ascendant nobility, and the bishops coming from these families.[13]

It is worth considering the prince's generosity by relating it to the sums he spent on other things. In this context, at first glance, he does not seem particularly generous. He occasionally paid 1 guilder for his favourite weekly bath and regularly lost ½ or 1 guilder in gambling.

In the autumn of 1500, when he gave the Dominicans of Szeged 1 orth,[14] he bought a horse for 8 guilders.[15] Compared to other donations, the amounts given to the friars are not at all high. Chanting schoolchildren, for example, usually received 1 orth. The cumulated sum the prince spent on alms was about 10 to

---

[11] P. Kozák (ed.), Rationes (note 10 above), p. 24.

[12] The church of Fehéregyháza (today on the territory of Budapest III) was allegedly the burial place of Duke Árpád. Somewhen before the Mongol Invasion (1241), a Holy Virgin's Chapel was built at the site which became a place of pilgrimage in the late Middle Ages. That chapel was entrusted to the Paulines by King Mathias Corvinus in 1480. B. F. Romhányi, Kolostorok és társaskáptalanok a középkori Magyarországon [Monasteries and Collegiate Chapters in medieval Hungary], Budapest 2000, p. 24.

[13] B. F. Romhányi, A koldulóbarátok szerepe a XV–XVI. századi vallási megújulásban [The role of the mendicant friars in the religious reforms of the 15th and 16th centuries], in: B. F. Romhányi / G. Kendeffy (eds.), Szentírás – hagyomány – reformáció, Budapest 2009, pp. 144–155.

[14] Orth was a Polish coin, the quarter of a Thaler.

[15] P. Kozák (ed.), Rationes (note 10 above), p. 61.

12 guilders per year, only in 1500 it was much higher, about 25 guilders, due to a single Good Friday donation. Knowing the price conditions of the time, it can be said that every year Sigismund used the price of a good horse and the related horse gear to support the mendicants and the Paulines, which is not a small sum.

The friars did indeed receive much higher donations from other people. The testaments contain bequests of 5–10 guilders without any special obligation attached. There are also much higher sums of up to 100 guilders for funeral funds, and several noblemen have donated 1000 guilders or more to the friaries they supported. However, these donations were single payments. Larger sums of several hundred guilders went to friaries for specific purposes, such as the support of construction, and the annual interest rate on the donated capital was roughly equivalent to smaller one-off amounts. That is, the friars could actually spend these smaller amounts, usually less than 10 guilders, for their own purposes.

The picture that comes to us from Prince Sigismund's accounts differs from both the bequests and the regular interest income on capital. The friars asked for alms; they usually received small sums; and often they gave gifts or services in return. The repetition of the sums given as alms shows that this is not a regular business relationship, even if apparently something was given in return.

For what reason did the friars turn to the Polish prince when he was visiting Hungary? Their action was obviously not exceptional; the difference was that similar cases were less well documented. The expression *cum supplicatione* of the account book, which very often appears in connection with such donations, coincides with supplications known from the *formularia*.[16] We see the forms of mendicant practice, the begging itself. Another way of collecting alms was to visit the area around the towns, generally at harvest time. Perhaps it was because of the lack of a supplication that on 24 March 1501 the begging Carmelites (*monachis mendicantibus*) were given only 5 deniers. By the way, the pattern is the same as that of a door-to-door beggar: on 24 January 1501, a pauper from the hospital begging with a bell at lunchtime was given only 3 deniers.[17] Perhaps we could also include the Austin Hermits who were asking for money for bread, although they received the relatively high sum of 14 deniers.

The importance of collecting alms and begging is emphasised by the fact that the local friars immediately appeared before the prince when he arrived in a town. This happened in Nagyszombat, in Nyitra, in Trencsén or in Székesfehérvár. Sometimes the friars went to meet the guest who had not yet arrived, or they followed him after he had left. It is interesting to note that only two or three examples refer to the begging *stricto sensu*: the Franciscans at the Buda town gate,

---

[16] Formularium maius Ordinis S. Pauli primi Heremitae, eds. B. F. ROMHÁNYI / G. SARBAK, Budapest 2013.

[17] P. KOZÁK (ed.), Rationes (note 10 above), p. 87.

the Carmelites begging from gate to gate, and perhaps the Austin Hermits mentioned above. It is no coincidence that the Dominicans do not appear in this context.

As far as the use of the alms is concerned, it is striking that a specific purpose is rarely indicated in the text of the supplications. When a purpose was given, it could be for Advent oil, for general expenses, for wine, or for the repair of the roof, but these were exceptions. Sometimes it is added in the book entry that the friars applied for alms *cum supplicatione pro elemosina*, but it is not always clearly indicated. Anyhow, donations of such a small amount helped to defray the everyday costs of living.

It would be difficult to determine to what extent this revenue covered the needs of each friary. We do not know, for instance, how often the friars turned to their supporters in this way, and whether the sums known from Prince Sigismund's account books represented the average amount given to the friars as alms. We do not even know exactly how many friars lived in a given friary. However, a proportional comparison of the share given to each order suggests that the Observant Franciscans made the highest demand for this income. The fact that they received about half of the amounts, reflects the extent to which the community depended on direct donations. For the other orders, other sources of income, for instance the revenues of their modest estates, greatly reduced the importance of alms, and thus the frequency of begging. In addition, these estates sometimes made it easier for the friars to gain the goodwill of their supporters, because they enabled them to make a delicious gift to those who supported them.

Last wills and *pro anima* donations

Among the best indicators of the social relationships of mendicant orders and their livelihood are the last wills and *pro anima* or pious donations. Although there are differences between the two types of donation (for example, the *pro anima* donation was not necessarily made in connection with the impending death), it is worth discussing them together. In many cases, despite the apparent differences, even the classification of the charters would be difficult. It is important to emphasize that *pro anima* donations were always alms, which is often also expressed in the text itself. The two provisions are also linked in the sense that both were intended to secure the spiritual salvation of the donor and of his or her relatives. Since regular, possibly perpetual masses for the deceased would often have been too burdensome for the parish clergy, the faithful turned increasingly to the mendicant friars in the late Middle Ages.[18] In some cases, the relation was

---

[18] L. SOLYMOSI, Két középkor végi testamentum Szabolcs vármegyéből [Two late medieval testaments from Szabolcs County], in: Á. KOVÁCS (ed.), Emlékkönyv Rácz István 70. Születésnapjára, Debrecen 1999, pp. 203–225.

established not with individuals but with whole communities, for instance guilds, as it happened in the Buda Carmelite friary where the guild of the butchers had their altar. Unfortunately, the data are too sporadic, thus we can only register the phenomenon, without knowing anything about the kind and quantity of income these relations produced for the friaries.

Slightly more than 2,000 wills have survived from medieval Hungary, most of which were urban wills.[19] The number of documents that can be used for our topic is over 350, which is nearly 17 per cent of the total. Most of the data is real wills, but there are some other sources (lawsuits, receipts, account books, registers) which contain specific references to wills. Still, the picture is deceptive, as almost half of our sources – more than 150 – come from Pressburg.[20] In addition, there is a relatively large number of wills mentioning mendicant and/or Pauline convents issued in Sopron (23),[21] Schässburg (28)[22] and Kolozsvár (18+4).[23] This, of course, also means that the number of Franciscan friaries among the beneficiaries is extremely high, because there were only Franciscan friaries in both Pressburg and Sopron, competing only with a Pauline monastery close to the town.

Nevertheless, half of the benefitting institutions were Dominican priories (7) and Franciscans (6), who were in second place. Their share was split between the two branches of the order. While the conventuals are at the beginning of the ranking scale, the observants are at its end (Sóvár, Kolozsvár, Medgyes). In addition, two of them benefitted in conjunction with a different mendicant friary: Sóvár besides the Carmelites of Eperjes, and Kolozsvár next to the Dominican friary of the town. In these cases, the two mendicant communities usually appear in the same will.

We can only make very limited statements about the proportion of the different social classes who mentioned the mendicant friaries in their wills: they were citizens, nobles, magnates, and ecclesiastics. Perhaps the only notable feature is the low proportion of clergymen (~6 per cent). Similarly, it would be misleading

---

[19] Das Preßburger Protocollum Testamentorum 1410 (1427)–1529, 2 vols., eds. J. MAJOROSSY / K. SZENDE, Vienna 2010–2014, vol. 1, p. 6. The medieval charter collection (DL and DF) of the Hungarian National Archives (MNL) contains about 2,000 testaments in original or photocopy. Almost 40 per cent of them come from Pressburg alone.

[20] For the detailed analysis see J. MAJOROSSY, Church in Town: Urban Religious Life in Late Medieval Pressburg in the Mirror of Last Wills. PhD Thesis, CEU, Budapest 2006.

[21] For the detailed analysis see K. SZENDE, Otthon a városban: társadalom és anyagi kultúra a középkori Sopronban, Pozsonyban és Eperjesen [At home in the town: society and material culture in medieval Sopron, Pressburg and Eperjes], Budapest 2004.

[22] K. FABRITIUS, Zwei Funde in der ehemaligen Dominikanerkirche, in: Archiv des Vereins für siebenbürgische Landeskunde 5 (1861), pp. 4–19.

[23] J. ESZTERHÁZY, A kolozsvári ferencziek egyházának története [The history of the Franciscan church in Kolozsvár], in: Magyar Sion 4 (1866), pp. 561–585.

to draw conclusions for each monastery solely on the basis of their share of the bequests, since even at first glance it is clear that our data is extremely incomplete. The central areas of the country are almost literally absent, the only exceptions being the Dominican friary in Pest and the Saint Lawrence's monastery of the Paulines. Considering the one-off references, nearly half of the mendicant friaries that existed around 1500 have received a donation, but some large southern friaries, such as the Franciscan monasteries of Szeged or Újlak, are missing from this list. We can hardly assume the believers would not have supported them in this way. Given our knowledge of a small donation left to the Szeged Dominicans, this is all the less likely. However, in this case, the original will did not survive, only a private letter about it.[24] The fact that friaries do not appear as beneficiaries of last wills in the medieval kingdom's southern regions must be attributed to the large-scale destruction of written evidence, caused by the Ottoman wars. In other cases, however, mainly in the case of the friaries in the market towns – most of which were Observant Franciscan – the lower standard of literacy may also be the reason for the lack of wills.

A few words need to be said about the Austin Hermits. Although the Austin friary in Bártfa is one of the most frequently mentioned houses, other communities of the order were very rarely mentioned in the wills (21), and several of them (8) were issued in the thirteenth and fourteenth centuries, when testaments were much less common than in the fifteenth – sixteenth centuries. One of the telling examples is the case of Eperjes. While the burghers regularly left bequests to the nearby Franciscan friary of Sóvár, the neighbouring Augustine friary of Sáros was not at all on their spiritual map. Eperjes is 4 km from Sóvár and 6 km from Sáros, so if the Sáros Augustine monastery did not benefit from the wills of the burghers, it was certainly not because of its distance. The burghers of Pressburg, for example, donated regularly smaller or larger sums to the Paulines in Thal, although the monastery was about 15 kilometres from the town.

In contrast to the examination of the social strata, the analysis of the content of wills promises much more success, especially if we look not only for the relationships within one order, but also for the differences and similarities between the orders. The vast majority of the wills mentioned one, sometimes two or three monasteries among the beneficiaries. A larger number of institutions occur only in exceptional cases, as does the donation for the central administration of the province or of the whole order itself (for example, Queen Elizabeth in the fourteenth century or Bishop Oswald of Zagreb at the end of the fifteenth century).[25]

---

[24] MNL OL DL 56612 (mid–fifteenth century).

[25] Codex diplomaticus Hungariae ecclesiasticus ac civilis, ed. G. FEJÉR, 45 vols., Buda 1829–1866, vol. 9/5, n. 114; I. K. TKALČIĆ (ed.), Monumenta historica lib. reg. civitatis Zagrabiae metropolis regni Dalmatiae, Croatiae et Slavoniae (Povjestni spomenici slob. kralj. grada Zagreba.), vol. 3, Zagreb 1890, n. 394.

About half of the testaments involved money, the remainder being movable or immovable property.

As far as the chronological distribution of these sources is concerned, the preserved wills were made mainly in the fifteenth and sixteenth centuries. Of the pre-1400 period, there are only 32 relevant wills, but towards the end of the Middle Ages, there is a noticeable increase in the number of sources. About 73 per cent of the wills (83 per cent if we include the wills in Pressburg) were issued between 1450 and 1550, and even within this period we know more sources from the first decades of the sixteenth century than from the second half of the fifteenth century.

The Dominicans were the largest recipients of bequests, followed by the Franciscans. The division between the two branches of the Franciscan Order is very interesting. At first sight, it seems that Conventuals were more often beneficiaries of last wills in the given period (37 : 29). However, the order is reversed when we take into consideration the single friaries mentioned in the testaments, since there were 50 references to the Observants and only 38 to the Conventuals. The reason for this is that there are several wills mentioning more than one Observant friary. For instance, the widow of George Kőfaragó (stonemason), a burgher of Kolozsvár, left different amounts of money to a dozen of Observant friaries all around the country, besides commemorating of course the Dominican and the Franciscan friary of her town.[26] While the monasteries of the two branches of the Franciscan order accounted for 60 per cent of the late medieval mendicant monasteries in Hungary, their share was much smaller in the last wills, slightly over 40 per cent.

Indeed, the share of the Dominican friaries in the testaments was much higher than their proportion in the mendicant network. Between 1450 and 1550 they appear as beneficiaries in around 47 per cent of the wills, though they accounted for only 20 per cent of the mendicant friaries around 1500. Between 1350 and 1450, they were mentioned in over 50 per cent of the known wills.

In total, between 1450 and 1550, about 87 per cent of the wills with bequests in favour of mendicant friaries mentioned either Dominican or Franciscan friaries. The proportion of Observant Franciscans was the lowest, though the number of both their friaries and friars were the highest. This phenomenon cannot be explained by differences in the attitudes towards real estates or cash income. Instead, it reflects the different strategies of each order in building and nurturing social relationships. The Observant Franciscans were supported, on the one hand by their supporters from aristocratic and noble circles, in whose wills they often appear, and on the other hand by the burghers of the market towns, who, however, only rarely made written testaments in the late Middle Ages. In addition,

---

[26] E. JAKAB, Kolozsvár története [The history of Kolozsvár], Buda 1870, n. 237.

Observants seem to have preferred to embrace confraternity, and invite lay supporters to join their community in a way that was less formal than tertiary communities. In this case, being member of the confraternity may be interpreted as an alternative to the will.

The Austin Hermits were significantly less frequent among the recipients: they appear in about 7 per cent of the wills between 1450 and 1550, while their friaries represented almost 18 per cent. Similarly, the Carmelites are rarely mentioned, although due to the wills preserved in the archives of Eperjes their share in the last wills is higher than the proportion of their friaries (5.33 per cent / 2.14 per cent).

It is also typical that in the wills, these two orders were represented by one friary at a time, and that they often have to share bequests with the friaries of the larger orders. The popularity of the larger orders is eloquently demonstrated by the wills of Eperjes, as the burghers of the town supported not only the local Carmelites but also the Observant Franciscan friary of Sóvár, just 4 kilometres from the town's centre. Indeed, the will of Caritas, the widow of Gregor Fillach, not even mentioned the local Carmelite friary, while it benefitted the Franciscans in Sóvár.[27]

There are also some cases where the testator wished to be buried in a friary, without specifying any bequest. As examples we can refer to the wills of Benedict Csáki in 1490[28] or of Emeric Török of Enying in 1515.[29] The former wanted to be buried in Szalárd and the latter in Futak. Since in both cases, the testators were patrons of the friary in question, we can be sure that they and their family members supported the friars, but for some reason it was not important to mention it in the testament, as well. There is one known exception: Nicholas Daróci of Daróc wanted to be buried in the Perecske (today part of Villány) friary as he put it in his will of 1501, but he did not leave anything to the convent although he was not the patron. We do not know the reason, maybe there was a longer relationship in the background.[30]

As for the types of donations, the Dominicans very often received cash or annuities, a form of support hardly ever found in the case of the Franciscans, especially the Observants. If documents from the confraternities are included, it is possible to say that the Franciscans received the most alms in the fifteenth and

---

[27] B. IVÁNYI, Eperjes szabad királyi város levéltára 1424–1509 [The archives of the free royal town of Eperjes], Szeged 1932, n. 750 (1497): *Item cingulum argenteum parvum fratribus ad Sowar legavit.*

[28] A Körösszegi és Adorjáni gróf Csáky család történetéhe, ed. L. SZABÓ, 2 vols. [Charters to the history of the Counts Csáky], Budapest 1919, vol. 1, pp. 471–472.

[29] J. BESSENYEI, Enyingi Török Bálint, Budapest 1994, pp. 1–3.

[30] MNL OL DL 25160 (1501).

sixteenth centuries, but the Dominicans received considerably more cash. In addition, the Dominicans were increasingly given real estates after 1475, often by families with which the Order had already been on good terms for a longer period (for instance the Somkeréki family, Michael Szobi or Benedict Túri).

A comparison of two registers from the Bistritz friary reveals how the Dominican approach to incomes and finances changed during the fifteenth century.[31] According to the first list compiled in 1413 in the Dominican friary of Nösen, the friars had a total of 59 rundlets (hung. akó) of wine (in Hungary 1 rundlet was about 53.7 litres) from seven vineyards. On the reverse side of the list, a later hand recorded the annuities of four more vineyards, amounting to an additional 17 rundlets. This could roughly correspond to the annual needs of the monastic community in Bistritz which consisted of 22 friars according to the Fabri list. The annuities were derived from wills and provided the payment for everlasting remembrance: *Ista autem testamenta sunt legata pro fratribus ordinis et claustri supra scripti ad ministerationem spiritualium, ut istis a quibus exierunt refrigeria eveniant sempiterna.* However, forty years later, in 1454, the friary made a new list. It shows that by then the situation had changed radically. The annuities known at the beginning of the century had all disappeared and were replaced by four vineyards owned by the Dominicans. This change can also be observed when other items on the list are considered, for instance arable land instead of grain rent. The question is why a Dominican friary on the frontier of Western Christianity exchanged its existing annuities for landed estate ten years before the order received papal permission to own property. Since the friars certainly had more wine of their vineyards than out of the annuities, financial considerations were probably behind the change. As it was customary in the country only to issue wine-licences to vineyard owners in the town, the Dominicans in Bistritz acquired the right to run a pub as soon as they became vineyard owners. And that was a good source of income.

Donations in cash

Although some monasteries received money, including annuities (for instance the Franciscan friary of Szemenye [today Muraszemenye]), as early as in the thirteenth century, the quantity of data is insufficient for an analysis before the mid-fifteenth century. Besides the cash donations I also include the salt incomes at the guilder value, because often they were paid out in cash anyway, and a major part of the salt received in kind was also sold by the friars.

---

[31] Urkundenbuch zur Geschichte der Deutschen in Siebenbürgen, eds. F. ZIMMERMANN / C. WERNER / G. GÜNDISCH, 7 vols., Cologne 1872–1991, vol. 3, n. 1715 and vol. 5, n. 2914.

In the last decades of the Middle Ages, two mendicant communities received larger amounts of regular subventions from the ruler: the Dominicans and the Observant Franciscans. From the mid-1450s, the Dominicans received grants under various titles, but always in connection with a particular friary. The sum reached its highest value in 1481, when it amounted to approximately 242 guilders a year. Of this sum 92 guilders were paid in Kronstadt, fifty in Kolozsvár. The order received another 100 guilders through the Pest monastery. The friars received about 200 guilders in salt, and the rest was paid in cash. The Observant Franciscans, though strongly supported from the outset by the most distinguished sections of society, received such income only from the 1490s, and in a peculiar way through their monastery in Kolozsvár. King Matthias assigned an unspecified amount of salt to the construction of the monastery he founded in the town. This was gradually transformed into an annuity from the mid-1490s, and the amount was fixed at 300 forints till the mid-sixteenth century. Similar amounts of money were given to the Conventual Franciscans in 1525 or to the Paulines from the late fourteenth century to support the annual meeting of their chapter.

The testament of Queen Elizabeth the Elder from 1379[32] is an important source for the relationship between the royal dynasty and the mendicant orders which – if only the cash amounts are considered – listed a total of 2,200 guilders for various mendicant communities. The Franciscans, Dominicans and Austin Hermits received the usual 300 guilders, the queen left 200 for the Paulines and 100 for the Carmelite friary under construction in Buda. The remaining 1,000 forints were shared by two Franciscan friaries which were also under construction at that time, namely Aracs and Beregszász. Of course, the amounts in the will are not to be confused with annuities, still, their magnitude evokes that of the regular subventions. It is also worth emphasising that, at the end of the fourteenth century, the queen mother made no distinction between the three great mendicant orders present in the kingdom. The younger order of the Paulines was given two-thirds of the above sum. A century later, the ranking was to be quite different.

It would be difficult to give an estimate of the sums received by the individual orders in Hungary because our data is fragmentary. However, the tendencies are clear: the Dominicans tended to receive their income in cash, while the Franciscans – both Conventuals and Observants – preferred not to accept such donations. The sixteenth-century account book of the Sopron friary proves that direct alms in cash were rather marginal as late as in the 1520s. One of the results of this difference is reflected in the number of friars sent to study abroad: while

---

[32] Codex diplomaticus Hungariae, ed. G. FEJÉR (note 25 above), vol. 9/5, n. 114.

many Dominicans spent several years mainly at Italian *studia generalia*, we can hardly find one or two Franciscans studying outside Hungary.[33]

An interesting episode that happened in the Carmelite friary of Eperjes sheds light on the use of the money coming from these sources. In a lawsuit between the town and its former mayor, Ladislaus Szőcs the latter was accused of having embezzled about 500 guilders left by burghers to the Carmelite friary. Indeed, we do not know how long this sum had been accumulated, but apparently it served as a fund managed by the town. Another aspect of the story reveals the relation between the sums mentioned in the documents and the amount of money discussed in the lawsuit: the latter is seven times higher than the sum known from the preserved testaments.[34]

Donations in kind

Livestock

A substantial part of the donations in kind were actually indirect money donations, such as horses and oxen, or more generally wine. Another part served the table of the brethren, which could be both one-off gifts and regular grants. Horses, sometimes with harness or the arms of the donor, regularly appear in last wills from the thirteenth century onwards. Giving the horse which had been used in the funeral procession to the church was a widespread practice in Hungary. The tradition was followed in both a noble and an urban environment.[35] The value of the horses varied between 0,9 and 26 guilders; the first was probably a jade, while the other must have been steeds.[36]

Another form of donating horses is represented by the annuity given by Blaise Kenderesi in 1465 in favour of the Dominican friary of Pest.[37] In this case, the economic activity of the donor is reflected. Such annuities, however, were usually given in wine.

Not all the horses were sold, at least some data show that the friaries had dray-horses, too. In 1428 Prior Isaiah of Bártfa mentioned the friary's cart and

---

[33] B. F. ROMHÁNYI, Egyetemjáró szerzetesek a késő középkori Magyarországon (Ki, hova és miből?) [Friars at universities in the late Middle Ages. Who, where and who paid for?], in: P. HARASZTI SZABÓ / B. KELÉNYI / Z. SIMON (eds.), „Mindenki vágyik a tudásra, de az árát senki sem akarja megadni": Az oktatás financiális háttere és haszna a középkorban és a kora újkorban, Budapest 2019, pp. 117–140.

[34] B. F. ROMHÁNYI, Kolduló barátok (note 1 above), p. 187.

[35] For instance, MNL OL DL 30356 (1270–1278), 33655 (1280–1290), 36398 (1492), 35727 (1492), 74407 (1525), MNL OL DF 213582 (1456).

[36] J. HÁZI, Sopron szabad királyi város története [The history of the free royal town of Sopron], 2 vols., in 13 parts, Sopron 1921–1943, vol. 2/5, n. 26 (pp. 367, 374).

[37] MNL OL DL 16159 (1465).

the horses belonging to it. In the Sopron account book, the cart, the cost of shoeing and the fodder used in the friary refer to the horse. The general presence of horses in the friaries can be presumed based on the decisions of the Salvatorian Provincial Assembly in the 1530s forbidding the friaries to have carts. Although we do not have written evidence for carts and dray-horses from any Dominican friaries, the fact that they possessed manors suggests that they did have such animals.

Oxen appear only rarely in testaments or other *pro anima* donations. One example is the last will of Lady Ursula, the widow of John Várdai, who left oxen for four Franciscan friaries.[38] We do not know what happened with those animals but according to the account books of the Sopron friary according to which beef was regularly on the table of the friars, it cannot be excluded that they were consumed. However, the same account books contain other data about selling the meat and the leather of oxen received by the friary. The value of the oxen seems to have been somewhat lower than that of the horses, but our impression maybe false because of the scarcity of data.

Along with horses and cattle, sheep and pigs also appear in some of the testaments around 1500. In 1498, the Dominicans of Schässburg, together with their estates in Hétúr, received not only cattle, but sheep and pigs as well (it is probably not by chance that one of the friars living in Schässburg in this period was a butcher). In 1520, "a good man" gave them eight pigs. The source has been preserved at an extraordinary location: it was recorded on the wall of the kitchen by the steward of the friary.[39] The Dominican friary of Simontornya, built around 1516, also received a large number of sheep, altogether a thousand, given by the founder Moses Buzlai. Periodically, Franciscan friaries had livestock (sheep, swine and poultry), as well, which the friars had received as alms. In 1554, the provincial chapter allowed the Franciscan friaries to have hens, since they could not get them any more by the quest.

To sum up, Franciscans and Austin Hermits received livestock (horses and cattle) mainly for sale, while some of the late medieval Dominican friaries owned manors with large stocks, mainly sheep and swine. These were also reared to be sold on the market, but the economic context was completely different.

Similar provisions were made for certain crops: emphasizing the avoidance of cash, monasteries were allowed to plant flax, barley and oats. The former served

---

[38] MNL OL DL 83023 (1517–1526).

[39] A. IPOLYI, Adalékok a magyar domonkosok történetéhez, in: Magyar Sion 5 (1867), pp. 561–609, at p. 602.

to make oil and the latter two were fodder. The permit for fodder plants emphasized that beer should not be brewed.[40] All these data also reflect the growing difficulty in collecting alms.

Grain and wine

Grain, wine and lard[41] were the basic victuals which mendicant friars asked for when they went on their regular tour in their zones of quest. Sometimes, especially in connection with Franciscan friaries, these products also appear in last wills and *pro anima* donations, but usually they were part of the alms collected by the brethren. Indeed, the planning of the quest belonged to the most important tasks of the local superiors since they needed to ensure the acquisition of the annual provision for the community without accepting any superfluous donation. The form in which these products were given to the friars changed considerably over time. The Austin Hermits and the Carmelites – just like the Paulines – had estates from early times on, supplying their communities with the necessary food and drink. As for the Paulines, some of their monasteries were even able to sell their surplus on the market – for instance wine in north-eastern Hungary, or grain in Slavonia – but the basic function of their landed estates was to produce food for the order's monasteries.

In addition to the more frequent donations mentioned above, the friars occasionally received other necessities, such as candles for their churches,[42] oil, building materials,[43] or even wood. An example of the latter is the entry in the accounts of the tax collectors of Sopron in 1452–1453, stating that heating wood worth of 224 Viennese deniers were sent to the Franciscan friary.[44]

It is also interesting that certain items never appear among the donations. This includes vegetables and fruits: they were either produced in the garden of the friaries or given to the friars in small quantities as occasional gifts. Poultry and eggs are also missing, but these got into the friaries only as alms or gifts, at least until the mid-sixteenth century.

---

[40] V. BUNYITAY / R. RAPAICS / J. KARÁCSONYI (eds.), Egyháztörténelmi emlékek a magyarországi hitújítás korából, 2 vols., Budapest 1902–1904, vol. 2, p. 522: *Liceat fratribus, ubi commode et sine pecuniis fieri potest, seminari facere lium ad excutendum oleum ad usum fratrum. Item ordeum sive avenam ad sustentanda animalia, non autem ad vendendum aut faciendam cervisiam.*

[41] Zs. JAKÓ (ed.), A kolozsmonostori konvent jegyzőkönyvei. 1289–1556 [Registers of the place of authentication of the Cluj–Mănăstur abbey], 2 vols., Budapest 1990, vol. 2, n. 2832: ...*Item fratribus ordinis predicatorum in Coloswar degentibus legavit septem lardones cum spatulis et arvinis.*

[42] Preßburger Protocollum, eds. J. MAJOROSSY / K. SZENDE (note 19 above), vol. 1, n. 29.

[43] I. K. TKALČIĆ (ed.), Monumenta historica (note 24 above), vol. 3, n. 185.

[44] J. HÁZI, Sopron szabad királyi város története (note 36 above), vol. 2/1, n. 32, p. 388.

Termini

In Hungary, we have relatively little data on the *termini*.[45] The earliest, but less informative, source referring only to the existence of a *terminus* is a charter dating from 1385. In this, Bartholomew, the new prior general of the Austin Hermits elected at the general chapter of Esztergom, informs the friars of the monasteries of Bruck and Marchegg (Lower Austria) that Matthias of Torda, prior provincial of Hungary, had allowed them to collect alms within the Hungarian province, i.e. at such places which were outside the interest of the Hungarian friars.[46] At that time, the friary of Pápoc was the Hungarian house closest to the two Austrian friaries, but it was also almost 100 km from Bruck and more than 130 km from Marchegg. Thus, the boundary of the zone of quest was located about 50–60 km from the friary. The same distance appears several times in the Transylvanian vicariate of the Dominicans in the late fifteenth century. Of course, this gives only a very superficial picture and actually raises several questions. The most important conclusion is that such a distance would necessitate a network providing due lodging for the friars on the way, however, we have hardly any hint of that. On the one hand, we look in vain for "Termineihäuser" known in Germany. On the other, there is very little evidence for the confriars of the monasteries hosting the friars on the quest. The only case is a confriar of the Dominicans of Schässburg, mentioned in the notes of Prior Anton Fabri.[47]

The extent of the *termini* is not known. The charter issued by Mathew Vicedominis in 1414, following a complaint from the Franciscans in Pressburg, according to which some parsons required one half or a quarter of the alms collected in their parishes, threatening to prohibit the quest, does not provide any detail. The vicar of the archbishop of Esztergom ordered the parsons and rectors of the diocese to welcome begging monks in their territory and not to obstruct

---

[45] Mostly I use the term *terminus* uniformly for the zone of quest, but there were differences in the contemporary terminology used by the orders themselves. While the Dominicans and the Austin Hermits usually labelled their area this way, the Franciscans used the word *contrata* or rarely *questus* in Latin sources. However, in medieval German-language sources, *terminey* also appears.

[46] Codex diplomaticus Hungariae, ed. G. FEJÉR (note 25 above), vol. 10/1, nn. 258–259: ...*venerabilis et religiosus vir, frater Mathias de Thorda, Provincialis Ungarie, inedie vestre gravitate pensata, liberam vobis, vestrisque subditis dedit licenciam in sua provincia eleemosynas petendi in eis duntaxat locis, ad que fratres de Ungaria ire non consueverunt, cuius et super hoc vidimus litteras cum sigillo pendenti.*

[47] A. IPOLYI, Adalékok a magyar domonkosok történetéhez (note 39 above), p. 609. *Insuper adiuravit filios et heredes* (sic) *proprios per nomen Dei vivens perpetuis temporibus, quatenus forent, semper fautores et confratres, necnon receptores hospicio patrum et fratrum loci istius.* The village in question, Bord (today Romania) was 65 kilometres from the friary.

them in collecting alms.[48] This suggests a specific interpretation of the *quarta canonicalis*. However, the problem remained, as a century later, Pope Leo X repeated the same order in his letter *Exponi nobis fecerunt*, issued in 1518.[49]

Slightly more information is provided in a letter dated 1459, written in the Hainburg friary in Austria by the Franciscan Ludwig von Tulln to the town of Pressburg, because of a dispute between the Austrian friars and the Franciscans in Pressburg. With a distance of only 16 km the two settlements are very close to each other. The wording of the letter suggests that the Austrian friars went beyond Pressburg and wanted to transport the alms collected through the town (*...ut scribitur in decreto Quod et ipsi diligentissime fecerunt et duxerunt usque ad praenominatam vestram civitatem, volentes ducere ad conventum nostrum*). Together with the above-mentioned charter for the two Lower Austrian friaries of the Austin Hermits, this suggests that the Austrian friars occasionally collected alms in Western Hungary, too. At the same time, the fact that the two friaries are so close to each other indicates that the *terminus* did not have a circular shape with the monastery in its centre. Similarly, in the early sixteenth century, when many friaries had to be abandoned and the zones of quest needed to be reorganised, several bits of information suggest that the zones of quest comprised an area of 50–60 kilometres basically in one direction from the friary, for instance the Observant Franciscan friaries of Kőrösszeg and Sóvár. This assumption is supported by some data from Germany and France, such as the *terminus* of the Austin Friary of Erfurt,[50] some Franciscan friaries in Burgundy and Auvergne,[51] and – as a Hungarian example – the Franciscan friary of Sopron. Many factors had to be considered in defining the *terminus*: the population and capacity of the area, the transport facilities, the interests and possibly the area of other monasteries, even those belonging to other orders, the expected number of friars and the content of the agreement made with the founder and his family.

Only the practice of mendicancy at the end of the Middle Ages is attested by the testimony of two witnesses in the lawsuit of the Austin friary in Körmend, while a third witness mentioned the name of the village (*Egedy*) they went to (in the first two cases the monks collected alms only in Körmend).[52] Even if we cannot determine the exact extension of the *terminus*, it was relatively extensive

---

[48] Zsigmond–kori Oklevéltár vol. 4, ed. E. MÁLYUSZ, Budapest 1994, n. 1698 (1414).

[49] N. KAIZER, A gyöngyösi zárda oklevéltára, Budapest 1930, p. 12.

[50] J. E. A. MARTIN, Verzeichnis der Termineien der Erfurter Einsiedler des Augustinerordens in Thüringen, in: Zeitschrift des Vereins für thüringische Geschichte und Altertumskunde NF 5 (1887), pp. 132–137.

[51] P. BERTRAND / L. VIALLET, La quête mendiante: espace, pastorale, réseaux, in: J.–L. FREY / C. PEROL (eds.), L'Historien en quête d'espaces, Clermont–Ferrand 2004, pp. 347–369.

[52] G. ERDÉLYI, The Register of a Convent Controversy (1517–1518). Pope Leo X, Cardinal Bakócz, The Augustinians and the observant Franciscans in contest, Budapest/Rome 2006, pp. 80, 121–122.

because, at least in local terms, a friar was sent to "more distant places."[53] If *Egedy* can be identified with a deserted village in Zala County, the distance from Körmend was about 50 km. This, in turn, corresponds to the average distance known from other sources. Although the zone of quest has not been mentioned in the list of witnesses, mapping the data yields thought provoking results. The places of origin of the witnesses,[54] apart from a few settlements (Kölked, Rádóc, Hollós, Hídvég), are located south-southwest of Körmend and are mostly concentrated along the road to Szentgotthárd. This is not to say that they necessarily reflect the area of the *terminus*, but in any case, according to testimonies, people in these villages had the most opportunity to meet the Austin Hermits of Körmend. By the way, the distance between Hídvég, which is slightly outside this circle, and Szentmihály on the opposite extremity of the area described above is only 30 km.

The most detailed data comes from the Transylvanian vicariate of the Dominicans at the end of the fifteenth century. In 1497, the Dominican Provincial Johann Epi reorganised the zones of quest of the Transylvanian friaries by defining the new boundaries. The convent of Kronstadt received the whole Burzenland, and it shared the territory of the seats of Sepsi and Kézdi with the friary of Székelyudvarhely. The friars of Székelyudvarhely were allowed to beg for alms throughout the Szeklerland all the way to Szászrégen. The *terminus* of the friary of Schässburg comprised the seats of Maros, Keresztúr and Udvarhely, while the friary of Nösen received the region around Szászrégen.[55] The office of the *terminarius* appears in several convents in the list of 1529. The *terminarius* of Gyulafehérvár and both the Saxon and the Hungarian *terminarius* of Kronstadt belonged to the leadership of the given friary, however, the *terminarius* of the Nösen friary at that time was a lay brother.

If we look more closely at the 1497 arrangement, we find a surprising result regarding the *terminus* of the Székelyudvarhely friary. While the zones of quest of the friaries of Kronstadt, Nösen and Schässburg were at most 50–60 km from the town where the friary was located – which, however, is not a small distance and certainly impossible to walk in one day – that of Székelyudvarhely extended up to Szászrégen which means that the two extremes of the *terminus* were almost 200 km apart! The size of the zone of quest was obviously influenced by the population density and the economic capacity of the area. However, this enormous distance also raises the question of how and how often the friars were able to collect alms in their assigned territory – not to mention their confession and

---

[53] Ibid., p. 161.
[54] Ibid., p. 38.
[55] K. VESZELY, Erdélyi egyháztörténelmi adatok [Church historical data on Transylvania], vol. 1, Kolozsvár 1860, pp. 392–393.

preaching duties.⁵⁶ A good example for the link between the collection of alms and pastoral care is a charter issued in 1524, with which Prior Valentine Kőrösszegi of the Komár Dominican friary sent the priest Benedict to the nearby village of Baráti and its area in order to preach in Lent and to hear the confessions of the faithful.⁵⁷

As one can see, there are already major difficulties in identifying and describing the zones of quest within the same order. The available data is even less suitable for a comparison of the zones of quest of friaries belonging to different orders which coexisted in the same settlement. We know, for instance, that the Franciscan friaries of Buda and Pest, as well as the Dominican monasteries of the two towns had close contacts with the northern part of the Great Plain, but there is not even the faintest indication that their zones of quest were identical and there is no information on conflicts between the convents.

The infrastructure of the *terminus*,⁵⁸ which is much better known in Germany, remains obscure in Hungary. We do not know whether the friars had maintained *terminus* houses, which at the same time served as accommodation for the friars and as a storehouse for the collected alms. The friars in Körmend do not seem to have had such houses, at least the friars going farther from Körmend were accommodated at the local parsonage.⁵⁹ However, it is possible that the list of the Austin Hermits' friaries in Hungary, compiled in the mid-sixteenth century, referred to such a house under the name of Kissáros.⁶⁰ The locality is only 4 km away from Sáros where an Austin friary existed since the last decades of the thirteenth century. In any case, it would be very surprising if there were two friaries of the same order in two such nearby settlements at the same time, especially since it is clear that our sources in Hungary only know about the Sáros friary. At the same time, we have to see that there are misspellings and repetitions elsewhere in the list, so it is possible that this is just a duplication of the friary of Sáros. Furthermore, although much less written evidence survived from medieval Hungary than elsewhere in western and southern Europe, it is suspicious that not a single clear reference to such a house has been found so far.

---

56 Cf. H. HOOGEWEG, Die Stifter und Klöster der Provinz Pommern, 2 vols., Stettin 1924, vol. 1, pp. 1–12 (about the dispute between the Austin friaries of Anklam and Helmstedt).

57 V. BUNYITAY / R. RAPAICS / J. KARÁCSONYI (eds.), Egyháztörténelmi emlékek a magyarországi hitújítás korából (note 40 above), vol. 1, p. 124.

58 Cf. K. ELM, Termineien und Hospize der westfälischen Augustiner–Eremitenklöster Osnabrück, Herford und Lippstadt, Bielefeld 1977.

59 G. ERDÉLYI, The Register of a Convent Controversy (note 52 above), p. 122: *Dicit etiam testis se scire, quod dum cum eodem fratre Anthonio in mendicando semel proficisceretur in quadam villa Egedÿ vocata in domo plebani absente ipso plebano ad hospitium descendisset (…)*.

60 B. F. ROMHÁNYI, Kolostorok és társaskáptalanok a középkori Magyarországon (note 12 above), p. 36.

One set of information from the Fabri list of the Schässburg friary can be interpreted to mention an alternative to maintaining a *terminus* house. According to this, Nicholas Bordys of Bord (today in Romania), who was himself a confriar of the Dominicans, obliged his sons and heirs in his will to always welcome the friars of Schässburg (*Insuper adiuravit filios et heredes (sic) proprios per nomen et confratres, necnon receptores hospitio patrum et fratrum loci istius*).[61] The village is located about 65 km from Schässburg, on the border of their area established at the end of the fifteenth century.

It is also possible that the system was only typical for the Austin Hermits in Germany, and it is not inconceivable that similar practices have never been developed in Hungary at all. The reason for this may have been that the Austin friars partially produced the food they needed on their estates, so that they were less dependent on the alms, or that a smaller *terminus* might be sufficient to supply a monastery. On the other hand, *terminus* limits can be calculated for some friaries of other orders, and they imply that several days were needed to reach the areas of the quest. This also means that they were too remote to be involved in any daily practice of begging.[62]

The sixteenth-century list of the Dominican friary in Schässburg provides an interesting addition to the collection of alms. On one page there is a German-language record of the friary's grain pits in the town,[63] a total of thirteen. The census maker noted that six were full, and about one he explicitly stated that it was empty. For some pits, we also find the caretakers' identity: some burghers and guilds appear on the list. One of the stacks looks like a depository for casual alms: *dy hot eyn man gefolt fom sches*. We know from other places that burghers gave grain as alms to mendicant friaries (e. g. Sopron), but this is our only source for the storage – and it cannot necessarily be generalised. In any case, it is interesting that the grain in Schässburg was not stored in a larger granary in the friary but was stored in grain pits all around the town, usually near burgher houses.

---

[61] A. Ipolyi, Adalékok a magyar domonkosok történetéhez (note 39 above), p. 609.

[62] Although the evidence is from a much later period, it is still interesting that in 1763, when Count Anthony I. Grassalkovich founded the Capuchin Friary in Besnyő, one of the main difficulties in obtaining the permit was that the zones of quest of two already existing friaries, Buda and Hatvan, could not be reduced (the story was recorded in the *Historia Domus* of the friary, today preserved in the friary of Mór). Thus, the friary of Besnyő had hardly any *terminus* (essentially limited to a few neighbouring villages, including Isaszeg). Therefore, the founding family undertook the support of the friars, as it often happened in the Middle Ages. Hatvan was 26 km, Buda 36 km from Besnyő.

[63] A. Ipolyi, Adalékok a magyar domonkosok történetéhez (note 39 above), pp. 773–774.

Manual labour – workshops and craftsmen

Manual labour and the wages paid for it also played an important role in the economy of mendicant and Pauline monks. However, we have very little data on workshops and craftsmen. In the case of workshops, written sources are particularly rare. There is only limited information, mostly in fourteenth-century papal charters permitting the establishment of new friaries, as in the case of the foundation of the friary in Diakovar in 1347.[64] Similar wording appears in the papal charters of 1372 and 1373, authorizing the foundation of the Carmelite friaries of Pécs and Buda. Apart from these I only know of a single mendicant friary where a workshop was discovered. Zoltán Soós was able to identify two workshops at the Franciscan friary in Marosvásárhely: a bone-cutter and a bronze-melting workshop.[65] Fragments of melting pots were found at Tövis, too, but no workshop could be identified so far.[66]

At the beginning of the sixteenth century there was a slight increase in the data on friars' identity, and it emerges that there were quite a few craftsmen among the lay brothers. Some of these were crafts that were not part of the daily needs of the monastery. One of the natives of the Dominican monastery in Schässburg (a friar who made a vow there) was a goldsmith, who stayed at Lábatlan in 1529.[67] Of course, it is possible that he created a liturgical object for the friary, but it cannot be ruled out that he worked for someone else – the patron of the friary or another client in the area.

An interesting note is a letter from the end of the fifteenth century, written by the Buda goldsmiths' guild to the goldsmiths of Kolozsvár. The letter informs the guild of Kolozsvár that there is a man named Lawrence who did not learn the craft in the usual way and place but was trained by a friar named John in the Dominican priory[68] – who was obviously a goldsmith, but not a guild member. In addition, the letter testified that he was dealing with something that was not accepted: teaching his craft. We do not know, of course, whether Lawrence was a novice for a while or not, and thus his apprenticeship was not illegal at all. In any case, he certainly did not become a friar, and he may never have wanted to join the order, perhaps he simply learned the craft from friar John.

---

[64] F. SEBŐK (ed.), Anjou oklevéltár (Documenta res Hungaricas tempore regum Andegavensium illustrantia 31), Budapest/Szeged 2007, n. 235 (1347).

[65] Z. SOÓS, Bronze Objects from the Excavation of the Târgu Mureş Franciscan Friary, in: Marisia 31 (2011), pp. 315–338. The findings have not been published yet.

[66] I am grateful for the information kindly provided by the archaeologist Adrian Andrei RUSU.

[67] A. IPOLYI, Adalékok a magyar domonkosok történetéhez (note 39 above), p. 670.

[68] K. SZABÓ, Az Erdélyi Múzeum oklevelei IV [The charters of the Transylvanian Museum], in: Magyar Történelmi Tár 1890, p. 331 (n. 429).

We hardly know anything about the personal composition of the Carmelites in Hungary, and this also applies to the management of convents. However, a craftsman appears even in this meagre material. In 1458, one of the friars of the Pécs convent, a lay brother called Peter, sent a petition to the Pope asking his approval to enter the Benedictine Order. The petition reveals that Peter, who was a native Hungarian speaker (*merus Ungarus*), was a carpenter. He was in contact with the friary in Pécs. He had a good relationship with the then head of the monastery and entered the order as a lay brother. But later, after the prior was replaced by a new superior who did not speak Hungarian, his relationship with the monastic community deteriorated and he eventually left the order. He turned to Rome because his friends persuaded him to clarify his status in the Church.[69]

One of the most valuable sources is the list of Transylvanian Dominicans of 1528. There were several craftsmen among the friars of the eight friaries, including a miller (*molendinator*), a cooper (*doleator*), a butcher (*carnifex*), a saddler (*corrigiator*), a wainwright (*currifex*), a stonemason (*lapicida*), two masons (*murator*), three blacksmiths (*faber*), as well as seven tailors (*sartor*) and seven cobblers (*sutor*). These 25 craftsmen represented about 14 per cent of the Dominicans in Transylvania. Beside them there was a *magister piscinae* in the friary of Bistritz, obviously to supervise the work on the fishponds of the monastery.[70] Although not handicraft, the *procuratores* of the monastic estates in the friaries of Kolozsvár and Schässburg should be mentioned, as well as of the lay brother of the Hermannstadt friary, Quintinus Hyspanus, who was sent to the estate of Zsuk (today Juc, Romania).[71] A total of fifteen friars had crafts related to clothing. Six were able to use their knowledge at construction sites (1 stonemason, 2 masons, 3 blacksmiths), but the activities of blacksmiths were, of course, not limited to construction work. The craft of the miller, the cooper and the wainwright, as well as the skill of the master of the fishponds, were obviously useful in relation to the monastic estates. We do not know whether these skills were acquired in the order or whether the persons in question were craftsmen before entering the friary. The only person who does not seem to fit into this group at first glance is the butcher but knowing that the Schässburg friary had a manor with livestock and the butcher was living in that friary, the connection is obvious.

---

[69] I. Petrovics, A középkori Pécs idegen származású polgárai [The burghers of foreign origin of the medieval town of Pécs], in: G. Mikó / B. Péterfi / A. Vadas (eds.), Tiszteletkör. Történeti tanulmányok Draskóczy István egyetemi tanár 60. születésnapjára, Budapest 2012, pp. 283–292, at p. 286; F. Szakály, Schreiber Farkas pécsi bíró (1527–1542) [Wolfgang Schreiber, judge of Pécs], in: A Janus Pannonius Múzeum Évkönyve 20–21 (1977), pp. 75–102, at p. 79; K. Regényi, Die ungarischen Konvente der oberdeutschen Karmelitenprovinz im Mittelalter, Budapest/Heidelberg 2001, pp. 75, 79–81.

[70] A. Ipolyi, Adalékok a magyar domonkosok történetéhez (note 39 above), p. 774.

[71] Ibid., p. 770.

However, trained lay brothers represent only one side of the coin. There are examples where the friars employed externals to do the work for a salary. The fact that a friar was a good carpenter did not mean that he would have been sent to another friary if his expertise were needed. Such cases hardly appear in the sources. The only master sent out from his convent is the goldsmith brother of the Dominican monastery of Schässburg working in Lábatlan.[72] At the same time, the accounts of the church of the Dominican friary in Schemnitz show that the town had the roof of the church repaired every year, while candles were made for the church by a local woman, probably a widow.[73]

In the light of the data, it can be concluded that lay brothers were always present in the mendicant orders. Lists made at the beginning of the sixteenth century show that their proportion was not negligible: 9 per cent of Franciscans and 14 per cent of Dominicans. Unfortunately, we do not have such good information about the other orders but based on normative sources we can presume that such lay brothers played an important role in the Pauline Order. Some of them may have worked for the monastery, but most undertook external work for which they were paid or received alms. According to the Franciscan regulations, payment was likely to be in kind, but the members of other orders accepted money. The range of crafts mentioned in the sources was relatively wide, but also somewhat incidental. Mendicant orders neither dealt with elementary education nor did they teach their members craft skills, except maybe in some very special cases. Whoever had a profession must have learned it before he entered the order. In the case of the Paulines, it is not impossible that professional skills could be acquired within the order (the Directorium mentions cobblers, tailors and blacksmiths),[74] but we cannot fully support this with sources. However, the construction of a more expensive workshop would have been contrary to the flexibility with which the mendicants dealt with their business-related affairs. The references to the workshops in the charters can be interpreted partly as a survival of an earlier tradition and partly as an indication that, depending on the skill of the friars living in the community, any kind of workshop could be set up, an enterprise which also answered market needs. Therefore, most of the lay brothers in question had everyday professions, there were just a few who had a 'more elegant' craft, such as goldsmith, stonemason or organ-builder. We know very little about the organisation of the work itself. In a couple of cases, there was more than one friar working in the same field (for instance, there were five tailors in the friary of Ivanić in 1535) which suggests a sort of 'mass production'. The

---

[72] Ibid., p. 70.
[73] V. BUNYITAY / R. RAPAICS / J. KARÁCSONYI (eds.), Egyháztörténelmi emlékek a magyarországi hitújítás korából (note 40 above), vol. 1, nn. 223 and 274.
[74] G. SARBAK (ed.), Gyöngyösi Gergely: Directorium singulorum fratrum officialium Ordinis Sancti Pauli Primi Heremite sub regula Beati Augustini episcopi militantium, Budapest 2011, pp. 32–33.

Directorium of the Paulines contains references to employees, however, we do not have any evidence how they cooperated with the monks in practice, nor do we know about sales of their products or the modes of payment.

We have no information on the interaction of these monastic workshops with the guilds of the towns or market towns. It is unlikely that they caused serious conflicts because they do not appear in urban sources and there is no criticism of their operation. The only exception is a goldsmith living in the Dominican friary in Pest. However, he was not directly accused. Instead, his disciple had acted irregularly in entering the guild of Kolozsvár, violating the guild rules. All this proves that, as long as the relationship between the local community and the monastery was balanced, the work done by the friars and the income out of it did not cause any conflict.

Management – principles and practices

The late medieval and early modern economy of the mendicant orders can obviously not be described as that of a modern institution. From this point of view, our sources are very limited, and we cannot accurately assess the assets of the friaries, the size and structure of their revenues and expenditures, the management of their real estate, the risks or the strategies used to mitigate them. However, even if we do not get a complete picture from the fragmentary data, we can identify certain trends and also discover differences between the different orders.

Possible risks in the management of a mendicant community include damage to monastic buildings, demographic or economic changes in the environment or in the zone of quest, and deterioration in the relationship between the patron or the local community and the religious community. Occasionally, as some examples show, there may have been risks in the management of the estates caused by disadvantageous contracts. In addition, war was a very real threat in this period: the Ottoman wars from the 1390s in the South, the Hussite raids in the first half of the fifteenth century in the North, and the occasional domestic wars.

Theoretically the size of the community may have exceeded the limits of its resources, but the mendicant orders and the Paulines handled this problem well. Since the friars, unlike the older monastic communities, did not enter the friary but the order, the province provided for the number of religious living there, considering the capacity of each friary. Thus, in Alvinc there were only four monks in the 1520s because the monastery was in ruins due to an earlier Ottoman invasion. In the worst case, the friary was even abandoned if the friars saw no hope for improvement. Changes in the relationship between the lords and the friaries may also have led to the abandonment of a friary.

As for the management models, mendicant orders followed two slightly different strategies. The Franciscans and Dominicans initially based their livelihoods on various forms of alms, while the Austin Hermits and the Paulines based their economy more on their landed estates. The difference between the latter ones was, that the Paulines relied much more on the incomes of the real estates, and alms played only a complementary role. Sadly, not enough data is available for the Carmelites. By the end of the Middle Ages, the Dominicans also had moved towards landed estates, and regular cash benefits played a major role. At the same time the role of alms slightly increased in the Pauline economy. The degree of dependence on alms apparently affected social relationships and thus the popularity of the single monastic communities, as well.

The inclusion of monastic administrators in the system led to a reduction of the risks in farming. Although the need for these persons was mostly due to the friars' commitment to poverty, the letter of the Carmelite provincial to the town council of Eperjes in the early fifteenth century reveals a different angle, for there is no word on mendicancy or poverty. The provincial asked the town to manage the monastery's economic affairs because the friars proved unfit for the task: the friary's assets were lost, thereby endangering its existence. Precisely because they did not have a great deal of property, mendicant friaries needed a person or body with the right economic background to help the friars with alms or annuities in case of trouble. The administrator, or through him the town, or in other cases the patron should provide the necessary support. In the case of the Paulines we can also see the role of the order's centre, which not only occasionally helped distressed monasteries, but also prevented them from getting into trouble. To this end it also intervened in managing the monastery's assets, sometimes causing outrage in the community. For similar reasons, the patron appointed the *vitricus* of the Austin friary in Körmend, and in the first half of the sixteenth century, it was the town that tried to manage the friary's property in Bártfa. In both places, the lay management of the friary seems to be a new development. In other Austin friaries, however, the prior, or possibly a vicar, managed the property. An example is the sale of properties in the Dés friary in the mid-sixteenth century.

It is common to the orders under consideration that the friars were not charged with the maintenance of the monastic buildings, and they did not borrow money for repair and maintenance. With the exception of the Paulines, it is also typical that incomes, whether from alms or from farming, were not accumulated. Avoiding borrowing also meant that individual friaries could not become indebted. The only known case is that of the Dominicans of Kassa, who negotiated loans from the town in 1524, 1525 and 1527 to cultivate their vineyards. The repayment was probably made with the income from the sale of wine. Although the case is economically understandable, it is a sign of change. In the past the friars would have been more likely to receive help in the form of a grant, that is alms, at least on the basis of the accounts of the Franciscans of Sopron. Indeed, there are no more such examples. The *provisores* of the friaries, elected by the town council and involved personally in the economic affairs of the friary, were also responsible for filling the gaps in management, and they mostly fulfilled this task (see the examples from Sopron, Kassa, Eperjes and Schässburg).

Last but not least it is worth mentioning that trust played a very important role in the management of the friaries. Obviously, it was also a good thing that they were working in a transparent, relatively small social environment where everyone was, so to speak, known. However, the confriars also had a very important role to play. They were committed supporters of the orders and sought to manage the economic affairs of the friaries in the best possible way. Some of these people helped the monastic community as *provisores*, others provided accommodation when the friars went to the *terminus*, and others may have contributed regular alms to maintain the friary. All this combined to provide a basically friendly environment for the friars, the value of which would be difficult to quantify, but it certainly made economic activities considerably simpler and less expensive.

The two key features of accounting, income and expenses, cannot be defined without accurate and detailed record keeping, so we cannot produce the balance sheet of mendicant economic management. Even though the orders were sometimes accused of greed, there is no doubt that they were not business associations. It was not their purpose to make profit, and in some cases their own production did not even cover the friars' requirements. This is shown by the fact that they needed financial support not only for the construction of a new monastery, like the monastic orders, but also for its maintenance. Throughout the Middle Ages, alms were an important source of income for every mendicant community, including the pseudo-mendicant Paulines. The difference to the mendicants' revenue consisted of the forms of alms and in their proportion of the total revenue. In this context, even the money-lending activities of Paulines or Dominicans helped to reduce management risks and should not be considered as actual banking activities. It is important to emphasize that much less data on lending is available from mendicant friaries than from the Paulines. The reason for the difference is the mendicant economy which did not allow the transformation of real estates, given as security for a loan into a permanent property. While Paulines received a number of *pro anima* donations which – at a closer look – turn out to be real estate loan securities, there are almost no such cases in the sources of mendicants. The two exceptions are related to the Dominicans of Pest and the Austin Hermits of Pápoc.[75] Both cases follow exactly the pattern that is

---

[75] V. BEDY, A pápóci prépostság és perjelség története [The history of the Collegiate Chapter and of the priory in Pápoc], Győr 1939, p. 57; L. BÁRTFAI SZABÓ (ed.), Pest megye történetének okleveles emlékei 1002–1599–ig [Written evidence of the history of Pest County], Budapest 1938, n. 1339.

so often encountered in loan agreements made by Pauline monasteries:[76] the borrower, being unable to repay the loan, turned his mortgaged property into a pious donation to the monastery that had provided the loan.

The income page should list wills, pious donations, as well as crafts and, of course, the income derived from the estates. Some of the latter were in kind and were used directly to serve the friars, so we have no data on the size of this part. A special real estate was the garden that was probably much more common, than documented. However, gardens are mentioned in connection with several monasteries (e. g. Bistritz, Eperjes, Gyula, Kolozsvár, Körmend, Szatmár, Németi, Schässburg, Sopron, Vasvár, Zagreb). Their importance is shown by the fact that even among the few data we have, one is speaking about a garden (*hortus*) established on a meadow (*pratum*). Some products appear in our sources because they were sold or given as gifts. The rest of the garden produce went straight to the kitchen and then to the table, so it would not make sense to record it.

The revenue from the friaries' own real estates is best seen in the case of the Franciscan friary of Sopron. The biggest item was undoubtedly the income from wine, due to the friary's wine-licence, which made up about 50–60 per cent of the annual income. However, the wine did not come necessarily from their own vineyard alone, as it is clear from the book that the friars went to their zone of quest at the time of harvest and some of the wine was derived from donations.[77] In the second place we can find different fees (12 per cent) and other donations received as alms. Of these, cereal and fodder donations were especially important, due to their value in use, not in cash. Special mention should also be made of the support provided by the *provisores*. However, this is not always easy to identify. Such support may have been received directly in cash, but more often through the purchase of real estate or movable property given to the friary as donation in kind. When summing up the scattered data for the other monasteries, it appears that the proportion of property producing income in cash was high among the estates. Of these, 32 per cent are vineyards and mills, and another 16 per cent are miscellaneous, producing annuities, salt income, and cash. This property structure is characteristic of the Paulines, who are much more well-known in this respect. Paulines based their economy mainly on these and the leasing of their town houses in the fifteenth century, in a pre-capitalist way of estate management.[78]

The only detailed sixteenth-century source of monastic expenditure are the Sopron account books. It is not possible to generalise any conclusions drawn

---

[76] B. F. ROMHÁNYI, Pauline Economy in the Middle Ages: "The Spiritual Cannot Be Maintained without the Temporal …", Leiden 2020, pp. 125–129.

[77] J. HÁZI, Sopron szabad királyi város története (note 36 above), vol. 2/5, n. 18 [257]: *Item mer hab ich gebnn bruder Anthoni, so er ist gefaren in das lesen, zu zerung facit LXXV den.* (around 1520).

[78] B. F. ROMHÁNYI, Pauline Economy (note 76 above), pp. 130–135.

from. When analysing the expenses, it should be borne in mind that not all money seemed to flow into the friars' hands, but a significant part went through the hands of the *provisor*. Such persons were appointed for Dominican and Austin Hermits' friaries in the late Middle Ages. It is also from the Sopron records that we know that the *provisor* gave the friary money for food, and these amounts did not need to be recorded. Thus, the picture from the account books is definitely incomplete. There are two items that are regularly bought on the market: fish and meat, the latter mainly beef. It also appears that more and better-quality food was served on the table when guests arrived. However, it still accounted for a smaller proportion of the expenditure. Much larger sums were spent on clothing, various repairs, and occasional travel, but the largest item on the expenditure side was related to the cultivation of vineyards.

By grouping the data of the Sopron register into categories, we see that the monastery's net income covered its daily living costs. But little was spent on investment, only the necessary repairs were financed from this revenue. The cultivation of vineyards brought the greatest returns, but it also had the greatest risks, and the costs were considerable. It is no coincidence that both *provisores* of the friary tried to offset the losses of the worst years with extra revenue: Christoph Gräzer sold a vineyard and Paul Moritz sold almost twice the usual amount of wine in one year. The question is, of course, whether the previous year was such a good year that the own product could be turned into cash, or whether the friars received more than usual alms in the form wine.

Ideally, three account books should be available to reconstruct the revenue and expenditure of a friary because it seems that three types of records were kept. The first is the book of the church, the second, made by the *provisores*, records the friary's cash, and the third is the book of the friary's superior. Although specimens of all three types have survived, they are not related to the same friary and were not made at exactly the same time. What is more, it is clear that the incomes out of wills have been recorded only to a very limited extent, and even if they appear in the books of account, they record proceeds from the sale of higher value movable and immovable property. The sale of lower value movables is never mentioned in these sources and the value of the assets that were directly used – which increased the friary's assets – is usually unknown.

The maintenance cost of buildings was very low, as far as one can see from the accounting books. In the case of the monastery church in Schemnitz, it is evident that only the annual maintenance costs are shown, while in Sopron we find some costs for minor repairs and for the increase of the comfort provided by the building. The larger-scale renovation and, in particular, the expansion of buildings exceeded the financial strength of the religious communities. In any case, it was initiated and funded by the patron or one of the well-off supporters, as we know of many examples in various wills.⁷⁹ It is no accident that the accounts relating to the construction of the Eperjes friary were preserved in the town and not in the order. This may also be the reason for the distinction in certain wills between the provision for monks and for buildings.⁸⁰

In fact, the friars were not necessarily considered to have full ownership of the buildings, they were merely users of the friaries. This way we can understand the letter formulated by John, the provincial of the Carmelites in 1437, in which he gave the town council extraordinary powers over the economic affairs of the Eperjes friary. According to later documents, the town actually acted as owner, so that Judge Ladislaus Szőcs, also called Saylich, at the end of the fifteenth century handled the Carmelites' finances as if they were his own property. But this is also how we understand the outrage of the Council of Schemnitz when, in 1536, they were confronted with the fact, that the Dominicans had sold their property before they left the town, for it followed the Reformation.

Specialities of the Pauline Economy

At the time when the Pauline Order emerged (around 1300), the community, being of eremitic character, received small parcels of land. Vineyards were an essential part of the early estates, but some hermitages received ploughlands, meadows, forests or even fisheries depending on local conditions. In this early phase, the monasteries lived to some extent in symbioses with the patrons or with other ecclesiastic institutions, e. g. monasteries or the bishop's household.⁸¹ This early, autarchic estate structure began to change from the mid-fourteenth century. One of the first documents for this is the document issued in 1359 for the Remete monastery in Bereg. In it, the Count of Bereg granted that the Paulines got enough parcels of land for the vineyards and that only they and their tenants were allowed to fish in a certain section of the river. In addition, they were allowed to have pasture in the wood, and, above all, no one should build a mill near their mill. The privileges were granted by the king and the queen mother.⁸²

---

[79] ELTE University Library, Budapest, Kaprinai coll. II, 452 (1507).

[80] Zs. JAKÓ (ed.), A kolozsmonostori konvent jegyzőkönyvei, vol. 2, n. 1153 (1455); V. BUNYITAY / R. RAPAICS / J. KARÁCSONYI (eds.), Egyháztörténelmi emlékek a magyarországi hitújítás korból (note 40 above), vol. 1, n. 18 (1520).

[81] É. KNAPP, Pálos gazdálkodás a középkori Baranya megyében [Pauline economy in Baranya County], in: G. SARBAK (ed.), Pálos rendtörténeti tanulmányok (Varia Paulina 1), Budapest 1994, pp. 62–103, at pp. 81–100; B. F. ROMHÁNYI, Heremitae – monachi – fratres. Szempontok a pálos rend történetének újragondolásához, [Points of view to the early history of the Pauline Order], in: G. SARBAK (ed.), Pálosaink és Pécs, Budapest 2016, pp. 9–23.

[82] B. GYÉRESSY / F. L. HERVAY / M. TOTH (eds.), Documenta Artis Paulinorum, 3 vols. (A Magyar Tudományos Adadémia Művészettörténeti Kutató Csoportjának forráskiadványai, 10,

Fishing and pig farming were a part of self-provision. Vineyards and mills, however, were clearly sources of cash from the earliest times. These two elements of the economy always had a special importance for the Paulines because of the early ban on accepting tenant plots. Vineyards can be cultivated with relatively little manpower, and they can be profitable even in small parcels. As for the mills, they used to be rented out in the late Middle Ages. Mills were rather industrial equipment to which different rules were applied. They were important because thirlage and multure assured a constant and predictable income. These estate types prevailed even in the late Middle Ages, despite the fact that the order had already tenant plots and villages. Furthermore, the order tried to establish measures concerning the size of their estates in order to avoid taking on the burden of an oversized estate that would have exceeded the administrative capacity of the hermit community (see the story about the first prior of Nosztre (today Márianosztra) in Gyöngyösi's *Vitae fratrum*). Thus, the importance of cash incomes increased. In addition, the Paulines tended to align themselves to the mendicant orders from the end of the fourteenth century. This not only meant a move towards more intensive participation in pastoral care or the – eventually failed – attempt to send members of the order to foreign centres of study. In the fifteenth century the Paulines received alms, too, especially through last wills and *pro anima* donations. However, despite the increasing sums received by the order, alms could never cover the necessary costs of the monasteries and begging remained prohibited throughout the Middle Ages. Thus, a unique, mixed economy emerged containing both monastic and mendicant elements.[83]

Due to one of the main patrons of the order, King Louis I of Anjou (1342–1382), the Paulines received considerable incomes and many of their privileges originated in his time. A good number of the mills and the first tax exemptions were granted by Louis. His support was so substantial that even the yearly salt worth of 300 guilders was later connected to him. Tax exemptions were linked to the production of food and other goods necessary for the monks' daily life.[84] Even the origin of the possession of urban houses can be connected to King Louis I, at least within the kingdom of Hungary, as he donated the former royal

---

13, 14), Budapest 1978, vol. 1, p. 10. The rights of the Bereg monastery were confirmed by several charters in the fifteenth century.

[83] The first summary of the typical Pauline estates was given in 1373, in a charter of King Louis I for the monastery of Diósgyőr: Zs. BÁNDI, Északkelet–magyarországi pálos kolostorok oklevelei [Charters of Pauline monasteries in north–eastern Hungary], Miskolc 1985, p. 564.

[84] MNL OL DL 6254 (1375); 6830 (1381). The privileges seem to have been impinged upon quite regularly, as it is indicated both by their multiple confirmations (e.g. MNL OL DL 8825 (1383); 7084 (1384); 8825 (1406 and 1419)), and by the lawsuits and acts of might (in Latin *potentia*, the term was used in Hungarian customary law for violent attacks on property and/or tenants of a noble landlord). A special case of tax exemption was when the king renounced his royal right to property connected to the landed estate.

palace, the Kammerhof of Buda to the order.[85] In fact, this was the period when the urban houses in Buda and in other towns became an integral part of the Pauline estate structure, and influential patrons appeared around the order such as the Kont, the Cudar or the Kanizsai families. The monasteries received regular incomes in cash, allowing them to use wage labour on their manors (which sometimes led to conflicts with the neighbourhood) and to buy or rent estates. The proliferation of monasteries began to end from the last decade of the fourteenth century, but this did not mean decline or stagnation.

To some extent the Pauline economy was double-faced. On the one hand, there were monasteries with considerable assets. Their incomes originated partly from their landed estates, partly from renting out different elements of the asset (urban houses, mills, and vineyards). On the other hand, there were small, hermitage-like monasteries which were basically self-sufficient or even needed some support from the other monasteries of the order. Manors and urban houses, partly in market towns and boroughs, played a role in self-sufficiency, but they were also essential for marketing the produce from the monastic estates. Manors could receive market rights and urban houses had wine-licences. While the average estate structure of the Pauline monasteries can be reconstructed based on the charters, almost all the larger monasteries were specialised to some extent, meaning that a significant part of the incomes came from a given estate element or product. Such income sources could be vineyards, mills, grain, and in some cases also animal husbandry.

The second half of the fifteenth century was a second period of the order's economic development, due to the excellent relations with King Matthias and his successor, King Wladislaus II Jagiello. The most important change was the taking over of former Benedictine abbeys and Premonstratensian monasteries (Zsámbék, Csút [today Budapest-Háros], Visegrád, Váradhegyfok [today part of Oradea], Szentjobb),[86] however, the salt income granted to certain Pauline monasteries, landed estates and privileges – including the general tax exemption of the Slavonian monasteries – were also the result of the good relations between the religious and the monarchy.[87] The strength and the feudal character of the order

---

[85] This merits special emphasis because urban properties and the rent of townhouses appeared much earlier in Dalmatia, see, for example, the townhouses of the Senj monasteries (Croatia).

[86] B. F. ROMHÁNYI, Königliche Stiftungen des Spätmittelalters in Ungarn, in: Gy. KOVÁCS (ed.), Quasi liber et pictura: tanulmányok Kubinyi András 70. születésnapjára, Budapest 2004, pp. 167–172.

[87] MNL OL DL 15253 (1458). Since the charter was issued about six months after Matthias's election, the decision is likely to have been that of his advisors and family members, and not (or perhaps only partly) by the king himself. However, Matthias continued to support the order until the end of his life, and their excellent rapport was recorded by Gregorius Gyöngyösi. Thus, the charter of 1458 can be considered as the overture of a long and fruitful relationship.

was also reflected by the privilege of high justice granted by Matthias.[88] The order also profited from the effective support of the prelates, e.g. Cardinal Thomas Bakóc or Archbishop Peter Váradi. The good relations with the clergy were also due to the fact that a relatively high portion of the order's members were clergymen who abandoned their diocesan career for the order. At the turn from the fifteenth to the sixteenth centuries, the Paulines aimed to maintain a similar relationship with courts outside Hungary, too, as is attested by a formula preserved in the sixteenth-century formulary which proves that Paulines monks served in the imperial court as chaplains.[89]

Around 1500, there is evidence for the order's increasing financial activity. The religious were regularly involved in mortgage cases.[90] Money lending and acquisitions were covered by the cash incomes of the vineyards, mills and less frequently tolls and salt. Among these transactions, there were two unusually high loans, both granted by the central monastery of Saint Lawrence: first two thousand guilders were lent to the town of Buda, then the same amount was granted to the town of Vienna.

However, despite the stable management, it is clear that the order needed additional sources to ensure the funding of its central administration and sometimes even to help sustain the monasteries. Royal support was granted in the form of the two salt donations with a total value of 400 guilders. Entries in the Pauline *formularium* show that the monks regularly urged the payment of this sum even in the 1530s. In addition, there were the pious donations and the last wills, as it is reflected in both the formulary and the preserved charters, mainly dating from the sixteenth century. Alms were either in cash, or in the form of real estates, sometimes movables were bequeathed which could easily be converted into cash. There were usually single donations, but one can find annuities and even interest payments on loans. The supporters were basically recruited from three social groups: prestigious urban burghers, members of the lesser nobility and – for a smaller part – magnates.

---

[88] MNL OL DL 16297 (1466). The same feudal character may have been recognised by Pope Eugenius IV when he appointed the prior general of the order as papal judge in 1446: Gy. BÓNIS (ed.), Szentszéki regeszták. Iratok az egyházi bíráskodás történetéhez a középkori Magyarországon [Documents on the history of ecclesiastical justice in medieval Hungary], Budapest 1997, n. 2600.

[89] Formularium maius Ordinis S. Pauli primi Heremitae, eds. B. F. ROMHÁNYI / G. SARBAK (note 16 above), pp. 80–81 (ff. 55ʳ–55ᵛ). The addressee was Emperor Charles V, the letter was probably issued between 1532 and 1536. A Pauline monastery existed in Wiener Neustadt since 1480.

[90] About this type of financial service provided by other orders see N. G. SZABÓ: Monasztikus férfikolostorok társadalmi kapcsolatai a 15–16. században a végrendeletek tükrében [Social relations of monasteries in the 15th and 16th centuries as reflected in the last wills], in: Századok 143 (2009), pp. 451–466; B. F. ROMHÁNYI, A koldulóbarátok szerepe a XV–XVI. századi vallási megújulásban (note 13 above), pp. 123–126.

Conclusion

The late medieval Hungarian Kingdom accommodated the largest mendicant communities in East Central Europe, with the exception of the Carmelites. Their existence and expansion were simultaneously influenced by religious and political considerations, and they sought to secure their economic background by different strategies.

Since a significant increase in the number of sources can be observed in the second half of the fifteenth century – contrary to Western and Southern Europe – the economic management of mendicant orders can best be studied from sources dated after the 1450s. However, earlier data must not be ignored either. In the case of the Austin Hermits, a comparison of early – thirteenth century – and late sources show a long-lasting, in most cases undisturbed possession of landed estates. Data on early Dominican estates is much more random. Nevertheless, it is certain that some of their monasteries received estates in the early period. An example of this is the friary of Vasvár, albeit the odd contract between the order and the Gersei Pető family shows, that the order was either not able, or not willing to manage the estate. At the end of the Middle Ages, half of the mendicant friaries had some kind of property or regular income. There are no major differences in the distribution of data: data were preserved concerning 22 Dominican friaries (57.9 per cent), 21 Conventual Franciscan (48.8 per cent), 18 Austin Hermits (54.6 per cent), and two Carmelite friaries. In contrast to this, more or less all the Pauline monasteries had some real estate.

In order to avoid a premature conclusion, one has to keep in mind that written evidence suffered very serious losses, especially in the sixteenth and seventeenth centuries, but also later. It is important that the mendicant friaries which had more than one landed estate or source of income, were almost without exception on the periphery of the country. The central and southern areas of the medieval Hungarian Kingdom are clearly missing due to the Ottoman wars. However, it is also true that mendicant communities regarded real estate in a different way, and they did not always consider the preservation of their documents and proof of ownership as an important task. Very often, they held the estates only temporarily. From this point of view, the Paulines were the most monastic, preserving several thousands of charters. But we also have to emphasize, that there was one more major difference between the Paulines and the other orders: the prior general of the Paulines resided in Hungary, that may also have contributed to the better preservation of their archives.

The overall picture is quite consistent. Except for the Franciscans, the economy of the mendicant and Pauline communities was increasingly money-based at the dawn of early modern period. Real estates, producing cash income, were key elements of the system. The most important were vineyards and mills, and as a third element specific to the Paulines, there were urban houses. It needs to be emphasised, however, that none of these monasteries and friaries, not even the central monastery of Paulines, became landlords comparable to the higher nobility. Besides the real estates, there was also direct cash income, such as annuities, tolls, rents and revenue from salt. The high level of royal support was also a feature common to all. This and the dependence on alms that remained a factor throughout the Middle Ages, suggest that the income of the estates balanced basically the uncertainties of alms and temporary donations. The differences between the orders consisted mainly in the inner structure of the assets (the Dominicans, for instance, seem to have preferred those estates that required less manpower). Last but not least, the complex system of real estates, regular cash incomes and temporary alms was based on a dense social network, which provided for the balanced finances of the discussed orders, until the surrounding society was friendly and supportive. As soon as the relation changed, either because the non-Catholic population became the majority, or because of conflicts of interest, the friars had to leave.

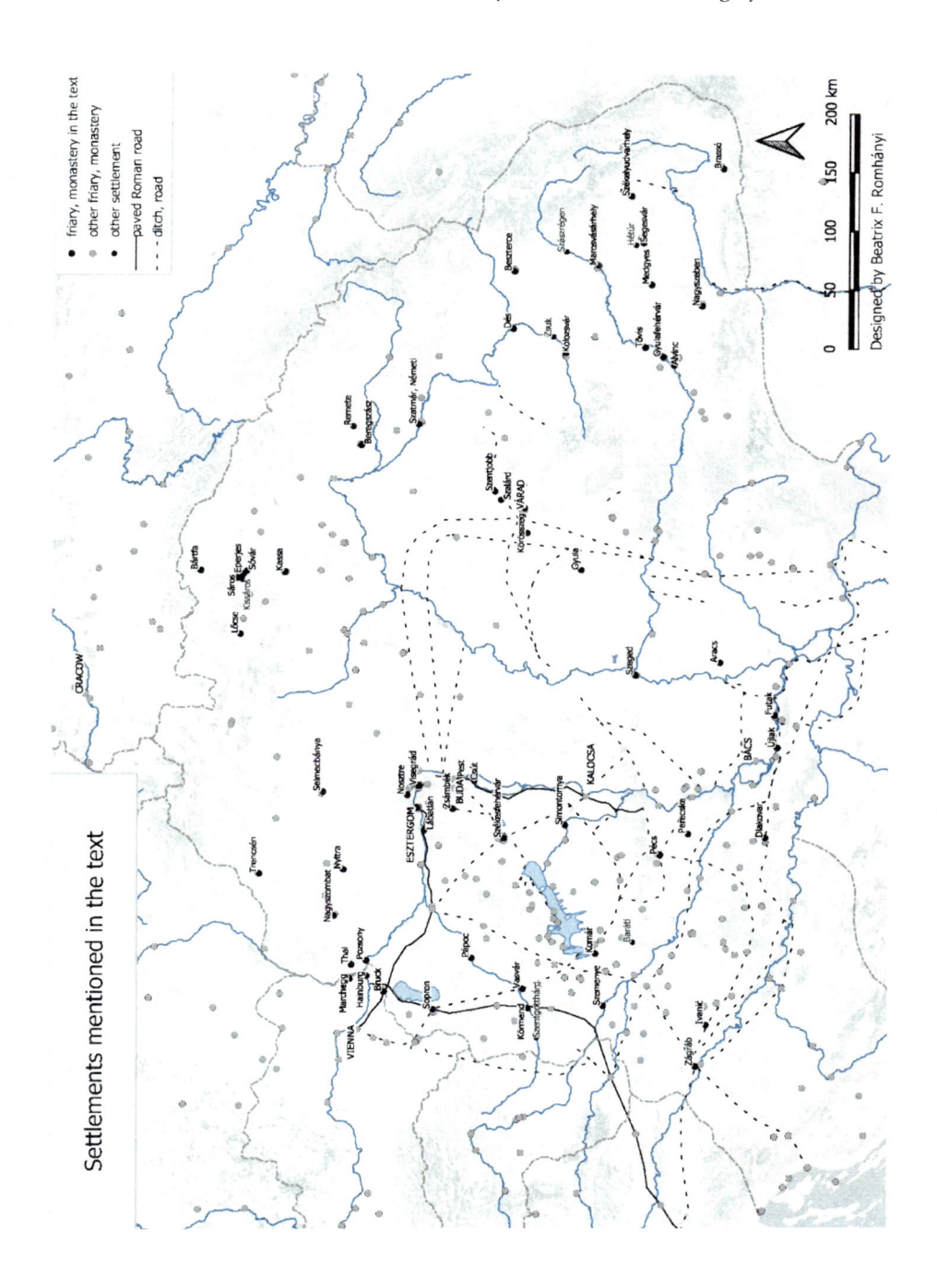

Mendicant and Pauline Economy in Late Medieval Hungary

Concordance of often-used historical place names

Hungarian	German	Present-day (with country)
Alvinc	Winzendorf, Wänts	Vinţu de Jos (RO)
Aracs		Arača (SR)
Bártfa	Bartfeld	Bardejov (SK)
Beregszász	Lampertshaus	Beregove (UKR)
Beszterce	Bistritz, Nösen	Bistriţa (RO)
Brassó	Kronstadt	Braşov (RO)
Buda	Ofen	Budapest I (HU)
Dés	Deesch, Burglos	Dej (RO)
Eperjes	Eperjes, Preschau	Prešov (SK)
Futak		Futog (SR)
Gyulafehérvár	Karlsburg	Alba Iulia (RO)
Hétúr	Marienburg b. Schässburg	Hetiur (RO)
Kassa	Kaschau	Košice (SK)
Kissáros		Maly Šariš (SK)
Kolozsvár	Klausenburg	Cluj-Napoca (RO)
Kőrösszeg		Cheresig (RO)
Lőcse	Leutschau	Levoča (SK)
Máriavölgy	Thal	Marianka (SK)
Marosvásárhely	Neumarkt	Târgu Mureş (RO)
Medgyes	Mediasch	Mediaş (RO)
Nagyszeben	Hermannstadt	Sibiu (RO)
Nagyszombat	Tyrnau	Trnava (SK)
Nagyvárad, Várad	Wardein	Oradea (RO)
Németi (right bank of the Szamos River)	Sathmar	Satu Mare (RO)
Nyitra	Neutra	Nitra (SK)

Hungarian	German	Present-day (with country)
Óbuda	Altofen	Budapest III (HU)
Pest	Pest	Budapest V (HU)
Pozsony	Pressburg	Bratislava (SK)
Remete, Beregremete		Nizhny Remety (UKR)
Sáros, Nagysáros		Velky Šariš (SK)
Segesvár	Schässburg	Sighişoara (RO)
Selmecbánya	Schemnitz	Banská Štiavnica (SK)
Sopron	Ödenburg	Sopron (HU)
Sóvár	Salzburg	Solivar (SK)
Szalárd		Sălard (RO)
Szászrégen	Rennmarkt, Reen	Reghin (RO)
Szatmár (left bank of the Szamos River)	Sathmar	Satu Mare (RO)
Székelyudvarhely	Oderhellen	Odorheiu Secuiesc (RO)
Szentjobb		Sîniob (RO)
Tövis	Dreikirchen	Teiuş (RO)
Trencsén	Trentschin	Trenčín (SK)
Újlak		Ilok (HR)
Zágráb	Agram	Zagreb (HR)

LES MÉCANISMES DE CONTRÔLE ÉCONOMIQUE À L'ŒUVRE DANS LA PROVINCE FRANCISCAINE OBSERVANTE DE HONGRIE À LA FIN DU MOYEN ÂGE (V. 1450–V. 1530)

Marie-Madeleine de Cevins

L'espace centre-européen offre un terrain d'observation privilégié pour l'histoire du franciscanisme réformé à la fin du Moyen Âge. En position de périphérie géographique et mentale de la chrétienté latine, les Franciscains observants implantés en Hongrie, en Pologne et en Bohême se sont vu assigner *ab initio*, en plus de leur vocation pastorale, la tâche de convertir les « Schismatiques », hérétiques et autres « Infidèles ». Ce « paradigme de la frontière » (Jerzy KŁOCZOWSKI) traverse tout particulièrement l'histoire de l'Observance franciscaine polonaise et hongroise.[1] En outre, la circonscription regroupant les couvents franciscains observants du royaume de Hongrie dans ses limites politiques du XVe siècle illustre un développement institutionnel singulier. La vicairie (*vicaria*) puis (après 1517) province (*provincia*) de Hongrie, qualifiée en 1523 de salvatorienne pour la différencier de celle des Conventuels, marianiste –, est née du détachement des Observants hongrois de la vicairie de Bosnie en 1448. Soumise comme cette dernière au vicaire de la *familia cismontana*, elle échappe ensuite pendant un demi-siècle (1458–1502) à l'autorité du vicaire cismontain pour être placée sous celle, plus distante, du ministre général. Et lorsque la vicairie de Hongrie retourne dans le giron cismontain en 1502, elle conserve une large autonomie : l'accord du chapitre provincial est nécessaire pour appliquer une décision émanant de l'échelon cismontain ; la province de Hongrie a pour principal interlocuteur le pape (ou ses représentants), à une période où la montée de la pression ottomane (qui conduit en 1526 à la défaite chrétienne de Mohács puis à la chute de Buda en 1541) et la propagation du luthéranisme (qui entraîne des fermetures de couvents en série à partir des années 1530) font des couvents hongrois, aux yeux de la papauté, un bastion de la chrétienté assiégée.

On le sait, le rapport des Franciscains observants à l'économie diffère sensiblement de celui des conventuels à la fin du Moyen Âge. Ils doivent relever trois défis économiques inhérents au *propositum* mendiant et franciscain observant (ou réformé).[2] Les problèmes de subsistance des frères, tout d'abord, susceptibles de

---

[1] Sur ces aspects généraux, on me permettra de renvoyer à: M.–M. DE CEVINS, Les franciscains observants hongrois de l'expansion à la débâcle (vers 1450–vers 1540), Rome 2008.

[2] Voir les volumes collectifs F. MEYER / L. VIALLET (dir.), Identités franciscaines à l'âge des réformes, Clermont–Ferrand 2005 et N. BÉRIOU / J. CHIFFOLEAU (dir.), Économie et religion. L'expérience des ordres mendiants (XIIIe–XVe s.) (Collection d'histoire et archéologie médiévales 21), Lyon 2009, ainsi que L. VIALLET, Les sens de l'observance. Enquête sur les réformes franciscaines entre l'Elbe et l'Oder, de Capistran à Luther (vers 1450 – vers 1520)

nuire à l'accomplissement des tâches liturgiques et pastorales qui leur incombent, voire de les mener à la famine. Ils découlent d'un modèle économique fondé sur la précarité matérielle (à savoir, pour faire court, l'absence de biens et de revenus stables, notamment fonciers) et sur la dépendance par rapport aux donateurs, dont la générosité est par définition aléatoire. Le deuxième risque est la prolifération de pratiques s'écartant ouvertement du modèle économique propre aux franciscains réformés, un modèle décliné en plusieurs variantes par les textes normatifs issus de l'Observance franciscaine dans un ajustement permanent, une interaction continue avec les pratiques. Troisième écueil à éviter: les « scandales », accusations et autres signes de perception négative par les fidèles des pratiques économiques des frères, de manière à conserver le soutien des fidèles et à préserver la réputation de l'ordre (ou de la province), dans un contexte d'anticléricalisme croissant, notamment dans les villes. Les critiques tournent alors essentiellement autour de deux thèmes : l'enrichissement (collectif et surtout personnel) de frères qui n'auraient de pauvres que le nom ; la dilapidation par incurie, négligence ou cupidité des aumônes, des objets liturgiques et des autres biens cédés ou confiés aux religieux par les fidèles.

Il semble que, dans la Hongrie des années 1450 à 1530, ces défis aient été relevés. Les frères de la vicairie puis province de Hongrie ne se plaignent pas de difficultés alimentaires[3], contrairement aux conventuels à la même période.[4] Deuxièmement, les couvents hongrois de l'Observance franciscaine appliquent scrupuleusement l'exigence de pauvreté absolue. En témoigne l'absence de biens ou revenus tirés de la terre dans les ressources des quelque soixante-dix couvents de la vicairie puis province de Hongrie – à la différence des Dominicains, des Ermites de saint Augustin et des Franciscains conventuels.[5] Les aumônes et le pro-

---

(Vita regularis 57), Münster 2014 et de M.–M. DE CEVINS / L. VIALLET (dir.), L'économie des couvents mendiants en Europe centrale (Bohême, Hongrie, Pologne, v. 1220–v. 1550), Rennes 2018. Les couvents de Clarisses confiés à la tutelle spirituelle des Franciscains observants et les communautés de tertiaires qui dépendaient d'eux avaient un fonctionnement économique différent de celui des couvents masculins. Ils resteront donc à l'écart de cette étude.

[3] Vue d'ensemble dans: M.–M. DE CEVINS, Les franciscains observants hongrois (cf. n. 1), p. 216–217. Détail dans les notices de la base de données par couvent du programme de recherche MARGEC: http://margec.univ-bpclermont.fr/fr/notices.

[4] Ce n'est qu'après 1530 que la pénurie se fait jour: les frères ne reçoivent alors pratiquement plus d'aumônes en raison des destructions causées par les guerres ottomanes, qui privent la population alentour de ses propres moyens de subsistance, et de l'adhésion des habitants et des seigneurs–patrons au protestantisme. M.–M. DE CEVINS, Les franciscains observants hongrois (cf. n. 1), p. 428–437.

[5] Un contre–exemple: le couvent franciscain de Cluj / Kolozsvár, de fondation royale, percevait certes depuis 1494 une rente annuelle sur la production des mines royales de sel d'une valeur de 300 florins, ainsi qu'une fraction de loyer urbain jusqu'en 1510. Kolozsvár története, Oklevéltár I. (Kolozsvár története első kötetéhez), éd. E. JAKAB, Buda 1870, p. 352 n° 219 et n° 196 p. 317–318. Encore cela pouvait–il être considéré comme un don récurrent. Voir *infra*, note 29, à propos des aumônes annuelles.

duit de la quête itinérante constituent une part significative des ressources, y compris dans les couvents dotés à leur fondation d'une subvention confortable ou bénéficiant du soutien d'un puissant *patronus*.[6] Ce modèle perdure jusque dans les années 1530 incluses.[7] D'ailleurs, les fidèles ne s'y trompent pas. Ils lèguent aux Franciscains observants des sommes d'argent pour les travaux à effectuer sur les bâtiments, la confection d'objets liturgiques ou la célébration de tricénaires. Tandis qu'ils cèdent aux membres d'autres ordres (ou branches d'ordre) des biens fonciers et consentent des dons individuels à des religieux.[8] Les entorses à la réglementation générale se cantonnent chez les Observants hongrois à l'utilisation de vêtements et vaisselle liturgiques de valeur, à propos desquels le vicaire de Hongrie Oswald de Laskó et les membres du chapitre obtiennent du pape en 1507 un assouplissement de la législation en vigueur dans la famille cismontaine.[9] Enfin, les fidèles ne semblent pas avoir reproché aux frères observants d'éventuels manquements à la pauvreté ou une gestion médiocre des ressources communautaires.

Difficile de mettre ce bilan *a priori* satisfaisant au compte des destructions d'archives ou des campagnes délibérées d'expurgation des sources : les couvents des autres ordres mendiants implantés en Hongrie ne présentent pas le même

---

[6] Deux couvents franciscains observants illustrent cette configuration, l'un en milieu urbain, le second en milieu rural: celui de Cluj et celui d'Egervár. Voir les notices correspondantes dans la base de données du programme MARGEC: http://margec.univ-bpclermont.fr/fr/content/couvent–franciscain-obs–ste–marie–de–cluj–kolozsvar et http://margec.univ-bpclermont.fr/fr/content/couvent–franciscain-obs–ste–marie–degervar.

[7] Une erreur s'est glissée à ce propos dans mon livre sur les Franciscains observants de Hongrie (2008): en 1533, le chapitre provincial n'autorise pas les Mineurs observants de Cluj à exploiter des vignes sur le mont Felvinc mais seulement à étendre leur territoire de quête à ce secteur: *Item vesta vinaria possessionis Felwyncz assignatur ad conventum Coloswariensem*. Monumenta ecclesiastica tempora innovatae in Hungaria religionis. Egyháztörténelmi emlékek a magyarországi hitújítás korából, Budapest, Szent István Társulat, éd. V. BUNYITAY / R. RAPAICS / J. KARÁCSONYI, 5 vols., Budapest 1902–1912, vol. 2, p. 473.

[8] Ces dons différenciés apparaissent particulièrement bien dans deux testaments féminins de Cluj: celui d'Élisabeth Weymer en 1503 et celui de Madeleine veuve du lapicide Georges en 1531. Voir http://margec.univ-bpclermont.fr/fr/content/couvent-franciscain-obs-ste-marie–de–cluj-kolozsvar. Lorsque des biens fonds sont légués aux Mineurs observants, il peut s'agir en réalité de leur prix de vente, même si le texte ne le précise pas. C'est le cas du testament de Benoît Boros de Csigle en faveur des frères de Pápa, qui leur lègue une ferme (22 juin 1480). MNL DL 45830. Rare exception: une vigne léguée conjointement au même couvent de Pápa ainsi qu'aux Ermites de saint Paul de Porva en 1501, ce qui indiquerait une possession (ou jouissance) partagée entre deux établissements n'appliquant pas le même modèle économique. Z. MEZEI, A pápai ferencesek története a XV–XVIII században [L'histoire des franciscains de Pápa du XVe au XVIIIe siècle], dans: S. ŐZE / N. MEDGYESY–SCHMIKLI (dir.), A ferences lelkiség hatása az újkori Közép–Európa történetére és kultúrája – Die Wirkung der Franziskanischen Spiritualität auf die neuzeitliche Geschichte und Kultur Mitteleuropas, Budapest–Piliscsaba 2005, vol. 1/1, p. 216–226, p. 219.

[9] M.–M. DE CEVINS, Les franciscains observants hongrois (cf. n. 1), pp. 226–229. Voir aussi *infra*.

tableau, en particulier les Ermites de saint Augustin[10] et les Dominicains[11], ainsi que les Franciscains conventuels jusqu'aux années 1450.[12] La réussite à la fois économique et spirituelle des Observants hongrois résulte manifestement de l'existence de mécanismes de contrôle et de régulation du fonctionnement matériel des couvents particulièrement efficaces. Cette étude a pour objectif de les identifier, de les caractériser et d'apprécier leur application.

Les textes normatifs dominent le corpus documentaire exploitable. Pour mémoire, la législation qui régit la vie des Franciscains observants de Hongrie se compose – outre les textes généraux, dont l'appropriation par les Franciscains hongrois mériterait une étude approfondie –, de trois ensembles : les Constitutions adoptées en 1499 au chapitre vicarial réuni à Šarengrad / Atya[13] puis révisées en 1518 en appliquant le nouveau vocabulaire découlant de la bulle *Ite vos* (1517)[14] ; les actes des chapitres de la vicairie puis province de Hongrie (réunis tous les deux ans et dont on a conservé le texte presque continuellement entre 1505 et 1567), qui prennent des dispositions ponctuelles[15] ; les « exhortations »

---

[10] Le cas le plus célèbre est celui du couvent d'Ermites augustiniens de Körmend, finement analysé par Gabriella ERDÉLYI dans plusieurs articles et livres, dernièrement G. ERDÉLYI, A Cloister on Trial. Religious Culture and Everyday Life in Late Medieval Hungary (Catholic Christendom, 1300–1700), Farnham 2015.

[11] M.–M. DE CEVINS, Les Ermites de saint Augustin en Hongrie médiévale: état des connaissances, dans: Augustiniana 62 (2012), p. 77–117; EAD., Les frères mendiants et l'économie en Hongrie médiévale: état de la recherche, dans: Études franciscaines, n. s. 3 (2010), p. 4–45; B. ROMHÁNYI, Adalékok a soproni ferences kolostor gazdálkodásához [Données sur la gestion du couvent franciscain de Sopron], dans: Soproni Szemle 64 (2010), p. 181–184; EAD., Domonkos kolostorok birtokai a későközépkorban [Les possessions des couvents dominicains à la fin du Moyen Âge], dans: Századok 144 (2010), p. 395–410; EAD., *Koldulórendi barátok, gazdálkodó szerzetesek. Koldulórendi gazdálkodás a késő középkori Magyarországon* [Frères mendiants, frères exploitants. L'économie mendiante dans la Hongrie médiévale], Mémoire inédit pour le doctorat de l'Académie hongroise des Sciences, Budapest 2013.

[12] M.–M. DE CEVINS, Les franciscains observants hongrois (cf. n. 1), p. 106–107.

[13] Les localités aujourd'hui situées hors des frontières politiques de la Hongrie sont nommées selon leur forme actuelle, suivie de leur nom hongrois.

[14] I. BATTHYÁNY (éd.), Leges ecclesiasticae regni Hungariae et provinciarum adiacentium, 3 vols., Cluj Napoca 1827, vol. 3, p. 609–635. Une édition plus rigoureuse prenant en compte l'ensemble des manuscrits reproduisant ces Constitutions – notamment celui conservé à Alba Iulia: Bibl. Batthyaneum, ms R. II. 148 – est actuellement en préparation. L'édition critique du Prologue des Constitutions a déjà effectuée par Balázs KERTÉSZ: B. KERTÉSZ, A magyarországi obszerváns ferencesek 1499. és 1518. évi konstitúcióinak prológusa, dans: Történelmi Szemle 58 (2016), p. 643–655.

[15] Partiellement édités dans: I. BATTHYÁNY (éd.), Leges ecclesiasticae regni Hungariae (cf. n. 14), vol. 3, p. 647–649 [1505], p. 650–653 [1507], p. 667–669 [1515]; V. BUNYITAY / R. RAPAICS / J. KARÁCSONYI (éd.), Monumenta ecclesiastica tempora innovatae in Hungaria religionis. Egyháztörténelmi emlékek a magyarországi hitujítás korából, 5 vols., Budapest 1902–1912, vol. 2, p. 464–469 [1531], p. 470–476 [1533], p. 476–489 [1535], p. 489 [1539], p. 489–500 [1542], p. 501–504 [1544], p. 504–508 [1546], p. 508–512 [1548], p. 512–516 [1550], p. 516–519 [1552], p. 520–522 [1554], p. 523–524 [1558], p. 524–526 [1559], p. 526–529 [1561], p. 528–

des vicaires puis ministres provinciaux transmises par les formulaires copiés à usage interne au début du XVIe siècle.[16] Aucune source comptable issue d'un couvent franciscain observant hongrois n'a malheureusement subsisté. Mais on dispose de textes situés à mi-chemin entre sources normatives et sources découlant de la pratique : les éléments de correspondance datés des années 1510 à 1530 (mandats, lettres de réclamation, dispenses, dérogations, etc.) figurant dans les formulaires mentionnés précédemment. Ils reflètent des situations réelles mais de manière indirecte, après avoir été sélectionnés et partiellement réécrits pour répondre aux besoins d'autres frères.[17]

Quatre outils assurent le bon fonctionnement matériel des couvents de l'Observance franciscaine hongroise d'après cette documentation : (1) la législation provinciale hongroise, (2) les membres de l'ordre chargés de contrôler ou d'assurer la gestion des couvents de Hongrie, (3) les agents externes ou procureurs, (4) les patrons.

1. La législation provinciale hongroise à caractère économique: le prisme de la pauvreté

Les divers textes en vigueur dans la province salvatorienne – les Constitutions de 1499–1518, les actes des chapitres, les exhortations des vicaires puis ministres – forment un tout cohérent, dont le contenu n'évolue guère avant les aménagements rendus nécessaires par les troubles des années 1540–1550.[18] Sans dominer l'ensemble, les questions économiques y apparaissent de façon récurrente, presque toujours sous l'angle de la pauvreté.

Un premier groupe de prescriptions, peu original, impose aux religieux de mener une existence sobre. Cela passe par la rusticité de l'habit, dont la matière, la coupe et les dimensions sont détaillées dans les Constitutions de 1499, de même que par une alimentation frugale, une literie et un couchage sommaires, et l'obligation de se déplacer à pied plutôt qu'à cheval.[19] La législation provinciale

---

529 [1565], p. 530 [1567]. Jean–François Morvan en prépare actuellement l'édition critique et l'analyse compare.

16 Formulaires inédits conservés à la Bibliothèque Nationale Széchényi: Budapest, Országos Széchényi Könyvtár (OSzK) [Bibliothèque Nationale Széchényi], Kézirattár [Département des manuscrits], Cod. Lat. medii aevi n°432 et Oct. Lat. n°775.

17 Voir les références données à la note précédente.

18 M.–M. DE CEVINS, Les franciscains observants hongrois (cf. n. 1), p. 434–435.

19 Ibid., p. 96–97. Source: I. BATTHYÁNY (éd.), Leges ecclesiasticae regni Hungariae (cf. n. 14), vol. 3, p. 620, 623. Les actes du chapitre de 1505 précisent sur quels marchés les frères doivent s'approvisionner pour se procurer le tissu nécessaire à la confection de leur habit. Ibid., vol. 3, p. 648.

sanctionne par ailleurs, à plusieurs reprises, les ornements superflus sur les bâtiments (église et couvent confondus). C'est dans cet esprit qu'elle condamne l'accumulation (*thezaurisatio*) dans les couvents d'objets liturgiques de grande valeur – dans les Constitutions de 1499[20], les actes du chapitre de 1505[21] ou encore dans les exhortations du vicaire Blaise de Dézs au milieu des années 1510. Ils sont décrits comme autant de *superfluitates* susceptibles d'éveiller des convoitises et de nuire à la réputation de l'ordre. Est également sanctionnée l'accumulation de vivres dans les couvents – en 1499 et 1507.[22] La quête doit subvenir aux besoins présents, et non anticiper sur les besoins à venir : les frères ne sauraient solliciter des dons quand ils disposent déjà du nécessaire. Le chapitre de 1507 précise que si les quêteurs obtiennent l'équivalent d'un quartier de lard pour deux frères, ils doivent rentrer au couvent, sauf si la pièce reçue est de taille insuffisante, ce que le gardien entouré des « discrets » du couvent est tenu d'apprécier.[23]

D'autres articles règlementent la pratique de la quête. Celle-ci se restreint au périmètre affecté au couvent par le chapitre provincial (*contrata*), précisent les Constitutions de 1499[24], réitérées sur ce point en 1515.[25] Pour prévenir toute contestation, les quêteurs se dotent au début du XVIe siècle d'un mandat établi au nom du provincial, qui précise dans quel secteur ils ont autorisation de quêter. La législation salvatorienne n'impose pas l'utilisation de ces mandats *ad contratas* mais les formulaires des années 1510–1530 en fournissent plusieurs exemples, ce qui indique un procédé courant.[26] La quête ne peut être confiée qu'à des frères expérimentés et intègres (*probati, maturi et spiritu roborati*) selon le vicaire Barthélemy de Sáros en 1488 ; ils sont sélectionnés par leur supérieur (le gardien) en vertu des Constitutions de 1499.[27] Il va sans dire que les quêteurs doivent rapporter à leur couvent l'intégralité des biens (en nature ou en argent) qu'ils ont

---

[20] Item paramenta pretiosa, calice, monstrantie, thuribula et huiusmodi, que capiunt thesaurizationem in nostris locis non multiplicentur, si vero contrarium quis fecerit importetur visitatio sua ad capitulum discutienda. Ibid., vol. 3, p. 624.

[21] Ibid., vol. 3, p. 649.

[22] Ibid., vol. 3, p. 652 (*De mendicatione alimentorum*).

[23] Item pro duobus fratribus recipiatur unum lardum, et si larda fuerit nimis parva et macilenta, possit pater guardianus cum dictis discretis defectum resarcire ad equivalens in quibus et premisssi eorum conscientiam oneramus. Ibid., vol. 3, p. 652.

[24] Item fratres ad contratas aliorum locorum questum facere non vadant, contra facientes puniantur ad arbitrium suorum prelatorum. Ibid., vol. 3, p. 626 (transcription fautive: « contractas », rectifiée au vu du manuscrit conservé à Alba Iulia).

[25] *Item, non vadant ad questus aliorum locorum, si qui contrarium fecerint, puniantur per custodes; et si custodes negligentes fuerint, tunc per sequens capitulum et ipsi puniantur.* Ibid., vol. 3, p. 667.

[26] M.–M. DE CEVINS, Les franciscains observants hongrois (cf. n. 1), p. 218–219.

[27] *Ad quod ordinat reverendus pater vicarius unacum capitulo, quod omnes fratres vadant pro eleemosynis aquirendis prout regula dicit iuxta discretionem prelati precipientis, cuius arbitrio committitur discernendum, qui congrue mittendi sint pro eleemosyna, vel qui non.* I. BATTHYÁNY (éd.), Leges ecclesiasticae regni Hungariae (cf. n. 14), vol. 3, p. 625.

récoltés : le mandat *ad contratas* qu'ils portent sur eux le rappelle, en écho aux Constitutions de 1499, qui imposent un délai maximal de huit jours.[28]

La hantise de la simonie motive plusieurs dispositions relatives à l'exercice de la pastorale. Pas question de tirer de celle-ci des revenus récurrents, y compris pour les sépultures. Les pères assemblés en chapitre à Esztergom en 1507 interdisent aux religieux de réclamer quelque rétribution que ce soit à ceux des fidèles qui souhaiteraient être inhumés dans l'enceinte du couvent.[29] Tous les testateurs dont on sait par la documentation qu'ils ont élu sépulture chez des frères observants leur consentaient des dons, généralement importants. Mais ils avaient (en principe) un caractère spontané. Que ce soit dans le cadre de la pastorale ou non, les Constitutions de 1499 condamnent ceux des frères qui réclament aux fidèles des biens ou revenus matériels, en particulier viagers ou périodiques : les aumônes doivent toujours résulter de l'initiative du donateur, rappellent-elles.[30]

Les questions de propriété et de possession affleurent dans plusieurs articles de la législation provinciale hongroise. Ils sanctionnent la possession de biens personnels par la privation de sépulture chrétienne.[31] Les actes du chapitre de 1515 interdisent toute « propriété ou forme de propriété » à l'intérieur des couvents, quel que soit leur objet : cens, rentes, maisons, prés, viviers à poissons, paysans dépendants, services, jusqu'aux vivres et enfin aux objets liturgiques.[32] On notera en revanche que la législation salvatorienne n'interdit pas formellement la jouissance – à titre communautaire – de biens stables, fonciers ou non, ou, si l'on préfère, la perception de revenus récurrents. Dans les faits, les fondations de services perpétuels (anniversaires notamment) ne se rencontrent pas chez les Franciscains observants de Hongrie, alors qu'elles sont monnaie courante chez les Franciscains conventuels, les Ermites de saint Augustin, les Dominicains et les Carmes. Implicitement, les Observants hongrois s'appuyaient donc

---

[28] *Sed omnes eleemosynae quorumcunque fratrum assignentur ad manus confratris conventus sive loci. Quas quidem eleemosynas infra octo dies postquam sui prelati habuerint presentiam eidem integraliter teneantur reversare.* Ibid., vol. 3, p. 623.

[29] *Item pro sepultura in ecclesiis nostris nihil exigatur a quocunque quovis quesito colore.* Ibid., vol. 3, p. 652.

[30] *Inhibet insuper, quod nullus frater per se vel per alium inducat personam aliquam ad faciendum vel ordinandum eleemosynam aliquam perpetuam ad vitam sibi vel ordini exhibendam. Si quis contrarium attentaverit, semel in pane et aqua ieiunet et disciplinatus coram fratribus in terra sedeat. Eleemosynam autem sic ordinatam fratres nullomodo exigant. Si vero quis ex donatione annuatim aliquam vult facere eleemosynam, absque scrupulo consciencie a fratribus potest recipi.* Ibid., vol. 3, p. 626. On observe au passage qu'un don récurrent n'est pas considéré comme incompatible avec le *propositum* observant – ce dont on a de nombreux exemples dans la documentation hongroise. Voir les notices de la base MARGEC mentionnée supra.

[31] *Item quicunque frater inventus fuerit in morte proprietarius, ecclesiastica careat sepultura.* Ibid., vol. 3, p. 626.

[32] *Primo ordinatum est, quod cum exacta diligentia ex quo periculum est in mora conventus, et loca in quibus aliqua proprietas seu saltem tendens ad proprietatem, ut in censibus, reditibus, domibus, pratis, territoriis, piscinis, jobbagionibus ac quibusdam oneribus, servitiis, nec non angariis secularium et huiusmodi forsitan invenitur, et ne dum in talibus, sed etiam in victualibus.* Ibid., vol. 3, p. 667.

sur la législation réformée antérieure, notamment sur les « Constitutions martiniennes » rédigées par Jean de Capistran et confirmées par Martin V en 1430. Les Constitutions provinciales hongroises interdisent en 1499 aux frères de manipuler l'argent, y compris pendant leurs déplacements, en renvoyant précisément aux lettres du pape Martin V. Elles étendent cette prohibition aux nouveaux moyens de paiement, les « lettres de banque » (*litere banke*).[33] Au nom de la pauvreté individuelle, garder de l'argent dans sa cellule est passible de sanctions.[34] D'où l'obligation faite aux couvents de recruter un intendant extérieur à l'établissement et à l'ordre, le *procurator*.

Bien que la généalogie de la législation salvatorienne reste à établir[35], on y reconnaîtra facilement les thèmes et le vocabulaire employés par les dirigeants italiens de l'Observance franciscaine, relayés ou encadrés par la papauté, depuis 1430 environ. Les dispositions hongroises font également écho aux accusations portées contre les Conventuels de Hongrie : leurs détracteurs, à savoir les souverains, aristocrates et évêques partisans de l'Observance, leur reprochaient de mener une vie confortable, de posséder des biens personnels, de détourner à leur profit les objets liturgiques précieux donnés à l'établissement.[36] Mais la principale singularité hongroise se trouve probablement du côté des agents chargés de faire appliquer les prescriptions observantes.

2. La surveillance exercée par les contrôleurs internes

Sans entrer dans le détail de l'organisation administrative de la vicairie puis province de Hongrie[37], il convient d'en rappeler l'architecture générale. Trois niveaux de décision se superposent alors dans la province de Hongrie : le chapitre vicarial ou provincial (qui a autorité sur toute la vicairie-province), le custode (responsable de sa custodie), le gardien (dans chaque couvent). Tous interviennent dans la vie économique des couvents.

À l'intérieur de la vicairie puis province hongroise, c'est le chapitre (vicarial puis provincial) qui a la haute main sur le contrôle des couvents du royaume – ne

---

[33] *Item fratres euntes ad vias non audeant secum ducere [–] bursarios, nec deferant literas bankas, si quis vero sine superiori licentia contrarium facere presumpserit scienter, pena proprietarii puniatur.* Ibid., vol. 3, p. 622.

[34] Ibid., vol. 3, p. 623.

[35] En attendant l'achèvement d'une enquête en cours sur ce sujet, voir les propositions de Balázs KERTÉSZ, à propos du Prologue des Constitutions de 1499: son auteur, le provincial Oswald de Laskó s'appuie sur la bulle *Sacrae religionis* d'Eugène IV (1444) pour légitimer son pouvoir de doter la vicairie de Hongrie d'une législation propre. B. KERTÉSZ, A magyarországi obszerváns ferencesek (cf. n. 14), pp. 645–649.

[36] M.–M. DE CEVINS, Les franciscains observants hongrois (cf. n. 1), pp. 103–108.

[37] M.–M. de CEVINS, L'Observance franciscaine en Hongrie dans les années 1500 à 1530: une centralisation ratée?, dans: F. MEYER / L. VIALLET (dir.), Identités franciscaines (cf. n. 2), pp. 431–462; M.–M. DE CEVINS, Les franciscains observants hongrois (cf. n. 1), pp. 165–183.

serait-ce que parce qu'il est la seule instance légiférante. *Secundo*, c'est lui qui nomme (par élection) les agents de contrôle économique dont il sera question plus loin : custodes, gardiens et visiteurs. Troisièmement, c'est le chapitre provincial qui délimite les zones de quête (*contratae*) affectées à chaque couvent. Il révise la carte en vigueur à la demande des intéressés (qui peuvent lui adresser des réclamations), suite à la suppression d'un couvent (comme après la fermeture des couvents de Solivar / Sóvár en 1536 et de Kőröshegy en 1542[38]), après la fondation d'un nouveau couvent (afin de lui assurer des moyens de subsistance), ou pour des raisons qui nous échappent.[39] Entre les sessions du chapitre, c'est le vicaire ou ministre provincial qui agit. Il peut redistribuer le produit des aumônes d'un couvent à un autre – sauf ce qui provient des legs ou de dons faits explicitement à tel établissement, précisent les Constitutions de 1499.[40] Il doit s'assurer, lorsqu'il visite les couvents de Hongrie (au moins une fois tous les deux ans au moins, selon les Constitutions), que les frères se contentent du « nécessaire »[41] et n'accumulent pas de denrées superflues par des quêtes injustifiées.[42] Enfin, il est consulté par les custodes à chaque fois que ceux-ci doivent prendre une décision matérielle importante : construire (ou non) de nouveaux bâtiments[43], procéder à des transferts de vivres et autres biens meubles d'une certaine valeur à l'intérieur de la custodie, etc.

Les *visitatores*, au nombre d'une dizaine, soit autant que de custodies dans la province salvatorienne, émanent directement des instances provinciales : c'est le chapitre qui les nomme et ils rendent des comptes de leur activité au chapitre suivant, deux ans plus tard. Recrutés parmi les gardiens – ce qui garantit une certaine connaissance, par l'expérience, des problèmes économiques d'un couvent –, ils visitent une fois en deux ans tous les couvents de la custodie qui leur est confiée. À en juger par les noms de ces visiteurs, celle-ci est toujours différente de leur custodie d'origine – gage d'impartialité. Le déroulement des visites

---

[38] V. BUNYITAY / R. RAPAICS / J. KARÁCSONYI (éd.), Monumenta ecclesiastica (cf. n. 15), vol. 2, p. 589 et 498.

[39] La zone de quête du couvent de Jászberény est modifiée sans motif apparent par le chapitre provincial en 1539 puis 1550. J. KARÁCSONYI, Szent Ferencz rendjének története Magyarországon 1711-ig [Histoire de l'ordre de saint François en Hongrie jusqu'en 1711], 2 vols., Budapest 1922–1924, vol. 2, p. 84.

[40] *Item reverendus pater vicarius de eleemosynis pecuniariis indistincte provenientibus de consilio discretorum loci illius si opus fuerit possit facere provisionem, aliis locis magis indigentibus; se de datis determinate, ad aliquod datis vel legatis nullomodo se intromittat, quod si secus fecerit, fratres non debeant ei in hac parte obedire.* I. BATTHYÁNY (éd.), Leges ecclesiasticae regni Hungariae (cf. n. 14), vol. 3, p. 611.

[41] *Item vicarii provincie teneantur semel in quolibet anno vel qui visitant loca fratrum visitare res concessas ad usum fratrum nec permittant eos tenere superflua et non necessaria.* Ibid., vol. 3, p. 653.

[42] Chapitre De receptione alimentorum: *Et reverendus pater vicarius et custos quando visitant loca teneantur inquirere et contemplari quomodo hec constitutio observetur.* Ibid., vol. 3, p. 652.

[43] *Item nova edificia notabilia in sua* [= le custode] *custodia fieri sine licentia reverendi patris vicarii non permittant.* Ibid., vol. 3, p. 613 (Constitutions de 1499).

suit un protocole déjà très élaboré à l'époque des Constitutions de 1499 : en témoigne le long paragraphe intitulé *De officio patrum visitatorum*. Il ne cesse de se perfectionner dans les décennies suivantes, d'après les actes capitulaires et les directives du provincial transmises par les formulaires des années 1510–1530.[44] Dans la liste des points à contrôler par les *visitatores* et à transmettre oralement ou par écrit au chapitre[45], plusieurs concernent le respect de la pauvreté : l'ornementation des bâtiments et la valeur des objets liturgiques, l'utilisation de montures, selon les Constitutions de 1499[46] ; l'abondance ou non de vivres stockés, l'état de l'infirmerie, les méthodes de quête, l'utilisation éventuelle de montures, selon le formulaire des années 1510–1525.[47] C'est sur la foi des déclarations des *visitatores* que les autorités provinciales décident de déplacer des biens d'un couvent à un autre, de prononcer la condamnation de tel frère délinquant ou de déposer tel gardien négligent. La documentation conservée n'offre malheureusement pas d'exemple de telles actions faisant suite aux déclarations des visiteurs. Mais l'abondance d'écrits sur ces derniers dans les formulaires du XVIe siècle oriente vers une activité soutenue.

Courroie de transmission des décisions provinciales, les custodes interviennent eux aussi, à leur niveau, dans la régulation économique des couvents hongrois. Les demandes d'autorisation, les décisions et mandats recopiés dans les formulaires internes du début du XVIe siècle en sont la preuve. Les dix custodes de la vicairie puis province de Hongrie ont en moyenne de six à huit couvents sous leur autorité vers 1500. Conformément à la tradition franciscaine, ils exercent leur autorité de façon principalement itinérante. En Hongrie, chaque couvent reçoit en principe la visite du custode au minimum deux fois par an. C'est à cette occasion que les custodes vérifient l'état matériel des couvents et s'assurent du respect de la pauvreté individuelle et collective. Leur position intermédiaire et la fréquence relative de leurs visites permettent aux custodes d'avoir une vision globale de leur custodie. S'ils constatent un déséquilibre criant entre les couvents

---

[44] OSzK, Cod. Lat. n° 432, fol. 73v, 75–76v (*Modus visitationis*); édition: M.–M. DE CEVINS, Les franciscains observants hongrois (cf. n. 1), n° 11, pp. 515–517.

[45] À compter de 1514, les visiteurs doivent résumer les infractions majeures sur une fiche écrite (*cedula*). M.–M. CEVINS, L'Observance franciscaine en Hongrie (cf. n. 37), pp. 457–458.

[46] *Visitatores (…) significent capitulo fideliter si custodiam visitatam invenerit vitiosam in sumptuositate aedificiorum, sacrarum vestium ac vasorum vel aequitatura seu relaxacionis regularis disciplinae.* I. BATTHYÁNY (éd.), Leges ecclesiasticae regni Hungariae (cf. n. 14), vol. 3, p. 616.

[47] OSzK, Cod. Lat. n° 432, fol. 72, 73.

de leur circonscription, ils effectuent des transferts d'argent, d'objets, de nourriture entre eux.[48] Ils peuvent procéder à la vente des objets qu'ils trouvent superflus, précisent les actes du chapitre de 1533.[49] Les Constitutions de 1499 confient tout particulièrement aux custodes en tournée la vérification de la prise en charge des frères malades, outre la conformité de l'habit.[50] Leur revient également le soin de vérifier que les couvents n'empiètent pas sur la zone de quête d'autres établissements et de punir les éventuels coupables, indiquent les actes du chapitre de 1515.[51] Les prérogatives des custodes restent toutefois limitées par leur obligation de consulter le provincial pour les décisions engageant des sommes élevées, on l'a dit, ainsi que par des clauses protégeant le « temporel » des couvents : les custodes ne doivent pas ponctionner de plus de 6 à 10 florins le produit des aumônes d'un couvent[52] ni confisquer ses objets liturgiques.

Le gardien apparaît comme le responsable de la gestion matérielle du couvent qu'il dirige. Même si la comptabilité est assurée par un intendant extérieur (le procureur), c'est à lui que les autorités de l'ordre viennent demander des comptes. La législation hongroise confie plus particulièrement au gardien le soin d'établir les rations alimentaires, en prenant conseil auprès des « anciens » du couvent. À lui également de décider à quel moment il faut interrompre les quêtes itinérantes pour éviter l'accumulation de vivres au couvent.[53] Le gardien ne dispose pas pour autant d'une grande marge de manœuvre. Il en réfère à son supérieur direct, le custode, avant d'engager de lourdes dépenses à partir de biens reçus en aumône, selon les Constitutions de 1499.[54] Les frères peuvent se plaindre de la mauvaise gestion de leur gardien au custode, aux visiteurs ou au provincial lors de leur

---

48   On lit dans les Constitutions de 1499: *Item pater custos providentiam habeat ne superfluas eleemosynas patiatur ad loca fratrum congregari, si autem contrarium contigat, extunc ex fratrum discretorum illius loci, vel aliorum locorum consilio distribuat aliis locis magis indigentibus vel aliis egentibus, quibus secundum Deum melius viderit expedire.* I. BATTHYÁNY (éd.), Leges ecclesiasticae regni Hungariae (cf. n. 14), vol. 3, p. 613. Selon le chapitre de 1507, les custodes doivent veiller à ce que certains couvents n'accumulent pas de vivres tandis que d'autres seraient menacés de famine. Ibid., vol. 3, p. 652.

49   *Item patres custodes possint vendere et vendant res fratrum illorum, qui censentur superfluas tenere et ab eisdem auferant non necessarias.* Ibid., vol. 3, p. 473.

50   *Item ordinat reverendus pater vicarius una cum capitulo predicto, quod quilibet custos loca sue custodie teneatur ad minus bis in annum perlustrare et in quolibet loco infirmarios instituere, de vestitura providere, pacem et concordiam inter fratres ordinare…* Ibid., vol. 3, p. 613.

51   *Item, non vadant ad questus aliorum locorum, si qui contrarium fecerint, puniantur per custodes; et si custodes negligentes fuerint, tunc per sequens capitulum et ipsi puniantur.* Ibid., vol. 3, p. 667.

52   *…quod certitudinaliter in singulis locis sue custodie resciant eleemosynam locorum, nec exponant notabilem eleemosynam frustra absque scitu guardiani loci et aliquorum fratrum discretorum illius loci, notabiles vero eleemosynas dicimus 6, 7, 8 et decem florenos et supra.* Ibid., vol. 3, p. 613.

53   *Item patri guardiani habeant providentiam discretam de fratrum quotidiano victu. Propter hoc tamen non congregentur victualia multa ad fratrum loca. Sed compescant discursus inutiles pro eleemosynis aquirendis, et hoc fiat secundum sanctam paupertatem, ex fratrum maxime senum consilio, et quod secundum sanctam paupertatem fratrum faciant fratribus coquere.* Ibid., vol. 3, p. 614.

54   *Item patri guardiani notabilem fratrum eleemosynam non exponant sine scitu patris custodis…* Ibid., vol. 3, p. 614.

passage dans l'établissement. Ces derniers lui imputent la responsabilité des éventuelles irrégularités qu'ils constatent. La documentation provenant des gardiens est trop sporadique pour permettre de savoir comment les gardiens hongrois s'acquittaient de leur tâche. Au mieux, on les voit demander la confirmation de privilèges antérieurs (à Șumuleu Ciuc / Csíksomlyó en 1519[55]), informer le patron de la remise de dons importants (en 1510 à Voćin / Atyina[56]), assister comme témoin à l'expression des dernières volontés d'un fidèle (en 1525 à Albeşti / Fehéregyháza[57]). Alors que chez les Conventuels, les gardiens transcrivent des chartes relatives aux biens et revenus de leur couvent, défendent les intérêts de leur établissement devant les juridictions laïques, dressent des quittances, des actes de location ou des déclarations de vente. Celui qui tient ce rôle dans les couvents observants, c'est le *procurator*.

3. Le rôle des procureurs

Au nom de l'interdiction de manier l'argent déjà évoquée, la législation hongroise impose à chaque couvent le recours à une « personne interposée », le *procurator*, pour gérer les aumônes (dont les legs) et le produit des quêtes, ceci de façon systématique et exclusive. L'obligation figure dans les Constitutions de Šarengrad. Le *procurator* est mentionné dans de nombreux actes capitulaires du XVIe siècle, de 1505 jusqu'aux années 1540 incluses.[58] La disparition des actes des chapitres hongrois antérieurs à 1499 ne permet pas de savoir à quelle date les dirigeants hongrois ont introduit pour la première fois son recrutement dans leurs règlements. Il remonte probablement à l'époque de la fondation de la vicairie observante de Hongrie : les Conventuels hongrois le font apparaître dans leurs propres statuts réformés en 1454. Quoi qu'il en soit, côté observant, la pratique est ancienne. Elle caractérise les couvents de la vicairie de Bosnie, matrice de celle de Hongrie, dès la seconde moitié du XIVe siècle. Sigismond de Luxembourg confirme officiellement en 1428 le recrutement d'un intendant dans quatre couvents franciscains fondés par Louis Ier (1342–1382) au sud du royaume, en prolongement de la décision prise par son prédécesseur angevin à la demande des

---

[55] K. Szabó (éd.), Székely oklevéltár 1219–1776, 8 vol., Budapest 1872–1934, vol. 1, p. 340–342 n° 242; MNL DL 29090.

[56] MNL DL 104224; B. Kertész (éd.), A magyarországi obszerváns ferencesek eredetiben fennmaradt iratai 1448–1526. The original surviving documents of the Hungarian observant Franciscans 1448–1526 (Fontes Historici ordinis Fratrum minorum in Hungaria. Magyar ferences források 7), Budapest 2015, p. 124–125 n° 49.

[57] K. Fabritius (éd.), Urkundenbuch zur Geschichte des Kisder Kapitels vor der Reformation und der auf dem Gebiete desselben ehedem befindlichen Orden, Hermannstadt 1875, p. 59 n° 112.

[58] I. Batthyány (éd.), Leges ecclesiasticae regni Hungariae (cf. n. 14), vol. 3, p. 623–624 et 647.

frères.⁵⁹ Le couvent de Șumuleu Ciuc / Csíksomlyó a son *procurator* dès 1442. Au total, le procureur n'est formellement mentionné qu'à propos de sept établissements hongrois⁶⁰, soit moins d'un sur dix. Mais c'est probablement là le résultat des pertes documentaires. La nomination d'un procureur par le patron est encore posée comme indispensable à la création d'un nouveau couvent en 1544 (à Suseni / Felfalu).⁶¹

Les textes normatifs (hongrois ou généraux) ne fixent pas de nombre précis de procureurs. Les sources n'en mentionnent généralement qu'un seul à la fois par couvent. Le couvent de Șumuleu Ciuc / Csíksomlyó constitue à ce titre un cas atypique et toujours énigmatique. Selon la confirmation accordée en 1519 par le voïvode de Transylvanie, au nom du roi Louis II, des privilèges obtenus respectivement de Jean de Hunyad puis de Mathias Corvin en 1442 et 1462, 32 « confrères » – dont les tâches ne sont pas définies dans la charte – sont placés au service des frères de ce couvent depuis les années 1440.⁶² Diverses hypothèses ont été avancées pour expliquer ce nombre étonnamment élevé dans un couvent d'envergure modeste – il abritait 14 frères en 1535. La moins fantaisiste considère qu'il ne s'agit pas d'intendants mais de personnel mis à la disposition des frères pour accomplir divers travaux, à commencer par les travaux de construction, inachevés au milieu du XVᵉ siècle.⁶³ Or le vocabulaire employé pour désigner ces agents, les exonérations qui leur sont accordées simultanément par le roi, de même que les formules qui marquent leur obéissance par rapport aux frères les apparentent à des procureurs. Peut-être l'église de ce couvent attirait-elle des pèlerins (ceux qu'évoque la bulle d'indulgences de 1445⁶⁴) suffisamment nombreux pour générer des dons élevés nécessitant la mobilisation d'une véritable équipe de comptables. Cet exemple isolé mis à part, le nombre de procureurs par couvent a manifestement augmenté au fil du temps. Les pères assemblés au chapitre de 1507 prennent acte du fait que les procureurs se doublent parfois de remplaçants, adjoints ou collaborateurs. Ils précisent que, dans cette configuration, il

---

59   ... *eisdem fratribus annuimus et consensimus, concessimusque gratiose, quemadmodum per felicis reminiscentiae condam serenissimum dominum Ludovicum regem Hungariae, socerum nostrum charissimum, suas per litteras, quae in specie coram nobis productae fuerant, comperimus factum fuisse,* ... E. FERMENDŽIN (éd.), Acta Bosnae potissimum ecclesiastica cum insertis editorum documentorum regestis ab anno 925 usque ad annum 1752 (Monumenta spectantia historiam Slavorum Meridionalium 23), Zagreb 1892, p. 128.

60   Il s'agit des couvents de: Brașov / Brassó, Jászberény, Pest, Sacoșu Turcesc / Cseri, Șumuleu Ciuc / Csíksomlyó, Suseni / Felfalu et Voćin / Atyina. Voir les fiches correspondantes dans la base de données MARGEC.

61   V. BUNYITAY / R. RAPAICS / J. KARÁCSONYI (éd.), Monumenta ecclesiastica (cf. n. 15), vol. 2, p. 503.

62   K. SZABÓ (éd.), Székely oklevéltár (cf. n. 55), vol. 1, p. 340–342 n° 242; MNL DL 29090.

63   F. BOROS, Az erdélyi ferencrendiek, Cluj–Kolozsvár 1927, pp. 27–30.

64   *ad ecclesiam beate Marie* [...] *ingens fidelium multitudo devocionis causa confluere consueverit, ac dietim non cessat confluere.* K. SZABÓ (éd.), Székely oklevéltár (cf. n. 55), vol. 1, pp. 153–154, n° 124.

doit y avoir un « gestionnaire en chef », le *summus procurator*.[65] Pas question donc de diluer les responsabilités. C'est dire leur importance.

Le nom donné aux intendants des couvents fluctue selon les textes. L'appellation la plus fréquente est celle de *procurator* – terme ambigu puisqu'il peut également désigner ceux des membres de la province qui ont la charge de défendre en justice les intérêts d'un couvent, d'une custodie, ou encore de la province entière.[66] Le mot *confrater* arrive presque à égalité, souvent en association avec le précédent vocable, devant *vitricus*. Les termes d'*administrator*, *œconomus*, *sindicus* ou *actor* demeurent rares, surtout isolément.[67] Derrière cette taxinomie instable, qui n'est pas propre aux Observants hongrois, les tâches confiées aux procureurs semblent partout les mêmes et se retrouvent à l'identique chez les Conventuels.[68] Les règlements observants n'en détaillent pas le contenu : ils se contentent de justifier l'activité des procureurs par l'interdit de manier l'argent. De fait, l'essentiel de leur travail consiste à réceptionner et comptabiliser le produit des aumônes (legs compris) et des quêtes. Ce sont les procureurs que l'on voit manipuler les espèces sonnantes et trébuchantes, tandis que la répartition entre frères ou entre couvents des stocks de vivres, des vêtements, du mobilier et des livres revient aux *officiales* de l'ordre, du gardien au provincial.

Dans l'esprit des responsables de la province salvatorienne, l'activité des intendants laïques n'a pas seulement pour vocation d'éloigner les frères de l'« argent corrupteur ». Elle soulage les frères des tracas matériels, leur laissant ainsi davantage de temps pour s'adonner à la méditation et célébrer l'office divin (comme l'écrit le roi Sigismond en 1428)[69], plus de temps aussi pour prier pour l'âme du patron et fondateur (ajoute Wladislas II en 1501).[70] Le recours aux procureurs a

---

[65] *Item singula loca habeant unum summum procuratorem et non plures, qui tamen poterit alium, vel alios substituere si necesse sit, quod autem eleemosyna pecuniaria teneatur in sacristia nunc reliquitur pro futuro capitulo, quia non licet simpliciter.* I. Batthyány (éd.), Leges ecclesiasticae regni Hungariae (cf. n. 14), vol. 3, p. 653.

[66] La confusion est d'autant plus aisée que l'intendant laïque d'un couvent peut lui aussi défendre les intérêts de celui-ci devant des personnes ou tribunaux civils, sous le même nom de *procurator*. M.–M. de Cevins, Les franciscains observants hongrois (cf. n. 1), p. 220–221.

[67] Ibid., p. 219. On trouve ainsi dans une charte royale de 1501 copiée dans le formulaire des années 1510–1525 l'énumération: *in sindicum, actorem, iconomum sive procuratorem, quem communi vocabulo confratrem vocant...* OSzK, Cod. Lat. n° 432, fol. 136v; édition: Ibid., n° 42 p. 550.

[68] Ibid., p. 112.

[69] *... Volentes religiosos viros guardianos ceterosque fratres ipsius ordinis minorum, qui sunt in claustris de Chery, de Sebes, de Hatsak et Orsava, et qui etiam pro tempore erunt, ab omni prorsus procuratione et opera servili ipsorum claustrorum esse semotos et rellegatos, ut eo liberius eoque devotius et sedulius contemplationi dediti intra divina officia vacare possint et debeant, quo maioris commoditatis suavitute pacisque et tranquilitatis dulcedine senserint se munitos,...* E. Fermendžin (éd.), Acta Bosnae potissimum ecclesiastica (cf. n. 59), p. 128.

[70] *... ut igitur in dicto novo nostro claustro officia divini honoris per fratres inibi commorantes liberius et devotius [...] peragantur, et iidem pro nostra ac nostrorum salute vitaque liberius orare valeant.* OSzK, Cod. Lat.

également une dimension morale et spirituelle dans la mesure où elle facilite le renoncement des frères à toute forme d'appropriation. Le chapitre de 1515 précise que les procureurs doivent placer les liquidités ainsi que les objets précieux à distance des profès, afin d'éviter que ceux-ci ne s'en considèrent les possesseurs.[71] En préservant les religieux des tentations, les procureurs deviennent en quelque sorte les remparts de la pauvreté vécue.

Nul doute que les *procuratores* ont contribué à éloigner le triple spectre des difficultés de subsistance, du délabrement des bâtiments, du gaspillage des revenus par incompétence ou malhonnêteté des frères. On ne saurait oublier toutefois qu'ils ne prennent aucune initiative. Que ce soit dans la répartition des « recettes » ou la ventilation des dépenses, les procureurs ne font qu'appliquer les décisions du gardien, parfois du custode. Les textes normatifs insistent fortement sur l'obligation pour le procureur de leur obéir, sous peine de destitution ou de transfert dans un autre couvent, dès le règne de Louis le Grand (dans la confirmation accordée par Sigismond de Luxembourg à propos de quatre couvents en 1428)[72], en 1442 et 1462 (selon la confirmation établie en 1519 en faveur du couvent de Șumuleu Ciuc / Csíksomlyó[73]), puis dans les Constitutions de 1499.[74] Instrument de ce contrôle, les bilans et les rapports que les procureurs fournissent au gardien, au custode, au visiteur[75], de même qu'au patron. Ce que l'on attend avant tout d'un procureur, c'est qu'il mette à la disposition des frères les

---

432, fol. 136; édition: M.–M. DE CEVINS, Les franciscains observants hongrois (cf. n. 1), n° 42, p. 549.

[71] *Et caveant fratres, ne dum ab exteriori proprietate, sed etiam ab interiori, et intrinseca rerum preciosarum quarumcunque proprietaria detentione. Ita quod monstrantie turribula ac alia utensilia sumptuosa distrahantur per procuratores et de cupreis habeantur et subveniatur exinde locorum necessitatibus.* I. BATTHYÁNY (éd.), Leges ecclesiasticae regni Hungariae (cf. n. 14), vol. 3, p. 667.

[72] *...ut iidem fratres minores ipsos homines eligendi et conservandi ac dum placuerit ab officio eorum removendi et deponendi ac alios loco eorum constituendi et proficiendi plenam et commodam potestatis habeant facultatem. Ita videlicet, ut tales homines per ipsos fratres depositi, et a servitio seu eorum officium remoti, de collectis et aliis solutionibus instar caeterorum hospitum earumdem civitatem modo pristino respondere teneantur.* E. FERMENDŽIN (éd.), Acta Bosnae potissimum ecclesiastica (cf. n. 59), p. 128.

[73] *ea tamen condicione, ut iidem confratres ipsorumque successores universi modo consuetudo ad predictum claustrum inservire, iussaque fratrum exequi teneantur, si qui contumaces obedire nollent, alii loco ipsorum assignentur.* K. SZABÓ (éd.), Székely oklevéltár (cf. n. 55), vol. 1, pp. 341–342.

[74] *Quemadmodum aliarum ecclesiarum administratores sive procuratores, quam exhortari possunt et inducere etiam debeant custodes et guardiani quod in re sibi commissa fideliter se habeant. Quem si ex certa cognitione, non ex opinione, que sepe fallit ad id inutilem compererint, valeant prelati ex fratrum discretorum consilio ab huiusmodi cura absolvere, et alium loco illius magis idoneum nominare.* I. BATTHYÁNY (éd.), Leges ecclesiasticae regni Hungariae (cf. n. 14), vol. 3, p. 624.

[75] Les procureurs des couvents hongrois ont été néanmoins dispensés par le chapitre cismontain de 1504 de présenter un bilan périodique. M.–M. DE CEVINS, Les franciscains observants hongrois (cf. n. 1), p. 220.

biens reçus pour répondre sans délai à leurs besoins.[76] La poignée de documents qui montre ces agents à l'œuvre les présente dans ce rôle. Ainsi, à Voćin / Atyina, le gardien (Valentin de Kemlék) déclare par écrit au patron du couvent (Balthazar de Batthyán) en 1510 que le « confrère Luc » (*Lucas confrater noster*) lui a remis l'offrande donnée au couvent par un évêque (non nommé) pour la célébration de messes dans le couvent pour le salut de l'âme du donateur.[77]

Principe grégorien et indépendance régulière obligent, le recrutement du procureur émane de la volonté des frères. Dans les couvents fondés par Louis Ier dont Sigismond de Luxembourg a confirmé les privilèges en 1428, ce sont les frères de chaque communauté qui élisent leur procureur, sans consultation du roi.[78] Même désignation par élection au couvent de Șumuleu Ciuc / Csiksomlyó, dont les privilèges remontent (selon la confirmation de 1519) à 1442.[79] Au fil du temps, le *patronus* se trouve néanmoins investi de la tâche de trouver des candidats parmi ses dépendants. Ceux-ci doivent remplir au moins deux critères : résider ou avoir des biens dans la localité même[80] et avoir un minimum d'instruction (celui de Voćin / Atyina est qualifié de *clericus* en 1496[81]). On comprend ainsi que, dans les couvents des grandes villes, les procureurs sortent des rangs de bourgeoisie (à Buda en 1526, à Pest en 1522)[82], tandis qu'ailleurs, c'est-à-dire dans la plupart des couvents de Hongrie, ils sont généralement issus de la paysannerie (à Voćin / Atyina en 1496[83], comme à Suseni / Felfalu en 1544[84]).

Une fois élus, les procureurs sont rétribués par un moyen indirect : l'exonération des taxes seigneuriales ou royales. Elle apparaît dès la fin du XIVe siècle,

---

[76] Le chapitre provincial de 1544 le précise à propos du procureur du couvent de Suseni/Felfalu: *qui ex apostolico indultu oblata et legata fratribus habet [sic] dispensare ad eorum usum*. V. BUNYITAY / R. RAPAICS / J. KARÁCSONYI (éd.), Monumenta ecclesiastica (cf. n. 15), vol. 2, p. 503.

[77] *Is Lucas confrater noster, presentium scilicet ostensor fideliter nobis administravit elemosinam reverendissimi domini episcopi*. MNL DL 104224; B. KERTÉSZ (éd.), A magyarországi obszerváns ferencesek eredetiben fennmaradt iratai 1448–1526 (cf. n. 56), p. 124–125 n° 49.

[78] E. FERMENDŽIN (éd.), Acta Bosnae potissimum ecclesiastica (cf. n. 59), p. 128.

[79] *... ut nemo omnino hominum eosdem vitricos sew confratres ecclesie predicte ad aliquod officium sew servicium sine ipsorum fratrum voluntate eligere, nullusque ad deponendum juramentum citare, aut quoquomodo iudicare posset et valeret*. K. SZABÓ (éd.), Székely oklevéltár (cf. n. 55), vol. 1, p. 341.

[80] *... ut ipsi nunc et semper in praedictis civitatibus, videlicet in Chery unum et Sebes unum, in Hatsak unum, et in Orsova unum, similiter homines, fundos curiarum seu domos in eisdem habentes, sponte se offerentes eligere valeant atque possint*. E. FERMENDŽIN (éd.), Acta Bosnae potissimum ecclesiastica (cf. n. 59), p. 128.

[81] Cf. n. 83.

[82] M.–M. DE CEVINS, Les franciscains observants hongrois (cf. n. 1), pp. 219–220; J. KARÁCSONYI, Szent Ferencz rendjének története Magyarországon 1711–ig (cf. n. 39), vol. 2, p. 138.

[83] Voir *infra*.

[84] *Preterea idem* [patronus] *deputet fratribus loci illius* [Felfalw] *unum confratrem sive procuratorem ex suis jobagionibus, qui...* V. BUNYITAY / R. RAPAICS / J. KARÁCSONYI (éd.), Monumenta ecclesiastica (cf. n. 15), vol. 2, p. 503.

sous Louis le Grand, à propos des couvents fondés près de la frontière serbe.[85] Elle est encore octroyée par le roi de Hongrie Wladislas II en 1501, d'après un extrait de charte copié dans le formulaire interne des années 1510–1525.[86] Du milieu du XVe siècle aux années 1540, les frères s'acharnent à obtenir du roi ou du patron que leur procureur soit exempt de toute contribution royale (à Șumuleu Ciuc / Csiksomlyó en 1442, 1462 puis 1519, à Jászberény en 1480[87], au moment même du transfert de ce couvent à l'Observance), ou seigneuriale (condition posée à la fondation d'un nouveau couvent à Suseni / Felfalu en 1544[88]). Au couvent frontalier de Șumuleu Ciuc / Csiksomlyó, les procureurs sont de surcroît exempts de tout service armé.[89] Cette insistance des frères à demander l'obtention ou la confirmation de ces avantages fiscaux – qui se retrouve à la même période chez les Franciscains conventuels[90] – d'une part, et à impliquer le patron dans le processus pour qu'il désigne des « volontaires », d'autre part, trahit la difficulté à trouver des candidats. Il faut dire que l'emploi n'offre guère de perspective d'enrichissement personnel ou de promotion sociale. C'est même le contraire, si l'on en croit les exemples connus chez les Conventuels, où le procureur est responsable sur ses biens propres de la gestion du couvent.[91]

IV. Les patrons

On sait l'importance du patronage laïque sur le fonctionnement des établissements ecclésiastiques en Europe centrale. Si les patrons n'y exercent pas autant de prérogatives sur les couvents mendiants que sur les églises paroissiales ou les abbatiales bénédictines, les frères eux-mêmes admettent que le *patronus* contribue de manière décisive à la viabilité économique de chaque établissement. Par sa

---

85 E. FERMENDŽIN (éd.), Acta Bosnae potissimum ecclesiastica (cf. n. 59), p. 128.

86 OSzK, Cod. Lat. 432, fol. 136–137v; édition: M.-M. DE CEVINS, Les franciscains observants hongrois (cf. n. 1), n° 42 pp. 549–551.

87 J. KARÁCSONYI, Szent Ferencz rendjének története Magyarországon 1711–ig (cf. n. 39), vol. 2, p. 83.

88 V. BUNYITAY / R. RAPAICS / J. KARÁCSONYI (éd.), Monumenta ecclesiastica (cf. n. 15), vol. 2, p. 503.

89 *Insuper quod idem serenissimus Matthias Rex eosdem triginta duos confratres, futurosque eorum successores, ab omni expedicione bellica tam generali quam particulari, ingressioneque lustracionum, domos etiam eorum ab omni censuum, taxarum, decimarum, nonarum, capeciarum, serviciorum quorumlibet plebeorum et civilium exhibicione, contribucionum nostrarum tam ordinariarum quam extraordinariarum solucione exemptos et immunes semper esse voluerit, concesserit et iusserit.* K. SZABÓ (éd.), Székely oklevéltár (cf. n. 55), vol. 1, p. 341 n°242; MNL DL 29090.

90 J. KARÁCSONYI, Szent Ferencz rendjének története Magyarországon 1711–ig (cf. n. 39), vol. 1, p. 227; E. KÓSA, Antiquarii provinciae sanctae Mariae in Hungaria ordinis Minorum a.p.n. Francisci strictioris observantiae collectanea 1206–1774, inédit (1774), pp. 172–174 (1521).

91 M.-M. DE CEVINS, Les frères mendiants et l'économie en Hongrie médiévale (cf. n. 11), (exemple du couvent franciscain de Sopron).

position juridique comme par sa puissance sociale, le patron a la charge de protéger l'établissement contre ses prévaricateurs ou ennemis. Sa qualité de fondateur ou d'héritier du fondateur en fait également le responsable de l'entretien des bâtiments et, plus largement, de la viabilité matérielle des nouveaux couvents. Après 1500, le patron reste un pilier du fonctionnement matériel des couvents mendiants hongrois, à en juger par la multiplication des mentions relatives aux *patroni* dans les actes capitulaires de la première moitié du XVIe siècle.[92]

Les *patroni* trouvent de nombreux avantages à ce système. Leurs armoiries se déploient dans les églises des couvents (murs, tableaux d'autel, vitraux, vaisselle liturgique). Fonder un couvent sur une terre fraîchement reçue du roi permet à un noble ou à un aristocrate mal implanté d'y consolider l'ancrage géographique et politique de son lignage. Certains patrons utilisent « leurs » couvents comme lieu de conservation de biens meubles ou d'archives. Le testament d'Étienne Csupor, neveu du fondateur et probablement patron du couvent de Moslavina, qui demande le 24 décembre 1492 à être inhumé devant le maître-autel de l'église franciscaine et lègue des sommes importantes à l'établissement (plus de 600 florins), révèle qu'il y stockait des espèces (240 florins) ainsi que des documents seigneuriaux.[93] Les fondateurs-patrons obtiennent par ailleurs des contreparties spirituelles : être associé aux prières de recommandation dont bénéficient les bienfaiteurs du couvent, éventuellement la sépulture sur place. À partir des années 1500 (au plus tard), le patron (ou son épouse) recrute son confesseur parmi les frères du couvent dont il assure la protection. Le chapitre provincial pourvoit à cet « emploi » de manière officielle à partir du milieu des années 1530 : les registres provinciaux mentionnent expressément la fonction de confesseur du patron à propos des couvents de Buda et de Vinogradov (en 1535, 1542, 1548, 1552).[94] Le même phénomène de « privatisation » s'observe un peu plus tard à propos de la charge de prédicateur : un prédicateur est affecté par le chapitre au service du patron du couvent de Vinogradov, puis à celui de son épouse, en 1550 et 1552.[95]

L'intervention des patrons a-t-elle été positive pour l'Observance franciscaine hongroise ? A-t-elle conduit les frères à mieux respecter l'exigence de pauvreté tout en les mettant à l'abri du besoin ? Impossible de généraliser tant les indices

---

[92] V. Bunyitay / R. Rapaics / J. Karácsonyi (éd.), Monumenta ecclesiastica (cf. n. 15), vol. 2, *passim*.

[93] A. Theiner (éd.), Vetera monumenta historica Hungariam sacram illustrantia, maximam partem nondum edita ex tabulariis Vaticanis deprompta collecta ac serie chronologica disposita, 2 vols., Rome 1859–1860, vol. 2, p. 360 n° 542.

[94] J. Karácsonyi, Szent Ferencz rendjének története Magyarországon 1711-ig (cf. n. 39), vol. 2, p. 22 et 185; V. Bunyitay / R. Rapaics / J. Karácsonyi (éd.), Monumenta ecclesiastica (cf. n. 15), vol. 2, p. 496, 510, 517.

[95] Ibid., vol. 2, p. 514 et 517.

et les situations qu'ils décrivent diffèrent d'un couvent à l'autre. On peut néanmoins dégager quelques tendances. Le patron joue manifestement un rôle décisif dans la phase de « lancement » d'un couvent. C'est souvent lui qui obtient du pape l'autorisation de fondation, en amont, ou la demande de transfert à l'Observance (à Sárospatak[96]). Il supervise et rend possible la construction ou la réfection des bâtiments en fournissant matériaux et main d'œuvre. Sans son aide, le couvent est menacé de fermeture, comme à Zalatárnok en 1504[97] ou à Körmend en 1519–1521.[98] Il équipe l'église en objets liturgiques. Il fournit les réserves initiales de vivres pour assurer aux religieux leur subsistance alimentaire pendant les premiers mois de leur installation. Il leur donne du bétail en période de pénurie, comme à Suseni en 1544.[99] C'est encore le patron qui s'occupe de solliciter du pape ou de l'évêque des bulles d'indulgences pour stimuler la fréquentation de l'église conventuelle et augmenter du même coup le produit des aumônes.[100] Enfin, on l'a vu, le patron s'implique dans le recrutement du procureur.

Une fois cette étape franchie, le patron s'efface. Plusieurs *patroni* continuent d'œuvrer au développement du couvent fondé par leurs ancêtres : Laurent d'Újlak, fils du fondateur, fait agrandir le couvent de Hlohovec / Galgóc vers 1492[101] ; Éméric Czibak, évêque d'Oradea et nouveau seigneur de la citadelle de Gyula, obtient en 1531 du chapitre provincial la promotion du couvent de Gyula en *conventus* et y fait installer un orgue[102] ; d'autres proposent de tenir à leur frais le chapitre vicarial ou provincial dans « leur » couvent pour en accroître le rayonnement. Mais le patron n'intervient jamais dans les choix gestionnaires. Seuls les

---

[96] J. KARÁCSONYI, Szent Ferencz rendjének története Magyarországon 1711–ig (cf. n. 39), vol. 2, pp. 145–146.

[97] Le patron du couvent de Zalatárnok, Jean Botka de Széplak, n'ayant pas apporté aux frères les fonds nécessaires à l'achèvement du couvent, le vicaire demande au pape Jules II l'autorisation de fermer l'établissement. Ibid., vol. 2, p. 195. Peut–être cette démarche a–t–elle fait réagir le patron car le couvent semble fonctionner jusqu'en 1537.

[98] Parce que l'archevêque Thomas Bakócz n'a manifestement pas effectué les travaux d'aménagement nécessaires au transfert de ce couvent d'Ermites de saint Augustin aux Franciscains observants décidé en 1517, il périclite très rapidement. G. ERDÉLYI, A Cloister on Trial (cf. n. 10), pp. 55–56.

[99] V. BUNYTAY / R. RAPAICS / J. KARÁCSONYI (éd.), Monumenta ecclesiastica (cf. n. 15), vol. 2, pp. 503–504.

[100] Nombreux exemples, qui ont fait l'objet d'une communication présentée à l'Université de Lille le 22 juin 2018, sous presse.

[101] J. KARÁCSONYI, Szent Ferencz rendjének története Magyarországon 1711–ig (cf. n. 39), vol. 2, p. 53.

[102] V. BUNYITAY / R. RAPAICS / J. KARÁCSONYI (éd.), Monumenta ecclesiastica (cf. n. 15), vol. 2, p. 469.

objets liturgiques précieux suscitent parfois des réclamations, le *patronus* conservant un droit de regard sur ceux-ci.[103]

Dans l'ensemble, la viabilité matérielle des couvents hongrois ne repose pas en priorité sur le *patronus*. Même soutenue par un protecteur influent, une communauté ne saurait subsister sans les dons des populations alentour. En 1496, Brice d'Egervár, évêque de Knin et neveu du fondateur, demande au roi de Hongrie Wladislas II d'accorder des exemptions fiscales à tous ceux qui viendraient s'installer sur les lopins en friche et inhabités situés à proximité du couvent franciscain d'Egervár.[104] Plus tard, au temps de la pénurie généralisée des années 1530–1540, ce n'est pas au *patronus* que les frères réclament une aide d'urgence, mais à leurs supérieurs : les gardiens alertent les custodes, les custodes le ministre ou le chapitre provincial, d'après les modèles de lettres transcrits dans le formulaire des années 1530.[105] La seule chose qu'ils demandent au patron est de conserver en lieu sûr les objets liturgiques précieux. De nombreux documents rapportent la livraison de ces pièces au patron ou à son représentant, au moment où les progrès du protestantisme et l'avance ottomane contraignent la plupart des établissements hongrois à fermer leurs portes.[106]

Le traitement des objets liturgiques illustre bien la fonction du *patronus* : il doit préserver les biens du couvent de l'appétit d'éventuels spoliateurs, à commencer par lui-même, mais aussi contre les frères qui voudraient les aliéner. Si un patron n'a pas le droit de retirer aux frères les objets précieux offerts au couvent par ses prédécesseurs, de leur côté, les frères ne sont pas autorisés à mettre en vente ces objets pour subvenir à leurs besoins ou à ceux d'un autre couvent de la province. En 1517, François Bodó, descendant des fondateurs du couvent Saint-Grégoire de Györgyi, se plaint au pape de ce que les frères ont vendu la vaisselle liturgique dorée et incrustée de pierreries du couvent pour financer la réparation d'un autre établissement de la province. À nouveau saisi en 1519, le pape ordonne aux frères de Györgyi de conserver pour leur usage les objets liturgiques afin d'éviter toute réclamation semblable.[107] De la même façon, lorsque les dirigeants de la province décident de fermer un couvent pour raisons de sécurité, ils remettent les bâtiments conventuels (église et cloître) au patron.[108] On ne s'étonnera pas que, dans

---

[103] Voir *infra*.

[104] MNL DL 20518.

[105] M.-M. DE CEVINS, Les franciscains observants hongrois (cf. n. 1), pp. 428–429, à partir de OSzK Oct. Lat. 775.

[106] Nombreux exemples dans J. KARÁCSONYI, Szent Ferencz rendjének története Magyarországon 1711-ig (cf. n. 39), vol. 2, *passim*.

[107] Ibid., vol. 2, p. 70.

[108] Comme à Perecske, pour cause d'avance ottomane, sur décision du chapitre provincial réuni en 1533: *Item locus de Perechke, qui est in faucibus Turcarum, ubi periculosum est fratribus propter illos demorari, loci patrono resignetur et fratres de eo extrahantur*. V. BUNYITAY / R. RAPAICS / J. KARÁCSONYI (éd.), Monumenta ecclesiastica (cf. n. 15), vol. 2, p. 474.

un tel système, la conversion de nombreux *patroni* au protestantisme dans les années 1530 à 1550 ait eu des effets aussi désastreux sur les couvents : les bâtiments tombent en ruines faute d'entretien ; parfois, le patron encourage ses hommes à y mettre le feu pour chasser les frères, décide de les démolir ou les affecte à un autre usage.[109]

Au total, la législation de la province salvatorienne et les agents de contrôle qui étaient chargés de l'appliquer ont permis aux Franciscains observants hongrois de relever les trois défis de la subsistance des frères, du respect de la pauvreté absolue et de l'adhésion des fidèles. Les procureurs, bien que dépourvus d'autonomie, ont contribué à ce succès, de même que les patrons. Ils corroborent le principe de biens utilisés mais non possédés par les frères (notamment dans le cas des objets liturgiques de grande valeur) ; et les patrons ont aidé au recrutement des procureurs ainsi qu'à la construction et à l'entretien des bâtiments, principal poste de dépenses dans le budget des communautés. Conjugués, ces quatre outils expliquent que les franciscains observants aient pu s'épanouir en Hongrie sans perdre leur popularité.

Le grand absent, ce sont les fidèles. Alors qu'à Körmend, on les voit dénoncer à l'archevêque d'Esztergom (Thomas Bakócz), membre du lignage des patrons et seigneurs du lieu, les abus commis par les frères du couvent d'Ermites de saint Augustin vers 1510[110], ils ne paraissent pas s'être exprimés sur le fonctionnement matériel des couvents franciscains observants. Pourquoi ? À cause du comportement exemplaire des frères, répond l'historiographie traditionnelle, volontiers laudative. La discrétion des habitants peut aussi d'expliquer par le fait que la plupart des couvents hongrois ont pour fondateur un membre de la noblesse, de l'aristocratie ou de la famille royale, plutôt qu'une communauté d'habitants. Difficile par conséquent pour les fidèles de s'ériger en agents de contrôle de ces couvents. Troisième explication, liée à la précédente : le *patronus* remplissait déjà ce rôle. C'est sans doute là que réside la principale singularité hongroise par rapport à ce que l'on observe en France, en Italie ou en Angleterre à la même période. Loin de décliner, le rôle du patron s'accroît au début du XVIe siècle, dans un contexte de diminution des aumônes qui se renforce après 1530. L'histoire du couvent de Šarengrad / Atya, fondé vers 1405 par le ban de Mačva / Macsó Jean de Marót, qui avait reçu depuis peu la bourgade et ses environs du roi Sigismond de Luxembourg, en fournit un bon exemple. C'est Jean de Marót qui sollicite (avec succès) du pape Jean XXIII des indulgences en 1415, en effectuant le déplacement jusqu'à Constance. À l'extinction du lignage des Marót en 1476, les Geréb de Vingárt leur succèdent comme *patroni* du couvent et contribuent à leur tour au rayonnement de l'établissement. Ce sont eux qui auraient insisté pour

---

[109] J. KARÁCSONYI, Szent Ferencz rendjének története Magyarországon 1711-ig (cf. n. 39), vol. 2, *passim*.

[110] Voir note 10.

qu'il accueille les chapitres vicariaux de Hongrie de 1495, 1499 (celui qui accouche des célèbres « Constitutions » provinciales) et 1511. Plusieurs membres de ce lignage choisissent de se faire ensevelir sur place.[111] En dernière analyse, le rôle central du patron dans le fonctionnement matériel des couvents franciscains observants hongrois reflète une réalité propre à la Hongrie (et dans une moindre mesure à la Pologne) : l'implantation principalement rurale (ou semi-rurale) des couvents franciscains observants. Elle est synonyme de relations privilégiées avec la noblesse (aristocratie incluse), bien plus engagée dans la promotion de l'Observance franciscaine que la bourgeoisie. Illustrant une situation intermédiaire entre celle des couvents de la péninsule Ibérique et celle des grandes villes de l'Empire germanique (jusqu'en Silésie), l'exemple de la Hongrie confirme que le fonctionnement économique des couvents franciscains observants s'est adapté à leur environnement.

---

[111] Voir http://margec.univ–bpclermont.fr/fr/content/couvent–franciscain–obs–st–esprit–de–sarengrad–atya.

Index

Ablauff, Eberhard 176 n. 28; 30, 31, 32, 177 n. 35; 36, 38, 39; 178 n. 43; 179 n. 44; 45, 46

Aegean / Ägäis 124

d'Agen, Guillaume, patriarch of Jerusalem 136

Aigueblanche, Peter of, bishop of Hereford (1240–1268) 77, 78

Aimont 127

Al-Andalus 15, 25

Alba Iulia .... 226 n. 14

Albești / Fehéregyháza 234

Albrecht of Brandenburg, cardinal and archbishop of Mainz 172, 180

Albrecht, duke of Saxony 159

Albric de Vere .... 53 n. 67

Alexander II., pope (1161–1173) 54

Alexander IV., pope (1254–1261) 77

Alexandria 134

Alfonso I. 'the Battler' king of Aragón and Navarra (1104–1134) 26

Alfonso III., king of Aragón (1285–1291) 140

Alfonso III., king of León (866–910) .... 15, 17 n. 13

Alfonso VI., king of León (1067–1109) 17, 18, 19, 25, 27, 31

Alfonso VII., king of León and Castile (1126–1157) 17, 20, 26

Alfonso VIII., king of Castile (1158–1214) 26

Alfonso of Valladolid, almoner of Sahagún (1316–1335) 115, 116 n. 66

Alfonso, Juan, lawyer 118

Allix, Edgard 8

Almanza, Juan de, cellarer of Sahagún (1358) .... 115 n. 59

Almanzor .... see al-Manṣūr

Almoravids 26

Alps 5, 169

Alsace-Burgundy 143

Althaus-Kulm 128

Álvarez, Diego, nephew of abbot Diego of Sahagún 120

Álvarez, Domingo .... 120 n. 98

Álvarez, Juan, nephew of abbot Diego of Sahagún 120

Alvari, Didacus 33

Alvinc, Paulines 208, 220

Amesbury, Michael of 91

Amposta 130

Anklam, Austin Friars .... 203 n. 56

Anselm, archbishop of Canterbury (1093–1109) 55

Anthony, friar, king's preacher 187

Anthony I., count Grassalkovich ..... 204 n. 62

Antonius 1

Antwerp 131

Apolinarius 179

Aquitaine 145

Aracs, Franciscan friary 196, 220

Aragón 12, 125, 129, 130, 140

Arbas, abbot of 118

Arias, cellarer of Sahagún .... 30 n. 56

Asensio, Domingo, chamberlain of Sahagún (1304–1313) ..115 nn. 58; 62, 116 n. 66

Assassins 134

Assisi 1, 174

Athanasius 1

d'Aubussons, Pierre 141

Aunderstat, William de, brother of the Teutonic Knights .... 99 n. 345

Austria / Österreich 143, 167, 169, 184, 185, 186, 200, 201

Auvergne 201

Avignon 56

Baibars, sultan (1260–1277) 136

Bakóc / Bakócz, Thomas, cardinal 216, 241 n. 98; 243

Balga 163

Baltikum 124, 142

Baráti 203

BARBER, Malcolm 124

Barcelona 124, 131, 138, 140

Barking, abbess of 62

Bartenstein 164

Bártfa, Austin priory 192, 209, 220

Bártfa, Isaiah of 198

Bartholomew, prior general of the Austin Friars 200

Bath, Robert of 90

Bath and Wells, bishop of 71, 90

Battle, abbot of 81

Baugy 127

Bechyně 170, 174

Bechyně, friary of the Assumption of the Virgin Mary 177

Belgium 8

Belgrade 174

BELL, Adrian 11

Benchovich, Benedict 173, 174

Benedict XII., pope (1334–1342) ...101, 103, 113, 122

Benedict, priest 203

Bereford, Sir William 89

Bereg, count of 213

Beregszász 220

Beregszász, Franciscan friary 196

Berganza, Francisco de, chronicler of Cardeña 102

Berkshire 81

Bernardus, monk of Cluny 17, 18, 19

Besnyő, Capuchin friary .... 204 n. 62

Bistritz, Dominican friary 195, 206, 211, 220

Blanche of Castile (1188–1252) 136

Blois, Henry of, bishop of Winchester (1129–1171) 53

Bodó, Francis 242

Bodrum 146

Bohemia / Böhmen 143, 167, 168, 169, 170, 171, 172, 173, 174, 175, 176, 177, 178, 179, 180, 184, 185, 186

Bohun, Eleanor de, nun 94

Bolevec 169

BOLTON, Jim 96

Boniface VIII., pope (1294–1303) 55, 87

Bordys, Nicholas, of Bord, Dominican friar 204

Borek 169

Boros, Benedict, of Csigle .... 225 n. 8

Bosak / Bosatz 169

Bosnia / Bosnie 223, 234

Botka, John, of Széplak 241

BOUCHARD, Constance 11
Bovadilla, Juan de, cellarer of Sahagún (1330–1342) 115
Bozen 143
Brakelond, Jocelin of 89
Bramfield, Edmund, monk of Bury St. Edmunds 56
Brandenburg .... 154 n. 21; 159, 161, 163
Brandenburg, elector of 144
Braşov / Brassó, Franciscan Observants .... 235 n. 60
Brathean 157
BREAY, Claire 45
Brno 173, 175, 176, 179
Brno, Franciscan friary 170
Brok, Keno tom 126
Brokhampton, John of, abbot of Evesham (1282–1316) 85
BROOKS, Chris 11
Bruges 139
Buckfast, abbot of 62
Buda 186, 187, 188, 204, 215, 216, 223, 233, 240
Buda, Austin Friars 187
Buda, Capuchin friary .... 204 n. 62
Buda, Carmelite priory 187, 191, 196, 205
Buda, Dominican priory 203
Buda, Franciscan friary 187, 190, 203
Buda, Franciscan Observants 187
Buda, Kammerhof 215
Buda goldsmiths 205
Budapest 188, 215
Burgundy 6, 11, 143, 201
Burnell, Robert, bishop of Bath and Wells (1275–1292), royal chancellor .... 79 n. 226

BURTON, Janet 11
Burton, abbot of 62, 78
Burton, annalist of .... 58, 61 n. 121; 77
Bury St. Edmunds, town 56
Bury St. Edmunds, royal mint 62
Bury St. Edmunds, abbot of . 62, 73, 74, 80
Bury St. Edmunds, abbot Hugh of 92
Bury St. Edmunds, abbot Samson 80, 93
Bury St. Edmunds, prior of 65
Burzenland 202
Busse, Franz, Rentmeister of the Teutonic Knights 162, 163, 164, 165
Bütow 126, 148, 157
Buzlai, Moses 198

Cambridge .... 8, 45 n. 29
Cambridgeshire 42
Camino de Santiago 15
Capistrano, John of 167, 171, 230
Cardeña, chronicler of 102
Carinthia, Michael of, OFM, chronicler. 176 nn. 28, 30, 31, 32; 177, 178 n. 40; 179 nn. 44, 45, 46, 47
Carlisle 93
Carolingians .... 16, 18, 19 n. 23; 37
Caspe 130
Castile 12, 15, 16, 67, 101, 102, 103, 121
Caux, John of, abbot of Peterborough, Treasurer (1260–1263) 78
DE CEVINS, Marie-Madeleine 13
Champagne 129, 130
Chancery (England) 48, 76
Charles I., king of Sicily (1266–1285) 141

Charles II., king of Naples (1286–1309).................................141
Charles V., emperor (1520–1558)....216 n. 89
Chery, Franciscan Observants 235 n. 69; 237 n. 80
CHEW, Helena 51
Chomutov...179
Christburg...158
Chrzyen, Nicholas 170
Cilli, Margareta of 178
Cîteaux, abbot of ....135 n. 58
Cluj / Kolozsvár, Franciscan friary.223 n. 5; 224 nn.6, 7, 8
Cluny................................. 17, 18, 19, 32
Cluny, abbot of 136
Colditz family 177
Cologne 32
Colowrat family.....................................177
Constance / Konstanz........................243
COULTON, George Gordon...................8
Cranach, Lukas........................... 171, 174
Croatia .... 185, 215 n. 85
Csáki, Benedict......................................194
Csupor, Étienne....................................240
Cudar family 215
Cuevas, Alfonso....................................121
Curia, papal............ 59, 60, 80, 84, 90, 91
Cyprus / Zypern................ 131, 145, 146
Czech Lands 167, 173, 180
Czibak, Émeric, bishop of Oradea..241
Czomer, Melchior................................177

Dalmatia ....215 n. 85
Damerkow 126
Danzig (Danczk) / Gdansk 155, 156

Daróci, Nicholas. of Daróc...............195
Dartmouth 131
DELISLE, Leopold.....................................7
Dés, Austin Friars......................209, 220
Devon 131
Dézs, Blaise de OFM 228
Diakovar, Paulines...............................205
Diaz, Alfonso 120
Didacus, abbot of Sahagún (c. 1090–1110).........................27, 29, 32, 33, 34
Diego II., abbot of Sahagún (1329–1357)............................113 n. 49; 114
Dirschau 148, 156, 157
Domínguez, Juan, almoner of Sahagún (1312–1314)........................115 n. 60
Dominicus II., abbot of Sahagún 30, 105
Dominicus III., abbot of Sahagún.....30
Dominicus, chamberlain............33 n. 77
DONKIN, Robert......................................11
Dordrecht...131
Dorset ....69 n. 172; 72
DOUGLAS, David 50
Douzens 129
DRYBURGH, Paul 11
DUBY, Georges 32
DUGDALE, William................................47
Dungun, Ralph..........................86 n. 273

Eastry, Henry of, prior of Christ Church Canterbury (1285–1331) 39, 92, 93
Ebros..131
Edmund, son of king Henry III of England......................................76, 77
Edward the Confessor, king of England (1042–1066)..............................52

Edward I., king of England (1272–1307).. 55, 58, 66, 67, 68, 74, 76, 80, 83, 84, 86, 88, 89, 91, 94

Edward II., king of England (1307–1327)...........61, 76 n. 205; 79, 85, 94

Edward III., king of England (1327–1377).....................58, 61, 95

Egedy .... 201, 202, 203 n. 59

Eger, river 172

Egervár, Franciscan Observant friary.................................. 225 n. 6; 242

Egervár, Brice, bishop of Knin 242

Egypt..1, 3

Eisenhofen, Ulrich von, Tressler of the Teutonic Knights 149

Elbing........................128, 129, 158, 161

Eleanor of Castile, queen of England (1274–1290).....................................67

Elizabeth, queen of Hungary (1305–1380) 193, 196

Elizabeth, princess, daughter of king Edward I. of England....................87

ELM, Kaspar 4, 12

Ely, Isle of...52

Emmanuel College, Cambridge 8

Engelsburg.................................154 n. 21

England .... 6, 8, 9, 11, 12, 40, 41, 44, 49 n. 49; 50, 51, 52, 53, 55, 77, 84, 87, 95, 130, 131, 132, 142, 145, 146

Eperjes 192, 194, 209, 210, 211, 213, 220

Eperjes, Carmelites 192, 197

Epi, Johann, Dominican Provincial 202

ERDÉLYI, Gabriella ....226 n. 10

Erfurt, Austin Friars 201

Erlichshausen, Konrad of, Hochmeister of the Teutonic Knights... 153 n. 17

Ermegíldiz, Gundisalvus 35

Ermland, bishopric.............................159

Erzgebirge 171, 174, 179

ESMEIN, Charles 7

Essex 127, 130

Esztergom 200, 229

Esztergom, archbishop of.................200

Eugenius IV., pope (1431–1447) 216 n. 88; 230 n. 35

Europe 4, 5, 6, 11, 13, 167, 168, 169, 172, 175, 180, 182, 183, 184, 185, 186, 203, 217, 239

Evesham, prior of.................................79

Evesham, Ranulph abbot of 81

Exchequer (England) ..9, 44, 48, 61, 62, 64, 65, 68, 69, 72, 74, 85, 86

Eye, Simon, abbot of Ramsey (1316–1343)...81

Fabri, Anton 195, 200, 204

Facundo, cellarer of Sahagún (1306–1317) ....115 n. 59

Facundus (Sant Facundo).. 15, 16 n. 10; 29 n. 56

Faricius, abbot of Abingdon (d. 1117) ....84 n. 253

Fayum 1

Fehéregyháza, church................ 188, 234

Ferdinand I., emperor (1556–1564)....................................... 172, 180

Fernández, Alfonso, almoner of Sahagún (1353) . 115 n. 60; 117, 120

Fernández, Domingo, chamberlain of Sahagún (1326–1329) 115 n. 58; 118

Fernández, Juan ....117, 120 n. 100

Fernández, Ruy, cleric..............116 n. 66

Fernández Cidiel, Gonzalo .. 120 n. 100

Ferrer, Jean, French merchant..........138
Filipec, Jan, bishop of Oradea / Nagyvárad..176
Fillach, Caritas, the widow of Gregor..194
Flanders...6
Florence...135, 138
Fluvià, Antoni...146
France..8, 12, 76, 84, 95, 127, 136, 146, 186 n. 9; 201, 243
Francis of Assisi (Francesco Bernardone)............................. see St. Francis
Frederick I., prince of Legnica and Brzeg...177
Frederick II., emperor (1220–1250).75, 76, 77, 84, 141
Frisia / Friesland..................................126
Futak..194, 220

Gaetani, Benedetto.....see Boniface VIII.
García de las Cuevas, Juan ... 121 n. 102
García, Nuño........................ 121 n. 102
García, Simón, confectioner..............119
GARCÍA GONZÁLEZ, Juan José........103
Gascony..79
Gaul..17
GÉNÉSTAL, Robert..............................7, 8
GENNEVOISE, Joseph...............................8
Genoa..7
Geoffrey Fitz Peter, justiciar...............59
George the Bearded, duke of Saxony...172, 180
George of Poděbrady, king of Bohemia (1458–1471)......... 169, 170, 177
Geréb family...243
German lands...... 11, 12, 200, 201, 203, 204, 244

Gersei Pető family................................217
Glastonbury, abbot of.................. 84, 91
Glastonbury, John of 90
Glatz..173
Glatz, Laurentius, of Starý Dvůr.....178, 179
Glatz, Ursula, of Starý Dvůr....179, 180
Głogów, friary of Sts. Peter and Paul and St. Bernardine.......................178
Gloucester..58
Gloucester, earl of (Gilbert de Clare, 1243–1295)...86
Godstow, abbess of..............................38
Gollub...154 n. 21
Gonzalo, cellarer (1318–1327) and chamberlain of Sahagún...27, 115 n. 58; 116 n. 66; 120 n. 100; 121
Goto, wife of Gonzalo Núñez .27 n. 46
Grajal... 20, 21
Grand-Selve...127
Gras, Richard le, abbot of Evesham, royal Chancellor (1240) 78
Graudenz...158
Gräzer, Christoph.............................212
Grebin.......................................148, 154 n. 21
Gregory VII., pope (1173–1185) 17, 18
Gregory IX., pope (1227–1241).........75
Gregory X., pope (1271–1276) 87
Gross, Valentinus 177
Grossglogau, Jakob of, Franciscan Bohemian provincial vicar 173
Großendorf...125
Grünberg, Lukas of, Franciscan provincial minister...............................173
Gutierri, Petrus......................................34
Gyöngyösi, Gregorius..183, 214, 216 n. 87

Györgyi, Franciscan Observant friary 214
Gyula, Franciscan Observants. 211, 241
Gyulafehérvár 202, 220

Haff 161, 163
Hainburg, Franciscan friary 201
Hampshire 38
HARRISON, Julian 45
HARVEY, Barbara 9
Hasištejnský, Jan, of Lobkowicz 178
Hassenstein castle 174
Hassensteiner, lords of Lobkowicz . 178
Hassensteiner, Bohuslaus Felix, of Lobkowicz 172
Hassensteiner, Jan, of Lobkowicz ... 179
Hassensteiner, Sidonia, of Lobkowicz 179
Hastings 50, 52
Hatsak, Franciscan Observants ... 236 n. 69; 238 n. 80
Hatvan, Capuchin friary .... 204 n. 62
HEALE, Martin 89
Helmstedt, Austin Friars .... 203 n. 56
Hemmingford .... 53 n. 67
Henry I., king of England (1100–1135) 39 n. 11; 43, 55, 60, 61, 64, 69
Henry II., king of England (1154–1189) ... 43, 57, 69, 70, 80, 83, 90, 98
Henry III., king of England (1216–1273) .. 43, 56, 57, 61, 62, 72, 73, 75, 76, 77, 78, 83, 84, 85, 89, 96, 97
Henry V., king of England (1413–1422) 61
Hermannstadt, Dominican friary 206, 220
Hétúr 198, 220

Hídvég 202
Hilary, bishop of Chichester (1147–1169) 57
Hladik, John 170
Hlohovec / Galgóc 241
Hlohovec, Peter of, Franciscan provincial vicar 169
Hollós 202
Holy Land 55
Honorius III., pope (1216–1227) ...... 75, 135 n. 58
Hopko, knight 173
Horažďovice 170
Horažďovice, friary of St. Angels 177
Hradec family 178
Hradec, princess Anna of 178
Huesca 125
Hungary 13, 181, 183, 184, 186, 187, 189, 191, 195, 197, 199, 200, 201, 203, 204, 206, 215, 216, 218, 244
Hungary, Aegidius of, OFM obs. 173
Hunyad, János 235
Hyde, abbot of .... 73, 78 n. 219
Hyde, John abbot of 80
Hyspanus, Quintinus, Dominican lay brother 206

Iberia 19
Innocent II., pope (1130–1143) .. 17, 18
Innocent III., pope (1198–1216) 91
Innocent IV., pope (1243–1254) 77
Iohanes, Alfonso, scribe 117
Iohannes, abbot of Sahagún (1182–1194) 21, 33
Iohannes, cellarer of Sahagún ... 30 n. 58
Isabella, queen of England (1308–1258) 79

Italy.....1, 7, 67, 74, 78, 85, 91, 127, 135, 139 n. 79; 140, 142, 155, 167, 168, 173, 197, 230, 243

Ivanić, Paulines 207

Jaffa 133
Jan II., prince of Opole and Brzeg..178
Jászberény, Observant Franciscan friary.............. 231 n. 39; 235 n. 60; 239
Jemnice 175
Jerusalem.... 32, 34, 123, 133 n. 46; 136, 174
Johann Friedrich, elector of Saxony 172, 180
John XXIII., pope (1410–1419).......243
John, king of England (1199–1216) .38, 61, 75, 76, 77, 84, 89, 97
John, the provincial of the Carmelites..213
John, Dominican of Kolozsvár........205
Julius II., pope (1503–1513) ...241 n. 97
Jungingen, Konrad von, Hochmeister of the Teutonic Knights..............154

Kadaň170, 171, 172, 175, 178, 179, 180
Kadaň castle................................179, 180
Kadaň, church of Virgin Mary 179
Kadaň, Franciscan friary of St. Michael................................ 170, 171, 174
Kadaň, Observant Friary of the Fourteen Holy Helpers 171, 174, 178, 180
Kadaň, George of, OFM obs. 173
Kampen...131
Kanizsai family....................................215
Kassa, Dominicans 209, 210, 220
Kemlék, Valentin de OFM obs........236

Kenderesi, Blaise..................................198
Kent 88
Keresztúr..202
KERTÉSZ, Balázs....230 n. 35; 226 n. 14
Ketzerdorf...169
Kézdi..202
KING, Edmund......................................92
Kinsberg, Eberhard von, Tressler of the Teutonic Knights....................159
Kissáros, Austin Friars..............203, 220
KŁOCZOWSKI, Jerzy 223
KNOWLES, David...........9, 40, 41, 42, 49
Koblenz 128, 131, 139, 143
Kőfaragó, George, citizen of Kolozsvár 193
Kölked 202
Kolozsvár 191, 192, 193, 196, 205, 206, 208, 211, 220, 224 n. 5
Komár, Dominican priory 203
Königsberg.......132, 151, 159, 160, 161, 162
Kont family..215
Körmend 201, 202, 203
Körmend, Austin friary .. 201, 202, 203, 209, 211, 226 n. 10; 241, 243
Kőröshegy / Kőrösszeg, Observant Franciscan friary 231
Kőrösszegi, Valentine, prior of the Komár Dominican priory...........203
Kos 146
Krabice, Sebastian, of Weitmühle....179
Krakow...170
Kremmen..125
Kronstadt 196, 220
Kronstadt, Dominican piory.............202
Krupka..177

Kulmerland 144, 157

Lábatlan 205, 207
La Forbie 145
Lagow 125
Lanfranc, archbishop of Canterbury (1070–1089) 50, 52
Langham, Simon, abbot of Westminster, royal Treasurer (1360–1363) 78
Laskó, Oswald de, vicar of the Observant Franciscans in Hungary 225, 230 n. 35
Laurensin, Claude, of Lyon 138
Lawrence, goldsmith of Kolozsvár 205
Legnica, friary of Holy Trinity 177
Leicester 130
Leipe .... 148 n. 120; 157
Lemberg 132
Leo X., pope (1513–1521) 201
León 15, 18, 19, 25, 26, 28, 29, 120, 121
Lerrersteig 173
Lichtenstein, Hans von, master of the mint of Thorn (Torun) 139
Litlyngton, Nicholas of, abbot of Westminster (1362–1386) 78
Livonia 173
Lobkowicz, family ... 171, 172, 174, 178, 179
Lombardy 135
London 55, 97
London, New Temple .... 86 n. 273
Lorraine 6
Louis I. of Anjou, king of Hungary (1342–1382) 214, 215, 234, 238
Louis II., king of Hungary (1516–1526) 186, 187, 235

Louis VII., king of France (1137–1180) 136
Louis IX., king of France (1226–1270) 237, 238
Lübeck 132
Ludmila, princess of Legnica and Brzeg 177
Lyon 138

Mačva / Macsó 243
Malmesbury, Robert of, abbot 80
Malta 131
Mameluken 124, 136
Manfred, king of Sicily (1258–1266) 77
Marchegg 200
Marienburg .... 128, 132, 144, 148, 150, 153 n. 20; 154, 155, 156
Marienburg near Schässburg 220
Marlborough, Thomas of 57, 59, 97
Maros 202
Marosvásárhely, Franciscan friary ... 205, 220
Marót, Jean de 242
Marseille 131, 132
Marseille, St. Viktor 7
Martin II., abbot of Sahagún (1317–1329) 114, 117, 120, 121
Martin IV., pope (1281–1285) 135 n. 58
Martin V., pope (1417–1431) 230
Martín, almoner of Sahagún (1340) . 115
Martín, chamberlain of Sahagún (1335–1336) .... 115, 116 n. 66
Martinez, Alfonso .... 120 n. 98
MARTÍNEZ LIÉBANA, Evelio 21
Martinis, Michele de, of Rhodes 138
Martinus, cellarer of Sahagún ... 30 n. 58

Mary, princess, daughter of king Edward I., nun at Amesbury 94

Masovia 155

Mathias Corvinus, king of Hungary (1458–1490) .... 188 n. 12; 235

Matilda, empress (1102–1167) .. 39 n. 11

Matilla 34

Matthew Paris 51

Mauger, bishop of Worcester (1199–1212) 57

Maximilian II., emperor (1564–1576) 172

Mayor, donor to Sahagún 34

Medgyes 191, 220

Mediterranean 5, 11, 84

Memel 148, 163

Meselanz 148

Michaelis, Petrus, chamberlain . 33 n. 77

Miedelsum 126

Mínguez, Pedro, gatekeeper 118

Mirow 125

Mohács 223

Montau 148

Montpellier 131

Mór .... 204 n. 62

Moravia 169, 173, 174, 175, 176

MORETA VELAYOS, Salustiano 103

Moritz, Paul 212

Morlyn 126

Moslavina, Observant Franciscans .. 240

Nagyszombat 190, 220

Narbonne 131

Nebílovy 170

Neidenburg 161

Neisse 173

Németi 211, 220

Nessau 157

Neumark 125, 126, 144, 159

Neumarkt, Eusebius of, Minister Provincial of the Bohemian province 179, 220

Nicholas IV., pope (1288–1292) 84

Nicholas V., pope (1447–1455) 137

Nicolas II., abbot of Sahagún (1301–1316) 114, 116, 119

Normandy / Normandie .. 8, 52, 54, 55, 127, 145

Norreys, Roger, abbot of Evesham (1190–1213) 55, 92, 97

Northwold, Hugh of, abbot of Bury St. Edmunds 65

Nösen, Dominican priory 195, 202, 220

Nosztre, prior of (today Márianosztra) 214

Núñez, Gonzalo, prior of Sahagún .. 27, 28

Nuremberg 173

Nyitra 190, 220

Nysa 175, 176

Óbuda 187, 221

Oder river 169

Odo of Bayeux 52, 53

Olomouc 174, 176

Olomouc, friary of St. Bernardine and the Virgin Mary 176

Olomouc, Basil of, OFM obs. 173

Opava 175

Orense, church of 121

Orsava, Franciscan Observants .... 236 n. 69

Orseln, Werner von, Hochmeister of the Teutonic Knights 147
Osterode 126
Oswald, bishop of Zagreb 193
Ottheinrich, count Palatine of the Rhine (1522–1559) 147
Ottobuono, cardinal 87
Ottomans 184, 192, 208, 217
Ow, Johann von .... 138 n. 72
Oxenedes, John de 58, 76, 77

PAGE, Frances Mary 49
Palencia, cathedral chapter 102, 120
Pandulf Verraccio, papal legate, bishop of Norwich (1215–1226) 55
Pápa .... 225 n. 8
Papau 157
Pápoc, Austin Friars 200, 211
Paris .... 131, 136, 137 n. 70; 145, 150
Pecham, John, archbishop of Canterbury (1279–1292) 39
Pécs, Carmelite priory 205, 206
Perecske (today part of Villány) ...... 195, 242 n. 108
Pérez, Alfonso, abbot's gatekeeper 111, 116 n. 66; 119
Pérez, Juan, almoner of Sahagún (1301–1309) 115
Pérez, Juan, brother of abbot Diego of Sahagún 120
Pérez, Juan, cleric 121
Pérez, Juan, scribe 119
Pérez, Ruy, cleric 117
Pest 187
Pest, Austin Friars 187
Pest, Dominican priory ... 192, 196, 198, 208, 211, 221

Pest, Franciscan friary 203
Pest, Franciscan Observant friary .... 235 n. 60; 238
Peter, Carmelite lay brother of Pécs 206
Peterborough, abbot of 65
Peterborough, chronicler of 75
Petri, Munius 32
Petri, Romanus, debtor to Sahagún (1096–1097) 32
Philip IV., king of France (1285–1314) 76
Philip VI , king of France (1328–1350) 95
Piasca, prior of .... 114 n. 54; 116 n. 71
Pilsen, Franciscan friary of the Virgin Mary 169, 170
Pilsum, Enno von 126
Pius II., pope (1458–1464) 170
PLATELLE, Henri 8
Plauen, Henry of, Hochmeister of the Teutonic Knights 143
Plumpton 131
Poitou 73
Poland 185, 186, 187, 188
Poland-Lithuania 167
Pommerellen 144
Portsmouth 73
Portugal 142
Porva, Paulines .... 225 n. 8
POWER, Eileen 49
Prague 167, 169, 170, 173
Prague, cathedral church 169
Prague, Dominicans 171
Prague, Franciscan friary of St. Ambrose 170
Prague, Martin of, Franciscan conventual provincial minister 170

Pressburg........... 191, 192, 193, 201, 221

Pressburg, Franciscans.............. 200, 201

Preußisch-Holland.............................. 163

Přísečnice 174

Provins...129, 130

Prunéřov.. 171

Prussia / Preußen 124, 126, 128, 131, 139, 140, 143, 144, 148, 150, 151, 153

Prussia, Alexius of, OFM obs. 173

Prutz, Hans.. 137

Pyrenees... 19

Quadrones................................... 29 n. 56

Rádóc... 202

Ragnit... 148, 163

Rakowitz, Thomas von....................... 126

Ramiro, brother of king Alfonso I 26

Ramsey, abbot of 80, 83, 87

Ramsey, Hugh abbot of... 80, 83, 87, 96

Ranulph Flambard, bishop of Durham (1099–1128)....................................... 54

Ratibor 169

Reading, abbot of 89

Reading, Simon abbot of..................... 80

Reglero de la Fuente, Carlos 12

Religious Houses

Abbotsbury Abbey...... 38 n. 5; 51 n. 59; 58, 68 n. 170; 72, 74, 86

Abellar... 29 n. 51

Abingdon Abbey....................... 38 n. 5; 51, 53, 54, 57, 64, 68 n. 170; 70, 73, 80, 84, 82 n. 230; 84, 86, 88 n. 282; 91

Alcester Priory 97

Amesbury nunnery..................... 38 n. 5; 94, 97

Athelney....................................... 51 n. 60; 57, 69

Barking... 38 n. 5; 51 n. 60; 65, 69, 89

Bath.. 39

Battle Abbey...............................38, 43, 57, 60, 65, 66

Beaulieu Abbey........................... 38

Bereg, Remete, monastery........ 213, 214 n. 82

Bruck monastery 200

Burton Abbey .... 38 n. 5; 51 n. 60; 69

Bury St. Edmunds...................... 38 n. 5; 42, 45, 51 n. 59; 56, 59, 60, 66, 71, 72 n. 187; 74, 75, 76 80, 82, 85, 88 n. 282; 89, 92

Canterbury Cathedral Priory .... 9, 38 n. 5; 39, 45, 49, 51 n. 59; 59, 82 n. 239; 83, 86, 88, 91, 92, 93, 96

Cardeña monastery 102, 103, 104, 106, 109, 110, 111, 113

Cerne .... 38 n. 5; 51 n. 59; 59, 63 n. 134; 68 n. 170; 70, 72, 83

Chatteris.......................................42, 95

Chertsey .... 38 n. 5; 51 n. 59; 68 n. 170; 72, 75, 83, 96, 98

Cluny 17, 18, 19, 32, 136

Coventry Cathedral Priory........39, 51 n. 59; 56, 63 n. 135; 68 n. 170; 72 nn. 184, 187

Crowland Abbey......................... 38 n. 5; 39, 49, 59, 60, 64, 68 n. 170; 86, 88 n. 286

Csút monasteri (today Budapest-Háros).. 215

Diósgyőr monastery................... 214 n. 83

Religious Houses (cont.)

    Durham Priory........45, 53, 76, 82 n. 239; 88 n. 282; 96

    Ely, Abbey and Cathedral Priory.38 n. 5; 39, 51, 60

    Evesham Abbey ... 38 n. 5; 51 n. 59; 53, 55, 57, 59, 61, 66, 68 n. 170; 70 n. 175; 72 n. 187; 83, 85, 88 n. 282; 91, 93, 97

    Eynsham........38 n. 5; 53, 69, 76, 86

    Faversham..........................39, 75, 86

    Fontevraud..98

    Glastonbury......38 n. 5; 45 n. 34; 51 n. 59; 53, 67 n. 158; 68 n. 170; 71, 72 n. 187; 88 n. 282; 90, 91, 92

    Godstow nunnery..........................98

    Great Malvern Priory........39, 75, 97

    Hornillos Priory..........103, 104, 108

    Hyde Abbey near Winchester.....39, 45, 51 n. 59, 65, 67, 68 n. 170; 71, 72 n. 187

    Lindisfarne..2

    Malmesbury......38 n. 5; 51 n. 59; 53, 58, 59, 64, 68 n. 170; 72 n. 187; 74, 75, 76, 83, 86

    Mave priory....................................110

    Medina del Campo Priory...........113

    Milton...38 n. 5; 51 n. 59; 68 n. 170; 70 n. 175

    Muchelney........38 n. 5; 51 n. 59; 66

    Nogal..........................114 n. 54; 115

    Norwich Cathedral Priory39, 56, 95

    Obarenes Abbey.......103 n. 11; 108, 113 n. 47

    Pershore Abbey.... 38 n. 5; 51 n. 59; 67 n. 158; 70 n. 145; 72 n. 187; 80, 83, 97

    Peterborough Abbey........9, 38 n. 5; 40, 51, 52, 53, 57, 58, 63, 65, 68 n. 170; 72 n. 187; 76, 82, 85, 86, 88, 92

    Ramsey Abbey...........38 n. 5; 40, 46 n. 35; 51 n. 59; 53 n. 67; 56, 57, 58, 61, 62, 63 n. 133; 65, 67, 68 n. 170; 70, 72 n. 187; 73, 74, 77, 79, 81, 83, 84, 85, 87, 88, 89, 93, 95, 96

    Reading Abbey......39, 43, 57, 61, 62 n. 126; 66, 72 n. 187; 78 n. 219; 88 n. 282; 92, 94, 95

    Rochester Cathedral Priory..........39

    Romsey......................38 n. 5; 88, 94

    Saelices de Mayorga.............28 n. 51

    Sahagún abbey.....12, 15, 16, 17, 18, 19, 20, 21, 22, 23, 25, 26, 27, 28, 29, 30, 31, 32, 33, 34, 35, 36, 101, 103 n. 11; 104, 106, 108, 111, 112, 113, 114, 116, 117, 118, 119, 120, 121

    San Juan de Burgos priory.....103 n. 11; 104, 110

    San Pedro de Arlanza.......103 n. 11; 105

    San Pedro de Cardeña.......103 n. 11

    San Pedro de los molinos, nunnery dependent on Sahagún........20, 27 n. 46; 103 n. 11

    San Salvador de Oña..........103 n. 11

    San Salvador in Tejadillo.....29 n. 54

    San Salvador de Villacete....32 n. 71

    San Salvador de Villaverde .31 n. 68

    San Zoilo de Carrión 103 n. 11; 104 n. 12; 105, 107 n. 20

    Santervás... 26 n. 41; 114 n. 54; 115, 116 n. 71

    Santo Domingo de Silos 103 nn. 9, 11; 105

    Santo Toribio de Liébana prior 103 n. 11; 110 n. 34

    Selby Abbey... 38, 53, 61, 67, 69, 88, 95

    Shaftesbury Abbey 38 n. 5; 51 n. 59; 67, 68 n. 170; 73 n. 187; 74, 87

    Sherborne ....51 n. 59; 68 n. 170; 70, 73 n. 187; 74, 79, 80

    Shrewsbury Abbey.... 38, 56, 58, 68, 86

    St. Albans.......38 n. 5; 51, 56, 59, 76, 77, 80, 83, 85, 97

Religious Houses (cont.)

    St. Amand 8

    St. Augustine, Canterbury .. 51 n. 59; 58, 59, 75, 95

    St. Benet Holme ... 38 n. 5; 51 n. 59; 58, 64, 76, 77, 95

    St. Denis 2

    St. John, Colchester ... 39, 54, 67, 96

    St. Martin of Troarn 8

    St. Mary, Winchester ..... 51 n. 60; 69

    St. Mary, York. 39, 53, 78, 88 n. 282

    St. Oswald, Gloucester ...... 82 n. 243

    St. Peter, Gloucester ... 38 n. 5; 51 n. 60; 54, 58, 59, 60, 63, 66, 68 n. 170; 69, 76, 79, 82, 86, 88, 96, 97

    St. Swithun, Winchester .. 39, 57, 58, 67, 73, 83 n. 245; 88 n. 282; 91, 94

    St. Victor of Marseille 7

    St. Werburgh, Chester 63, 68, 78, 86

    Tavistock 38 n. 5; 60, 63, 68 n. 170; 72 n. 184; 73 n. 187; 75, 88, 96

    Tewkesbury .... 68 n. 170; 73, 77, 80, 88 n. 282; 97

    Thorney Abbey ... 38 n. 5; 59, 64, 66

    Vicogne 8

    Villagarcía Priory .... 116 n. 64

    Westminster Abbey 38 n. 5; 42, 43, 51 n. 59; 59, 63 n. 135; 65, 67, 68 n. 170; 71, 73 n. 187; 78, 83, 85, 88, 91, 94, 96, 98

    Whitby Abbey 39, 53, 69

    Wilton .... 51 n. 59; 68 n. 170; 70 n. 175

    Winchcombe 38 n. 5; 51 n. 59; 70 n. 175; 73 n. 187; 97

    Worcester Cathedral Priory .. 39, 73, 74, 84, 88 n. 282; 95

Religious Orders

    Augustinian Canons 38, 40

    Austin Friars ... 224, 226, 229, 241 n. 98

    Benedictines ..... 10, 12, 17 n. 13; 18, 38, 40, 41, 47, 48, 49, 51, 53, 54, 55, 73, 78, 91, 92, 95, 121, 206

    Carmelites .. 182, 183, 187, 188, 189, 190, 194, 199, 206, 209, 213, 217, 229

    Carthusians 38, 47

    Cistercians 2, 6, 10, 11, 12, 17 n. 15; 38, 39 n. 15; 40, 47, 69

    Cluniacs 39 n. 11; 40, 47, 50, 104 n. 13

    Dominicans 182, 183, 186, 187, 188, 190, 193, 195, 196, 197, 200, 202, 204, 206, 209, 210, 218, 224, 226, 229

    Franciscans 2, 12, 57, 109, 167, 168, 182, 183, 186, 187, 188, 193, 195, 196, 197, 198, 218, 224, 226, 229, 239

    Franciscan Observants .... 13, 167, 168, 170, 171, 173, 174, 175, 177, 178, 180, 187, 188, 190, 193, 194, 195, 196, 197, 198, 218, 223, 224 n. 2; 225, 226, 229, 241 n. 98; 243

    Gilbertines 38

    Grandmont 2

    Hospitallers / Johanniter 12, 13, 123, 124, 125, 127, 129, 130, 131, 132, 133, 134, 137, 138, 139, 140, 144, 145, 146, 147, 149, 150

    Paulines (Hermits of St. Paul) ... 181, 183, 185, 187, 188, 189, 192, 196, 199, 207, 208, 209, 210, 211, 214, 216, 217, 218

    Premonstratensians .. 12, 38, 40, 215

    Savignacs 69

    St. Anthony, order of 12

    St. Bridget, order of 12

    St. Clare, order of .... 224 n. 2

    Santiago, order of 125

    Sisters of the Common Life 12

    Templars .... 12, 13, 123, 124, 125, 126 n. 17; 127, 129, 130, 132, 134, 135, 136, 137, 139, 140, 141, 145, 146, 149, 150

Religious Orders (cont.)

   Teutonic Knights / Deutscher Orden ... 12, 13, 99, 123, 124, 125, 126, 128, 129, 131, 133, 139, 140, 142, 146, 147, 149, 150, 151, 152, 165

   Williamites (Hermits of St. William) 181

Retz, Matthias of 174

Revel, Hugues 142

Rhein 163

Rhineland 12, 181

Rhodes 130, 131, 133, 134, 138, 141, 146, 147, 150

Riccardi 99

Richard I., king of England (1189–1199) 73, 74, 84

Richard II., king of England (1377–1399) 67

Rio Cinca 129

Robert, duke of Normandy (1087–1106) 55

Robert I., king of Scotland (1306–1329) .... 76 n. 205

Robertus, Cluniac monk 17

Rodríguez, Sancha .... 121 n. 102

Roger, bishop of Salisbury (1102–1139) 53

Roggenhausen 157

Roman Empire 5, 172, 180

Romania .... 200 n. 47; 204, 206

Rome 57, 59, 75, 77, 78, 112

ROMHÁNYI, Beatrix 13

Ros, Bernardino, of Rhodes 138

RÖSENER, Werner 11

Rožmitál, Margaret of 170

Rumpenheim, Johann von, Komtur of Elbing, Teutonic Knights 158

Rusdorf, Paul of, Hochmeister of the Teutonic Knights 144, 154

RUSU, Adrian Andrei ....205 n. 66

Rýzmburk, castle 177

Sacoșu Turcesc / Cseri, Observant Franciscan friary ....235 n. 60

Sahagún, town 20, 21, 35, 113

Sainte-Eulalie-du-Larzac 127

Salamanca, Alfonso bishop of 121

Salisbury 53

Samland, bishopric of 161, 162, 164

Samson, abbot of Bury St. Edmunds (1182–1211) 65, 80, 90

San Benito de Sahagún 15

San Felices, Domingo de ....116 n. 64

San Mancio, Juan de, cellarer of Sahagún (1344–1347) 120

San Mancio, prior of ...... 115, 116 n. 71; 117 n. 72; 120 n. 100

San Pedro de Arlanza ...... 103 n. 11; 105

San Pedro de Cardeña ...102 n. 6; 103 n. 11

San Pedro de los molinos, nunnery dependent on Sahagún ..... 20, 27 n. 46

San Pedro de Dueñas, prior of .... 116 n. 71

San Zoilo de Carrión priory ...103 n. 11; 104 n. 12; 105, 107 n. 30

Sancha, sister of king Alfonso VIII ...26 n. 41

Sancho III. the Great, king of Navarre (c. 992–1035) 16

Sant Facundo / Sant Fagunt (Facundus) 15

Santervás, prior of .. 26 n. 41; 114 n. 54; 115, 116 n. 71

Santiago, Camino de 15

Santiago de Compostela 19, 26, 136

Santo Domingo de Silos, town 109

Šarengrad / Atya 226, 234, 243

Sáros, Austin Friars 192, 203

Sáros, Bartholomew of 228

Sárospatak, Franciscans 241

Sarrasin, Pierre 136

Saxony / Sachsen, duke of (Henry the Lion) 70

Saxony, duke Albrecht 159
Saxony, Friedrich von, Hochmeister of the Teutonic Knights 149, 152, 159, 160, 161, 165
Saxony, duke George of 180
Schässburg 191, 210, 220, 221
Schässburg, Dominicans of 198, 200, 202, 204, 205, 206, 207, 211
Schemnitz 221
Schemnitz, Dominican friary ... 207, 213
SCHICH, Winfried 11
Schippenbeil 164
Schivelbein .... 159 n. 54
Schlick, Albrecht 172, 179, 180
Schönburg, Frederick of 171
Schwamberg, Henry of 177
Schwetz 157
Scotland .... 73, 76 n. 205; 78, 84, 95
Sebes, Franciscan Observants .. 236 n. 69
Seehesten .... 147 n. 120; 164
Semovit, duke of Masovia 155
Senj monastery, Croatia .... 215 n. 85
Sepsi 202
Shrewsbury 68
Shrewsbury, abbot of .... 78 n. 222
Shropshire .... 78 n. 222
Sicily 76, 77, 96, 130, 140, 141, 142
Sidon 140
Siena 135
Sigismund, emperor (1433–1437) ... 234, 236, 237, 238, 243
Sigismund Jagiello, king of Poland (1507–1548) 187, 188, 190
Sigismund, brother of king Wladislaus II. of Hungary 186
Silesia 169, 173, 174, 175, 176, 177, 178, 184, 185, 186
Silos, abbot of 103
Simontornya, Dominicans of 198
SMITH, David M 45
SMITH, Reginald 9, 39, 49, 96

Smyrna / Izmir 133
SNAPE, Robert Hugh 8, 48
Solivar / Sóvár, Observant Franciscans 191, 192, 194, 201, 221, 231
Somerset .... 69 n. 172
Somkeréki family 195
Somme 127
Soós, Zoltán 205
Sopratello / Sobradillo 22, 27, 28
Sopron 191, 199, 204
Sopron, Franciscan friary 191, 197, 198, 201, 210, 211, 212, 213, 221
Spain .... 17, 18, 104 n. 13
Spalding, prior of 81
St. Albans, abbot of 83, 85
St. Benedict ..... 1, 3, 16, 17, 28, 29 n. 31; 39, 45, 101, 102, 105
St. Benet Holme, chronicler of 76, 77
St. Francis 2, 174, 176, 180
St. Ivo 96
St. Mary's, York, abbot of 78
St. Werburgh, Chester, abbot of 78
Starý Dvůr 178, 179
Stephen, king of England (1135–1154) .... 39 n. 11
Sternberg, Ladislav of 177
STEVENS, John .... 47 n. 37
Styria 185
Suffolk 42, 60
Sully, Henry of 90
Şumuleu Ciuc / Csíksomlyó ... 233, 234, 235, 237, 238, 239
Suseni / Felfalu ...... 235, 237 n. 76; 238, 239, 241
Švihov, family 177
Švihov, Jindřich of 177
Sweden 12
Szalárd 194, 221
Szászrégen 202, 221
Szeged, Dominicans 189, 192
Szeged, Franciscan friary 192

Székelyudvarhely 221
Székelyudvarhely, Dominicans 202
Székesfehérvár............................... 187, 190
Szeklerland 202
Szentgotthárd 202
Szentjobb monastery................. 215, 221
Szentmihály..202
Szobi, Michael 195
Szőcs, Ladislaus (alias Saylich). 197, 213

Tachov 170, 173
Tannenberg.................. 13, 143, 152, 158
TANNER, Thomas 47
Teresa, daughter of Goto and Gonzalo Núñez ....27 n. 46
Tewkesbury, abbot of 73
Tewkesbury, Alan abbot of................80
Tewkesbury, annalist of................ 58, 77
Thal, Paulines 192, 220
Thorda, Mathias de...................200 n. 46
Thorn / Torun........................... 139, 156
Thüngen, Hans von, Rentmeister of the Teutonic Knights 161, 162, 163, 164, 165
Thurstan, abbot of Glastonbury (c. 1077–c. 1096) 52
Toledo... 18, 101
Toledo, archbishop of 105
Torda, Matthias of, prior provincial of the Austin Friars in Hungary 200
Török, Emeric, of Enying 194
Tortosa 125
Tövis 205, 221
Transylvania..200
Transylvania, Dominicans 202, 206
Trencsén 221
Troyes 129
Tuchel 157, 158
Tulln, Ludwig von 201
Túri, Benedict......................................195
Tuscany..182

Tuwernicz, Andreas............ ....154, 165
Tuwernicz, Johannes 154, 157, 165

Ucles...125
Udvarhely 202
Újlak 221
Újlak, Franciscan friary 192
d'Újlak, Laurent...................................241
Ulldecona 131
Upper Lusatia 169, 174
Urban IV., pope (1261–1264) 132
Urbino..171
Urraca, queen of León (c. 1080–1126) 20

Valderas, archdeacon of .... 121 n. 102
Valencia, kingdom of 125
Valencia, town 129
Valero, Alfonso, de Valladolid, almoner of Sahagún (1346–1351, 1354–1357) 115
Valladolid 34, 115
Váradhegyfok monastery...... 215
Váradi, Peter, archbishop 216
Várdai, Lady Ursula, the widow of John 198
Vasvár, friary............................. 211, 217
Vellitiz, Isidoro....................... ...32 n. 71
Vellitiz, Petro ....29 n. 52
Venice / Venedig....................... 133, 138
Vergerio, Pier Paolo, papal legate ...172, 180
Vicedominis, Mathew 200
Vichiers, Renaut de, marshal of the Templars 136
Vienna..216
Vikings..2
Vingárt 243
Vinogradov 240
VIOLANTE, Cinzio 10
Visconti, Tedaldo see Gregory X.......87

Visegrád monastery 215
Visigothic kingdom 18, 19
Vitzthum family 179
Vitzthum, Appel, of Šumburk 179
Vitzthum, Dietrich, of Egerberg 179
Voćin / Atyina 234, 235 n. 60; 237, 238

Wales 9, 11, 73, 78, 84
Walsingham, Thomas 54, 77, 85
Walter, Hubert, archbishop of Canterbury (1193–1205) 57
Ware, Richard, abbot of Westminster (1258–1283) 78
Watt, Paulus 163
Werle, lords of 125
Werther, Dietrich von 160, 162, 165
Westminster, abbot of 68
Wettin, family 172
Weymer, Elisabeth .... 225 n. 8
Wiener Neustadt, Paulines ...... 216 n. 89
William I., king of England (1066–1087) 34, 43, 52, 53
William II., king of England (1187–1100) 55, 64
Wiltshire 64
Wimar, priest 64

Wittbach, Christopher of, OFM obs. 173
Wittenberg 172, 180
Wladislaus II., king of Hungary (1490–1516) 186, 215, 236, 238, 242
Wladislaus Jagiello, king of Bohemia (1471–1516) 171, 178
Wobeke, Burghard von 155, 158
Worcester, bishop of 59
Worcester, Florence of 53

Yarmouth 97

Zagreb 211, 221
Zala County 202
Zalatárnok, Franciscans 241
Zdeněk, Břetislav 177
Zdeněk, Jindřich 177
Zdeněk, Lev 177
Želina 170
Znojmo 170
Zöllner, Konrad, von Rotenstein, Hochmeister of the Teutonic Knights 139
Zsámbék monastery 215
Zsuk / Juc 206

Vita regularis
Ordnungen und Deutungen religiosen Lebens im Mittelalter – Abhandlungen
hrsg. von Mirko Breitenstein und Gert Melville

Clemens T. Galbam
Propst Georg Muestinger und die Einführung der Raudnitzer Reform im Stift Klosterneuburg 1418 – ca. 1421
Das Konzil von Konstanz und die mit ihm erreichte Beendigung des päpstlichen Schismas setzten in der gesamten Kirche und insbesondere in den Orden lange aufgestaute Reformenergien frei. Infolge der österreichischen Visitation von 1418/19 wurde das altehrwürdige Stift Klosterneuburg Teil der Raudnitzer Reformbewegung der Augustiner-Chorherren und erfuhr unter seinem neuen Propst Georg Muestinger eine kulturelle Blüte. Die im Buch dargestellten Ereignisse zeigen, wie Reformkräfte sowohl zusammenwirkten als auch miteinander konkurrierten, um das Ordensleben zu erneuern. Im Mittelpunkt steht die Einführung der Raudnitzer Statuten im Stift Klosterneuburg und damit Georg Muestingers ganz eigene Adaption dieser Gesetzgebung für sein Haus.
Bd. 80, 2022, 340 S., 34,90 €, br., ISBN-AT 978-3-643-51085-3

Mirko Breitenstein; Gert Melville (Eds.)
Between Community and Seclusion
Defining the Religious Life in the South Asian Traditions, in Buddhism, and in Eastern and Western Christianity
The fact that certain cultures and religions produced a way of life which, for the sake of self-perfection, expected its adherents to withdraw from various obligations to the world and to enter into the organisational structure of a monastic community obviously represents a constant anthropological foundation. The spectrum of monastic life within these various cultures was extremely diverse in its manifestations. It was the result of a high degree of flexibility in the face of constantly changing ideas about piety, social needs and concepts of community and individuality.
However, an interreligious study with the aim of a scholarly analysis of comparable key elements across different monastic cultures does not exist yet. The editors as well as the authors of this volume are particularly interested in how monastic life was realised communally in many ways according to fixed norms and rules, how it shaped the understanding of community and civilisation and therefore made a decisive contribution to the formation of our cultural identity.
Bd. 79, 2020, 202 S., 29,90 €, br., ISBN 978-3-643-14875-9

Gert Melville; James D. Mixson (Eds.)
Virtuosos of Faith
Monks, Nuns, Canons, and Friars as Elites of Medieval Culture
For over a thousand years, monks, nuns, canons, friars, and others under religious vows stood at the pinnacle of Western European society. For their ascetic sacrifices, their learning, piety, and expertise, they were accorded positions of power and influence, and a wide range of legal, financial and social privileges. As such they present an important opportunity to consider the nature and dynamics of an "elite" in medieval culture. Using medieval religious life as their interpretive lens, the essays of this volume seek to uncover the essential markers of elite status. They explore how those under vows claimed and manifested elite status in complex spiritual, temporal, and social combinations. They explore the workings of elite status from day to day, across region and locale – who earned recognition and how, whether through specific achievements or the deployment of specific capacities; who recognized, conferred, or helped maintain elite status, how and why; how elite status could be redefined, contested or rejected. The essays also seek to understand how medieval European religious elites compared to those found in other cultures and settings, from Syria and South Asia to the early modern transatlantic world.
Bd. 78, 2020, 338 S., 49,90 €, br., ISBN 978-3-643-91363-0

LIT Verlag Berlin – Münster – Wien – Zürich – London
Auslieferung Deutschland / Österreich / Schweiz: siehe Impressumsseite

Clemens T. Galban
Provost Georg Muestinger and the Introduction of the Raudnitz Reform into Stift Klosterneuburg, 1418 – ca. 1421
The Council of Constance and the conclusion of the Papal Schism released long pent-up energies of reform throughout the Church and in the religious Orders in particular. The Austrian Visitation of 1418/19 which propelled Georg Muestinger to the highest position in Stift Klosterneuburg and introduced the Raudnitz Reform of canons regular into his ancient monastery, illustrates how these energies both cooperated and competed with each other to achieve a reform of religious life. The centerpiece of this work is the introduction of the Raudnitz Statutes into the monastery and Muestinger's adaptation of that legislation.
Bd. 77, 2020, 324 S., 34,90 €, br., ISBN 978-3-643-91197-1

Stephanie Righetti-Templer
Der spanische Franciscanismo in der Neuen Welt
Eine Untersuchung zum Transfer der franziskanischen Theologie im 16. Jahrhundert nach Lateinamerika anhand der Werke von Fray Toribio de Benavente Motolinía
Nach der Entdeckung Amerikas entwickelte sich die Mission in der Neuen Welt zu einer zentralen Aufgabe für viele Brüder des Franziskanerordens. Einer der wirkmächtigsten unter ihnen war Fray Toribio de Benavente Motolinía, dem die vorliegende Arbeit gewidmet ist. Anhand dreier besonders aufschlussreicher Bereiche lässt sich sein spezifisch spanisch-franziskanisches Profil, sein *Franciscanismo*, deutlich aufzeigen: sein eschatologisches Verständnis, seine franziskanischen Ideale, die er lebte und öffentlich präsentierte, und seine Missionsarbeit. Die Schriften Motolinías dienten vielen späteren Missionaren als Orientierungshilfe und Vorbild.
Bd. 76, 2019, 336 S., 49,90 €, br., ISBN 978-3-643-14408-9

Nikolas Jaspert; Imke Just (Eds.)
Queens, Princesses and Mendicants
Close Relations in a European Perspective
The decades between ca 1280 and ca 1380 were marked by a striking affinity to the Mendicant orders on the part of many female members of royal and princely courts. And yet, "Queens, Princesses and Mendicants" is both an innovative and comparatively neglected juxtaposition in medieval studies, for historical research has generally tended to neglect the relationship between Mendicants and aristocratic women. This volume unites twelve articles written by experts from seven European countries. The contributions cover a wide array of medieval European kingdoms in order to facilitate direct comparisons. Was affinity towards the Mendicants a prevalent phenomenon in the late Middle Ages? Can one even term "philomendicantism" a late medieval European movement? The collection of essays provides answers to these and other questions within the field of gender, religious and cultural history.
Bd. 75, 2019, 308 S., 44,90 €, br., ISBN 978-3-643-91092-9

Steven Vanderputten (Ed.)
Abbots and Abbesses as a Human Resource in the Ninth- to Twelfth-Century West
This volume provides a record of the response, by eight expert scholars in the field of medieval monastic studies, to the question "To what extent did abbots and abbesses contribute as a 'human resource' to the development of reformed monastic communities in the ninth- to twelfth-century west?" Covering a broad geographical area, papers consider one or several of three key points of interest: the direct contribution of abbots and abbesses to the shaping of reformed realities; their influence over future modes of leadership; and the way in which later generations of monastics relied upon the memory of a leader's life and achievements to project current realities onto a legitimizing past.
Bd. 74, 2018, 184 S., 29,90 €, br., ISBN 978-3-643-91070-7

LIT Verlag Berlin – Münster – Wien – Zürich – London
Auslieferung Deutschland / Österreich / Schweiz: siehe Impressumsseite

Wolf Zöller
Regularkanoniker im Heiligen Land
Studien zur Kirchen-, Ordens- und Frömmigkeitsgeschichte der Kreuzfahrerstaaten
Das vorliegende Buch beschäftigt sich mit einer kaum beachteten Ausprägung der mittelalterlichen *vita religiosa*, nämlich dem Regularkanonikertum in den Kreuzfahrerstaaten. In Folge der lateinischen Eroberung der Heiligen Stätten entwickelte sich speziell das Königreich Jerusalem zu einem Verdichtungsraum der hochmittelalterlichen Kanonikerreform. Die Studie, die an der Grenze zwischen Ordens- und Kreuzzugsforschung angesiedelt ist, untersucht das wechselvolle Schicksal von acht Augustinerchorherrengemeinschaften des lateinischen Ostens und leistet damit einen wichtigen Beitrag zur Kirchen- und Frömmigkeitsgeschichte des hochmittelalterlichen Palästina.
Bd. 73, 2018, 572 S., 69,90 €, br., ISBN 978-3-643-14159-0

Simon Falch
Das Predigtoeuvre des Rebdorfer Augustiner-Chorherren Balthasar Boehm († 1530)
Zugänge zur Machart von Musterpredigtsammlungen des Spätmittelalters
Das in autographen Codices in der UB Eichstätt sowie in der BSB München überlieferte Predigtœuvre Balthasar Boehms entstand (um 1500) im Kontext der Reformen der Eichstätter Humanistenbischöfe und des Anschlusses des Klosters Rebdorf an die Windesheimer Kongregation. Der Kompilator schuf eine dem Umfang und der Systematik nach einmalige, den liturgischen Anlässen und Propria der Diözese und des Ordens verpflichtete Musterpredigtsammlung – gleich einer *summa praedicandi* – am Vorabend der Reformation. Das Werk kommt einem Gattungsarchiv gleich, das seiner Anlage nach, vom *registrum* bis zum *argumentum*, Schlüssel zur *bibliothèque imaginaire* des Christentums offeriert.
Bd. 72, 2018, 388 S., 59,90 €, br., ISBN 978-3-643-14045-6

Florian M. Lim
Die Brüder vom Gemeinsamen Leben im 15. Jahrhundert in Deutschland
Vom Münsterschen Kolloquium zum Oberdeutschen Generalkapitel: Eine kirchenrechtsgeschichtliche Untersuchung über Eingliederung und Gemeinschaftsform der süddeutschen Kanoniker
Die „Brüder vom Gemeinsamen Leben", die aus der *Devotio Moderna* Ende des 14. Jh. hervorgingen, strebten ein frommes und innerliches Leben an und banden sich mit Gütergemeinschaft durch einen privatrechtlichen Vertrag aneinander. 1401 kamen sie nach Deutschland und breiteten sich von Münster bis nach Württemberg aus. Auch wenn schon viel über die süddeutschen Brüder geforscht worden ist, so blieb die kirchenrechtliche Bindungsform doch bislang weitgehend offen. Die hier vorgelegte Untersuchung der Eingliederung der Brüder lässt nun auf eine vollgültige Aufnahme in die *vita religiosa* schließen.
Bd. 71, 2017, 224 S., 34,90 €, br., ISBN 978-3-643-13802-6

Stefanie Neidhardt
Autonomie im Gehorsam
Die dominikanische Observanz in Selbstzeugnissen geistlicher Frauen des Spätmittelalters
Im Zentrum dieser Arbeit steht die Frage nach Autonomie im Ordensgehorsam von observanten Dominikanerinnen im südwestdeutschen Raum. Chroniken, Briefe und private Berichte geben Einblicke in Reformabläufe, Widerstand, Alltag und Umgang mit altem Wissensgut und ermöglichen den Fokus auf eine kleine Gruppe gebildeter Frauen aus Niederadel und Bürgertum, die die Vorgaben des Ordens aufnehmen, an die Gegebenheiten innerhalb des Klosters anpassen und für sich nutzbar machen konnten. So öffnet sich ein seltener Einblick in Abläufe, Gestaltung und Kommunikation zwischen Dominikanern und Schwestern.
Bd. 70, 2017, 486 S., 54,90 €, br., ISBN 978-3-643-13583-4

Jörg Sonntag (Hg..) unter Mitwirkung von Petrus Bsteh, Brigitte Proksch und Gert Melville
Geist und Gestalt
Monastische Raumkonzepte als Ausdrucksformen religiöser Leitideen im Mittelalter
Dieser Band diskutiert, inwieweit sich spirituelle Leitideen in den Raumkonzepten religiöser Gemeinschaften des Mittelalters widerspiegeln. Hierfür nimmt er vergleichend die Klausur betonenden Orden und Verbände ebenso in den Blick wie die Mendikanten oder die Beginen. Er begibt sich dabei hinein in die Spannungsfelder aus Anspruch und Wirklichkeit, Transzendenz und Immanenz, Altem und Neuem, Ritual und Performanz sowie Faktizität und Illusion. „Geist und Gestalt" beleuchtet auch darum einen grundlegenden Aspekt europäischer Kulturgeschichte.
Bd. 69, 2016, 408 S., 49,90 €, br., ISBN 978-3-643-13405-9

Jens Röhrkasten; Coralie Zermatten (Eds.)
Historiography and Identity
Responses to Medieval Carmelite Culture
The Carmelites' role as one of the four great mendicant orders was not unchallenged. Originating as an association of hermits on Mount Carmel, the order experienced a dramatic transformation in the thirteenth century while its name was a reminder to origins which were obscure and its first form of religious life was diametrically opposed to the mendicant ministry. In addition the 'White Friars' were unable to find legitimization in a charismatic founder figure, unlike the Franciscans and the Dominicans. These factors led the Carmelites to create an identity finding their roots with the prophets Elijah and Elisha, who appear in texts and were represented in altar pieces and other works of art. The ten articles published in this volume address these underlying issues and deal with the order's historiography as well as its regional representation in different phases of its history.
Bd. 68, 2017, 220 S., 29,90 €, br., ISBN 978-3-643-90737-0

Mirko Breitenstein; Julia Burkhardt; Stefan Burkhardt; Jörg Sonntag (Hg.)
Identität und Gemeinschaft
Vier Zugänge zu Eigengeschichten und Selbstbildern institutioneller Ordnungen
Der vorliegende Band eröffnet anhand der Leitbegriffe „Identität" und „Gemeinschaft" Zugänge zu Eigengeschichten und Selbstbildern institutioneller Ordnungen des Mittelalters. Vier einander ergänzende Perspektiven erlauben es, die Zusammenhänge von Genese, Verstetigung, Neukodierung, Auflösung oder Verlust von Identitäten im Spannungsfeld individueller Bedürfnisse und institutioneller Ansprüche zu untersuchen. Ein erster Abschnitt thematisiert dabei Mechanismen zur Perfektionierung des Normativen im Spiegel klösterlicher Regelkommentare. Die Beiträge der zweiten Sektion diskutieren spirituelle Leitideen als Generatoren und Stabilisatoren kollektiver Identitäten in der Vita religiosa. Im Mittelpunkt des dritten Abschnittes stehen Überlegungen zur Schaffung, Etablierung und schließlich Übertragung kollektiver Identitäten. Der vierte Abschnitt schließlich befasst sich mit übergeordneten Vorstellungswelten des Mittelalters und Versuchen ihrer Ordnung bzw. Positionierung.
Bd. 67, 2016, 338 S., 44,90 €, br., ISBN 978-3-643-13242-0

Katrin Rösler
Einheit ohne Gleichheit
Aspekte der Konstruktion prämonstratensischer Identität im 12. und 13. Jahrhundert
Die vorliegende Arbeit untersucht den Prozess der Identitätsbildung des Prämonstratenserordens im hohen Mittelalter. Ziel der Studie ist es zu zeigen, wie es den Nachfolgern des Norbert von Xanten gelungen ist, eine tragfähige kollektive Identität auszubilden, die den von Beginn an bestehenden Spaltungstendenzen des entstehenden Ordens erfolgreich entgegenwirken konnte.
In den Blick genommen werden neben normativen, formativen und administrativen Texten des 12. und 13. Jahrhunderts auch Quellen, welche die Selbst- und die Außenwahrnehmung insbesondere der sächsischen Ordensstifte zeigen. Wurde in der bisherigen Forschung der Fokus oftmals eher auf das innerhalb des Prämonstratenserordens vorhandene Konflikt- und Spaltungspotential gelegt, so arbeitet die Studie die Ausprägung von Vorstellungen heraus, welche erfolgreich Bilder von Dauer und von Einheit unter den Nachfolgern Norberts erzeugen konnten.
Bd. 66, 2020, 336 S., 44,90 €, br., ISBN 978-3-643-13211-6

LIT Verlag Berlin – Münster – Wien – Zürich – London
Auslieferung Deutschland / Österreich / Schweiz: siehe Impressumsseite

Tobias Schöneweis
Die Architektur zisterziensischer Wirtschaftsbauten
Den Zisterziensern eilt seit jeher der Ruf vorbildlicher Asketen und tüchtiger Agrarpioniere voraus. Plakativ ist das Bild von Mönchen als Managern, die durch innovative Organisationsstrukturen und strenge Betriebsführung einen frühkapitalistischen, europaweit expandierenden Klosterkonzern schufen. Dieses Buch widmet sich den mittelalterlichen Wirtschaftsbauten des Ordens. Unter den angenommenen Vorzeichen einer protomodernen Wirtschaftspraxis ist es reizvoll, in den monumentalen Ökonomiegebäuden frühe, fabrikähnliche „Kathedralen der Arbeit" zu sehen, die der herausragenden Wertschätzung für die monastische Handarbeit in der Zisterzienserspiritualität architektonisch Ausdruck verleihen sollten.
Bd. 65, 2021, 672 S., 99,90 €, gb., ISBN 978-3-643-13140-9

Thomas Krämer
Dämonen, Prälaten und gottlose Menschen
Konflikte und ihre Beilegung im Umfeld der geistlichen Ritterorden
Durch die vielfältigen Kontakte und Aktivitäten der Johanniter, der Templer und des Deutschen Ordens blieben Konflikte mit anderen geistlichen Gemeinschaften nicht aus. Anhand von Beispielfeldern wird gezeigt, dass nicht nur Versuche, die eigenen Interessen durchzusetzen, sondern ebenso die umfassende Privilegierung der Ritterorden und eine z. T. schwankende kuriale Politik Konflikte auslösten. Meist gelang deren Beilegung durch ein breites Instrumentarium im regionalen Rahmen ohne Beteiligung des Papsttums. Trotz aller Interessengegensätze und Konkurrenzen, die zu erbitterten Auseinandersetzungen führten, gingen die Kontrahenten dabei ausgesprochen pragmatisch und flexibel vor.
Bd. 64, 2015, 754 S., 89,90 €, br., ISBN 978-3-643-12960-4

Gert Melville; Leonie Silberer; Bernd Schmies (Hg.)
Die Klöster der Franziskaner im Mittelalter
Räume, Nutzungen, Symbolik
Die Mendikantenorden veränderten das Religiosentum des Hochmittelalters in den ersten Jahrzehnten des 13. Jahrhunderts gravierend und dauerhaft. Die Bettelbrüder prägten eine vita religiosa, die die Welt zum Kloster erklärte, und erhoben Armut, Predigt und Pastoral zu ihrer Berufung. Eine in den ersten Generationen elaborierte Spiritualität und Theologie prägte einen spezifisch mendikantischen Wirkungsraum mit durchaus ordensspezifischen Akzentuierungen, der sich auch in der Anlage der Konvente, in der Funktion der Räume und ihrer Symbolik konkretisierte. Der vorliegende Band dokumentiert die Beiträge eines Workshops, der auf eine gemeinsame Initiative des Interakademischen Projektes „Klöster im Hochmittelalter: Innovationslabore europäischer Lebensentwürfe und Ordnungsmodelle" (Sächsische und Heidelberger Akademie der Wissenschaften), des Instituts für Europäische Kunstgeschichte der Universität Heidelberg und der Fachstelle Franziskanische Forschung (Münster) hin zusammen mit der Forschungsstelle für Vergleichende Ordensgeschichte (TU Dresden) im November 2012 in Heidelberg stattfand.
Bd. 63, 2015, 284 S., 39,90 €, br., ISBN 978-3-643-12921-5

Piearantonio Piatti; Massimiliano Vidili (Ed.)
Per Sardiniae insulam constituti
Gli ordini religiosi nel Medioevo sardo
Il volume offre, anzitutto, un puntuale *status quaestionis* della capillare presenza in terra sarda degli Ordini, prima monastici e poi Mendicanti, secondo un'ampia diacronia che dall'alto Medioevo si estende sino ai primi decenni del Cinquecento. Ricostruite le coordinate cronologiche e geografiche della diffusione dei monaci e poi dei frati nella regione, sono state elaborate delle prospettive di ricerca di ampio raggio con un approccio interdisciplinare. L'indagine si è estesa anche all'ambito letterario attraverso l'analisi della produzione di scritture agiografiche e della loro circolazione tra la regione e il continente, alla luce delle labili sopravvivenze cultuali e delle scarne attestazioni devozionali riscontrabili fino alla piena Età moderna.
Bd. 62, 2014, 496 S., 74,90 €, br., ISBN 978-3-643-12838-6

Jörg Bölling
Reform vor der Reformation
Augustiner-Chorherrenstiftsgründungen an Marienwallfahrtsorten durch die Windesheimer Kongregation
Bd. 61, 2014, 264 S., 34,90 €, br., ISBN 978-3-643-12612-2

Mirko Breitenstein; Julia Burkhardt; Stefan Burkhardt; Jens Röhrkasten (Eds.)
Rules and Observance
Devising Forms of Communal Life
Bd. 60, 2014, 320 S., 39,90 €, br., ISBN 978-3-643-90489-8

Tobias Tanneberger
„... usz latin in tutsch gebracht ... "
Normative Basistexte religiöser Gemeinschaften in volkssprachlichen Übertragungen. Katalog – Untersuchung – Fallstudie
Bd. 59, 2014, 456 S., 49,90 €, br., ISBN 978-3-643-12484-5

Monasticum regnum
Religione e politica nelle pratiche di governo tra Medioevo ed Età Moderna. A cura di Giancarlo Andenna, Laura Gaffuri, Elisabetta Filippini
Bd. 58, 2015, 224 S., 34,90 €, br., ISBN 978-3-643-12444-9

Ludovic Viallet
Les sens de l'observance
Enquête sur les réformes franciscaines entre l'Elbe et l'Oder, de Capistran à Luther (vers 1450 – vers 1520)
Bd. 57, 2014, 400 S., 49,90 €, br., ISBN 978-3-643-12441-8

Guido Gassmann
Konversen im Mittelalter
Eine Untersuchung anhand der neun Schweizer Zisterzienserabteien
Bd. 56, 2013, 368 S., 31,90 €, br., ISBN 978-3-643-80161-6

Daniela Hoffmann; Tanja Skambraks (Hg.)
Benedikt – gestern und heute
Norm, Tradition, Interaktion
Bd. 55, 2016, 288 S., 44,90 €, br., ISBN 978-3-643-12387-9

Steven Vanderputten
Reform, Conflict, and the Shaping of Corporate Identities
Collected Studies on Benedictine Monasticism, 1050 – 1150
Bd. 54, 2013, 320 S., 34,90 €, br., ISBN 978-3-643-90429-4

Klaus Schreiner
Gemeinsam leben
Spiritualität, Lebens- und Verfassungsformen klösterlicher Gemeinschaften in Kirche und Gesellschaft des Mittelalters. Herausgegeben in Verbindung mit Mirko Breitenstein von Gert Melville
Bd. 53, 2013, 648 S., 64,90 €, br., ISBN 978-3-643-12177-6

Gerd Jäkel
... usque in praesentem diem
Kontinuitätskonstruktionen in der Eigengeschichtsschreibung religiöser Orden des Hoch- und Spätmittelalters
Bd. 52, 2013, 280 S., 29,90 €, br., ISBN 978-3-643-12176-9

LIT Verlag Berlin – Münster – Wien – Zürich – London
Auslieferung Deutschland / Österreich / Schweiz: siehe Impressumsseite

Philippe Josserand; Mathieu Olivier (Eds.)
La mémoire des origines dans les ordres religieux-militaires au Moyen Âge. Die Erinnerung an die eigenen Ursprünge in den geistlichen Ritterorden im Mittelalter
Actes des journées d'études de Göttingen (25 – 26 juin 2009). Beiträge der Göttinger Tagung (25. – 26. Juni 2009)
Bd. 51, 2012, 296 S., 29,90 €, br., ISBN 978"3-643-12008-3

Da Accon a Matera: Santa Maria la Nova, un monastero femminile tra dimensione mediterranea e identità urbana (XIII – XVI secolo)
A cura di Francesco Panarelli
Bd. 50, 2012, 296 S., 39,90 €, br., ISBN 978-3-643-11830-1

Achim Wesjohann
Mendikantische Gründungserzählungen im 13. und 14. Jahrhundert
Mythen als Element institutioneller Eigengeschichtsschreibung der mittelalterlichen Franziskaner, Dominikaner und Augustiner-Eremiten
Bd. 49, 2012, 744 S., 74,90 €, br., ISBN 978-3-643-11667-3

Mirko Breitenstein; Stefan Burkhardt; Julia Dücker (Hg.)
Innovation in Klöstern und Orden des Hohen Mittelalters
Aspekte und Pragmatik eines Begriffs
Bd. 48, 2012, 328 S., 29,90 €, br., ISBN 978-3-643-11523-2

Gert Melville; Anne Müller (Eds.)
Female *vita religiosa* between Late Antiquity and High Middle Ages
Spaces, Organisation and Symbolisation
Bd. 47, 2011, 456 S., 44,90 €, br., ISBN 978-3-643-90124-8

Katharine Sykes
Inventing Sempringham
Gilbert of Sempringham and the origins of the role of the Master. Preface by Brian Golding
Bd. 46, 2011, 280 S., 29,90 €, br., ISBN 978-3-643-90122-4

Gert Melville (Ed.)
Aspects of Charity
Concern for one's neighbour in medieval vita religiosa
vol. 45, 2011, 192 pp., 29,90 €, br., ISBN 978-3-643-11166-1

Michael Robson; Jens Röhrkasten (Ed.)
Franciscan Organisation in the Mendicant Context
Formal and informal structures of the friars' lives and ministry in the Middle Ages
vol. 44, 2010, 440 pp., 44,90 €, br., ISBN 978-3-643-10820-3

Giles Constable (Ed.)
The Abbey of Cluny
A Collection of Essays to Mark the Eleven-Hundredth Anniversary of its Foundation
vol. 43, 2010, 584 pp., 54,90 €, br., ISBN 978-3-643-10777-0

Franz J. Felten; Werner Rösener (Hg.)
Norm und Realität
Kontinuität und Wandel der Zisterzienser im Mittelalter
Bd. 42, 2. Aufl. 2011, 632 S., 69,90 €, gb., ISBN 978-3-643-10408-3

Jean-Marie Cauchies; Marie-Astrid Collet-Lombard (Ed.)
Le miracle du Saint Sang : Bois-Seigneur-Isaac 1405 – 2005
Actes du colloque organisé au prieuré des Prémontrés de Bois-Seigneur-Isaac (Belgique, Brabant wallon)les 13 et 14 mai 2005
Bd. 41, 2009, 512 S., 49,90 €, br., ISBN 978-3-643-10080-1

LIT Verlag Berlin – Münster – Wien – Zürich – London
Auslieferung Deutschland / Österreich / Schweiz: siehe Impressumsseite

Anne Müller; Karen Stöber (Eds.)
Self-Representation of Medieval Religious Communities
The British Isles in Context
vol. 40, 2009, 432 pp., 39,90 €, br., ISBN 978-3-8258-1758-9

Lars-Arne Dannenberg
Das Recht der Religiosen in der Kanonistik des 12. und 13. Jahrhunderts
Bd. 39, 2008, 512 S., 49,90 €, br., ISBN 978-3-8258-1042-9

Mirko Breitenstein
Das Noviziat im hohen Mittelalter
Zur Organisation des Eintrittes bei den Cluniazensern, Cisterziensern und Franziskanern
Bd. 38, 2008, 712 S., 49,90 €, br., ISBN 978-3-8258-1259-1

Jacques Dalarun
« Dieu changea de sexe, pour ainsi dire »
La religion faite femme (XIe–XVe siècle)
Bd. 37, 2008, 464 S., 39,90 €, br., ISBN 978-3-8258-1319-2

Sabine von Heusinger; Annette Kehnel (Eds./Hg.)
Generations in the Cloister. Generationen im Kloster
Youth and Age in Medieval Religious Life. Jugend und Alter in der mittelalterlichen vita religiosa
Bd. 36, 2008, 200 S., 29,90 €, br., ISBN 978-3-8258-1173-0

Jörg Sonntag
Klosterleben im Spiegel des Zeichenhaften
Symbolisches Denken und Handeln hochmittelalterlicher Mönche zwischen Dauer und Wandel, Regel und Gewohnheit
Bd. 35, 2008, 768 S., 69,90 €, br., ISBN 978-3-8258-1033-7

Gert Melville; Anne Müller (Hg.)
Mittelalterliche Orden und Klöster im Vergleich
Methodische Ansätze und Perspektiven
Bd. 34, 2007, 352 S., 49,90 €, br., ISBN 978-3-8258-1125-9

Christian Vogel
Das Recht der Templer
Ausgewählte Aspekte des Templerrechts unter besonderer Berücksichtigung der Statutenhandschriften aus Paris, Rom, Baltimore und Barcelona
Bd. 33, 2007, 408 S., 49,90 €, br., ISBN 978-3-8258-0776-4

Cristina Andenna
Mortariensis Ecclesia
Una congregazione di canonici regolari in Italia settentrionale tra XI e XII secolo
Bd. 32, 2007, 744 S., 59,90 €, br., ISBN 978-3-8258-0211-0

Susanne Krauß
Die *Devotio moderna* in Deventer
Anatomie eines Zentrums der Reformbewegung
Bd. 31, 2007, 528 S., 39,90 €, br., ISBN 978-3-8258-0172-4

Giorgio Picasso
Monachorum tempora seu gesta exquirere
Studi di storia monastica (secoli VI-XIII) a cura di Giancarlo Andenna e Cosimo Damiano Fonseca
Bd. 30, 2006, 424 S., 39,90 €, br., ISBN 3-8258-0089-X

LIT Verlag Berlin – Münster – Wien – Zürich – London
Auslieferung Deutschland / Österreich / Schweiz: siehe Impressumsseite

Uwe Israel (Hg.)
Vita communis und ethnische Vielfalt
Multinational zusammengesetzte Klöster im Mittelalter. Akten des internationalen Studientags vom 26. Januar 2005 im Deutschen Historischen Institut in Rom
Bd. 29, 2006, 288 S., 29,90 €, br., ISBN 3-8258-9726-5

Ramona Sickert
Wenn Klosterbrüder zu Jahrmarktsbrüdern werden
Studien zur zeitgenössischen Wahrnehmung der Franziskaner und Dominikaner im 13. Jahrhundert
Bd. 28, 2006, 472 S., 49,90 €, br., ISBN 3-8258-9248-4

Sébastien Barret; Gert Melville (Hg.)
Oboedientia
Zu Formen und Grenzen von Macht und Unterordnung im mittelalterlichen Religiosentum
Bd. 27, 2005, 472 S., 49,90 €, br., ISBN 3-8258-8926-2

Giancarlo Andenna; Mirko Breitenstein; Gert Melville (Hg.)
Charisma und religiöse Gemeinschaften im Mittelalter
Akten des 3. Internationalen Kongresses des „Italienisch-deutschen Zentrums für Vergleichende Ordensgeschichte" in Verbindung mit Projekt C „Institutionelle Strukturen religiöser Orden im Mittelalter" und Projekt W „Stadtkultur und Klosterkultur in der mittelalterlichen Lombardei. Institutionelle Wechselwirkung zweier politischer und sozialer Felder" des Sonderforschungsbereichs 537 „Institutionalität und Geschichtlichkeit" (Dresden, 10.–12. Juni 2004)
Bd. 26, 2005, 520 S., 49,90 €, br., ISBN 3-8258-8765-0

Cristina Andenna e Gert Melville (a cura di), con la consulenza scientifica di Cosimo Damiano Fonseca, Hubert Houben e Giuseppe Picasso
Regulae – Consuetudines – Statuta
Studi sulle fonti normative degli ordini religiosi nei secoli centrali del Medioevo. Atti del I e del II Seminario internazionale di studio del Centro italo-tedesco di storia comparata degli ordini religiosi (Bari/Noci/Lecce, 26-27 ottobre 2002/Castiglione delle Stiviere, 23-24 maggio 2003)
Bd. 25, 2005, 728 S., 69,90 €, br., ISBN 3-8258-8572-0

Albrecht Diem
Das monastische Experiment
Die Rolle der Keuschheit bei der Entstehung des westlichen Klosterwesens
Bd. 24, 2005, 480 S., 39,90 €, br., ISBN 3-8258-8556-9

Markus Schürer
Das Exemplum oder die erzählte Institution
Studien zum Beispielgebrauch bei den Dominikanern und Franziskanern des 13. Jahrhunderts
Bd. 23, 2006, 368 S., 34,90 €, br., ISBN 3-8258-8367-1

Reinhardt Butz; Jörg Oberste (Hg.)
Studia monastica
Beiträge zum klösterlichen Leben im christlichen Abendland während des Mittelalters
Bd. 22, 2004, 376 S., 24,90 €, br., ISBN 3-8258-7864-3

Jens Röhrkasten
The Mendicant Houses of Medieval London
1221–1539
vol. 21, 2004, 688 pp., 59,90 €, br., ISBN 3-8258-8117-2

LIT Verlag Berlin – Münster – Wien – Zürich – London
Auslieferung Deutschland / Österreich / Schweiz: siehe Impressumsseite

Giancarlo Andenna
Sanctimoniales Cluniacenses
Studi sui monasteri femminili di Cluny e sulla loro legislazione in Lombardia (XI – XV secolo)
Bd. 20, 2005, 240 S., 24,90 €, br., ISBN 3-8258-7462-1

Sébastien Barret
La mémoire et l'écrit: l'abbaye de Cluny et ses archives (X^e – XVIIIe siècle)
Bd. 19, 2004, 480 S., 45,90 €, br., ISBN 3-8258-7456-7

Elke Goez
Pragmatische Schriftlichkeit und Archivpflege der Zisterzienser
Ordenszentralismus und regionale Vielfalt, namentlich in Franken und Altbayern (1098 – 1525)
Bd. 17, 2003, 408 S., 29,90 €, br., ISBN 3-8258-6491-x

Gert Melville, Markus Schürer (Hg.)
Das Eigene und das Ganze
Zum Individuellen im mittelalterlichen Religiosentum
Bd. 16, 2002, 728 S., 50,90 €, br., ISBN 3-8258-6163-5

Anne Müller
Bettelmönche in islamischer Fremde
Institutionelle Rahmenbedingungen franziskanischer und dominikanischer Mission in muslimischen Räumen des 13. Jahrhunderts
Bd. 15, 2002, 360 S., 35,90 €, br., ISBN 3-8258-6159-7

Jürgen Sarnowsky
Macht und Herrschaft im Johanniterorden des 15. Jahrhunderts
Verfassung und Verwaltung der Johanniter auf Rhodos (1421 – 1522)
Bd. 14, 2001, 760 S., 51,90 €, br., ISBN 3-8258-5481-7

Gert Melville; Annette Kehnel (Hg.)
In proposito paupertatis
Studien zum Armutsverständnis bei den mittelalterlichen Bettelorden
Bd. 13, 2001, 248 S., 25,90 €, br., ISBN 3-8258-5340-3

Florent Cygler
Das Generalkapitel im hohen Mittelalter
Cisterzienser, Prämonstratenser, Kartäuser und Cluniazenser
Bd. 12, 2002, 544 S., 40,90 €, br., ISBN 3-8258-4996-1

Gert Melville; Jörg Oberste (Hg.)
Die Bettelorden im Aufbau
Beiträge zu Institutionalisierungsprozessen im mittelalterlichen Religiosentum
Bd. 11, 1999, 680 S., 45,90 €, br., ISBN 3-8258-4293-2

Eliana Magnani Soares-Christen
Monastères et aristocratie en Provence – milieu X^e – début XIIe siècle
Bd. 10, 1999, 632 S., 40,90 €, br., ISBN 3-8258-3663-0

Thomas Füser
Mönche im Konflikt
Zum Spannungsfeld von Norm, Devianz und Sanktionen bei den Cisterziensern und Cluniazensern (12. bis frühes 14. Jahrhundert)
Bd. 9, 2000, 384 S., 40,90 €, br., ISBN 3-8258-3443-3

LIT Verlag Berlin – Münster – Wien – Zürich – London
Auslieferung Deutschland / Österreich / Schweiz: siehe Impressumsseite

Anette Kehnel
Clonmacnois – the Church and Lands of St. Ciarán
Change and Continuity in an Irish Monastic Foundation (6th to 16th Century)
vol. 8, 1998, 368 pp., 30,90 €, br., ISBN 3-8258-3442-5

Giles Constable; Gert Melville; Jörg Oberste (Hrsg.)
Die Cluniazenser in ihrem politisch-sozialen Umfeld
Bd. 7, 1998, 596 S., 40,90 €, br., ISBN 3-8258-3441-7

Kay Peter Jankrift
Leprose als Streiter Gottes
Institutionalisierung und Organisation des Ordens vom heiligen Lazarus zu Jerusalem von seinen Anfängen bis zum Jahre 1350
Bd. 4, 1997, 272 S., 30,90 €, br., ISBN 3-8258-2589-2

Godula Süßmann
Konflikt und Konsens
Zu den Auseinandersetzungen zwischen cluniazensischen Klöstern und ihren rechtsabhängigen burgenses im Frankreich des 12. und 13. Jahrhunderts
Bd. 3, 1997, 400 S., 24,90 €, br., ISBN 3-8258-2588-4

Jörg Oberste
Visitation und Ordensorganisation
Formen sozialer Normierung, Kontrolle und Kommunikation bei Cisterziensern, Prämonstratensern und Cluniazensern (12. – frühes 14. Jahrhundert)
Bd. 2, 1996, 472 S., 24,90 €, br., ISBN 3-8258-2587-6

Gert Melville (Hg.)
De ordine vitae
Zu Normvorstellungen, Organisationsformen und Schriftgebrauch im mittelalterlichen Ordenswesen
Bd. 1, 1996, 400 S., 35,90 €, br., ISBN 3-8258-2586-8

LIT Verlag Berlin – Münster – Wien – Zürich – London
Auslieferung Deutschland / Österreich / Schweiz: siehe Impressumsseite

Vita regularis
Editionen
hrsg. von Mirko Breitenstein und Gert Melville

Jörg Sonntag
Sermones in regulam s. Benedicti
Die hier erstmals in Edition vorgelegte Predigtsammlung vom Beginn des 13. Jahrhunderts zählt zu den umfangreichsten Regelkommentaren des Mittelalters. Im französischen Pontigny entstanden, ist dies der einzige Kommentar aus zisterziensischer Feder, der die gesamte Benediktsregel in einem Werk erklärt und ihre Inhalte konsequent in übergeordnete, himmlische Kontexte einbettet. Es entsteht ein in vielerlei Hinsicht innovativer, enzyklopädischer Entwurf klösterlichen Lebens, der zugleich wertvolle Einblicke in grundlegende Ordnungsmuster europäischer Kulturgeschichte aus der Zeit um 1200 erlaubt.
Bd. 6, 2016, 846 S., 124,90 €, gb., ISBN 978-3-643-13428-8

Julia Bruch
Die Zisterze Kaisheim und ihre Tochterklöster
Studien zur Organisation und zum Wirtschaften spätmittelalterlicher Frauenklöster mit einer Edition des „Kaisheimer Rechnungsbuches"
Mit dem vorliegenden Band wird die Edition des *Kaisheimer Rechnungsbuches* vorgelegt. In diesem sind die jährlichen Abrechnungen von sechs Zisterzienserinnenklöstern (Kirchheim am Ries, Niederschönenfeld, Oberschönenfeld, Pielenhofen, Seligenthal und Zimmern) sowie zweier Zisterziensermännerklöster (Schöntal und Stams) enthalten. In ihrer umfangreichen Auswertung dieses bisher noch unerforschten Dokuments klösterlicher Wirtschaftsgeschichte kann die Autorin das dichte Beziehungsgefüge zisterzienscher Klöster aufzeigen. Dabei gelingt es nicht nur, die Mechanismen des ordensinternen Filiationssystems zu analysieren, sondern zugleich auch die Visitationspraxis im Orden zu beleuchten.
Bd. 5, 2013, 688 S., 69,90 €, br., ISBN 978-3-643-12370-1

Guido Caroboni
La via migliore
Pratiche memoriali e dinamiche istituzionali nel *liber* del capitolo dell'abbazia cistercense di Lucedio
Bd. 3, 2005, 256 S., 29,90 €, br., ISBN 3-8258-9161-5

Bruce C. Brasington
Ways of Mercy
The Prologue of Ivo of Chartres. Edition and Analysis
vol. 2, 2004, 176 pp., 24,90 €, br., ISBN 3-8258-7386-2

Mirko Breitenstein (Hg.)
De novitiis instruendis
Text und Kontext eines anonymen Traktates vom Ende des 12. Jahrhunderts
Bd. 1, 2003, 192 S., 24,90 €, br., ISBN 3-8258-7241-6

LIT Verlag Berlin – Münster – Wien – Zürich – London
Auslieferung Deutschland / Österreich / Schweiz: siehe Impressumsseite